Acclaim for Flexigidity

Former Chief Rabbi Lord Jonathan Sacks
The United Hebrew Congregations of the UK and the Common Wealth
"In Flexigidity, Gidi Grinstein has produced a work that is as innovative
in its understanding of leadership as it is in its insights about Jewish life.
This is a wonderful, mind-expanding work that should be read by everyone
concerned with the Jewish future, or simply seeking transformative
inspiration about the practice of leadership. A great book!"

Avraham Infeld
President Emeritus of Hillel: Foundation for Jewish Life on Campus:
"*Flexigidity* is not an easy read and it demands heavy contemplation, but it
is a must-read for contemporary Jewish lay and professional leaders and for
all those who seek to understand Judaism, the Jewish People and the State
of Israel. It cuts across denominational lines and stands to benefit readers of
all walks of life and all levels of learning and observance."

Dr. John Ruskay
Executive Vice President & CEO of UJA-Federation of New York:
"A must read for all focused on the Jewish Future. Gidi Grinstein brilliantly
unpacks the capacity of the Jewish people to adapt and persevere. The
volume is essential for all who seek to understand the challenges and
opportunities that face us."

Prof. Ricardo Hausmann
Director of the Center for ̶
Harvard Kennedy School
"Gidi Grinstein digs deep i̶ ̶ ̶ ̶ ̶ ̶ ̶ ̶ ̶ ̶ sent in order
to offer a much needed vision for the ̶ ̶ ̶ ̶ ̶ ̶ ̶ ̶ ̶ ̶ ld's most
successful economies. It is a must read for those i̶ ̶ ̶ ̶ ̶ ̶ ̶ ̶ Israel as
well as those that want to understand some of the avenues to success in the
21st century."

Lynn Schusterman
Co-founder and Chair of the Charles and Lynn Schusterman Family
Foundation
"The insights Gidi brings to the subject of Jewish history, as well as modern
challenges and trends, is sure to ignite constructive dialogue about the
future of Israel and the Jewish People"

Flexigidity®

Flexigidity®

The Secret of Jewish Adaptability
The Challenge & Opportunity
Facing Israel

Gidi Grinstein
Founder and President
The Reut Institute

Co-edited with Josh Gottesman

For information regarding permission to reprint material from this book, please send your request in writing to Gidi Grinstein at the Reut Institute, 126 Yigal Alon St., Tel-Aviv, Israel 67443 or by email at office@reut-institute.org.

ISBN-13: 978-0991306909

First limited edition: Adar 5774, February 2014

To Betty and to our children:
Eliyahu, Yosef (Sefi), Michael, Noa Sarah and Yael
Our very own links in the chain

"The eternity of Israel
shall not disappear."

Samuel I, 15:29

"There is no academy *(beit midrash)*
without innovation *(Hidush)*."

Tosefta Sotah 7:9

"All things are mortal but the Jew …
What is the secret of his immortality?"

Mark Twain, *Concerning the Jews*

"It is not the strongest of species that
survives, nor the most intelligent. It is
the most adaptable."

Leon Megginson on Charles Darwin's *On the Origin of Species*

The Flexigidity Project is a 21st century enterprise of Talmud wishing to inspire countless acts of Flexigid leadership.

It aspires to ignite a global conversation about the condition and future of the Jewish People and the State of Israel.

You are invited to enrich it with your insights, sources and personal stories.

www.flexigidity.com

Guidelines for Quick Reading

This book was written with busy people in mind who have varying degrees of knowledge and familiarity with its subject matters. It also aspires to engage a community of contributors who will continue to develop its ideas and sources. Therefore, the text is structured to help readers understand the broader framework, as well as to explore more deeply wherever they find interest. The following are brief guidelines for quick reading:

- In order to get the gist of the framework of Flexigidity, **please begin by reading the Table of Contents**. It is organized and detailed to capture the structure of the Flexigidity argument and its key insights;

- **Most chapters begin with a short description of their content framed by a box.** These boxes of text attempt to remind the readers of the chapter's place within the broader context of the Flexigidity framework;

- **Every paragraph contains a single idea that is captured in one or two bolded sentences.** The body of the paragraph usually develops that idea. Footnotes do *not* offer any new insights and mostly elaborate on sources and provide further data;

- **The electronic edition will include brief visual summaries of entire sections of the book** in the format of presentations, video clips, and links to additional sources;

- **All paragraphs are numbered to allow for easy referencing**.

Foreword by Avraham Infeld

Writing a foreword is a very novel experience for me, but I could not resist responding positively to Gidi Grinstein's invitation to do so for *Flexigidity: The Secret of Jewish Adaptability*, his recently completed very important work. *Flexigidity* is not an easy read and it demands heavy contemplation, but it is a must-read for contemporary Jewish lay and professional leaders and for all those who seek to understand Judaism, the Jewish People and the State of Israel. It cuts across denominational lines and stands to benefit readers of all walks of life and all levels of learning and observance.

I have known Gidi for nearly twenty years and have watched this work grow within him. Our relationship began when I was among those who chose Gidi to join a group of four carefully selected young Israelis to spend a month at the California-based Brandeis-Bardin Collegiate Institute (BCI). At the time, he was a young naval officer of exceptional character, educated as a typical secular Israeli. His lack of traditional Jewish knowledge was matched only by his evident intellectual curiosity and his obvious high intelligence, which would enable him to both engage with and critique that experience.

If ever there was veracity in the oft heard statement in Israel, "I went abroad as an Israeli and returned as a Jew," it was true in Gidi's case. He was, at that time, a typical and telling product of the successes and failures of the Zionist enterprise. His initial rootedness in Jewish life stemmed exclusively from his being Israeli, the success of Zionism. The relative ignorance with which Gidi came to BCI concerning the history and current realities of Diaspora Jewish life speak to Zionism's failures.

Gidi did not become a religious repentant. However, beginning with his return, his frame of reference in relating to things surrounding him was expanded. He came to view Israel and the Jewish People as a systemic whole with a mission to serve humanity. From that perspective, he was open and desirous to contend with his people's culture, memory, traditions, teachings and dreams. Shortly thereafter, he led a group of Israelis that concretized the vision of Birthright Israel into the outstandingly successful model that it is. I was honored to serve as the mentor and first director of that initiative. Later, he founded the Reut Institute, which contends with some of the toughest challenges facing the State of Israel and the Jewish People.

I have referred here to *Flexigidity* as a work rather than a book because of its novel approach. It is, in reality, an invitation to us, the readers, to participate

Join the conversation www.flexigidity.com

in a joint effort to understand the Jewish People with the aid of a designated web-platform and to impact its future. We are called upon to take the time to understand what Gidi is saying, to grapple with the ideas, to jointly develop them further and to take action. To my mind, it is well worth the effort, and the benefits that may accrue to the reader and the Jewish People are immense.

Flexigidity is innovative not only in its structure but also in its perspective. Gidi uses the discipline of 'Systems Thinking,' which enables applying astute scrutiny to existing phenomenon and allows for insights never before considered. The resulting product is an exceptionally interesting attempt to explain the survival, security, prosperity and leadership of the Jewish People and its repeated moments of renaissance through the tension between flexibility and rigidity that has driven Jewish adaptability throughout the millennia. It is not the first work to attempt to explain Jewish history and society, but it differs in significant ways that make it uniquely relevant to our times.

When Mordechai Kaplan first applied the emerging social science of sociology to the study of Judaism at the turn of the 20th century, he concluded that existing paradigms of religion and nationality were not enough to understand the complexity of the Jewish People. Using these tools, Kaplan concluded that Judaism was in actuality an evolving religious civilization. His insight eventually impacted Jewish community life profoundly, albeit in ways little known by most Jews in Israel and the Diaspora.

I'm the son of one who sought to do the same. My late father, Zvi Infeld z"l, in his book *Israel and the Decline of the West*, attempted to respond to Arnold Toynbee's vehement antisemitism, which was based on Oswald Spengler's Cyclic Theory of History. He applied that same theory to the development of a contrary and positive understanding of the Jewish People.

My father, who ultimately became secular, came out of a world rooted in Hasidic life and learning. By contrast, Gidi's decision to scrutinize the entire history of the Jewish People in Israel and abroad draws upon an awareness and engagement that only began developing in his adult life. The depth and breadth of *Flexigidity* reflects a phenomenon of significant Jewish thinkers that only came to Jewish learning late in their lives.

Flexigidity also provides a new outlook and vision for Zionism in the 21st Century, as well as a most intriguing analysis of Israel's historic achievements and challenges. Gidi's service as a thought leader in Israel for the last decade and his founding and steerage of the Reut Institute ensure that his ideas are rooted and well grounded. Reut has subjected Gidi's theses to the test of reality and that makes reading and contending with this work all the more essential.

As a septuagenarian with more than fifty years of involvement in informal Jewish education and leadership development, I cannot but view with excitement the potential impact of this work. This text is extremely timely and much needed. My thirty years as President of Melitz, my years as President of Hillel International and all of my other leadership involvement would have benefitted immensely from this work, which only now appears.

Avraham Infeld
President Emeritus, Hillel International
December 2013, Tevet 5774

Table of Contents

Flexigidity®

The Secret of Jewish Adaptability
The Challenge & Opportunity
Facing Israel

Prologue

The idea of Jewish Flexigidity posits that the survival, resilience, relative security, recurring prosperity and enduring leadership of the Jewish People stem from a societal system. This system optimizes the pace of collective adaptation by balancing new and old, innovation and tradition, flexibility and rigidity: Flexigidity. It is so reliably consistent that one of the few statements that can be made with confidence about humanity in the year 2500 is that there will be Jews lighting *Shabbat* candles on Friday night.

However, the great Jewish paradox of our time is the duality between power and vulnerability, placing the State of Israel and the Jewish world at a critical historical juncture. Jews have never been more economically, politically and militarily powerful as manifested primarily by the stature of the Jewish community in North America and in the achievements of the State of Israel and its people. Yet, the Jewish People has rarely been as vulnerable precisely due to its concentration in these two political, cultural and geographic centers.

Additionally, in recent decades, the Jewish world has experienced societal change unprecedented in its breadth and depth. The internal transformations in Israel and the Diaspora are compounded by the rapid pace of change in the world at large. In such a condition of permanent turmoil, many Jewish communities and individuals are relinquishing heritage and societal legacies that have served them for centuries and may be invaluable to their future. These trends excessively polarize Jewish society between the so-called 'progressives' and 'conservatives' and strain the Flexigid society.

The State of Israel is at the epicenter of this drama. Its successes are remarkable by any standard and astounding when considering that the point of departure of Zionism was only some hundred and thirty years ago. At the same time, Israel has come to represent a deep disruption to Jewish society. The Government of Israel and Israeli society evolved in directions that unnecessarily and deeply compromise institutions and practices that have been vital for the resilience and prosperity of the Jewish People. Without a change of course, Israel may evolve to compromise Jewish Flexigidity altogether.

Thus, the purpose of the Flexigidity Project is for Jews and their friends to explore this paradox, to point out the threats and opportunities that it creates, and to address the leadership challenges that stem from it. The underlying premise of this project is that leadership interventions into a complex society must be rooted in a framework that allows for broad and systemic societal

Join the conversation www.flexigidity.com

understanding. To be useful, such a framework must explain the historical evolution of the Jewish People and expose the distinct roles that key factions play, their interconnectedness and the unique dynamics among them.

The central target audience of the Flexigidity Project is Jewish leadership, broadly defined. It includes rabbis, lay leaders, activists, professionals, philanthropists, scholars, government agencies and non-governmental organizations across the political, ideological and religious spectrum in Israel and around the world. However, I also had novices and lay people in mind, as well as non-Jews who seek to understand Jewish history and society.

Zionists and Israelis are a particularly important group within the target audience of the Flexigidity Project. As mentioned earlier, Zionism and Israel have let go of many of the secrets of survival, security, prosperity and leadership of the Jewish People in favor of a model of statehood that is yet to prove its resilience. Thus, as Israel seeks to grow from strength to strength, the societal knowledge of the Jewish Diaspora may be invaluable to its future. While obviously history does not repeat itself in specific terms, certain patterns and structures persist over long periods of time, and much can be inferred from the past and present to a promising future.

Ultimately, the test of success for the Flexigidity Project will be whether many actually find it useful and inspiring: whether such a framework helps many Jews make sense of things, placing their personal and family stories within the broader context of Jewish history and society; whether it inspires people to assume responsibility and participate in the unique societal creation of the Jewish People with a benefit of a more nuanced outlook; whether, in exposing the inherent societal interconnectedness and interdependence among Jews, it increases tolerance and mutual respect within and among Jews and Jewish communities in Israel and the Diaspora across the inevitable fault lines; and whether it contributes to the legitimacy and understanding of the Jewish People, Zionism and the State of Israel in the eyes of the world.

Every societal system has its own logic from which generalizations can be deduced. This is the approach that underlies the Flexigidity Project. It holds that there are "no broken systems," which means that organizations, nations and people are aligned to create the outcomes they are producing, even if they are deemed by some of their members and outside observers dysfunctional.[1] These outcomes are shaped by forces, institutions, structures, values and incentives

---

1   See discussion at Heifetz, Grashow and Linsky, *The Practice of Adaptive Leadership*, Harvard University Press, p. 17-19.

that can be identified and explored. The interactions among them generate clashes, tensions, partnerships and collaborations, and shape societal symbols, heroes and festivals. Therefore, I have been guided by my confidence that there must be an explanation for the tremendous diversity yet remarkable similarities among Jewish communities and for the fact that Judaism has repeatedly housed some of the most progressive and conservative groups in human society, often simultaneously. I believe we can understand the Jewish world in all of its complexity and have been searching for a framework with which to do so.

This book offers such a skeletal framework for understanding Jewish history and society. Its *first section* explores Flexigidity as the secret to survival, general security, repeated renaissances and exceptional leadership of the Jewish People over more than two thousand years of exilic existence. The *second section* shows how Jewish Flexigidity underlay the remarkable success of Zionism over the past hundred and thirty years, embodied in the political, social, economic and military development and stature of the State of Israel. It also explores the challenges created by Jewish sovereignty in Israel to the Flexigidity of the Jewish People. The *third section* explores the ways in which the Flexigid legacy of Jewish Diaspora can and should inspire the revitalization of Israeli society in the coming decades. The *final section* discusses the requisites of Flexigid leadership.

I am fully aware that this framework challenges some Jewish and Zionist myths. There is no doubt that exile and life in the Diaspora prior to the establishment of the State of Israel represented a deep setback relative to life of sovereignty, independence and freedom of religion and practice in Zion. However, over time the Jewish People adjusted to life without these ideals. The Jewish People has even created alternative structures that ensured its survival and relative security, prosperity and communal, religious and spiritual freedom during most of its exile and throughout the Diaspora. Furthermore, the framework of Flexigidity implies that Judaism consciously preferred interaction with the Gentile world, risking the price of varying degrees of assimilation, as opposed to insularity. As a result, Jews have been a dynamic force throughout history rather than fossilized in it. Moreover, Judaism has favored diversity and dynamic adversity within its communities over uniformity, which may have been more conducive to internal peace. Therefore, the Zionist narrative of a Jewish fate of relentless insecurity, poverty and religious persecution in the Diaspora is simplistic, limited and incomplete.

The conceptual framework laid out in this book has a few obvious weaknesses. *First,* it required me to paint with broad brushstrokes. I wanted to capture the historical, societal and economic forces that shape Jewish destiny. Such forces take a minimum of decades, often generations and centuries, to evolve. Thus, central to this project is the assumption that if a certain phenomenon can be seen in snapshots that are centuries apart it must have existed throughout that timeframe.

The *second weakness* is generalization and simplification. Reality is not simple but complex. It does not progress in straight lines but often in evolving spirals with dialectical interplay among actions, ideas and a great variety of players. Nonetheless, I believe that it can be grasped by useful general observations that will not only shed light on the past and present but will also help shape determined action in the future. This required me to describe the forest without getting lost in the trees, which necessitated crystallizing the text into a compact narrative. Keeping footnotes to a minimum should not be seen as a disregard of those who came before me, as I fully realize that I am merely standing on their shoulders. I simply referred to the minimal amount of sources necessary to establish the crucial points of the Flexigidity framework.

In particular, a few teachers, writers, thinkers and leaders have heavily influenced my outlook, and some of them are extensively referred to in this text. They are: David Ben-Gurion's *Distinction and Destiny (Yichud ve Ye'ude)*; Edgar M. Bronfman, through our many conversations and his book, *Hope Not Fear*; Professor Yechezkel Dror's writings and teachings, and particularly his book, *Epistle to an Israeli Jewish-Zionist Leader*; my teacher Ron Heifetz's *Leadership Without Easy Answers*; my mentor and close friend, Avraham Infeld and particularly his vision in *Five Legged Table*; Paul Johnson's *A History of the Jews*; the teachings and coaching of Dr. Zvi Lanir, found in his recent book *The Fox Pocket Notebook;* Dr. Rabbi Binyamin Lau's trilogy, *Sages;* and Lord Rabbi Jonathan Sacks' *Future Tense*.

Another limitation stems from the scope of the project: two millennia of Jewish Diaspora, nearly one hundred and thirty years of Zionism and the coming decades of the State of Israel. The *first section* of this work offers an overview of history that took a minimum of decades and often centuries to evolve. The *second section* deals with near fourteen decades of Zionism and Israel. From this standpoint, for example, it may still be too early to assess the full effect of Jewish emancipation and Enlightenment (*Haskalah*) as of the 18th century and that of the devastation of European Jewry and the Shoah between 1933 and 1945. The *third section*, which deals with the coming decades, naturally requires a much higher resolution and refers to events that may never have qualified as historical from the broader perspective of Judaism.

Finally, this project does not engage in comparative analysis. I avoided statements that rank Judaism's successes, failures and contributions, and did not compare the Jewish outlook to that of other societies, religions and cultures. Suffice it to say that Judaism's unique force and voice in human history have been recognized by many Jews and non-Jews.

The architecture of the Flexigidity Project is designed to tap into the wisdom and knowledge of many individuals in order to continue to develop its ideas and explore their implications. The time when one person needed to articulate an entire framework with all its details and sources belongs to the past. In today's world, the 'wisdom of crowds' is likely to do a much better job than any single individual in describing a complex society, provided that proper structures and incentives are put in place to encourage them to do so.

Therefore, the Flexigidity Project is comprised of this book, as well as of a web-platform designed to allow for mass engagement, deliberation and participation. The skeletal framework for understanding the Jewish world within this book is organized to allow easy commentary, debate, reference and contribution. Each serially numbered paragraph presents a single idea, captured in bold type. Meanwhile, the web-platform was designed to enable a broad audience to further develop this framework and its specific themes and ideas through their additional insight, logic, sources, photos, music and videos. Such mass deliberation will hopefully contribute to the collective shared comprehension of Jewish past and present, as well as to the design of its future.

In conclusion, the Flexigidity Project calls for partnership in the service of our communities, people, nation and the world. Ensuring the security, prosperity and leadership of the State of Israel and the Jewish People into the 21st century is a formidable challenge, far greater than the capacity and resources available to any single individual or organization. Yet, as the Ethics of Our Fathers *(Pirkei Avot)* teaches, while it is not upon us to finish the task, neither are we free to desist from it.

Gidi Grinstein
Kislev 5774, December 2013

Join the conversation www.flexigidity.com

Part I
Introduction and
the Four Founding Stories

Introduction: Unprecedented Power and Rare Vulnerability

This section introduces the concept of Flexigidity – a blend of the words 'flexibility' and 'rigidity' – and its unique Jewish manifestation. It argues that the Jewish People have collectively optimized their pace of adaptation in response to external changes and internal tensions.

It then proceeds to describe the great paradox of present day Judaism and Israel: that the Jewish People has never been more powerful, but rarely has it been as vulnerable. This paradox is an outcome of the compounded effect of catastrophes and opportunities over the past one hundred and thirty years that caused mass destruction, relocation and societal transformation.

Finally, it describes the daunting challenges that face Zionism and the State of Israel, whose success has caused seismic shifts in Jewish society, compromising key mechanisms of Jewish survival, security, prosperity and leadership developed over nearly two millennia in exile.

The Permanence of Judaism and the Invisible Forces of Its Adaptability

1. **The concept of Flexigidity refers to the hybrid of flexibility and rigidity that exists in all human associations.** Every thoughtful corporation, not-for-profit organization, academic institution, nation and international organization creates its own particular form of Flexigidity. Rigidity may stem from a founding charter and from a legacy of deeply engrained values, patterns of conduct and incentives. Flexibility may come from faster moving decision making and action taking entities that respond to change. One can see these dynamics in the USA: its Constitution is a rigid document that is very difficult to modify, while Congress, individual states and local governments have much greater freedom to legislate within the confines of the Constitution.

2. **Jewish Flexigidity refers to the unique manner in which Judaism and the Jewish People have synthesized flexibility and rigidity in key areas of Jewish society** such as its mission, law, structure of communities, place, language and membership. It also captures the forces that drive the adaptation of the Jewish People, which stem from inherent structural tensions between unity and adversity, idealism and realism, powerlessness and security, wealth accumulation and social cohesion, and the existence of multiple centers of leadership. It aims to explain the vast geographic, cultural, philosophical, ethnic and communal diversity of the Jewish

People, as well as its surprising unity. While Judaism has given rise to some of the most innovative, creative, progressive, fast-moving and flexible communities and organizations in history, it has also simultaneously housed some of the most conservative, traditional and rigid elements of human society. Yet despite this, Judaism preserves its togetherness.

3. **Jewish Flexigidity produces societal mechanisms that optimize the pace of Jewish collective adaptation as if by an invisible hand.** It establishes an 'adaptation equilibrium' that balances the factions of Jewish society and effectively responds to sudden internal and external changes. It blends the enthusiasts and early adapters with the skeptics and latecomers, radicalism with conservatism, progressive ideas with ancient loyalties, the new with the old. It affects even the most traditional groups in Judaism whose pace of adaptation is slower than meets the eye. Judaism's societal forces optimize the pace of collective adaptation. It does so in a way loosely akin to Adam Smith's 'invisible hand,' which alludes to market forces that supposedly achieve 'efficiency' in economic markets by equilibrating the competing claims of supply and demand both in ordinary times, as well as in response to market shocks.

4. **The source of Judaism's Flexigid system is intensely debated.** Some view this reality and performance as the outcome of divine design resulting from the revelation at Mount Sinai, embodied in the Written Torah and Oral Torah *(Torah she'bictav* and *Torah she'ba'al-peh)* and manifested in Jewish law *(halacha)*. For many others, this approach is unsatisfactory: they view Judaism as an evolving civilization, an enterprise in society building, which, over time, has been cemented by and enshrined in religious texts, traditions, narratives, institutions and values.[2] **The underlying assumption of the Flexigidity Project is that any approach would benefit from a deeper understanding of the mechanisms of Jewish adaptation.**

5. **The quest for security, wellbeing and freedom of faith, as well as the service of Judaism's missions, are the engines of Jewish adaptation.** Where an environment of security and religious freedom existed, Jews congregated and developed flourishing, prosperous and cohesive communities. Deep insecurity, intolerance and discrimination usually resulted in a mass Jewish emigration and the eventual disintegration of Jewish community life and institutions. When the essential conditions were restored, Jews sometimes returned.

---

2   'Judaism as a Civilization' is a phrase coined by Mordechai Kaplan in his seminal work of that name.

6. Yet, **there are inevitable and inherent tensions among these quests for security, prosperity, freedom of faith and a particular mission**. Prosperity requires engagement with the world through trade, intellectual discourse and travel, which challenge Jewish particularism and allow for assimilation. As an economically successful minority, Jews were often the target of widespread resentment, which served to undermine security. Meanwhile, efforts to protect Jewish identity through insularity increased isolation and vulnerability, compromising the ability to accumulate wealth. Jews pledged loyalty to the local sovereign in exchange for security, but maintained contact with other Jews and Jewish communities across political borders, dreamt of returning to the Land of Israel, Zion, and, in recent times, supported Jewish political independence and the State of Israel. Finally, in an environment of tolerance, the Jewish tendency to nurture their particularism in practices, institutions, customs and costumes eventually challenged the dominant culture, which other Jews embraced and assimilated into. Jewish history can be described as an everlasting balancing act among these four conditions of security, prosperity, freedom of religion and association and the service of Judaism's particular missions.

7. The general rule is that **Jewish society, like others, goes through transformations when the existing institutions can no longer address the needs of the community.** When prevailing values, priorities, patterns of conduct and incentives fail to ensure security and prosperity, the gap between the old world and the emerging one requires adaptation and transformation. As it widens, the pressure for change grows as well, eventually legitimizing deep societal and institutional change.[3]

8. **Many Jewish transformations were ignited by radical changes in the outside world.** While in some cases these changes may have generated a crisis of security and poverty, in other cases, Jews suddenly had an opportunity for peaceful existence and prosperity: the destruction of the Second Temple and Jerusalem in 70 CE by the Romans ushered in Rabbinic Judaism; during the Golden Age of Spain of the 8th to 11th century, rationalism became integral to Jewish theology, laying the foundation for the work of Maimonides *(Rambam)*; Tsarist persecutions and the failure of emancipation in Western Europe ignited modern Zionism; the Shoah propelled the establishment of the State of Israel;

---

3   Based on the theory of Dr. Zvi Lanir, *The Fox Pocket Notebook* (in Hebrew), Mendele Electronic Books, Tel-Aviv, 2013.

and the prosperity and openness of the USA allowed for the flourishing of multiple denominations.[4]

9. Yet, **some transformations also came about because of internal crises.** Rabbinic Judaism, led by sages and rabbis, began to emerge as a leading political force prior to the destruction of the Second Temple primarily in response to the corruption of the Priests *(Cohanim)*. Universal education was embraced in a gradual process as of the 1st century BCE. The tools of rationalist philosophy became widely embraced in the 8th and 9th centuries during the debates with Karaite Jews who rejected Rabbinic Judaism. The world of *Hasidut* emerged in Eastern Europe during the 18th century in part as response to the failure of the Jewish leadership to meaningfully engage the masses in their religious and spiritual life. While the leadership emphasized scholarly mastery of the laws by a highly educated few, *Hasidim* focused on prayer *(tefilah)* and intent *(kavanah)*, which were relevant to every Jew. Rabbi Mordechai Kaplan and the Reconstructionist Movement responded to the threat of mass assimilation among American Jewry in the early 20th century with the idea of the Synagogue Center, which has evolved into the network of Jewish Community Centers and has affected many synagogues.

10. **Even the most dramatic calamities led to Jewish adaptation and, in a broader scheme, despite being traumatic and transformative, did not affect the unique stature of the Jewish People among nations.** The expulsion from Spain (1492) and the Shoah (1933-45) abruptly eliminated Jewish communities that rose to exceptional economic and political prominence and made remarkable contributions to the non-Jewish society at large. Both events left a deep scar on the collective Jewish psyche and memory and will be remembered for centuries to come. Yet, while the full effect of the Shoah is yet to be assessed, one can cautiously observe that in this case as well, the Jewish People rose to new heights shortly thereafter. As Former Chief Rabbi of Britain, Lord Rabbi Jonathan Sacks writes, "Jews have survived catastrophe after catastrophe, in a way unparalleled by any other culture. In each case they did more than survive. Every tragedy in Jewish history was followed by a new wave of creativity."[5]

---

4   Jonathan Sacks, *Future Tense, A Vision for Jews and Judaism in the Global Culture,* Hodder and Stoughton, 2009, P.54.

5   See Sacks, *Future Tense*, p. 54.

11. **These dynamics of adaptation persist as Judaism continues to face numerous formidable challenges from within and without:** Antisemitism tenaciously persists and Israel faces permanent adversity that challenges its existence; while China and India are rising in the East, Judaism and the Jewish People are predominantly located and invested in the West and must orient themselves toward these emerging powers; while about half of Diaspora Jews marry non-Jews, for the first time in history, many of these intermarried households want to remain a part of the Jewish People.[6] Such households often comprise a significant portion of progressive communities in the USA. Beyond these, there are multiple other challenges that keep Jewish leaders awake at night.

12. Yet, **the history and legacy of Judaism inspire confidence in the ability of Diaspora Jewry to continue to survive and thrive in spite of these dramatic challenges.** Following the destruction of the First Temple in 586 BCE, Diaspora Jewry has repeatedly proven its capacity to transcend crisis, which was shaped by the absence of power, sovereign land and a government. It transcended the decline of multiple great political powers, as well as the subsiding of prior golden epochs *(tor zahav)* of its greatest communities in places as diverse as Mesopotamia, Alexandria, Spain, Germany, Morocco and Poland. It adapted to the ever-changing economic and technological environment; to the challenges and assaults of Christianity, Islam and Communism; to the persecutions of the Roman Empire, the Crusaders, the Spanish Inquisition, Tsarist Russia and Nazism; and to the assimilative environment created by Hellenism, the Enlightenment, modernity and Americanism. It has survived calamities and evolved, repeatedly thrived and constantly led for two millennia in adverse conditions. In fact, the framework of Flexigidity implies that for most of this time, compared to the general society in which they resided, the majority of Jews lived in relative security, prosperity and religious, communal and cultural autonomy.[7] This legacy inspires confidence that Judaism will outlive even the inevitable decline of the USA over the centuries to come. Thus, **Judaism's vibrant societal mechanisms make**

---

6   According to the 2013 PEW Forum study, among Jews with a non-Jewish spouse, 20% say they are raising their children Jewish by religion, and 25% are raising their children partly Jewish by religion. Roughly one-third (37%) of intermarried Jews who are raising children say they are not raising those children Jewish at all. http://www.pewforum.org/2013/10/01/jewish-american-beliefs-attitudes-culture-survey/.

7   Johnson, *A History of the Jews*, Harper Perennial, 1988, p. 356: "...A survey of Frankurt in 1855 ... shows Jewish life spans averaged forty-eight years nine months, non-Jews thirty-six years eleven months."

it seem permanent in human terms. **One of the few statements that can be made about humanity in five hundred years from now with high certainty is that Jews will be lighting candles on Friday night.**

13. **It is Zionism and the State of Israel that face the critical challenge of Jewish adaptability.** The establishment of a Jewish sovereignty caused a dramatic transformation of the societal DNA of the Jewish community in Israel, which largely abandoned the legacy of the Diaspora. Yet, for the time being, Israel has not produced a unique outlook that engenders confidence in its ability to transcend the inevitable decline of nations, which has brought down even the world's greatest powers in history. This challenge is a primary subject of the Flexigidity Project.

The Jewish Paradox of Our Time: Power and Vulnerability

14. **At the beginning of the 21st century, Jews are celebrating unprecedented economic and political power.** It is concentrated primarily in the State of Israel and in North America, where about eighty percent of world Jews reside, as well as in other powerful Jewish communities around the world, such as Australia, leading European nations, Russia and Latin America. Power is also scattered among the hands of a disproportionally large number of families and individuals who reach professional, national and global prominence in business, academia, non-governmental organizations, civil service and politics, while being recognized as Jews and as part of the Jewish People. No sizeable Jewish community is under oppression, and relatively few nations officially discriminate against individual Jews and Jewish communities. In fact, most governments protect their Jewish populations. Such a phenomenon could not have happened before recent decades. Furthermore, in this environment of general prosperity and religious freedom in all developed nations and most countries of the world, the number of Jews who immerse themselves in the world of Torah has also reached historical records. In short, the Jewish People have never been more secure, prosperous, accepted and powerful.

15. Furthermore, **over the last three millennia, and particularly during the last two hundred and fifty years, the Jewish People has made a disproportionally significant contribution to humanity in all of its frontiers.** In its earlier periods, Judaism fostered radical new concepts that transformed humanity, such as monotheism, universal morality, the Sabbath, social justice and human rights. In modern times, individual

Jews such as Baruch Spinoza, Milton Friedman, Paul Samuelson, Benoit Mandelbrot, Sigmund Freud and Albert Einstein introduced and developed other transformative ideas in the areas of philosophy, theology, economy, both hard and social sciences, technology and finance.

16. **The paradox is that during the past two millennia, the Jewish People have rarely been as concentrated, and therefore as vulnerable, as they are now.** Jews are now congregated in two political and economic systems. Zionism has successfully attracted more than forty percent of world Jews and reached a point where half of all Jewish babies are Israelis. Another forty percent of world Jewry and nearly eighty percent of Jewish Diaspora live in the USA. Meanwhile, thousands of communities have disintegrated in North Africa and across the Moslem world, Central Asia, Latin America and Europe. In some cases – such as in the Caucasus, Iraq and India – they had lasted millennia and dated back to the days of the Babylonian exile, which ended the First Temple era some twenty seven centuries ago.[8] Such geographic concentration may have only occurred in Mesopotamia in the 3rd to the 7th centuries, and in the 16th to the 19th centuries in Central and Eastern Europe. Thus, **Jewish geographic diversity has dramatically decreased, and the resilience of the Jewish network-society significantly eroded.**[9] **A vast majority of the Jewish People's eggs are now placed in two geographic, cultural and political baskets.**

17. **This conundrum of power and vulnerability is the outcome of nearly one hundred and thirty years of radical and fundamental transformations in Jewish society.** It emanates from the compounded effect of repetitive disasters in Europe, as well as from the dramatic successes of Zionism and Americanism.

---

8   The Bible documents that only some of the First Temple exiles returned with Ezra in the fifth century BCE. Some four centuries later, "The Roman geographer Stravo (circa 64 BCE – 24 CE) said that the Jews were a power throughout the inhabited world. There were a million of them in Egypt alone. In Alexandria, perhaps the world's greatest city after Rome itself, they formed a majority in two out of five quarters. They were numerous in Cyrene and Berenice in Pergamum, Miletus, Sardis, in Phrygian Apamea, Cyprus, Antioch, Damascus, and Ephesus, and on both shores of the Black Sea. They had been in Rome for 200 years and now formed a substantial colony there and from Rome they had spread all over urban Italy, and then into Gaul and Spain and across the sea into north-west Africa." See Johnson, *A History of the Jews*, p. 132.

9   See http://www.economist.com/blogs/graphicdetail/2012/07/daily-chart-16.

18. **The demographic center of gravity of world Jewry has shifted dramatically**. On the one hand, Nazism eliminated a third of the Jewish People and an estimated seventy percent of all Jews in the areas of its conquests in Central and Eastern Europe, amounting to six million people and thousands of communities. Tsarist Russia and Communism in the Soviet Union, while not engaging in physical genocide, sought to destroy Judaism and systematically persecuted its communities and institutions for over a century. On the other hand, Zionism inspired millions of Jews to abandon their Diaspora life, relocate to Zion and become a part of an independent Jewish community. They were 'recreated' as 'Israelis' who are 'Hebrew' persons *(Ivrim)*. Meanwhile, the promise of the USA for freedom, acceptance, security and prosperity attracted millions of Jews who became the most economically and politically successful Jewish community in history and, arguably, the USA's most thriving minority. Thus, **while European Jewry was decimated, two communities that were demographically marginal one hundred and thirty years ago – those in North America and in Zion – are now the largest in the Jewish world**.

19. **The transformation was also cultural, societal, ethical and religious.** The Jewish People now houses manifestations of Judaism, which did not exist two hundred and fifty years ago. In Israel, a Jewish-Hebrew community that exercises a sovereign majority includes a national-religious faction that combines staunch nationalism with strict religious observance, a large 'secular' and 'atheist' constituency that still passionately identifies itself as Jewish, and a unique community of 'ultra-orthodox' Jews, *Haredim*. In the USA, the Modern Orthodox, Reform, Conservative and Reconstructionist denominations have now morphed into a plethora of religious practices and modes of congregations.

20. **Such rapid and deep societal relocation and transformation rarely occurred in Jewish history.** In the past it happened mostly in the aftermath of national traumas such as the exodus from Egypt, the two exiles from the Land of Israel and the expulsion from Spain – thirty five, twenty six, twenty and five centuries ago respectively. Such a transformation is taking place right now in our time, on our watch.

Zionism's Daunting Challenge: Israeli Prosperity and Jewish Vitality

21. **Zionism, the modern national movement of the Jewish People, emerged in the 19th century as a response to the crisis of European Jewry and as a solution with the intention of addressing its plight.** The first Zionist Congress of 1897 dealt with two major problems.[10] The *first* was framed as the "problem of Judaism," *(tzarat hayahadut)* which referred to the Jewish People being a scattered minority among many nations without sovereignty or self-determination. The *second* was the "problem of Jews," *(tzarat hayehudim)* which referred to individual Jews and Jewish communities being subjected to persecution and poverty. It therefore envisioned mass repatriation to Zion in order to remedy the conundrum of Jewish life in the Diaspora. The forbearers of Zionism and the leaders who followed in their footsteps expressed grave concerns for the future of European Jewry and acted with a deep sense of urgency. Sadly, history proved their fears realized.

22. **It took Zionism nearly a century to become a leading force in Judaism and a dominant movement within the Jewish People.** During its first decades, roughly from the 1860s until the late 1890s, Zionism had few supporters, and only a handful actually repatriated to Zion, compared to the hundreds of thousands of Jews who emigrated from Europe to the USA and other places during that same period. Under the Ottoman Empire, the Jewish community in Zion *(hayishuv hayashan)* was a minute and distant corner of the Jewish world, which was isolated from the major upheaval of European Jewry of the 19th century. Over the ensuing fifty years, beginning with Herzl's 'Political Zionism' *(Tziyonut Medinit)* and culminating with the establishment of the State of Israel in 1948, the *Yishuv* rapidly developed demographically, economically, ideologically, politically and militarily to create a new Hebrew society and civilization that was anchored in the legacy of the Diaspora, but embodied a broad adaptation of it. By 1967 – following the stunning victory over the Arab armies, the unification of Jerusalem under Israeli sovereignty, the liberation of the ancestral lands of Judea and Samaria commonly referred to as the 'West Bank' and the conquest of the Sinai Peninsula and the Golan Heights – Zionism established itself as the dominant force among world Jewry.

---

10 See Ahad Ha'Ahm, "The Jewish State and the Jewish Problem," Jewish Virtual Library: http://www.jewishvirtuallibrary.org/jsource/Zionism/haam2.html.

23. In this process, **Zionism turned against exilic mentality and existence *(galutiyut)* and against Diaspora itself *(golah)*.** As the conditions in Europe deteriorated in the late 19th and early 20th centuries, Zionism increasingly rejected life outside of Zion as a matter of ideological principle. It saw life in exile as morally inferior, demeaning for the individual and unsustainable due to assimilation and antisemitism. It envisioned dismantling the Diaspora altogether, and expected all Jews to repatriate *(*make *aliyah)*, not only viewing such collective and individual immigration as an ideological duty but also as an existential and practical necessity. The State of Israel would go to great lengths to encourage such a mass return. **This outlook legitimized arrogance toward the Diaspora and ignorance of its legacy.**

24. Consequently, **much of the societal DNA that ensured Jewish survival, security, prosperity and leadership in the Diaspora became lost in Israel.** Zionism originally stemmed from Diaspora society and the settlements of the first wave of immigration (1882-1903) *(*First Aliyah*)* were modeled after Diaspora communities. Over time, starting with the Second Aliyah (1904-1914), new societal models were entertained, gradually abandoning Diaspora communal structures. Furthermore, the Zionist movement attempted to transform the personal and communal outlook of the immigrants into that of 'pioneers' *(halutzim)*, later also 'Hebrews' *(Ivrim)* and ultimately 'Israelis' *(Israelim)* through a societal 'melting pot' (*kur hituch*). Those who were born in Zion came to be known as *sabras (tzabarim)*, named after the sweet and soft fruit of the cactus, which is prickly on the outside. As a result, it marginalized and was condescending to their communal legacies and heritage – be they from Morocco, Poland, Yemen or Romania. Indisputably, repatriation required inevitable adaptations, but the leadership of the *Yishuv* and then of the State of Israel had little patience for – or capacity to – sensitively deal with nuance. Thus, key vehicles of Diaspora Jewish society were abandoned under the pressure of Hebrew civilization and within the framework of Israeli statehood.

25. **Israel's dramatic successes now place it in a position to fundamentally affect Jewish history.** Naturally, the establishment of a sovereign Jewish majority after two millennia of exile in 1948 out of the ashes of the *Shoah* represented a dramatic milestone in Jewish history. However, at that time, only five percent of the remaining Jews lived in that tiny and feeble nation surrounded by enemies. Had the State of Israel failed to protect itself, Zionism could have turned into a brief and painful episode

in a century that was particularly torturous for Jews. However, Israel has been able to go from strength to strength, major challenges, setbacks and difficulties notwithstanding. At the dawn of the 21st century, amid rare global turmoil and instability, Israel proudly boasts of remarkable achievements across all areas of modern life including economics, technology, military and society, as well as of a flourishing Jewish and Hebrew culture and a thriving world of Torah. It now races to become the largest and fastest growing Jewish community in the world, housing the most diverse Jewish population ever to live in one polity. Thus, Israel's success means that a significant mass of Jews no longer possesses the DNA of Flexigidity that ensured Jewish longevity and leadership in the Diaspora. As such, its rise or decline will dramatically impact Judaism, Jewish society and history.

26. **After two millennia of Diaspora, there is a dearth of collective Jewish wisdom about sustaining prosperity and security when Jews are a majority and have the power of government.** No country exists forever, and the rise and decline of nations have been extensively documented.[11] Furthermore, Jewish history provides good reason to question Israel's prospects, as the People of Israel failed to sustain sovereignty three times in its past: the kingdom of Israel was destroyed by the Assyrians in 722 BCE, the Judean Kingdom was conquered by the Babylonians in 586 BCE, and the Jewish polity of the Second Temple era was conquered by the Romans in 70 CE. Indeed, Israel's painful reality is that the performance of its government and key sectors of its society fail to inspire.

27. Consequently, **Israel's dilemma is daunting: the outcome of Zionism, which sought to resolve the so-called 'Jewish problem' is a State of Israel that may threaten the future of Judaism.** Indeed, establishing a sovereign independent state for the Jewish People is paramount to making Jewish society whole on multiple levels, and Zionism pledged to resolve the entire predicament of Jews and Judaism within a Jewish nation state. Had the vision of classical Zionism been realized, all Jews would have relocated to Zion, Diaspora society would have been dismantled altogether and all Jewish eggs would have been placed in one political and cultural basket: the State of Israel. This would have dealt a

---

11 For a general discussion of the processes and dynamics of rise, golden eras and decline of nations and peoples, see Wald Shalom Salomon, *Rise and Decline of Civilizations: Lessons for the Jewish People*, Miskal – Yedioth Ahronoth Books and Chemed Books, 2013, p. 157-173 (in Hebrew).

deadly blow to Judaism's vitality, replacing a society that successfully developed mechanisms to ensure its immortality in human terms, as so eloquently articulated by Mark Twain. It would have done so in order to re-establish sovereign independence, this time in 'eternity,' without a robust approach that engenders confidence in the ability of Israel to succeed, despite three past failures.

28.   Indeed, **many changes to the DNA of Jewish Diaspora society in Zion were exaggerated and even unnecessary.** No doubt that a profound transformation occurs in Jewish society within the context of sovereignty in Zion and upon the establishment of a government and a legislature. Yet, other alterations, primarily the dismantling of community leadership and institutions that were in retrospect excessive and unnecessary, are painfully missing in Israel's present and their absence may jeopardize its future. Furthermore, while there is no doubt that Israel's vitality requires it to house a critical mass of Jews, beyond a certain tipping point it may compromise the vitality of the Diaspora.

29.   **The Flexigidity Project aims to offer a vision for Israel and the Jewish world that addresses these tensions, enhancing not only Israel's prosperity and security, but also the vitality of Diaspora Jewry.** It focuses on critical aspects of society building in both places that are essential for the collective Flexigidity of the Jewish People.

30.   **Such a vision requires leadership that is committed to building a Flexigid society, both in Israel and the Diaspora.** Naturally, most people can only lead on a narrow spectrum of society, building or directing an institution as lay leaders and professionals, speaking out for an idea, standing for a cause, designing a program and volunteering their time and money. However, it is from these individual contributions that Jewish Flexigidity emerges.

Four Founding Stories

> This section details the four meta-stories of Judaism: faith and covenant, peoplehood, nationhood and the mission to be a light unto the nations (*or la'goim*). For each story, the text presents the core mission, key themes, values, priorities, institutions, villains and heroes, as well as the calendar of events that enshrine it in Jewish life. The last part of this section shows how these four stories are ever present in Jewish life and society. These meta-stories are the foundation of Jewish Flexigidity.

31. **Four meta-stories comprise the foundation of Jewish Flexigidity, forming a common identity, vision and mission and framing Judaism's collective understanding of its past, present, future and destiny.**[12] **These stories explain Judaism in terms of faith and covenant** *(emunah ve brit)*, **peoplehood** *(amiyut)*, **nationhood** *(le'om or umah)* **and being a light unto the nations** *(or la'goim).*[13]

32. **Each story is distinct, establishing a specific framework, mission and logic for the Jewish People.** All four stories have a core narrative and stand for certain values. Each of them is manifested through distinct practices, is served by designated institutions, has a following among Jews, is enshrined in tales *(aggadot)* and is personalized through certain heroes and villains.

33. **The origins of these stories can be traced to the Biblical figure of Abraham.** He embodied faith and covenant in his willingness to perform the ultimate act of servitude to God in the binding of his son, Isaac;[14] he represents peoplehood as the 'father' of all Jews who received God's

---

12 For a discussion of an 'existence of destiny,' see Rabbi Joseph B. Soloveitchik in *Kol Dodi Dofek, Listen: My Beloved Knocks*, Yeshiva University Press, 2006, p. 5-11. Rabbi Soloveitchik writes: "...an existence of destiny ... is an active existence, when man confronts the environment ... with an understanding of his uniqueness and value, freedom and capacity; without compromising his integrity and independence..."

13 See Sacks, *Future Tense*, p. 36, about the two meta-stories of peoplehood and faith and covenant as follows: "Jews, 'the children of Israel', are described in the Bible as both an am, a people, and an edah, a religiously constituted congregation. They are both an extended family with the same biological ancestor, Jacob/Israel, and a community of faith bounded by the covenant they made with God at Mount Sinai."

14 Genesis 22

promise to him and his seed;[15] he received the pledge to inherit the land of Canaan from God,[16] thus crowning it as the 'The Promised Land,' and he bought the Tomb of the Patriarchs (*Me'a'rat HaMachpela*) in Hebron for its full price;[17] and it was Abraham who was told that his seed would be a blessing for the families of the earth.[18] He smashed his father's icons in his fight against paganism,[19] and there is extensive rabbinic literature that frames him as a person who sought to morally and spiritually elevate those around him.

34. **Each story also has sources in Jewish texts that epitomize it and support its attempt to claim primacy in Jewish thought and outlook.** The story of nationhood teaches that the settlement of the Land of Israel is equal to all other commandments (*mitzvot*) of the Torah.[20] The story of *or la'goim* draws upon the saying of Hillel the Elder *(Hillel HaZaken)*[21] that the entire Torah is captured by the commandment: "love thy neighbor as thyself"[22] *(ve'ahavta le're'a'cha kamocha)* and by the notion that all human beings were created in the image of God.[23] The story of faith views collective and individual observance as the secret of Jewish survival, as Ahad Ha'Ahm was known to say, "more than the Jews have kept *Shabbat*, *Shabbat* has kept the Jews."[24] And the story of peoplehood enshrines the maxim that all of Israel is responsible for each other *(kol Yisrael arevim ze bazeh)*, a principle that is rooted in the promised communal blessings and curses of Deuteronomy.[25]

---

15   Genesis 12:2-3

16   Genesis 13:14-18

17   Genesis 23:9

18   Genesis 12:3 and Isaiah 42:6

19   Genesis Rabbah, Chapter 38

20   Sifrei Devarim, 80

21   Babylonian Talmud Shabbat 31a

22   Leviticus 19:18. Hillel said: "Whatever you hate don't do to others that is the entire Torah". Rabbi Akiva is quoted as using Leviticus 19:18 in a similar context.

23   Genesis 1:27

24   Ahad Ha'Ahm, *On a Crossroads (Ahl Parashat Drachim)*, volume 3, p. 79

25   Deuteronomy 27

35.   **All four stories are ever present in Judaism, Jewish philosophy, life and society, both throughout the Diaspora and in the Modern State of Israel.** Two or more of these stories shape every major Jewish event, holiday and ritual. They inspired Zionism since its inception, shaped the foundations of the State of Israel in 1948 and continue to affect the direction of Israeli society. Many of the giant leaders of the Jewish People and their seminal works spoke to multiple stories, as did prominent Zionist and Israeli leaders.

Peoplehood

36.   **The story of Peoplehood *(amiyut)* is anchored in the view of Jews as a people *(ahm)* and as a tribe *(shevet).*** [26] This narrative embraces the entirety of the people of Israel *(klal ahm Israel)*. Its central themes are the intrinsic interconnectedness and mutual responsibility among all Jews, [27] which overshadow any other differences such as in faith, values, culture, practices, geography, education and affluence. According to this story, Jews connect through shared heritage, memories, stories and destiny, and relate to each other in language and through symbols that are used as though among family, which is incomplete without all of its individual members and very difficult to leave.

37.   **The question of 'who is a Jew?' i.e., who is a member of the Jewish family, is central to this meta-story.** All people who are born to a Jewish mother or converted to Judaism according to the strict requirements of the *halacha* are unequivocally seen as part of the 'family.' Meanwhile, there are heated disagreements as to who else may be admitted in a process of conversion. Some denominations and rabbis, partly in seeking to broaden the Jewish tent, accept as Jews people who are children of a Jewish father and a non-Jewish mother and lower the legal bar for conversion. Others expect proof of religious observance and trace only the maternal bloodline to verify Jewishness.

38.   **Distinct values underlie the story of Jewish Peoplehood.** It views the people of Israel as a whole *(klal ahm Israel),* which is judged as one by God and other humans, and is incomplete in the absence of any of its

---

26   Sacks, *Future Tense*, p. 36: "Jews, 'the children of Israel', are described in the Bible as both an *ahm*, a people, and an *edah*, a religiously constituted congregation. They are both an extended family with the same biological ancestor, Jacob/Israel..."

27   For brief discussion of the notion of mutual responsibility, see Sacks, *Future Tense*, p. 40-45.

members. This ideal underlies a strong sense of mutual responsibility *(arevut)* of every Jew to all other Jews.[28] It has been manifested in the ancient responsibility and practice of redeeming captives *(pidyon shvuim)*, in giving charity to struggling communities *(tzedaka)* and in the notion that every Jew is responsible and liable for the religious performance of other Jews. This relationship has roots in the communal blessings and curses of Deuteronomy,[29] and has extensive support in rabbinic literature. Mobilization on the behalf of Jewish Peoplehood occurs in modern times as well: a global Jewish movement "Let My People Go" fought to end Soviet oppression against its Jews; the Hassidic Chabad Lubavitch movement deploys 'Mitzvah Tanks' to motivate all Jews to perform *mitzvoth*; the State of Israel and Diaspora Jewish organizations reach out to help Jews in need around the world.

39. **The heroes of this story embodied in their philosophy and action the selfless service of and commitment to the entire Jewish People, and not to a specific faction within it.** They stood up for their fellow Jews at great personal risk and cost. Prominent examples include: Moses, who protected one of his brethren from the beating of an Egyptian;[30] Mordechai, who pushed his niece Esther into protecting the Jewish People from the decree of Haman[31] and Esther who risked her life on behalf of the Jewish People.[32] Modern day figures like Moses Montefiore, the Rothschilds, Herzl and the Lubavitcher Rebbe also carried a vision for and service to the entire Jewish People.

40. **The villains of this story are Gentiles who attacked the Jewish People and Jews because of their Peoplehood, as well as Jews who abdicated their responsibility toward other Jews.** Examples include Haman, who sought to kill all Jews because of his fury against Mordechai,[33] as well as modern antisemites who attack Jews for their connectedness to other Jews across political borders. This story also views as villains fellow Jews who turned against their brethren for ideology or other benefits. Examples include the Biblical figures of Datan and Aviram who,

---

28 For a discussion of the idea of collective responsibility, see Sacks *Future Tense* p. 40-45.

29 Deuteronomy 27 & 28

30 Exodus 2:11-12

31 Esther 4:13-14

32 Esther 5

33 Esther 3:1

according to tradition, threatened to turn in Moses to the Egyptians,[34] some of the Jewish police in the ghettos of Europe during World War II and the Jewish 'kapos' in the Nazi concentration camps,' Jewish leaders of the Bolshevik Party in the Soviet Union,[35] and, most recently, Jewish and Israeli intellectuals who deny the right of the State of Israel to exist.

41. **The practices that embody this story relate to the entire people of Israel** *(klal ahm Israel)*. A prime example is the general plural language of Jewish prayers, exemplified by the confessional prayers of the Jewish High Holidays.[36] It embodies the notion that Jews stand before God as a community and not as individuals, and that all Jews are bound by Jewish law purely by their membership in this 'family' irrespective of their personal faithfulness and observance. Another example is the multitude of obligations on individual Jews and Jewish communities to aid other members of the Jewish People in danger and need. Jewish history is full of examples of communal efforts to free imprisoned Jews and to ease their suffering. A recent example is the global campaign to free the Israeli soldier Gilad Shalit who was held in Hamas captivity in Gaza between 2006 and 2011.

42. **The masses of this story are Jews who feel bound to their fellow Jews on the basis of their being members of this 'familial tribe.'** They view Jews whom they may barely know as sharing a history and a destiny, and are willing to sacrifice some of their wellbeing for their favor. This may take the form of prayers, home hospitality, charity and political mobilization.

43. **Several events on the Jewish calendar highlight the peoplehood narrative and hail individuals that served this ideal.** On Passover *(Pesach)* Jews commemorate their transformation from twelve tribes into a people through the journey of the exodus from Egypt.[37] During the holiday of Pentecost *(Shavuot)* Jews retell the story of Ruth who, in talking to Naomi, preceded "your people are my people" to the

---

34   Exodus 2:13; Exodus Rabbah Parsha Aleph

35   See for example about Roza Luxembourg, in Paul Johnson, *A History of the Jews*, p. 448.

36   For an eloquent description of this approach, see Soloveitchik in *Kol Dodi Dofek*, p. 19.

37   The 70 members of the family described as descending with Jacob to Egypt in Genesis 46:27 have grown into a people whose men alone numbered six-hundred thousand strong by Exodus 12:37.

statement "your God is my God."[38] She joined the Israelites and bore the bloodline of King David.[39] The holiday of Purim recounts the leadership of Mordechai who invoked the sentiments of peoplehood and mutual responsibility in Esther, demanding that she risk her life for her people.[40]

44. *Finally,* **many Jewish institutions nurture, sustain and build the value of peoplehood.** The synagogues *(beit knesset)* serve as a place for religious practice, as well as for communal congregation. Every sizeable Jewish community throughout history had a committee *(va'ad or nesiut)*, which was built to represent and address collective concerns,[41] and a fund *(kuppah)* to underwrite communal needs such as education, food, defense and burial services.[42] Over the past centuries and in an increasingly globalized world, Jews have built global organizations in keeping with the vision of Peoplehood, such as the United Jewish Appeal, the Federation System, and the American Joint Distribution Committee for welfare; the French Alliance and similar associations in Germany and Britain for education; World Jewish Congress and American Jewish Committee for political representation; and the Maccabee Games for sport. Also, in times of crisis, ad hoc global organizations and movements were created by Jews to help other Jews, such as the Rescue Committees *(Va'ad HaHatzala)* during the Shoah and the National Council of Soviet Jewry. Finally, the largest Peoplehood project today is the very successful Birthright Israel program, launched in 1999, which grants every Jewish young adult a free visit to Israel as a matter of their right by birth. Birthright participants are Jews from Israel and the Diaspora, and it is funded as a joint venture between the Government of Israel and Diaspora Jewry.

38   Ruth 1:16

39   Ruth 4:22

40   Esther 4:13-14

41   See also the function of the 'lobbyist' *(Shtadlan)* on behalf of Jewish community representing its collective interests before the non-Jewish authorities. Johnson, *A History of the Jews*, P. 258.

42   Johnson, *A History of the Jews*, P. 203: "From Temple times, the kuppah or collecting box was a pivot around which the Jewish welfare-community revolved, Maimonides stating: 'We have never seen or heard of a Jewish community which does not have a kuppah."

Nationhood

45.   The story of 'nationhood' *(le'om or umah)* speaks of the Jewish
      People as bound by an unbreakable association with its land, Zion. It
      emphasizes that the People of Israel originated from a specific geographic
      location – the Land of Israel with Jerusalem, also known as Zion, at its
      heart. Nearly four thousand years ago, the Hebrews, later known as the
      Israelites, and then as the Jewish People – emerged in that territory.
      They preserved uninterrupted loyalty to, association with and presence
      in this land in spite of multiple forced departures. This story holds that
      a Jew's life is compromised by exile *(galut)* and by the condition of the
      Diaspora *(galutiyut)* and that a full Jewish life on personal, communal,
      national and religious levels can only be led in Zion. Thus, during their
      nearly two millennia of exile, Jews have always yearned to return to their
      motherland, live freely in it and realize their self-determination within
      independent sovereign institutions. This dormant dream was rekindled
      and realized in the 20th century by the call of Zionism and by the actions
      of Zionists. Thus **Zionism is the modern manifestation of this outlook.**

46.   **The central themes of this story are the legitimacy of the right of the
      Jewish People to the Land of Israel, the quest to realize this right
      and related dilemmas that have been facing Zionism and the modern
      State of Israel.** It emphasizes historic and legal arguments that establish
      the inalienable right of the Jewish People to their land, and stresses the
      uninterrupted Jewish loyalty to – and presence in – Zion throughout the
      generations. Since the inception of political Zionism in the 1880s, and
      particularly since the establishment of the State of Israel, the story of
      nationhood has been grappling with dilemmas relating to Jewish political
      and economic self-determination, sovereignty, being a majority, the
      role of religion in a modern Jewish polity, the relationship with Jewish
      Diaspora and to the ideal and vision of becoming a model society *(hevrat
      mofet).*

47.   **The values that underlie this story relate to Zion and Jerusalem and
      to their rebuilding under Jewish sovereignty.** They stem from their
      intrinsic sanctity to the Jewish People *(kedushat ha'aretz)*, and uphold
      the redeeming of the land from foreign hands and their transfer to Jewish
      ownership *(ge'ulat ha'aretz),* the repatriation of Jews to it *(aliyah),* the
      ingathering of the Diasporas to Zion *(kibbutz galuyot),* the settlement
      of the land *(hityashvut),* and its development and building *(bin'yan
      aa'aretz).*

48. **The heroes of this story are people who fought for these ideals.** In the Bible, we read about Joshua and Caleb (*Yehoshua* and *Calev*) who spoke well of the Land of Israel before Moses and the People,[43] King David who established the House and the Kingdom of David, with Jerusalem as its capital, the Maccabees who defeated the Greeks and achieved political and religious independence that lasted, to varying degrees, for nearly one hundred and thirty years (167-63 BCE), and Bar Kochva who led the rebellion against the Roman Empire (132-135 AD). They also include the 12th century poet and philosopher Yehuda HaLevi, who wrote in Spain about the love of Zion: "my heart is in the East and I am in the ends of the West," and the kabalists of Safed *(Tsfat)* in the 16th century who made that city sacred along with Hebron and Jerusalem. Modern Jewish leaders who are heroes of this story are Herzl (1860-1904), Chaim Weitzman (1874-1952), Ze'ev Jabotinsky (1880-1940), David Ben-Gurion (1886-1973), Moshe Dayan (1915-1981) and Yitzhak Rabin (1922-1995). Modern non-Jewish heroes of this story include the writer Marry Anne Evans, known by the pen name George Eliot (1819-1880), Foreign Secretary of Britain Lord James Balfour (1848-1930), and the thirty-third President of the USA Harry S. Truman (1884-1972). All of them believed in the association of the Jewish People to Zion and helped to legitimize and realize it.

49. **The villains of this story are those who either denied or undermined the historical claim of the Jewish People to their land or who ideologically rejected Zionism and the State of Israel.** This includes Biblical figures, such as the ten spies who spoke ill of the Land of Israel before Moses, as well as the Babylonian, Greek and Roman empires that exiled the Jews from their land. In modern times, they include Pan-Arab nationalism and the Islamic Republic of Iran, which reject the Jewish People's right to self-determination in their own nation-state, ultimately negating the State of Israel's right to exist. They also include Jewish groups such as the ultra-orthodox *Neturei Karta* community and the secular socialist Bund movement, as well as radical left-wing voices that reject the idea of Jewish nationhood on religious and ideological grounds.

50. **Many practices embody the story of nationhood by connecting Jews spiritually, financially and tangibly to Zion and the State of Israel.** Scratching the surface, this list includes passages in the three traditional daily prayers that invoke the Land of Israel and convey both a yearning for the return to Zion and for the reestablishment of the House of David

---

43   Numbers 14:17

and the Temple *(Beit Mikdash)* in Jerusalem "soon in our time" *(bimhera b'yameinu)*; the Jewish calendar that corresponds to the agricultural cycle of the Land of Israel, and therefore synchronizes Jewish life in the Diaspora to it;[44] the custom of pledging loyalty to Jerusalem and the breaking of the glass at weddings, as well as leaving an unfinished corner in one's home in order to commemorate the destruction of Jerusalem; religious commandments that can only be performed in Zion; and the Pesach Seder, which ends with a prayer for "the next year in Jerusalem *(la'shana ha'ba'ah bi'Yerushalaim)*.

51. **Prominent institutions were created to serve this story.** Older examples include institutions for the collection and distribution of funds *(halukah)* to support Jews living in Zion, which existed in many communities and provided vital economic support throughout the centuries.[45] In modernity, the national awakening of the Jewish People in the 19th century led to the establishment of many institutions of nationhood, such as the Zionist Congress, the Jewish National Fund, the Jewish Agency for Israel, Keren HaYesod, and the women's organization Hadassah. It also led to the Jewish settlement in the Land of Israel *(the Yishuv)* under the Ottomans and the British, which later served as the foundation for the plethora of institutions of sovereignty that make up the modern State of Israel.

52. **Several events in the Jewish calendar anchor this story into the Jewish lifecycle.** Chanukah is a celebration of the victory of the Maccabees over the Greeks and of the reinstitution of political independence. During Pesach, Jews remember the exodus from Egypt and the journey to the Land of Israel. The destruction of Jerusalem and the Temples in 586 BCE by the Babylonians and in 70 CE by the Romans is remembered and relived annually by many Jews, who fast and mourn these traumatic events on the 9th day of the month of Av *(Tisha b'Av)*. On *Lag Ba'Omer*, Jews remember the Bar Kochva rebellion against the Romans in 132-135, which led to brief Jewish independence before being crushed.

53. **Many Jews view Zionism and the State of Israel as realizing and epitomizing the hopes and aspirations of this this narrative for all Jews.** Secular Israeli Zionists often view Israel as the ultimate solution to the predicament of Jews and of Judaism in the Diaspora, while Diaspora

---

44 See Avraham Infeld's talk about the rain of the Jews falling in the Land of Israel at http://www.youtube.com/watch?v=el0NB1c_Ec4.

45 Though the specific term *"haluka"* emerged in the late middle ages, the practice of supporting the Jews in the Land of Israel likely goes back to early rabbinic period.

Zionists consider Israel as the realization of the right to self-determination of the entire Jewish People. Israel's national-religious faction views the establishment of Israel in 1948 and the 1967 victory, which led to the reunification of Jerusalem, renewed Jewish sovereignty over the Temple Mount *(Har HaBaiyt)* and to the liberation of the ancestral land of Judea and Samaria, as signs of the beginning of the redemption *(reshit tzmichat ge'ulatenu)*.

54. Meanwhile, **certain Jewish factions reject this Zionist notion**: Ultra-orthodox Haredi groups, especially *Neturei Karta*, agree with Zionism that Jews will only fully realize their Peoplehood and religious life upon repatriation to Zion, but they hold that the time of this eventual return may only be determined by God. Thus, they view Zionists as seeking to hasten redemption, and Zionism as heresy. Other Haredi groups simply view the State of Israel and its government as fundamentally secular, and therefore morally corrupt and oppressive toward their outlook. Zionism's non-orthodox critics view the State of Israel as failing to fulfill the vision of being a model society that is a light unto the nations, pointing primarily to its continued control of the Palestinians. For some of them, the ideal of a state whose identity is anchored in its Jewishness is a fundamentally ill-conceived notion, making Israel's policies and practices illegitimate altogether.

Being a Light unto the Nations

55. **This story is about the mission of the Jewish People to serve as a 'light unto the nations'** *(or la'goim)* **and to be a blessing for the peoples of the earth.**[46] Traditionally, this ideal was understood to mean that the Jewish People would lead other nations to recognize God and His presence on earth by modeling upstanding ethics, practices and values in its society. The modern take on this ideal is that Jews will repair the world *(tikkun olam)* through their innovations and their contributions to society and humanity. Both understandings saddle the Jewish People with a unique mission to fulfill in the service of humanity both in the areas of morality and ethics, as well as in providing leadership, resources and practical solutions to global problems.

---

46   As expressed in the Bible in Genesis 12:3 and Isaiah 42:6.

56. **Traditionally, the central themes of this story have been Judaism's quest for the creation of a model society that will inspire non-Jews, and the understanding of such society as a systemic whole that is based on relationships among God, humans, animals and nature.** It engages a broad spectrum of issues by establishing expectations for and among individuals, households and their communities relating to: family life and relationships among spouses, children and parents and wider familial circles; accumulation of wealth and the obligations to share it with the poor, the needy, the sick *(tzedaka)* and the community; protecting the rights of minorities within Jewish society; preserving the environment and protecting animals while still providing for human needs; and establishing the norms of conduct among neighbors, creditors and debtors, employers and employees, landlords and their renters. It is exemplified in the notion that proper conduct among human beings precedes the Torah and its ethical foundation *(derech eretz kadma la'Torah)*.[47]

57. **Distinct values underlie this story, establishing the ethical foundations of a society that would be a 'light unto the nations.'** Many of them establish general expectations of appropriate conduct that Judaism holds as a standard for any and all human societies, such as the notion that all human beings were created in the image of God *(be'tzelem Elokim)* and desire for peace, charity and love for one's fellow *(ve'ahavta le're'a'acha kamocha)*. In this context, the so-called 'Noahide Laws' or the 'Seven Laws of Noah' *(sheva mitzvot bnei Noah)*,[48] establish Judaism's most fundamental moral expectations for all humanity, sanctifying life, affirming the right to own property and calling for compassion for animals *(tza'ar ba'alei haim)*.

58. **The heroes of this story are individuals who articulated a broad vision for humanity as Jews and who worked to create a model society.** Examples include Moses, who introduced the Ten Commandments and a message of universal morality; the prophet Isaiah, who provided a pacifist vision for humanity by calling for the beating of swords into plowshares;[49] Hillel, whose enjoinment 'That which is hateful to you, do not do to your fellow[50] applies to all humanity; the Kibbutz settlements, which developed a unique model of an egalitarian society

---

47   Rabbi Israel Meir Lau, *Foundations*, p. 30

48   Tosefta Avodah Zara 9.4, quoted in Babylonian Talmud Sanhedrin 56a

49   Isaiah 2:4

50   Babylonian Talmud, Shabbat 31a

that served as a source of inspiration around the world; and Israeli and Jewish organizations and individuals who are disproportionally present in institutions and activities that tackle humanity's toughest challenges of human development.

59. **The mission of *or la'goim* is served by distinct institutions and practices.** There is an extensive body of Jewish Law relating to social justice and to the treatment of the poor, needy, sick, widow, foreigner *(gher)* and underprivileged. There are environmental laws relating to the treatment of the land, such as the obligation to give it a year of rest every 7th year *(shmita),* and laws regarding the treatment of one's animals *(tza'ar ba'alei haim).* Meanwhile, many Jewish prayers express yearning for harmony and peace in the world.

60. **The masses that uphold this story include numerous Jews around the world who refused to accept the prevailing moral condition and reality of humanity and fought to change them.** In antiquity, they included those who rejected the practices of the dominant Greek culture by condemning the gladiator bouts in the Coliseum.[51] In modernity, they include those who work to better society under the unifying banner of *tikkun olam.* Jews are often disproportionally represented in local nongovernmental not-for-profit efforts and organizations that fight poverty and hunger, help children at risk and reach out to the sick and the needy. They are also significantly present in dealing with global challenges, such as climate change, curing diseases, ensuring food and water security and promoting world peace.

61. **Another key Jewish practice related to the mission of being a 'light unto the nations' is the Jewish tendency to extract universal values, morality and ethics from particular and specific experiences of the Jewish People.** Every Jewish holiday can be understood to carry a general message for humanity. Every portion *(parasha)* of the five books of Moses *(Chumash* or *Torah)* and many verses in the Bible have been interpreted in a way that transcends Jewish particularism to deliver a broad, universal lesson about society. A prominent example is the story of the exodus from Egypt that has inspired many beyond the Jewish People. This tendency is rooted in the Jewish belief that the Torah embodies God's wishes for humanity that it be perfect, coherent and without contradiction, redundancy or lacking in letter, word and even

---

51 Babylonian Talmud, Avodah Zarah 18b commenting on Tosefta Avodah Zara chapter 2

the crowns on the letters *(ktarim)*.[52] This view has propelled Jews to seek to explicate 'unifying theories' that logically account for entire fields in science, philosophy and society, and for humanity at large. Rabbi Michael Paley calls this Jewish approach "oneness."[53] It may well lie at the heart of why an outstanding number of individual Jews – such as Sigmund Freud, Milton Friedman and Albert Einstein – were able to articulate a broad global framework for society within their individual fields.[54]

62. Here too, **several events stand out in the Jewish calendar anchoring this story to Jewish society.** Every *Shabbat*, Jews recite a verse or emphasizing that their day of rest is not only a Jewish right, but a universal one for every human and animals, as well. Many Jewish holidays such as the Festival of Booths *(Sukkoth)*, Pesach, Purim and Pentecost *(Shavuot)* establish expectations for societal responsibility in the form of charity, and carry a universal message about freedom, justice, free will, meritocracy, modesty and scholarship.

Faith and Covenant

63. **This story is about Judaism as a religion *(dat)* or faith *(emunah)* that** strives to inform, elevate and discipline, thereby sanctifying the life of every Jew and of the entire People of Israel.

64. **Its core narrative is about the covenant *(brith)* and a special relationship between God and the entire People of Israel *(klal ahm Israel)*, as well as between every individual Jew and God.**[55] This narrative views all Jews as a religious community and as having been personally present at the foot of Mount Sinai when the Torah was given

---

52 Deuteronomy, 4:2 instructs: "You shall not add to the word which I command you, nor shall you subtract from it…" The Babylonian Talmud in Eruvin 13a instructs a scribe: "…if you add or subtract even a single letter, [it is as if] you have destroyed the entire world!". The Rambam likewise emphasizes in his Mishne Torah that that if one letter is added to or missing from a Torah, it is invalidated and not fit for ritual use (Hilchot Sefer Torah 7:11).

53 On the idea of oneness see conversation between Rabbi Michael Paley and William Novak in "Kerem: Creative Explorations in Judaism", Jewish Study Center Press, Inc., Washington DC, 2012, volume no. 13 p. 35.

54 Johnson, *A History of the Jews*, p. 267

55 Jonathan Sacks, *Future Tense*, p. 36: "Jews, 'the children of Israel', are described in the Bible as both an *ahm*, a people, and an *edah*, a religiously constituted congregation … a community of faith bounded by the covenant they made with God at Mount Sinai."

to Moses. It therefore mandates each and every Jewish man and woman to realize their obligations under this covenant by living a 'life of Torah and *mitzvot*,' i.e. of religious observance. It invokes metaphors of shepherd and sheep[56] and of father and children to describe this unique association. This vision of the Jewish People calls for wholehearted acceptance of the sovereignty of God and obedience toward Him.

65. Thus, **the mission of the Jewish People, according to this narrative, is to determine God's wishes and execute His will.** This story holds that God's wisdom is captured in the Torah, which was given to Moses on Mount Sinai. The Ethics of the Fathers *(Pirkei Avot)* establishes that the Torah was then passed on from Moses to Joshua, and from him to the elders *(z'kenim)*, and from them to the prophets *(ne'vi'im)*, who passed it to the sages *(Knesset Gdola).*[57] The permanent quest to understand the wishes of God and to realize them continues through learning in the *beit midrash*, which attempts to bridge ancient texts with an ever-changing reality, thus perpetually developing Jewish law *(halacha)*.

66. **Some of the central themes of this story have much in common with other religions.** They include faith *(emunah),* doubt *(safek)* and repentance *(tshuvah);* obedience *(ki'yum mitzvoth)* and lack thereof *(averah);* sacrifice *(korbanot),* charity *(tzedakah)* and kindness *(che'sed);* prophesy *(ne'vu'ah)*; the coming of the messiah *(mashi'ach)* and redemption *(ge'ulah).* Within this narrative, there are extensive deliberations on the relationship between faith and reason, religion and science, determinism and free will and the historicity of the Bible and the relationship of Judaism to other religions.

67. **Distinct values underlie this story.** They include obedience *(ki'yum mitzvoth),* faith *(emunah)* and self-sacrifice *(kiddush haShem)* by serving the will of God in spite of tangible sacrifices such as poverty, hardship, risk and even martyrdom. These values are contrasted with actions that bring dishonor to God's covenant with the Jews *(hilul haShem)*.

68. **Jews who sacrificed to preserve the *brith (kiddush HaShem)* are heroes of this story.** Examples include the Maccabees, who rose against the Greeks and their attempts to suffocate the world of Torah; the ten

---

56   Psalms, 23:1: "The Lord is my shepherd, I shall not want..."

57   Ethics of the Fathers 1:1.

martyrs *(Aseret Harugei Malchut)*, rabbis who suffered torturous deaths at the hands of the Romans due to their devoted teaching of the Torah;[58] Jews who were burnt at the stake for defiance of the Spanish inquisitors; and the rabbis who sustained Jewish life in the Soviet Union during the dark days of communism at grave personal risk.

69. **Another group of heroes of this story of faith are the sages and prominent rabbis whose Torah scholarship echoed around the world and throughout the generations.** Hillel the Elder *(Hillel HaZaken)*; Rabbi Akiva; Rabbi Yehudah HaNasi, who redacted the *Mishnah* in the 2nd century; Rabbi Moshe Ben-Maimon, (Rambam, also known as Maimonides) who codified Jewish law in his Mishnne Torah in the 12th century; and Rabbi Elijah Ben Shlomo Zalman Kremer, known as the Vilna Gaon, and his student, Rabbi Chaim Volozhin, who revolutionized the yeshiva world in the 18th century. Every century produced a handful of towering intellectual religious leaders *(gedolei hador)* whose work impacted the entire Jewish world for generations.

70. **The villains of this story are Jews who betray the *brith* and Gentiles who try to sever the connection between the Jews, the Jewish People and God.** Prominent examples include the Greek King Antiochus, the Roman Caesar, Hadrian, the Crusaders, the Spanish Inquisitors and communist leaders who attacked the Jewish faith by banning its rituals, forcing religious disobedience, persecuting and often executing rabbis and destroying Jewish institutions. In each of these episodes, as well as in between them, there were Jews who turned against the *brith*. In antiquity, a converted Jew led the Roman legion against the Jews of Alexandria, and Hellenized Jews betrayed sages who taught Torah to be executed.[59] In Spain, some Jewish *conversos* spearheaded the persecutions of the Spanish Inquisition.[60] And, in the Soviet Union, the Politbureau was populated by several Jews who persecuted Judaism and their fellow Jews.[61]

---

58 The Ten Martyrs are remembered in part of the *Musaf* (literally, additional) prayer during Yom Kippur and during the prayers of the Ninth day of Av *(Tish'ah Be'Av)*.

59 See Wikipedia entry on Tiberius Julius Alexander leading his legions against Alexandria Jews and participating in the siege of Jerusalem: http://en.wikipedia.org/wiki/Tiberius_Julius_Alexander. See also Binyamin Lau, *Sages Volume II*, p. 100-102 (in Hebrew) about the *Yekum Elohimus*, the Hellenized High Priest *(Cohen Gadol)*, who surrendered and executed his uncle the sage, Yossie Ben Yoezer.

60 For example, see about the converso Alfonso de Spina in Johnson, *A History of the Jews*, p. 225.

61 See about Roza Luxembourg, in Johnson, *A History of the Jews*, p. 448.

71. In addition to the regular daily prayers, **during several annual events on the Jewish calendar Jews reaffirm their *brith* with God**. Examples include: the Jewish new year *(Rosh HaShana)*, which marks the day of divine judgment; the Day of Atonement *(Yom Kippur)*, when Jews plea for forgiveness; The Feast of Booths *(Sukkoth)*, when Jews remember the forty years in the desert and their complete dependence on God during that time; Passover *(Pesach)*, when Jews remember their exodus from Egypt as an outcome of powerful divine intervention; and Pentecost *(Shavuot)*, which marks the anniversary of the giving of the Torah to Moses on Mount Sinai.

72. **Many practices embody this story. They are commandments relating to the relationship between the individual and God *(mitzvoth bein adam la-makom)* and demonstrating the love for God *(ahavat haShem)*.** The most dramatic practice that reenacts the covenant is the act of circumcision *(brith milah)* of every Jewish boy at the age of eight days, and of any man who joins the Jewish People. Every Friday night at *Shabbat* dinner *(se'udat Shabbat)*, Jews testify to the existence of the covenant during the ceremonial blessing over the wine *(kiddush)*. Prayer represents the intimate connection between a Jew and God through their daily, weekly, monthly and annual routines. Particular prayers and blessings *(brachot)* are designed for specific human conditions such as sickness or health, grief or happiness, risk or survival, as well as for transitional moments such as births, coming of age *(bat-mitzva and bar-mitzva)*, wedding, parenthood and death of loved ones.

73. **The masses who uphold this story are Jews of faith who believe in God and preserve the *brith*.** To varying degrees, they espouse the values of this story, pray to God and observe the religious commandments *(mitzvot)*, even if they practice an individually particular set of *mitzvot* that fits their outlook and life.

74. **The institutions that serve, preserve and develop this story are places of worship, religious study and observance:** synagogues allow for prayer and worship; the *beit midrash* develops law *(halacha)*; religious schools educate all ages from toddlers at the age of three *(heder)* to children and adolescents *(yeshivot)* and, in more recent times, also for unmarried women *(ulpana)*, married men *(kolel)* and married women *(midrasha)*; a ritual bath *(mikveh)* is essential to allow for the observance of the laws of family purity *(teharat mishpacha)*; a designated institution provides burial services*(chevra kadisha)*; a court *(beit din)* resolves

disputes by the magistrate *(dayan)* based on Jewish law; and rabbis who serve as a source of religious authority.

75. **This story prides itself on the most distinct Jewish creation, the world of Jewish law *(halacha)* and Jewish tales *(aggadah)*, which underlie the unique way of Jewish life.** The Talmud, where the *halacha* was developed through debates among sages that lasted centuries, is seen by some as one of the greatest intellectual achievements of humanity. The world of *aggadah* offers context to formal *halacha* and therefore qualifies its rigid application. Together they provide a deep insight into the making of society, from the level of individual persons and their entire life cycle, to the levels of family, community, people and the world at large.

76. *Finally*, **the story of faith stands out among the four meta-stories of Judaism because it embraces, co-opts, and, thereby enshrines values and practices that emanate from the other stories and consistently serve the Jewish People.** Thus, Jewish religion serves to cement the DNA of Jewish society building. For example, there are commandments and prayers that emphasize Peoplehood by referring to the entire people of Israel *(klal ahm Israel)*, or to mutual responsibility *(arevut)*; to nationhood, by referring to the return to Zion and to the reestablishment of the house of David; and to *or la'goim* by establishing laws to protect and support the poor, needy, sick, the convert *(gehr)* and the alien resident *(gehr toshav)*, as well as norms for treating one's enemies.

Four Stories Ever Present

77. **The four meta-stories of Judaism are deeply rooted in Jewish heritage and tradition and will continue to shape Jewish destiny.**

78. **Two or more of these stories are present in shaping every major Jewish event, holiday and ritual.** Every Sabbath – beginning with its entry *(kabalat Shabbat)*, and continuing through the meals and blessings *(kiddush)* and its conclusion *(havdala)* – incorporates the four narratives. Throughout the Sabbath, Jews pray for the return to Zion, speak in plural on behalf of all the people of Israel, and testify about and re-commit to the covenant with God. They also remember that, as all human beings were created equal and in the image of God, the Sabbath was given not only to Jews but also to non-Jews within the Jewish domain, as well as to animals.[62]

---

62   See Rabbi Israel Meir Lau, Foundations, p. 170-171.

79. **All Jewish holidays can be understood and related to through two or more of these narratives.** The most prominent example of this phenomenon is the holiday of Passover *(Pesach)* and the text of its ritualized reenactment *(hagadah)*. It relates to the story of faith when remembering the 'strong arm' of God and His miracles that took the Israelites out of Egypt; to the story of Peoplehood through the discussion of the formation of the people through the forty-year journey in the desert; to the notion of being an *or la'goyim* through the themes of resistance to slavery and oppression and transformation into freedom; and to nationhood not only through the story of the long journey to Zion through the desert, but also in the *seder*'s concluding affirmation, "Next year in Jerusalem."

80. **Many great leaders of the Jewish People merged these stories into their vision and actions.** As mentioned earlier, Abraham is the source of all four stories through his life journey. Similarly, these stories can be found in the works leadership of Moses, prophets, leading Talmudic sages, Rambam, Herzl and David Ben-Gurion. In fact, that integration of multiple stories may have been essential for their ascendance to greatness.

81. **Non-Jews have also used these narratives to describe Jews.** The Roman historian Tacitus viewed the Jews through the prism of peoplehood, nationhood and religion.[63] During the Greek occupation of Judea, Jews were allowed a semblance of self-rule but denied, particularly during the reign of Antiochus IV Epiphanes, their identity as a religion.[64] In the 18th century, the French Stalinas Comte de Clermonte Tonnerre famously said, "The Jews should be denied everything as a nation, but granted everything as individuals."[65] Before the issuance of the 1917 Balfour Declaration, the British Government was also forced to consider whether Jews were a people, a nation or

---

63 See Tacitus, *Histories*, Book 5, section 5 writing about the Jews: "...the Jews are extremely loyal toward one another, and always ready to show compassion ... They sit apart at meals, and they sleep apart ... They adopted circumcision to distinguish themselves from other peoples by this difference ... the Jews conceive of one god only, and that with the mind alone: they regard as impious those who make from perishable materials representations of gods in man's image; that supreme and eternal being is to them incapable of representation and without end ... they set up no statues in their cities, still less in their temples; this flattery is not paid their kings..." Taken from: http:// penelope.uchicago.edu/Thayer/E/Roman/Texts/Tacitus/Histories/5A*.html.

64 II Maccabees, 6:1–11

65 Johnson, *A History of the Jews*, p. 306

a religion.[66] The 1947 United Nations General Assembly Resolution 181, which led to the establishment of the State of Israel, speaks of a 'Jewish State' and an 'Arab State,' effectively framing Jews as a nation.[67] Finally, while the Government of Israel presently demands the world to recognize it as the nation-state of the Jewish People, many, including some Arab and Palestinian leaders, reject the notion of Jewish peoplehood and nationhood, regarding Judaism as merely a religion.[68] Meanwhile there are numerous non-Jews who understand Judaism as a religious community of common descent, born of a certain location, and with a mission on behalf of all humanity.

82. *Finally,* **the Jewish vision for the end-of-days** *(acharit hayamim)* **as recounted in the Biblical book of Isaiah integrates the four stories, as well.** It embraces the story of religion by speaking about repentance *(tshuva)*, rebuilding of the Temple, renewal of sacrifices and the coming of the messiah *(be'viat hamashiach)*; the story of nationhood by envisioning the return to Zion, the ingathering of the exiles, and the reestablishment of Jewish independence under the House of David; the story of peoplehood by relating to the entire Jewish People that will assemble from the Diaspora; and to the story of *or la'goim* by the prophesy that a wolf shall dwell with the sheep,[69] and by envisioning global peace and harmony, free of strife and hardship: "They shall

---

66 See Jonathan Schneer, *The Balfour Declaration,* p. 145-147 concerning the necessity of the British cabinet to consider competing claims by Jews, most particularly Herbet Samuel and Edwin Montagu, as to the collective status of the Jewish People. Samuel argued that Jews were bound by a common relationship. Montagu argued that "There is no Jewish race as a homogenous whole. It is quite obvious that the Jews in Great Britain are as remote from the Jews in Morocco ... as the Christian Englishman is from the moor or Hindoo," viewing Judaism exclusively as a religion.

67 United Nations General Assembly Resolution 181, Part III, Section C, November 29, 1947.

68 Saeb Erekat, Palestinian Chief Negotiator, said: "There is no country in the world where religious and national identities are intertwined". See Jerusalem Post article titled: "Erekat: We Won't Accept Jewish Israel", December 11, 2007 (http://www.jpost.com/ Israel/Erekat-We-wont-accept-Jewish-Israel).

Also, the Government of Argentina refused to recognize the State of Israel as having any standing in the investigation of the Iran's involvement in the bombing of the Buenos Aires Jewish Community Center: "El atentado sufrido por el pueblo de nuestra patria el 18 de julio de 1994 no involucró a ningún ciudadano Israeli." See: http://www.mrecic. gov.ar/es/argentina-rechaza-el-pedido-de-explicaciones-formulado-por-israel.

69 Isaiah 11:6-8

beat their swords into plowshares and their spears into pruning hooks; nation shall not lift sword against nation, neither shall they learn war anymore."[70]

---

70 Isaiah 2:4. "Time after time it is settled that in the time of Mashia'ch nothing will be different in nature or the world only that Israel will be ruled by themselves and dwell in peace with the rest of the nations." Maimonides, *Mishne Torah*, Laws of Kings and Wars, Chapter 12, Halacha 1.

Join the conversation www.flexigidity.com

Part II
Pillars and Engines
of Adaptability

Ben-Zakai's Flexigidity Revolution

This section establishes the framework of Jewish Flexigidity and broadly explores the mechanisms that allow for Jewish survival, security, prosperity and leadership. Its first part presents the revolution led by Rabban Yochanan Ben-Zakai during the critical period of Yavneh, immediately following the destruction of the Second Temple in 70 CE, when the so-called 'rabbinical Judaism' was ushered in. The second part elaborates upon the six 'Pillars of Flexigidity,' i.e. the permanent associations between rigid and flexible elements in Jewish society in the areas of mission, law, community, membership, place and language. The third part explores the forces that drive Jewish adaptability, demonstrating that they emanate from permanent tensions that are inherent to, and structured into, Jewish society, never to be resolved. These tensions are between unity and adversity, insularity and openness, multiple centers of leadership, powerlessness and security, idealism and realism, and between inclusiveness and wealth creation. The final part of this section exposes the dynamics of Jewish adaptability, which optimize the pace of adaptation to the challenges and opportunities that the Jewish People faces, and then describe the crescendo of Jewish adaptability over the past one hundred and thirty years.

83. **Jewish Flexigidity as we know it today can be traced back to a critical period in Jewish history that followed the destruction of Jerusalem and the Temple in 70 CE. During this time, the Jewish People was led by Rabban Yochanan Ben-Zakai (~30BCE - 90CE).**

84. **The dramatic events of 70 CE ended nearly six centuries of varying degrees of Jewish sovereignty and religious freedom in Zion, called the Second Temple Era.** This period began with the return of the exiles from Babylon *(shivat Zion)* in 538 BCE under the reign of Cyrus the Great of Persia.[71] Shortly thereafter, Jerusalem again rose to become the religious center of the Jewish People and the political capital of the Jewish polity in Judea following the rededication of the Second Temple in 491 BCE and reinstitution of the offering of sacrifices therein *(avodat hakorbanot)*. Persian rule ended in 332 BCE with the conquest of Alexander and the rise of the Hellenistic Ptolemaic and Seleucid kingdoms, centered in the area of modern-day Syria. One hundred and fifty years later, between 167-160 BCE, the Maccabean Revolt ushered in the independent Hasmonean Dynasty, which would reign for one hundred

---

71   Ezra 6:3-5 and Josephus and *Antiquities of the Jews*, Book 11, Chapter 1

and twenty years until the rise to power of King Herod in 37 BCE. Herod would hold power for nearly four decades until 4 CE under the patronage of the rising Roman Empire, and was a great builder of the land and of Jerusalem. The Herodian renovated Temple, awesome by any standard, was his architectural *magnum opus*. As Rome became domineering in its religious and cultural outlook and imposed taxation and other restrictions, tensions with the Jews rose and the two civilizations clashed ethically, culturally and militarily.

85. **Over subsequent decades, Jews would become perhaps the only people to unsuccessfully rebel against the Roman Empire three times and they did so at a huge cost.** The First Jewish-Roman War, known as the Great Revolt, led to the destruction of Jerusalem and the Temple, ending with the fall of Masada in 73 CE. The second Jewish-Roman confrontation, known as the Kittos War or the Revolt of the Diasporas *(Mered Hatfutzot)*, took place in 115-117 in multiple locations across the Roman Empire, yet was inspired from and centered in Alexandria and Cetisephon. It was brutally suppressed. The third Jewish-Roman clash was the Bar-Kochva rebellion in 132-135. In this case, the Jews were initially successful, and saw the establishment of a short-lived politically independent entity, yet the rebellion was eventually quashed, leading to near utter destruction of the Jewish settlement in Judea, to the decimation of Yavneh and many other communities, to mass killing and exile, and to the eventual decline of Zion as the chief center of the Jewish People. Nonetheless, the cultural and religious defiance of the Romans would continue and last until Rome's ultimate decline some five hundred years later.

86. **Ben-Zakai was a student of Hillel the Elder, a leader of the Pharisees *(prushim)* and a bitter rival of the Sadducees.**[72] By the time of the Great Revolt, he was already one of the most prominent sages of the *Sanhedrin* in Jerusalem, who stood in opposition to the rebellion against Rome. He was particularly critical of the radical factions, the Sicarii *(Sikarikim),* who took extreme measures, such as burning the stored food of Jerusalem, in order to escalate the confrontation.[73] When Ben-Zakai felt that his leadership was no longer effective within besieged Jerusalem, and that the old societal structure was no longer redeemable, he left Jerusalem in order to recreate Judaism.

---

72 Babylonian Talmud Menahot 65a; Babylonian Talmud Baba Batra 115b

73 Babylonian Talmud Gittin 56a

87. **At the age of one hundred, the culmination of his life led him to a dramatic and daring period of leadership that would transform the course of the Jewish People.** According to the Talmud, Ben-Zakai was hidden in a coffin and carried out of embattled Jerusalem by his students, who pretended their great leader was dead.[74] He then met Vespasian *(Aspasyanus)*, the commander of the Roman Legion, and predicted that he would become Emperor of Rome, and that the temple would soon be destroyed. In that critical moment, Jewish history and destiny were in his hands. In return for his prophesies, Vespasian granted Ben-Zakai his wishes to salvage the community of Yavne, located just south of modern-day Tel-Aviv, as well as its sages, including the descendants of Rabban Gamliel, the Head of the *Sanhedrin*, who was of the Davidic dynasty.[75] For the next twenty years, Ben-Zakai led the Jewish People from Yavne, presiding over the Council of Sages *(Sanhedrin)*.

88. **The destruction of Jerusalem and the Temple was a pivotal moment for all Jews, both in Zion and across the ancient world.** For Diaspora Jews, Jerusalem and worship in its Temple were central to their religious practices. They made pilgrimages, sent money in tribute and offered sacrifices. For the Jews of Zion, the defeat obviously represented a calamity of being overpowered and suppressed by Rome, subject to its direct control. For both communities, it actually meant the collapse of the religious order and structure of power, which had been centered in the Temple for centuries, anchoring the political and societal stature of the priests *(Cohanim)* and of the faction of the Sadducees *(Tzdokim)*. In other words, **Judaism no longer had a central place of worship, a central source of political authority and a physical center of political power**. Therefore, the *Sanhedrin*, under the leadership of Ben-Zakai, had to institutionalize the adaptation of Judaism. Indeed, their work ushered in one of the most remarkable and resilient societal transformations in human history, as the ideas and processes that were instituted at that time underlie modern Judaism and vibrantly continue to develop until today, two thousand years later.

89. **Ben-Zakai's outlook and leadership during that critical time was shaped by a number of powerful debates and dynamics.** His actions indicate that he not only saw clearly the irredeemable corruption of the old power structure, but also had a vision for a Jewish People that could

---

74   Babylonian Talmud Gittin 56a&b

75   Babylonian Talmud, Gittin, 56a-b

only be realized on its ashes. As a student of Hillel the Elder and a leading Pharisee, Ben-Zakai sought to institute that outlook in Yavneh. Thus, upon meeting Vespasian, he knew exactly what to ask for. His principal request was for Yavne and its sages.[76]

90. *First,* **Ben-Zakai's outlook was shaped by the sectarian disputes that divided Jewish society during the Second Temple Era, primarily between the Pharisees and the Sadducees.**[77] The Pharisees *(Prushim)* (literally "set apart") were a political and social movement, as well as a school of thought that believed in the authority of sages *(chachamim)* to apply the Torah in order to design Jewish society and chart the course of the nation. Meanwhile, the Sadducees *(Tzdokim)* included mainly the priestly and aristocratic families and stood for the ancient priestly privileges and prerogatives based on the written Torah. Fault lines between the two groups evolved around issues of class between the wealthy and the poor; of culture between the Hellenists and those who resisted Hellenism; of religious practice between the Temple-centric outlook with its ancient rituals, and those that emphasized the study of Torah and its application to reality; and on issues of political power. In the absence of a king, for most of the Second Temple Era, power centered in the Temple in Jerusalem in the hands of the Sadducees. Yet, their power structure was deeply corrupted, particularly by the practices of the Hasmonean dynasty (140-37 BCE), which used the Temple and the position of High Priest *(Cohen Gadol)* for political legitimacy. These tensions ultimately led to a civil war, which took place during the Great Revolt and when the Romans were besieging Jerusalem. Thus, the destruction of the Temple decisively transferred power to the Pharisees.[78]

---

76   Babylonian Talmud, Gittin, 56a-b. Ben-Zakai made two other requests, one for the family of Rabbi Shimon Ben Gamliel and another requesting medical attention for Rabbi Tzadok, the great sage of the age who had fasted for forty years to stay the destruction of Jerusalem.

77   A third, much smaller social movement was the Essenes *(Isiyim)*, which flourished for about three hundred years from second century BCE. They congregated in communities who lived in urban areas and in the desert, dedicated to voluntary poverty, regular ritual immersion in a *Mikva*, charity, strict observance of Shabbat, and abstinence from worldly pleasures. They did not participate in the ritual sacrifices of the Temple, nor in political life. Wording of this description was influenced by *Wikipedia* entry on Essenes (http://en.wikipedia.org/wiki/Essenes). .

78   See Binyamin Lau, *Sages Volume 1*, p. 271-274 (in Hebrew), for description of the work of the sages during the Second Temple Era.

91. *Second,* **among the Pharisees there was tension between the generally more progressive and flexible House of Hillel *(Beit Hillel)* and the strict and rigid approach of the House of Shammai *(Beit Shammai)*.** This dispute began in the first century BCE and lasted several generations. The *midrash* teaches that the House of Hillel was founded by Hillel the Elder *(Hillel HaZaken)* (110 BCE-10 CE), who came to Jerusalem from Babylon at the age of forty as a poor man.[79] The House of Shammai *(Beit Shammai)* was founded by Shammai, Hillel's counterpart during an era when the rabbinic leadership of the People of Israel was in the hands of five subsequent pairs of religious authorities *(Zugot)*. There are only three documented disputes between Hillel and Shammai themselves, but hundreds of disagreements between their two academies over *halacha*.[80] Those tensions peaked in the aftermath of the destruction around the necessary outlook for the Jewish People in an age of internal and external turmoil. While both academies agreed that the sages had the authority and the tools to explicate the will of God from the Torah in new and different contexts in order to develop Jewish law and determine the best course for society, they differed in their understanding of how to go about doing so:[81] The Academy of Hillel espoused greater flexibility in interpretation of the Torah *(midrash)*,[82] opened the *beit midrash* to broader participation,[83] and set more relaxed expectations for conversion into Judaism *(giur)*.[84] Meanwhile, the House of Shammai followed a stricter reading of the commandments of the Torah, established highest standards of religious observance, was elitist by limiting the study of Torah and the participation in the *beit midrash* to worthy people of dedication, stature and means,[85] and increased insularity by putting higher barriers before non-Jews who sought to join Judaism.[86]

---

79   *Sifre,* Deuteronomy 357

80   Babylonian Talmud Shabbat 14b. See also Binyamin Lau, *Sages Volume 1*, p. 141-142 (in Hebrew).

81   Binyamin Lau, *Sages Volume 1*, p. 151-175 (in Hebrew)

82   Binyamin Lau, *Sages Volume 1*, p. 161-168 (in Hebrew)

83   Binyamin Lau, *Sages Volume 1*, p. 168-169 (in Hebrew)

84   Binyamin Lau, *Sages Volume 1*, p. 173-174 (in Hebrew)

85   Binyamin Lau, *Sages Volume 1*, p. 168 (in Hebrew)

86   Binyamin Lau, *Sages Volume 1*, p. 173-174 (in Hebrew)

92. *Third,* **Ben-Zakai's outlook was shaped by the legacy and practices of religious life centered on a distant Temple, developed particularly among the Diaspora communities in Babylon and Alexandria.** By his time, this revolutionary Jewish idea of life at a distance from a temple had been developing for over seven centuries. It was institutionalized by King Josiah *(Yoshiyyáhu)*, who reigned circa 649-609 BCE. Josiah waged a concerted war against paganism and destroyed all local shrines in the Judean Kingdom, thus concentrating all worship of the Jewish God in the Temple in Jerusalem.[87] Henceforth, many of the Israelites were forced to relate to a distant temple and to develop a religious philosophy and practices, such as prayer, pilgrimage and sacrifices that supported such religious life. The first exile and Diaspora *(galut)* to Babylon, which began in 586 BCE, led to further development of these practices and their supporting ideology. The exiles – a relatively small group of the political and economic elite, now residing in roughly the area of modern Iraq – adapted their religious practices to life without a Temple altogether, as encouraged by the prophet Ezekiel.[88] They developed and strengthened institutions essential for strong community life, most prominently the synagogues *(beit knesset)*, which served them as a 'small temple' *(mikdash me'at),* and ultimately also courts *(batei din)*, representative community institutions *(va'ad kehila or nesiut)* and communal funds *(kuppah)*.[89] Following the return from Babylon to Zion *(shivat zion)* in the 6th century BCE, a bi-polar Jewish world emerged as many of the exiles preferred life in Babylon to repatriation. Henceforth, a prominent Jewish Diaspora became a permanent reality for the Jewish People and by the 1st century of the Common Era large and prosperous Jewish communities existed not only in Babylon but also in Alexandria and other places. These communities in turn created a wealth of societal knowledge about life at a distance from a temple, which must have been invaluable to the community in Zion following the destruction of the Temple and to Ben-Zakai's leadership.

---

87 The law for the centralized ritual in Jerusalem first appears in Deuteronomy 12. Later enforcement of this edict during the reign of King Josiah (7th century BCE) can be found in II Kings 23.

88 Ezekiel 11:16: "Thus said the Lord GOD: Although I have removed them far off among the nations, and although I have scattered them among the countries, yet have I been to them as a little sanctuary in the countries where they are come." See also Sacks, *Future Tense*, p. 38-39. See also Johnson, *A History of the Jews*, p. 82-83: "...it was Ezekiel and his visions which gave the dynamic impulse to the formulation of Judaism ... it was during the Exile that ordinary Jews were first disciplined into the regular practice of their religion."

89 Johnson, *A History of the Jews*, P. 203: "From Temple times, the kuppah or collecting box was a pivot around which the Jewish welfare-community revolved, Maimonides stating: 'We have never seen or heard of a Jewish community which does not have a kuppah.'"

93. *Finally,* **Ben-Zakai's leadership was informed by centuries-long life among and in relationship with the dominant powers and cultures, and by the consequent challenge of assimilation, which emanated from such interaction.** Jewish tradition teaches about the challenge of resisting assimilation by the Hebrews during their enslavement in Egypt,[90] and mourns the disappearance of the ten tribes of the Northern Kingdom of Israel following their exile by the Assyrians between 733-722 BCE.[91] These legacies and trauma must have haunted the exiles in Babylon one hundred and fifty years later who, in spite of their efforts to preserve their identity, also experienced extensive intermarriage.[92] Two centuries after *shivat Zion* in the Judean kingdom, the tension and struggle with Hellenism during the Greek and Roman Empires was permanently present and repeatedly erupted into violence. Thus, by the time of Ben-Zakai in the first century, the phenomenon of 'assimilation' in names, spoken language and lifestyle had already been prevalent for hundreds of years. Life in the presence of a dominant culture had already been a challenge that inspired Judaism to develop multiple communal responses.

94. **Under Ben-Zakai's leadership, Yavne became the first widely accepted religious center of the Jewish People since the time of Solomon that did not rely on a physical Temple in Jerusalem.** As Rabbi Binyamin Lau explains, Ben-Zakai institutionalized the balance between the 'memory of the temple' *(zecher la'mikdash)* and life without a temple, where societal progress had to be made even in the harshest conditions. Referring to a passage in the Book of Hosea, "I desired mercy and not sacrifice,"[93] Ben-Zakai argued that prayers *(tfila)*, charity *(tzedaka)* and kindness *(che'sed)* could take the place of sacrifices *(korbanot)* as the vehicle for redeeming sins. Furthermore, prayers, both personal and in *minyans* in synagogues, and the study of Torah and its scholarly application to day-to-day life in a religious school *(beit midrash)* could replace presence at the Temple.[94]

---

90 BaMidbar Rabbah 13:20 and Vayikra Rabba 32:5 attest to Jews keeping their own traditions in Egypt.

91 II Kings 17

92 Ezra 9 & 10

93 Hosea 6:6

94 See Binyamin Lau, *Sages Volume 2*, p. 30-37 (in Hebrew). See also Johnson, *A History of the Jews*, p. 72: "...for the first time an Israelite thinker seems to envisage a religion of the heart, divorced from a particular state and organized society ... was received in a Judah which was terrified by the collapse of its northern neighbor and feared a similar fate."

95. Thus, **Ben-Zakai is one of the most important individuals in the legacy of Jewish Flexigidity.** Out of the ashes of destruction, he laid the cornerstone for Judaism's adaptive capacity. Ben-Zakai spent his final years teaching at Berur Hayil, near Yavne, and was buried in Tiberias. However, for his choice of Yavne over Jerusalem and of the sages over the priests, some have viewed Ben-Zakai as a traitor to Judaism and to the Jewish People.[95]

96. **Sixty years later that new societal architecture faced the utter destruction of Judea by the Roman Empire following the failed Bar-Kochva rebellion (132-135).** This calamity led to the near emptying of Judea from its Jews, with hundreds of thousands killed or sold as slaves.[96] The Yavne Academy was destroyed and many of the leading sages of the time, including Rabbi Akiva, were brutally executed *(Aseret Harugei Malchut)*. Others continued to live in the Galilee under harsh conditions, dispersed across the Roman Empire, or fled to Babylon.[97]

97. Yet, **by that time, the Jewish People had adapted to life without a temple.** The Jewish religion had become Flexigid, carried in the hearts and minds of Jews, as well as in the sacks on their backs. This transformation helped Jews escape the fate of all other small peoples who were exiled by great powers of antiquity, eventually to be fully assimilated and to disappear from history.

98. **In later centuries, the Jewish People would cope with and adapt to numerous challenges and radical changes in its circumstances,** such as the rise of Christianity and its official adoption as the state religion of the Roman empire as of the early 4th century; the disbandment of the *Sanhedrin* in 425; the rise of Islam at the beginning of the 7th century; the schism with Karaite Judaism, which challenged rabbinic rule between the 8th and 11th centuries; the end of the 'Golden Era' of Jews in Spain at the end of the 11th century; the brutal crusades of the 11th and 12th centuries; the decline of Jewish presence in Mesopotamia following the Mongolian conquest in the 13th century; the reign of the Inquisition in Spain and Portugal beginning in the 15th century; the expulsion from

---

95　In Binyamin Lau, *Sages Volume 2*, p. 57, 59-60 (in Hebrew), Rabbi Lau describes Ben-Zakai's fear before his death about how God will judge his leadership in transferring the heart of the nation from Jerusalem to Yavneh and how he will be remembered by future generations.

96　Cassius Dio, *Roman History*, section 69 12:1-14:3

97　Binyamin Lau, *Sages Volume 3*, p. 37-38 (in Hebrew)

Spain in 1492 and from other European polities throughout the Middle Ages; the false messiahs Sabbatai Zevi and Jacob Frank in the 17th and 18th centuries; the Khmelnitsky Massacre of 1648, which marked a the rise of state sponsored antisemitism in Eastern Europe; the schism between *Hasidim* and *Mitnagdim* in the 18th century; the emancipation of European Jews; the Jewish Enlightenment movement *(haskalah);* the rise of the European nation-state; the persecutions by the Russian Empire and by communism; the Shoah; and finally the establishment of the State of Israel.

99. **The full force of Jewish adaptability could only be framed within the perspective of centuries.** Exile and Diaspora represented a deep setback to a life of relative sovereignty, independence and freedom of religion and practice in Zion. In subsequent centuries, Jews were seen by others primarily through the prism of their resilience, steadfastness and religious tenacity. Judaism's inherent suspicion toward and resistance to the *zeitgeist*, to the spirit of their time, by its conservative factions created permanent challenges to the dominant culture, which often turned into adversity. In some cases, the Jewish People faced attempts to suppress, uproot and destroy it in specific areas or altogether by the Roman Empire, Christianity, Islam, Nazism and communism. But Judaism, remarkably, adjusted to life in exile and to a permanent condition of otherness, weakness and minority. Many Jews and Jewish communities have indeed suffered sustained periods of insecurity, poverty and religious persecution. They were often viewed as "fossilized in history." Yet, at the same time, many, and sometimes most Jews, have enjoyed relative security, prosperity and communal and religious autonomy for most of their exile, allowing Judaism to be a dynamic force in history, which would rise to global prominence in full force in the 20th century.

Pillars of Jewish Flexigidity

This section describes the six pillars of Flexigidity, which represent permanent associations between flexible and rigid elements in Jewish society: *Flexigidity of mission*, created by the four meta-stories of Judaism; *structure*, flowing from the rigid set of mandatory institutions in each and every Jewish community, yet of great variety among them; *law*, emerging from the rigid written law, the talmudic process and other sources of dynamism in society building; *membership*, found in the rigid law of matrilineal descent and in the flexibility of conversions; *place*, affirming loyalty to Zion, yet maintaining the ability to live in many Diasporas; and *Flexigidity of language*, balancing the rigid commitment to Hebrew with the freedom to use other languages.

Pillar of Flexigidity Defined

100. **Jewish society evolves around pillars of Flexigidity, which are hybrids of rigidities and flexibilities in key areas of Jewish society.** The rigid core of every pillar can very rarely be changed, negotiated, compromised or adjusted to context, as it has been deeply rooted in Jewish law, tradition and texts for millennia. Flexibility in these areas stems from inherent mechanisms in Jewish society, also deeply rooted in ancient traditions, which allow for experimentation, change, adaptation, evolution and sensitivity to context. Thus, each pillar embodies a permanent relationship between rigidity and flexibility, which is inherently present in Jewish society throughout its history and will remain in its future.

Flexigidity of Mission: Four Stories

> This section describes Judaism's Flexigidity of mission, which emerges out of the inherent tension between the rigid core of the four meta-stories of the Jewish People, on the one hand, and their inherent flexibility, on the other hand. It then proceeds to describe the interplay among the four meta-stories, never allowing one of them to dominate Jewish society, an essential component for Jewish adaptability, survival, security and prosperity.

101. **The first pillar of Jewish Flexigidity is its four stories about identity, vision and mission, as well as about the Jewish past, present and future.** These stories are about covenant and faith, nationhood, peoplehood and *or la'goim*. As mentioned earlier, these stories are ever present in Jewish psyche, texts, legacy, history and destiny, always competing for the hearts and minds of Jews.

102. As detailed earlier, **each meta-story has a rigid and uncompromising core, comprised of a coherent narrative that upholds specific values.** It is practiced through distinct priorities and patterns of conduct, served by designated institutions, enshrined in communal narratives and myths, and embodied by specific symbols, villains and heroes.

103. Yet, **the combined effect and synergy among the four stories creates great flexibility for Judaism, as Jews always have four powerful alternative frameworks with which to interpret and respond to the world around them.** Every story provides a distinct prism for understanding economic, political, technological and societal conditions, challenges and opportunities facing Jewish communities, and for designing responses to them. As Jews struggle with the challenge of adaptation, each story legitimizes different sources of inspiration and mobilization. It creates an alternative view of what is sacred and necessary, as opposed to what is expendable. All of these insights interplay in the Jewish public sphere.

104. **Attitudes toward Zionism and the State of Israel exemplify this point.**[98] *The framework of the story of Peoplehood* understands Israel to be the state of the entire Jewish People, in the same manner that France

---

98   On the debate among British Jewry on whether Jews were a 'people' or a 'nation' see Jonathan Schneer, *The Balfour Declaration – The Origins of the Arab-Israeli Conflict,* Chapter 10 p. 138-151, Bloomsbury, paperback edition 2011.

is the state of all French people. Thus, while Israel must serve the needs, concerns and aspirations of its citizens, it must also serve the needs of Diaspora Jews and be a force of unity for the entire Jewish People. This story also underlies the expectation of Diaspora Jews to unequivocally support Israel financially and politically. Meanwhile, *the meta-story of nationhood* emphasizes the historical obligation of Israel to reestablish Jewish sovereignty in Judaism's ancestral homeland. For some, this logic also requires Israel's permanent sovereignty in the areas of Judea and Samaria, which were liberated in 1967 and where a significant Palestinian population resides. This expectation exists despite the fact that Israel's control of these territories is challenged by the international community and by many Jews in Israel, and is a source of deep discord among many in the Diaspora. The *story of faith* conceives of Israel in a religious context, often viewing it as Jewish in the same manner that some other nations are Christian or Moslem, and placing its establishment and achievements within the process of ultimate redemption *(ge'ulah)*. Few even call for the introduction of *halacha* as the law of the land and the foundation for law making, judicial decisions and policy making. Finally, the story of *or la'goim* challenges Israel to be what Herzl referred to in *Altneuland* as a 'model society' of justice and ethics. In modern times, this outlook is often in conflict with Judaism's and Israel's particularism, and therefore may challenge the outlooks inspired by the stories of Faith, Nationhood and Peoplehood.

105.   Furthermore, **the four stories offer multiple and diverse gateways into Jewish life and society, legitimizing a broad range of conduct.** The proposition of Judaism to its followers and of the Jewish People to its members is not a take-it-or-leave-it one with any of these narratives. Rather, it is a menu of opportunities for meaningful spiritual, intellectual, religious and ethical engagement. This allows for a very diverse group of people to associate with Judaism to the point where loyalty to one story may constitute disobedience to another. Furthermore, every Jew who becomes disenchanted with a given story of Judaism has a choice of three alternative narratives to fall back upon. This happens particularly in the aftermath of a great calamity that shakes the foundations of Jewish life such as the Shoah, which led many Jews to reject Jewish faith, but to embrace the story of nationhood in its stead.

106.   Thus, **tensions among the four stories are inherent and inevitable, as their outlooks are different and sometimes conflicting**. For example, regarding conversions *(giyurim),* while the story of Peoplehood

emphasizes the desire for membership in the Jewish 'family' as the benchmark for inclusion,[99] the story of faith tests observance of *halacha*.[100] In recent decades, proponents of the story of nationhood in Israel have advocated that military service in the Israeli Defense Forces should constitute a de facto 'conversion by fire' and therefore allow Jewish burial to fallen soldiers who identified as such, even if their Judaism could be challenged by orthodox Jewish law.[101] Another example relates to the tension between the stories of nationhood and of *or la'goim* as they relate to Israel's reestablishing sovereignty over the Land of Israel and its settlement. For the former story, such a historical righting of the wrong done to the Jewish People provides legitimacy to actions that might otherwise be considered morally unjust, while for the story of *or la'goim,* such ethical compromises are unacceptable since the ultimate benchmark for the Jewish state is becoming a 'holy nation' and a 'model society' *(goy kadosh* and *hevrat mofet).*

107. **These tensions generate constant societal adaptation and innovation.** The clash among these outlooks in the Jewish public sphere produces new ideas that often emanate from two or more stories. The tension between the stories of peoplehood and faith continues to generate different approaches regarding conversion into Judaism *(giyur)* varying in their emphasis on the desire to be a part of the Jewish People as opposed to

---

99 Lecture by Rabbi Dr. Donniel Hartman on May 23, 2011 at the Samuel Bronfman Foundation Conference 'Why Be Jewish'. Rabbi Hartman referenced Babylonian Talmud, Yevamot 47a-b: "Our Rabbis taught: if at the present time a man desires to become a proselyte, he is to be addressed as follows: "What reason have you for desire to become a proselyte; do you know that Israel at the present time are persecuted and oppressed despised, harassed and overcome by afflictions? If he replies: "I know and yet am unworthy", he is accepted forthwith and is given instructions of some of the minor and some of the major commandments. He is informed of the sins of the neglect of the commandments of Gleanings *(shi'che'cha)*, Forgotten Sheaf *(leket)*, the Corner *(pe'ot)* and the Poor Man's Tithe *(me'a'ser ani)*."

100 Lecture by Rabbi Dr. Donniel Hartman on May 23, 2011 at the Samuel Bronfman Foundation Conference 'Why Be Jewish'. Rabbi Hartman referenced Tosefta Demai 2:4-5: "A proselyte who took upon himself all matters of Torah, and is suspected of [non-observance] with regard to one matter, even with regard to the entire Torah – behold, he is like an Israelite apostate. A proselyte who took upon himself all matters of Torah, excepting one thing, they don't accept him. Rabbi Jose son of Rabbi Judah says: "even [excepting] a small matter enacted by the scribes."

101 Orthodox rabbis found a different solution within *halacha*, according to which such fallen soldiers who tied their fate with the Jewish People are buried within the fence of the Jewish cemetery in a designated section. See Rabbi Yuval Sharlo at http://www.moreshet.co.il/web/shut/shut2.asp?id=9555.

strict observance of *halacha*. In Zionism and Israel, the tension between the stories of nationhood and *or la'goim* not only yielded the quest to build a model society, but also generated a large body of political thought, law and policy regarding the measured use of military force known as 'Purity of Arms' *(tohar haneshek)*.

108. **Israel is where these tensions manifest in greatest force, as it grapples to incorporate the stories of faith, peoplehood and *or la'goim* within the framework of modern Jewish nationhood.** These tensions unfold when Israel struggles to balance religious and secular authorities, Jewish heritage and modernity in areas such as law, justice, economics and education; when Israel shapes its relationship with Diaspora Jewry and with Israeli ex-pats; and when Israelis interpret and seek to actualize the vision of a model society in matters of welfare, minority rights, foreign assistance and military affairs.

109. **A minority among the Jewish People embraces one meta-story, de-facto rejecting others.** A particular group among the ultra-orthodox group of Judaism *(ha'edah haharedit)* expresses hostility to Zionism and little interest in associating with other Jews or in affecting humanity. Some communities in Israel have little regard for faith, Diaspora Jews or for the challenges facing humanity. Others, primarily in the USA, focus on the modern ideal of 'repairing the world' *(tikkun olam)* with mild if any religious observance, alienation from Israel and distance from anything that is perceived as communally 'Jewish.'

110. Yet, **most Jews and Jewish communities blend two or more of these narratives into their ethics, identity and action.** Throughout the Diaspora, communities varied in their tolerance toward the multiple possible frameworks of Judaism, but over the past few decades, Jews have had unprecedented freedom to create many individual and community hybrid identities. As such, peoplehood has been integral to modern Jewish nationhood as represented by Israel's caring deeply about Jews around the world. Meanwhile, many Diaspora communities not only feel deep responsibility to other Jews and Jewish communities within the spirit of peoplehood, but also want to help the tired, the poor and the huddled masses anywhere inspired by the values of *or la'goim* and *tikkun olam*.[102]

---

102 Taken from the poem "The New Colossus" by American Jewish Poet Emma Lazarus, the iconic lines which read, "Give me your tired, your poor, your huddled masses yearning to breathe free" are engraved on the base of the Statue of Liberty in New York City.

Join the conversation www.flexigidity.com

111. **In every period, one of these narratives seeks to dominate and shape the Jewish values and priorities of its communities and individuals.** In any given time and context, one narrative may better inspire and guide Jewish communities and individual Jews in their quest to achieve security, economic wellbeing and religious freedom. In some periods, one narrative is evidently more relevant than all others, so its proponents rise to leadership and authority across the Jewish world. That outlook then seeks to dominate Judaism and becomes domineering toward its other core narratives. Unable to eliminate them altogether, it attempts to contain, incorporate and co-opt them within its own framework.

112. Yet, **as if by an invisible hand, its domineering outlook is calibrated by a counterforce in Jewish society that holds on to the alternative narratives**. While the Bar Kochva Rebellion (132-135) was inspired by the narrative of nationhood and received the blessings of Rabbi Akiva, its opposition from within the Jewish leadership of that time stemmed from a concern for the world of Torah.[103] In the aftermath of the calamity that ensued and against the backdrop of the rise of Christianity, Judaism suppressed the narrative of nationhood and evolved around a hybrid of peoplehood and faith, i.e. dynamic religious adaptation that was designed to preserve the integrity of the people through the Diaspora. In later centuries, the story of religion prevailed. Nonetheless, the ideal of nationhood inspired the work of 12th century philosopher and poet Yehuda HaLevi who invoked the love of Zion and the yearning to repatriate. Following the Shoah and until recently, the story of nationhood has been dominant, under the banner of Zionism and the State of Israel.[104] However, in recent years, the narratives of peoplehood, and then of *tikkun olam,* have challenged Zionism for center stage. Thus, in this understanding, and what is perhaps somewhat of a paradox, anti-Zionist forces are inevitable within Judaism, and are as integral to Jewish society

---

103 See Binyamin Lau, *Sages Volume 2*, p. 260-274 (in Hebrew) on the debates between Rabbi Akiva's and other rabbis, primarily Rabbis Ben-Zoma, Elazar Ben Azaria and Rabbi Yehushua on the understanding of the story of the exodus from Egypt and on the appropriate approach toward the Romans. While Rabbi Akiva emphasized the narrative of nationhood, viewing political independence as a partnership between God and the People of Israel, the other rabbis interpreted the texts as establishing a more passive relationship, where political independence would come through the 'strong arm' of God.

104 Johnson, *A History of the Jews*, p. 160: "...after 135, in effect, Judaism ... implicitly renounced the state ... what happened at Yavneh ... was far more significant than what happened at Masada ... the lost fortress, indeed, was virtually forgotten until, in the lurid flames of the twentieth-century Holocaust, it became a national myth, displacing the myth of Yavneh."

as Zionism itself. No single outlook can be allowed to dominate Judaism. Not event post-Shoah Zionism.

113. *In conclusion*, **the dynamics of Flexigidity of mission are essential for Jewish society to preserve its vitality and to ensure its existence**. This dynamism gives Judaism the ability to constantly evolve its outlook through an authentic process of internal societal deliberation concerning its mission. It ensures that Judaism will not be dominated by a single myopic outlook that may prove ill-conceived and irrelevant. It guarantees that Judaism hedges its ideological risk and resources. This mechanism is vital not only for survival but also for Jewish security, prosperity and leadership.

Flexigidity of Structure: A Worldwide Web of Communities

This section describes Judaism's Flexigidity of structure, which stems from the rigid set of institutions that must exist in every Jewish community on the one hand, and the freedom to adjust these institutions to local context and conditions, on the other hand. Consequently, no two Jewish communities are alike. Its *first part* describes the basic units of Jewish society. The *second part* demonstrates how the Jewish People and its communities are organized as a worldwide web and network of communities, interconnected by powerful protocols. The *third part* explains why this architecture is critical not only for Jewish survival and resilience, but also for Jewish prosperity.

114. **The second pillar of Jewish Flexigidity is Judaism's architecture as a global network of communities.** Rigidity stems from a set of core elements that must exist in every sizeable Jewish community. Flexibility emanates from the countless variations not only of each of these institutions and the interaction and interconnectedness among them, but also of the systemic wholes, the communities, that they make up.

115. **The collective is essential for a complete Jewish life while solitude is a fundamentally compromising condition for Jews who must be part of a community to live Jewishly.** Jewish faith holds that Jews stand before God and are judged as a whole, bound by the covenant *(brith)* as individuals and as a community. The story of peoplehood stresses the familial nature of the Jewish People and the mutual responsibility among its members. The story of nationhood establishes that every Jew has a stake in Zion, not just those that dwell there. The mission of *or la'goim* requires the entire community to embody its ethics through the

cumulative action of all Jews. These ideas are manifested across Jewish tradition and life in countless ways.

116. **The household is the basic cell of Jewish society and community.** In the Jewish ideal, parents and teachers educate and groom children to join their community as adults, marry other Jews, build a household and educate their own children to do the same in due course. Many Jewish traditions prepare children for their roles as spouses and parents by establishing expectations about family life and about membership and participation in community and society.

117. **Jewish households needed to live in proximity to each other.** Observing the laws of Sabbath, which prohibit travel yet require congregating with other Jews, resulted in Jewish households being clustered together in communities that were geographically concentrated.

118. **A *minyan* establishes the smallest group of people that can constitute a Jewish community and the most basic association within large Jewish communities.** Traditionally, a *minyan* refers to ten men above the age of thirteen, which constitutes the quorum necessary for a full prayer service, for public reading of the Torah and for other religious activities. In remote areas, it typically required a few households to come together, and therefore served as the nuclear unit of a Jewish community. In larger Jewish communities, this rule allows for great communal agility, as anyone that qualifies is encouraged to participate in the basic activities of Jewish religious observance anywhere. Consequently, in all large Jewish communities multiple minyans *(minyanim)* take place.

119. Arguably, **the so-called egalitarian minyans, where adult women are also counted, represent a compromise of the logic of establishing a nuclear societal unit of minimal size.** While such egalitarian minyans address the perceived gender bias of Jewish tradition against women, they also decrease the minimal size of a Jewish community. In other words, **Judaism's traditional societal logic of Flexigidity should arguably have called for 'egalitarian minyans' to require a minimum of ten adult men or ten adult women.**

120. **Communities are the building blocks of the Jewish world, each made up of a particular set of institutions.** Over many centuries of Diaspora life since the First Temple exile to Babylon, these institutions have come to include a committee *(va'ad or nesiut)* to address collective needs and

a fund *(kuppah)* to underwrite them, ritual baths *(mikveh)*, schools for public education from the age of three to adulthood *(heder, yeshiva, kolel)*, synagogues *(beit knesset)* and courts *(beit din)*. Key civil service functions include the rabbi, who provides scholarly guidance; a judge *(dayan)*; cantor *(chazan or shaliach tzibur)*, who chants the prayers and the Torah in the name of the community; circumciser *(mohel)*; and butcher *(shochet)*.[105]

121. **Community building is at the core of the societal DNA of the Jewish People.** Jewish civilization has developed a wealth of wisdom regarding the makeup and management of each node community, the roles and functions of key institutions, as well as the protocols that ensure their interconnectedness. It has established a hierarchy of values, priorities, institutions and patterns of conduct to serve this structure, and has been adapting them continuously.

122. **All Jewish communities around the world have been interconnected in a way that has enabled communication, constant movement of individuals and a collective safety net in times of crisis.** Sages engaged in religious discussions and Jews traveled and communicated across the ancient world as early as the 1st and 2nd centuries.[106] Jewish traders of

---

105 See Babylonian Talmud, Sanhedrin 17b. The list includes: A court empowered to punish the guilty, a communal tzedakah fund, monies for which are collected by two people and distributed by three, a synagogue, a *mikveh*, sufficient bathroom facilities, a doctor, a blood letter, a scribe, a butcher and a Torah teacher for children. Found in the website of the Jewish Agency for Israel here.

See also Johnson, *A History of the Jews*, p. 112-113: "Herod ... provided funds for synagogues, libraries, baths, and charitable agencies, and encouraged others to do the same, so that it was in Herod's day that the Jews first became famous for the miniature welfare states they set up among their communities in Alexandria, Rome, Antioch, Babylon and elsewhere, providing for the sick and the poor, for widows and orphans, for visiting the imprisoned and bearing the dead."

See also Johnson, *Ibid*, p. 158: "In late antiquity, each Jewish community was ruled in effect congregationally, with a governing board of seven, which fixed wages, prices, weights and measures, and bye-laws, and had powers to punish offenders. The obligation to pay communal taxes was religious, as well as social. Moreover, philanthropy was an obligation too, since the word zedakah meant both charity and righteousness. The Jewish welfare state in antiquity, the prototype of all others, was not voluntary; a man had to contribute to the common fund in proportion to his means, and this duty could be enforced by the courts."

106 See Babylonian Talmud Horayot, 10a concerning Raban Gamliel II and Rabbi Yehoshua traveling on ship to or from Rome around the end of the 1st century.

the Middle Ages were known to import luxury goods from China and India.[107] Maimonides, while living in Egypt in the 12th century, served as a chief rabbinic authority for the Jews of Yemen, and responded to queries from around the Mediterranean and further east than Persia. The famous 12th century Jewish traveler, Benjamin of the city of Tudela, Spain, traveled across the Medieval world from the Iberian Peninsula to Persia, from one Jewish community to another, documenting his journey and the Jews that he met. This interconnectedness stems from Jewish law and tradition, which apply to each and every Jewish community around the world.

123. *First,* **Jews are obligated to assume mutual responsibility for their fellow Jews.** An entire body of Jewish law developed over centuries to establish the responsibilities of every individual and household to their community and to other individual Jews and communities. It is based upon the principle of "all the People of Israel are responsible for each other" *(kol Israel arevim ze ba'ze).* Within the logic of peoplehood, such hospitality and assistance was often extended to anyone who could communicate their Judaism, even if only by knowing basic Hebrew, Yiddish, blessings and prayers. In the 1st century, Jews from around the world rebelled against the Roman oppression of Jews, particularly in Palestine, in what became known as the Kittos War (113-115). In the 16th century Jews and Jewish communities in the Ottoman Empire and Eastern Europe provided help to Jewish refugees following the expulsions from Spain and from other areas in Western Europe. American members of the Jewish Territorialist Organization (ITO) helped immigrants from Russia to settle in America following the persecution at the hands of the Tsars, and the State of Israel provided refuge to Ethiopian Jews during and following the civil war there in the 1980s-1990s through Operations Moses, Joshua and Solomon. Even today, many Jewish children are told: when lost, look for a police station and for a *mezuzah*, which is the symbol of a Jewish home affixed to the frame of the door.

124. *Second,* **many Jews are guided by a virtually similar prayer book *(siddur)* that regulates all life and life cycle events, ranging from daily to bi-centennial rituals.** Regular and fixed prayers emerged in Judaism during the Second Temple era, and were further developed and formalized by Ben-Zakai and Rabban Gamliel II in Yavneh, as Jews

---

107 Johnson, *A History of the Jews*, p. 176: "Both Moslem sources and Jewish responsa show that at this time [8th to 11th centuries]… Jewish merchants were operating in India and China, where most of the luxuries originated."

became increasingly dispersed. The text continued to develop through the time of Saadia Gaon in the 10th century, who authored the oldest surviving effort to detail regular and festival prayers,[108] and the first printed *siddur* can be traced back to the 15th century. Though there are variations between the Sephardic and Ashkenazi liturgy, the text of the *siddur* is, by and large, common to all Jewish communities. It guides practices relating to births and deaths, sickness and health, weekday, Sabbath and holiday worship. Mastering the *siddur* granted every Jew the ability to join the motion, so to speak, with any Jewish community the world over. There are remarkable visual and practical similarities in the rituals of communities as diverse as Sana'a, Casablanca, New York City, Buenos Aires, Moscow and Tehran.

125.   *Third,* **Jews have a shared language: Hebrew.** The belief that the Torah was given by God to Moses on Mount Sinai mandates that its transcription on parchment scrolls must be identical to the original form. The slightest deviation, even of one letter, may disqualify the entire scroll from ritual use. Special expert craftsmen, called *sofrim* (scribes), mastered this art. Hence, all writing and reading of Hebrew around the world draws from an identical source. Prayers in Hebrew and the mandatory reading of the Torah three times every week meant that Hebrew literacy was prevalent among all communities. Furthermore, the central act of the *bar mitzvah* ceremony, celebrating Jewish youth coming of age, is reading from the Torah. Thus, the Jewish rite of passage has been effectively a literary exam in Hebrew.

126.   *Fourth,* **Jews share the Sabbath, with the core of its ritual performed by all active Jewish households, vast variations notwithstanding.** Observance of *Shabbat*, particularly by ceasing to 'work,' is a central obligation of a faithful Jewish person and a common practice among Jews. Core elements are universal, though the rituals of *Shabbat* have continued to evolve over time and may vary from one community to another. Thus, to a great extent, remembering and keeping *Shabbat* has been a central symbol of membership in the Jewish People. Furthermore, the custom of hospitality around the Sabbath table on Friday night and Saturday is paramount to introducing wandering Jews to the community. This underlies Ahad HaAhm's famous observation that, "more than Jews have kept *Shabbat*, *Shabbat* has kept the Jews," viewing it not just as a religious obligation but as a unique national and cultural attribute of the Jewish People.

---

108   See http://hebrewbooks.org/pdfpager.aspx?req=20685&pgnum=1.

127. *Fifth,* **Jews have lived by a unique lunisolar calendar that distinguishes their lives.** Its cyclicality is unique: the week begins on Sunday and ends on Saturday; each month follows the lunar phases; the annual cycle – from *Tishrei,* usually around September, to *Elul* – is adjusted to the solar calendar, keeping the holidays in their proper seasons;[109] and the holidays take Jews through a unique shared spiritual progression of sorrow and happiness, hope and fear, pride and mourning, anticipation and acceptance. Therefore, this calendar places Jews, in some respects, on a separate and unique annual cycle. It is no coincidence that one of the decrees issued by Caesar Hadrian following the Bar Kochva Revolt (132-135) forbade Jews from "keeping their times" and observance of *Shabbat.*[110]

128. *Finally,* **Jews have shared stories and memories, which often help them create immediate association.** For thousands of years, Jews have ritually retold the story of the exodus from Egypt at the Passover *seder (the hagadah)* and shared the tales of the Torah and the *aggada.* During the last few centuries, Jews have been increasingly and more frequently globally mobile, often across oceans and among continents within their worldwide web of communities. Hence, their need to 'plug and play' Jewishly has grown. Stories ease this movement, relating to immigration and the 'old country;' to the experience of persecution or the *Shoah;* to Israel, service in the IDF and to life on a Kibbutz; and to participation in a major Jewish political or social action campaign. They often help to reliably verify association and membership and to establish quick, personal relationships.[111]

129. **The network architecture of the Jewish People resembles other resilient systems in areas as diverse as biology, economics and the Internet,[112] and is essential to Jewish survival, security, prosperity and leadership.**

---

109 Exodus 13:4 establishes that Passover must remain in the Spring, and many Jewish holydays correspond with the agricultural cycle of the Land of Israel. Moslem holydays, in contrast, continuously change their season, as is the case with the fast of Ramadan, which takes place in about eleven days earlier each year.

110 For a thorough overview see the Wikipedia entry (Hebrew) סונאיירדא תורזג here.

111 Such a form of relationship among Jews is described in depth in numerous places in Kaplan's *Judaism as Civilization.*

112 On social networks, see: Albert-Laszlo Barabási, *Linked: The New Science of Networks,* (Basic Books, 2002); Yochai Benkler, *The Wealth of Networks,* (Yale University Press, 2006); J. R. McNeill, *The Human Web, A Bird's Eye View of World History,* (Norton & Company, 2003).

Join the conversation www.flexigidity.com

130.   *First,* **the Jewish People does not have a single unit that concentrates power and authority, and therefore, without a head, cannot be decapitated**. During the Second Temple Era and until the destruction of Jerusalem, the political life of the Jewish People was anchored in the Temple *(Beit HaMikdash)* in Jerusalem. Thus, the Romans were convinced that in physically destroying Jerusalem and the central institution of Jewish faith they would eliminate the vitality of the Jewish People. Nonetheless, under the leadership of Ben-Zakai and Rabban Gamliel II in Yavneh, Jews adjusted to life without a political center and the *Sanhedrin* assumed the supreme religious, judicial and political leadership of the Jewish People. However, its power and authority gradually waned since Jews further dispersed across the Roman Empire and immigrated to Babylon, particularly in the aftermath the Bar Kochva rebellion (132-135) and the Hadrianic persecutions that followed. This process gradually 'flattened' the Jewish world and made the *Sanhedrin* ineffectual. By the time it was dismantled in 425 with the death of Rabban Gamliel VI, its ordinary functions of 'government' were de-centralized to local communities.[113] Generally, in the absence of sovereignty, matters of physical security were entrusted to the hands of local sovereign authorities.[114] Meanwhile, internal matters were handled by the key community institutions: courts *(batei din)* established laws for the community and settled disputes, and an Exilarch *(Rosh Galutah)*, who chaired a committee *(va'ad)*, handled administrative affairs and external relations.[115] This structure has been present in a variety of forms and shapes since Babylon in every sizeable Jewish community around the world.[116] Thus, even Judaism's most powerful enemies could not locate and dispose of a 'king of the Jews' in order to solve their 'Jewish problem.' Such an entity simply did not exist.

---

113 See Johnson, *A History of the Jews*, p. 158: "In late antiquity, each Jewish community was ruled in effect congregationally, with a governing board of seven, which fixed wages, prices, weights and measures, and bye-laws, and had powers to punish offenders. The obligation to pay communal taxes was religious as well as social.."

114 A notable exception to this otherwise broad state of events is the rebellion of Mar-Zutra II against Persia in the latter part of the fifth century.

115 See Gafni, *The Jews of Babylon in the Talmudic Era*, p. 94-104.

116 Other famous examples include the Council of Four Lands *(Va'ad Arba Ha'Aratzot)*, which led the Jews of Poland between sixteenth and eighteenth centuries; the Boards of Deputies, which lead the Jews of England and South Africa; and the CRIF that leads the Jews of France. Even during the Shoah, similar institutions, most famously the 'Judenrats', operated in the Ghettos.

131. What is more, **this is why the conspiracy theory of the Elders of Zion is contrary to the architecture of the Jewish People.**[117] Created by the secret police of Tsarist Russia to legitimize their persecution of Jews, it describes the leadership of the Jewish People as a secret group of elderly scholars who manipulate world politics. Though still widely read around the world, even in places where few Jews live such as Japan and many Muslim nations, this fallacy is patently ignorant.

132. *Second,* **while each Jewish community is unique, all communities share core characteristics balancing rigid guidelines that shape their core institutions and capabilities, on the one hand, with independence of action, sensitivity to context, flexibility and innovation, on the other hand.** As described earlier, the building blocks of every Jewish community consist of a particular set of core institutions and functions, such as a committee, a fund, a synagogue, *beit midrash*, school and court. Meanwhile, each community is unique in structure, character, size and values, based on its own legacy, capacities and political, social and economic environment. For example, while France, the UK, Argentina and the USA all have rabbinical authorities and administrative councils *(va'adim)*, their structure, outlook and stature are fundamentally different.[118]

133. *Third,* **the Jewish network and its communities share consciousness, notwithstanding their vast differences.** The four meta-stories of Judaism, speaking of peoplehood, nationhood, faith and *or la'goim*, are present across the Jewish network. While each community may be distinct in terms of its outlook, it will always have other communities across the Jewish worldwide web with whom it has a critical mass of

---

117 For an overview of the history of the libel of the Elders of Zion, see Hadassa Ben-Itto, *The Lie That Wouldn't Die: The Protocols of the Elders of Zion,* Vallentine Mitchell, First Edition, 2005.

118 In England, the rabbi of the Great Synagogue of London came to be recognized as the official representative of Jewish faith and the Board of Deputies represents the affairs of the community before the British Government and crown. Thus the instillation of the current Chief Rabbi, Rabbi Ephraim Mirvis, was witnessed by Prince Charles. In France, the Consistoire Central Israélite de France (known as CRIF), established by Napoleon in 1808, served as the formal governing body of the Jewish community in France until 1905, and continues to represent the community. In the USA, Jewish institutions are not different from any other non-governmental religious organization and do not have any special status by law. Meanwhile, in Israel there are two Chief Rabbis – one *Sephardi* and one *Ashkenazi* – both recognized and funded by the state, enjoying legal jurisdiction over matters of civil status such as marriage, divorce, adoption and burial.

commonality in values, patterns of conduct and institutions, which would underlie their collaboration in times of crisis or opportunity.

134. *Fourth,* **the Jewish network has hubs, which are node communities with great influence on the Jewish People and on Judaism.** These hubs are large communities that have an extraordinary number of links to other communities and therefore great influence on Judaism's values, culture, strength and resilience in their time and beyond. Such communities are usually located in key metropolitan areas, where there is a combination of Jewish prosperity and security, as well as a healthy mixture of strong communal and religious institutions. The status of these nodes in the Jewish network is 'meritocratic' not only in that it is based on the quality and quantity of their connections with other nodes and the resources available to and in them, but also in that it is not determined by any one person's decision, rank or title. Presently, these hubs include New York, London, Jerusalem and Tel Aviv. In the past at different times, major centers of Jewish life included, for example, Alexandria in Egypt, Sura and Pompedita in Mesopotamia, Cordova in Spain, Meintz in Germany, and Vilnius in Lithuania.

135. *Fifth,* **the Jewish People progresses due to the commitment and efforts of 'catalysts,' who are individuals and institutions that are both dedicated to its security and wellbeing and possess the status and capacities to serve it.** The catalysts of the Jewish network are numerous community institutions, such as *beit midrash,* committees and funds, rabbis, lay leaders, funders and professionals. They work separately and collaboratively by developing Jewish ideology and theology; identifying threats and opportunities facing the community; preserving a sense of urgency; developing new node communities, strengthening existing ones, and interconnecting them; designing action plans; collecting information, turning it into relevant new knowledge and disseminating it; educating and training new 'catalysts;' defending the community and increasing its prosperity.

136. *Sixth,* **the structure of the Jewish network allows for mass mobilization of resources while minimizing inefficiencies.** The node communities and their 'catalysts' are able to rapidly adjust their attributes, enabling the network to divert resources across topical focuses and arenas with great dexterity. The fast flow of information and permanent movement across the network of communities allows the Jewish world to mobilize around critical issues with power and resources that have been significant relative

to its small size. In modern times this ability most clearly manifested in the response of world Jewry to the Damascus Affair in 1840, and in the global Jewish response to the plight of Soviet Jewry between the 1970s and the early 1990s. Therefore, the Jewish network, like other networks, possesses 'efficient redundancy' in the sense that duplications do not necessarily amount to inefficiencies.

137. Thus, **the Jewish network can withstand the sudden loss of a significant number of its hubs and nodes by shifting its center of gravity and rebuilding itself in other areas.**[119] As noted earlier, calamities – leading to a mass loss of a significant number of node-communities in one area of Jewish society – never paralyzed the Jewish People. In fact, they were often followed by a rise to great political and economic power in another area shortly thereafter. In other words, in times of crisis, other areas of the Jewish worldwide web of communities served as a safety net, mobilizing to support their fellow Jews, facilitating relocation, absorbing fleeing Jews and offering them opportunities for a fresh start. Furthermore, a spike of creativity to respond to the new reality often follows such calamities. Such renaissance often manifested itself in religious, communal and institutional innovation.[120]

138. Indeed, **over the past two millennia, the Jewish People and its web of communities suffered massive setbacks, which led to dramatic shifts in its geographic spread**: the expulsion of Jews from Spain in 1492 led to their migration across North Africa and the Mediterranean sea to Egypt, to the Ottoman Empire, and to Eastern Europe in Poland, Ukraine and Lithuania; the Khmelnitsky massacre in the Ukraine and Poland in 1648 led to significant Jewish migration back westward; the assault on Russian Jewry between 1880s and 1917 pushed many Jews to the Americas; and the disintegration of a Jewish presence in the Arab and Moslem world between 1948 and 1950s in North Africa led to Jewish migration to France, Canada and Israel.

139. Yet, **these assaults on Judaism did not reflect a deep understanding of the secret of its resilience**. As traumatic as these events had been, they were nonetheless attacks on a group of communities within a specific area, and not on the Jewish People and its web of communities in their entirety.

---

119 See: Barabási pp. 153-155, 287. See also Joshua Cooper Ramo, *The Age of Unthinkable*, p.236.

120 Sacks, *Future Tense*, p. 54: "Jews have survived catastrophe after catastrophe, ... every tragedy in Jewish history was followed by a new wave of creativity ..."

140. Tragically, **Nazi ideology correctly understood the sources of Judaism's resilience and therefore sought to destroy the Jewish network of communities**. Nazism concluded that the annihilation of the Jewish People required destroying the entire network of communities down to the last *minyan*, up to three generations back. While eventually seeking to eliminate all Jews, they prioritized the destruction of Jewish community institutions and the killing of rabbis and other leaders of Jewish communities.

141. **This is why Hitler stands together with other infamous figures such as Haman of the Book of Esther and the Roman Emperor Hadrian.** All three of whom sought to eliminate Judaism altogether and are therefore likened to the Biblical people of Amalek who sought to destroy the Israelites. Caesar Hadrian and Hitler were guided by a theory about the Jews that informed their decrees and persecutions. Both of them brought about a catastrophe on Judaism. It is estimated that about forty percent of the Jews perished in the wars against the Romans,[121] and by the time Nazism was reduced to ashes in 1945, a third of the Jewish People, amounting to six million people, were murdered, and thousands of communities had been destroyed.

142. **Nonetheless, shortly thereafter, Jews rose to prominence again due to the vitality of the Jewish web of communities**. By the 3rd century, the Jewish community in Babylon was thriving economically, culturally and religiously.[122] A century after the expulsion from Spain, Jewish communities flourished in the Ottoman Empire and in Poland.[123] And sixty years after the Shoah, the State of Israel and world Jewry are the strongest and most prosperous that they have ever been.

---

121 Johnson, *A History of the Jews*, p. 142 quotes Dio Cassius as saying: "580,000 Jews died in the fighting' and countless numbers of starvation, fire and the sword. Nearly the entire land of Judea was laid waste." In the late fourth century, St Jerome reported from Bethlehem a tradition that, after the defeat, there were so many Jewish slaves for sale that the price dropped to less than a horse."

122 Gafni, *The Jews of Babylon in the Talmudic Era* (Hebrew), is dedicated to describing Jewish prosperity in Babylon as of the 3rd century.

123 Regarding the rise of Polish Jewry, see Johnson, *A History of the Jews*, p. 231. Regarding the emigration of Jews to the Ottoman Empire following the expulsion from Spain, see Johnson, *ibid*, p. 239.

143. *In conclusion*, **a well-dispersed, diverse and closely interconnected network can preserve its vitality and core identity under harsh conditions.** The Jewish People has proven to have similar capabilities. Its flat architecture as a world-wide-web of communities has been key to its survival, security and prosperity, and underlies the ability of Jews to transcend crises. It lies at the very core of Judaism's Flexigidity.

Flexigidity of Membership: Who is a Jew?

This section describes Judaism's Flexigidity with regards to membership in the Jewish People. It emerges out of the inherent tension between the rigid law of matrilineal descent, which establishes that a child of a Jewish woman is a Jew, and the freedom of every ordained rabbi to convert people to Judaism *(giyur)*.

144. **The third pillar of Jewish Flexigidity addresses membership in the Jewish People begging the question: Who is a Jew?** Rigidity stems from the law of matrilineal descent, which establishes that a child of a Jewish mother is Jewish, with no further qualifications necessary. Flexibility is found in conversion, which is the other gateway into Judaism and the Jewish People. For some, flexibility can also be found in the law of patrilineal descent, which grants such membership based on the Jewish identity of the father. This approach is accepted by some progressive denominations and the State of Israel, yet rejected by the more conservative and orthodox circles.

145. **The rigid law of matrilineal descent accords irrevocable membership in the Jewish People to any child of a Jewish mother.** Questions regarding ideology, worldview, personal conduct, as well as the identity of the father or the circumstances of a child's conception are immaterial to the question of membership, as long as the mother is Jewish.

146. **This law of matrilineal descent applies even to Jews who are excommunicated or who reject their Judaism – as well as to their descendants.** For all intents and purposes, a person will remain Jewish even if they betray their covenant with God *(hilul haShem)*, with the Land of Israel and with the Jewish People.[124] Most rabbis hold that even

---

124 Babylonian Talmud Sanhedrin 44a (commenting on Joshua 7:11) quotes Rabbi Abba ben Zabda as saying that "Even though [the people of] Israel has sinned, they are still [called] Israel." *(Af al pi she'chata – Yisrael hu)*

conversion to other religions and public rejection of Judaism (becoming a *meshumad* or a *mumar*) does not remove a person from the Jewish People, although their ability to participate in community life may be qualified. Jews who are ex-communicated by the community *(herem)* certainly remain Jewish, and, if their ex-communication is lifted, they can rejoin the community as full members.

147. **Verifying the matrilineal bloodline is a technical evidence-based process**, which is performed by rabbis, most often prior to a Jewish marriage. In most cases it is a simple procedure, typically using the marriage certificates of one's parents. However, when there is doubt regarding family history, the process may also involve searching for records in community archives in order to verify the Jewish identity of the family. Rarely, when no such trusted references or straight forward documentation exists, such as following migration or war, this process may also require investigative collection of evidence and testimonials. Such probing and questioning may feel humiliating to people who are deeply committed to the Jewish People and identify themselves as Jewish. In a few instances it may even expose unpleasant family surprises and raise aggravating questions. In a growing number of cases, more conservative rabbis question the validity of past conversions along the matrilineal bloodline – of a mother, a grandmother and even further back – and require people who see themselves as Jewish to go through an orthodox conversion process to Judaism for them to bless the marriage.

148. **The law of matrilineal descent has been universally accepted by Jews for many centuries and was essential for exilic existence.** In Biblical and ancient times, it was actually the patrilineal bloodline that determined membership in the Jewish community. The switch to matrilineal logic likely took place following the destruction of the First Temple and the beginning of the Babylonian exile.[125] In that period, Jewish men increasingly travelled across foreign lands and among distant Jewish and non-Jewish communities, while women generally did not. Thus, this law established full responsibility to the community for all children born to its female members, and granted them basic support and protection, irrespective of the identity of the father. Meanwhile, it effectively abdicated its responsibility to children of Jewish men born to Gentile women, unless they converted to Judaism.

---

125 As noted elsewhere, the switch to matrilineal determination of Jewish status had taken hold by the time of Ezra, highlighted in Ezra 9 & 10.

149. Yet, **patrilineal descent is now reemerging in Jewish discourse as a consequence of dramatic societal changes.** This dilemma has intensified over the last decades as limitations on Jews nearly disappeared in most Western societies and Judaism has become a highly respected and attractive religion and way of life. In some cases, as many as half of the people who cross the doorways of Jewish institutions claiming membership, pledging loyalty and seeking participation are the product of a union between a Jewish father and a mother who either did not convert to Judaism or whose conversion is disputed by other Jews. More progressive denominations embrace these individuals unconditionally, considering patrilineal descent to be a legitimate test for membership in the Jewish People. Meanwhile, more orthodox groups demand that they go through a conversion process. This debate affects Jews, would-be Jews and Jewish institutions both in the Diaspora and in Israel.

150. **Flexibility of membership in the Jewish People stems from the ability to integrate non-Jews into Judaism through a conversion** *(giyur)*. Conversion to Judaism requires a non-Jew to go through a guided process of learning and practice in order to join the Jewish People, at the end of which he or she is formally recognized as a Jew. In many communities, at the end of that process a court *(beit din)* actually issues a formal certificate of conversion *(shtar giyur)*. Conversion dates back to the Bible, which documents individuals, such as Ruth, and entire communities that voluntarily joined the Israelites and the Jewish People.[126] Later Jewish texts of the early 1st millennium do so as well, and the issue of *giyur* remains central in the State of Israel and around the Jewish world today.

151. **Every ordained rabbi (one with *smicha*) has the authority to perform conversions.** Therefore, theoretically, Judaism allows as many gateways into the Jewish People, as there are rabbis, who can each apply and interpret *halacha* according to their discretion. Even among orthodox rabbis there are nuanced variances in the conversion process. Furthermore, in modern times, the spectrum of benchmarks for entry into Judaism and membership in the Jewish People has widened dramatically with the rise of the progressive movements. It ranges from demanding sustained religious observance *(shmirat mitzvot)* according to the orthodox approach to accepting converts "without any initiatory rite, ceremony, or observance whatsoever," according to the approach of the Reform Movement of the late 19th century.[127]

---

126 Regarding the conversion of Ruth, see Ruth 1:16. The Book of Esther 8:17 writes about many who joined the Jewish People.

127 CCAR Yearbook 3 (1893), 73–95; American Reform Responsa (ARR), no. 68, p. 236–237

152. **The debate about the authority to officiate over a conversion and its benchmarks for introducing new members into the Jewish People has been a heated one going on for millennia.** There is no gradualism of membership in the Jewish People. A Jew by Choice enjoys immediate access to all rights and privileges, to community institutions and to full participation in religious practices as an equal, even if some conversions were initially treated with suspicion.[128] Furthermore, the identity of a person as a Jew is naturally of critical importance to other Jews, as they perform certain commandments *(mitzvot)* that apply exclusively to Jews and contemplate marriages and family building for themselves and their children. These realities underlie the intensity of the debate regarding the authority to perform conversions and the benchmarks for such process. The Talmud documents a dispute between Hillel and Shammai regarding the necessary conditions for conversions.[129] Maimonides writes extensively about the topic. In modernity, in a growing number of cases, more conservative rabbis question the authority of progressive rabbis to perform conversions and the validity of their conversions. Additionally, in the State of Israel, conversions that were performed by the Military Rabbinate of the Israel Defense Forces have been contested by more orthodox authorities.

153. Indeed, **the benchmarks for conversions evolved in accordance with the dominant meta-story.** Where and when the governing story was peoplehood, the test for conversion emphasized the desire to be a part of the Jewish People.[130] This is also the case among many Jewish communities in the USA and around the world today. In other periods,

---

128 This is notwithstanding the fact that *halacha* prohibits a male from the priestly tribe (Cohen) from marrying a convert as such a marriage would disqualify the groom from service in the Temple. However, the majority of Jews *(Yisrael)* would not be so restricted.

129 Babylonian Talmud, Shabbat 135a and Gerim 2:2 among sources discussed in *The Way of the Boundary Crosser: An Introduction to Jewish Flexidoxy.* Lanham, MD: Rowman & Littlefield, 2005.

130 As noted earlier, this point is based on a lecture by Rabbi Dr. Donniel Hartman on May 23, 2011 at the Samuel Bronfman Foundation Conference entitled 'Why Be Jewish.' Rabbi Hartman referenced Babylonian Talmud, Yevamot 47a-b: "Our Rabbis taught: if at the present time a man desires to become a proselyte, he is to be addressed as follows: "What reason have you for desire to become a proselyte; do you know that Israel at the present time are persecuted and oppressed despised, harassed and overcome by afflictions? If he replies: "I know and yet am unworthy", he is accepted forthwith and is given instructions of some of the minor and some of the major commandments. He is informed of the sins of the neglect of the commandments of Gleanings *(Shi'che'cha)*, Forgotten Sheaf *(Leket)*, the Corner *(Pe'ot)* and the Poor Man's Tithe *(Me'a'ser Ani)*."

where the dominant story was faith and religion, the test for conversion was observance *(shmirat mitzvot)*.[131] Furthermore, in Israel, where the story of nationhood is dominant, some argue that service in the Israel Defense Forces qualifies as right-of-passage into the Jewish People, particularly in cases of burial of fallen soldiers whose identity as Jews is disputed by orthodox groups according to *halacha*.[132] This is an endless internal debate that has always been fought with great ferocity.

154. Furthermore, **the debate over conversions is also affected by the wellbeing of Jewish society.** The more orthodox calls for being stricter in eras of prosperity and security, in order to ensure that those who join the Jewish People are deeply committed to its faith, fate and outlook. Such rabbis would rather lose a potential convert who is not utterly committed to Judaism rather than embrace one whose commitment might be opportunistic. Meanwhile, the more progressive denominations establish lower benchmarks for entry, with the logic of broadening the Jewish tent and accommodating and retaining their intermarried households, as well as keeping Judaism relevant in a world of competing opportunities for spirituality.

155. *Finally*, **the controversy over legitimate conversions is also 'political' in that it stems from a challenge to the stature of the more progressive denominations within the Jewish world.** Since the emergence of the *Haskalah* and the birth of the Reform Movement in Germany in the early 19th century, orthodox rabbis have refused to recognize ordinations of rabbis of progressive movements, and therefore also the conversions that they perform. In other words, a conversion performed by a progressive rabbi according to the strict requirements of the *halacha* would not be recognized by some orthodox rabbis simply because of the identity of the rabbi who officiated over it. Rabbi Mordechai Kaplan, the founder of the Reconstructionist Movement, was ordained by the towering orthodox

---

131 As noted earlier, this point is based on a lecture by Rabbi Dr. Donniel Hartman on May 23, 2011 at the Samuel Bronfman Foundation Conference 'Why Be Jewish'. Rabbi Hartman referenced Tosefta Demai 2:4-5: "A proselyte who took upon himself all matters of Torah, and is suspected of [non-observance] with regard to one matter, even with regard to the entire Torah – behold, he is like an Israelite apostate. A proselyte who took upon himself all matters of Torah, excepting one thing, they don't accept him. Rabbi Jose son of Rabbi Judah says: "even [excepting] a small matter enacted by the scribes."

132 As noted earlier, orthodox rabbis found a different solution within *halacha*, according to which such fallen soldiers who tied their fate with the Jewish People are buried within the fence of the Jewish cemetery in a designated section. See Rabbi Yuval Sharlo at http://www.moreshet.co.il/web/shut/shut2.asp?id=9555.

rabbis of his time. Nonetheless, as his philosophy became increasingly progressive, he was expelled from the Union of Orthodox Rabbis in the USA and Canada in 1945, and therefore the ordinations and the conversions he performed were no longer recognized by his orthodox peers.[133]

156. **Membership remains a major challenge to the Jewish world and of critical significance to many Jewish individuals and households, as well as to entire communities.** Currently, the level of intermarriage among Diaspora Jews at the turn of the 21st century is around fifty percent. An estimated half of those Jews who marry non-Jews in the USA have no intention of remaining a part of the Jewish People. Their household is agnostic, void of any Jewish content, and even, in some cases, anti-Jewish and against the State of Israel. The other half builds households that seek to be a part of the Jewish People.[134] Their spouse often converts and together they build a family that is infused with Jewish values and traditions, and raise children who will continue the Jewish chain for generations. In other words, half of the children of intermarried families self-identify as Jews and practice Judaism to varying degrees. Hence, the issue of conversion and the status of converts in Jewish society in the Diaspora and Israel is of critical importance for Jewries with high levels of intermarriage such as in the USA, Russia, Western Europe and Australia. It is equally significant for Jewish immigrants to Israel, such as from Russia and Ethiopia, whose Judaism is challenged by the rabbinical authorities in Israel.

157. *In conclusion*, **Flexigidity of membership is a critically important mechanism of Jewish survival.** Its rigidity, through the law of matrilineal descent, establishes clearly and unequivocally for most Jews their membership in the community upon their birth. It also allows the boundaries of the Jewish community to be sensitive to local and historical context and responsive to change, making the contours of the Jewish People Flexigid.

---

133 About the ex-communication of Kaplan see: http://www.jta.org/1945/06/14/archive/prof-mordecai-m-kaplan-excommunicated-by-orthodox-rabbis-his-prayer-book-burned.

134 See the 2013 PEW Forum Report, *A Portrait of Jewish Americans*: "Among those who have gotten married since 2000, nearly six-in-ten have a non-Jewish spouse." See also: "Among Jews with a non-Jewish spouse, however, 20% say they are raising their children Jewish by religion and 25% are raising their children partly Jewish by religion. Roughly one-third (37%) of intermarried Jews who are raising children say they are not raising those children Jewish at all." http://www.pewforum.org/2013/10/01/jewish-american-beliefs-attitudes-culture-survey/.

Flexigidity of Law: Torah and *talmud*

> This section describes Judaism's Flexigidity of law. While the Torah and the Oral Torah are rigidly untouchable, the *Talmudic* process allows for interpretation of the ancient texts in order to explicate law *(halacha)* within an ever-changing reality throughout the generations. The *second part* of this section describes the institutions created within Judaism to uphold this process of *talmud* primarily the synagogue *(beit knesset)* and the academy *(beit midrash)*. The *third part* highlights different tools for the development of *halacha* such as systems of hermeneutic principles for interpretation, tales *(aggadah* and *midrashim)* and consensus building. The *fourth part* of this section deals with the freedom to establish *halacha* and its limits. The *final part* describes the manner in which Judaism honors and respects dissenting views within its midst, so long as they are for the 'sake of heaven' and the community.

158. **The fourth pillar of Jewish Flexigidity is Jewish law, which develops by means of a flexible process of interpretation and application called talmud, bridging the tension between the rigid text of the written law with an ever-changing external reality.**

159. **The written Torah and the Oral Torah, the pillars of Jewish law, are formulated and unchangeable.** 'Torah' refers to the five books of Moses *(chamisha chumshei Torah or Chumash)*. In addition, thirty one other books of Prophets *(Ne'vi'im)* and Writings *(Ktuvim)* were collated to create the Bible *(Tanach)* in a process that lasted centuries. Jewish faith holds that Moses received the Torah on Mount Sinai, and some carry the tradition that Ezra and Nehemia canonized the texts of the Tanach around 6th century BCE, while all others agree that it had been canonized by the time of Rabbi Akiva in the early part of the 2nd century.[135] The Oral Torah is the collection of the *Mishnah* of Rabbi Yehudah HaNasi; additional external texts *(Braitot)*, comprised of teachings that were not included in the *Mishnah*; additional rabbinic explanations of the text *(Midrashim)*; and further interpretation, application and legalization of the aforementioned texts, called the *Gemara*. Together, the *Mishnah* and the *Gemara* comprise the Talmud of which there are two versions: the Babylonian Talmud and the Jerusalem Talmud recording the discourses

---

135 Johnson, *A History of the Jews*, p. 87, 90, 95: "...the Torah was canonized as early as 622 BC. Other books were added gradually, the process being completed by about 300 BC ... before 400 BC there is no hint of a canon. By 200 BC it was there."

of the sages in the communities of Babylon and of the Land of Israel, respectively.

160. **This Oral Law is believed to have been transmitted by word of mouth from one generation to another for centuries.** According to tradition, this process began with Moses and continued to the days of Rabbi Yehudah HaNasi in the first half of the 3rd century.[136] During this period, the Oral Torah evolved to accommodate ordinary societal evolution including politics, social and economic development and new technologies. It also grappled with dramatic transformative events such as the exile of the First Temple *(hurban Bait Rishon)*, the return to Zion *(shivat Zion)*, the challenge of Hellenism and the destruction of the Second Temple.

161. **Related but also distinct, *talmud*, with a small 't,' refers to the permanent process of explicating new customs and laws for Jewish society *(halacha)*, bridging the dynamism of reality with the rigidity of the text.**[137] According to tradition, the *talmudic* process has been going on since the giving of the Torah to Moses on Mount Sinai, as the Ethics of Our Fathers *(Pirkei Avot)* documents the Men of the Great Assembly establishing law based on the Torah.[138] Until Hillel the Elder, in the 1st century BCE, Oral Law is believed to have been transmitted verbatim from one generation to another and applied in a straight forward manner. It was Hillel who introduced a new mode of interpretation of the text called innovation *(hidush)*, which allowed greater flexibility and adaptation of the law to the emerging needs of society.[139] His approach was contested by his contemporary, Shammai, who stood for a greater rigidity in the transmission and application of past wisdom.

---

136 Rabbi Israel Meir Lau, *Foundations*, p. 26-27

137 The distinction between Talmud the proper noun with a capital and talmud the verb and name of a process reflects an attempt at capturing an idea, which can be found in the Hebrew yet is lost in translation. Credit to Rabbi Nachum Braverman, of Los Angeles, California.

138 Avot 1:1. The men of the Great Assembly instruct that one should: be deliberate in judgment, raise many disciples, and make a fence around the Torah.

139 See Binyamin Lau, *Sages Volume 1*, p. 166-168 (in Hebrew).

162. **Hillel's student, Ben-Zakai, represents the beginning of another period, of the _Tannaim_,[140] who, in the absence of a Temple, institutionalized the development of Jewish Oral Law in the _beit midrash_ as inspired by Hillel.[141]** The Tannaim (literally: repeaters or teachers) continued to adapt Jewish law primarily to the harsh conditions which followed the destruction of Jerusalem. There were approximately one hundred and twenty known Tannaim, who operated for nearly one hundred and fifty years primarily in Yavneh, but also in Bnei Brak, Lod, Tiberias, and the Galilee.[142] They continuously contended with the tension between flexibility and rigidity, embodied by the disputes between Hillel and Shammai.

163. **The redaction and codification of key parts of the oral tradition into the Mishnah by Rabbi Yehudah HaNasi marked another major milestone in the transformation of Judaism into an adaptable and mobile civilization.** Rabbi Yehudah HaNasi lived in a particularly challenging period in the late 2nd century and early 3rd century. At this time, Roman oppression of Judea led to the mass departure of Jews from Zion and to the dispersal and atomization of the Jewish People into scattered communities across the Roman Empire and Mesopotamia. Additionally, Christianity began to emerge as a formidable challenge to Judaism. Living in the Galilee, Rabbi Yehudah HaNasi was concerned that the wisdom of the sages, Jewish faith and sense of peoplehood would be forgotten and lost. His idea of distilling and codifying the163 Oral Law into a set text that could be memorized and studied across geographic boundaries was a radical one. Under his leadership, sages curated and possibly also edited and formulated texts, which hitherto, according to tradition, had been transmitted orally from one generation to another.[143] This project met with great success, and the _Mishnah_ – divided into six orders _(Shisha Sidrei Mishnah)_ – has served as a cornerstone of _halacha_ ever since.

---

140 Technically, everyone quoted in the Mishnah is considered a Tana. This is notwithstanding the fact that this means there were "Tanaim" before the "first generation of Tanaim." Simon the Just, Antigonus and the five pairs (_zugot_) are all therefore Tanaim but lived before the "first generation."

141 See Binyamin Lau, _Sages Volume 2_, p. 30-55 (in Hebrew).

142 For a list of Tanaim broken down by generation see _Wikipedia_ page: http://en.wikipedia. org/wiki/Template:Tannaim.

143 Scholarly opinion is divided whether the _Mishnah_ was actually written down at this time or if the text was codified but still meant to be memorized. Regardless, the terse nature of the text and its consistent structure seem to have been designed to facilitate memorization.

164. **That period also established a very important principle of Jewish adaptability: that a different and even dissenting opinion, which is 'for the sake of heaven,' is documented, dignified and preserved for future generations.** Contemporary wisdom and commentaries that Rabbi Yehudah HaNasi did not include in the *Mishnah*, and yet still continued to be passed down, became known as Braitot (literally meaning 'outside' or 'external,' Braita in the singular). The Tosefta (literally 'supplement') refers to a compilation of Braitot that follows the same thematic and structural division of orders of the *Mishnah*. These texts would continue to feed future law making, cited regularly within the *Gemara*.

165. **The *Mishnah* marks the transition from period of the Tannaim to the era of the *Amoraim*, during which it was expounded upon and clarified to create the *Gemara*.**[144] Rabbis in the Land of Israel and in the Diaspora, primarily in Babylon, continued to relentlessly grapple with 'questions' on a range of issues, which span individual, household and communal life. They used accepted principles of interpretation to create precedents and further develop *halacha*. Altogether, hundreds of Amoraim (literally, 'those who speak to the people') operated in the Galilee and in Babylon in religious academies *(yeshivot)*, most notably those of Sura and Pumbedita in Mesopotamia.[145] Their rulings were eventually recorded in the Talmuds of Jerusalem and Babylon, around 400 and 492 respectively. The codification of the Babylonian Talmud also ushered in the period of the Savoraim, who further expounded upon the work of the Amoraim and possibly gave the Talmud its final form, likely in the 7th century.

166. **The prosperous period of the Geonim began in the early 7th century and lasted until the 11th century, during which the Jewish People and Judaism were largely led from Mesopotamia,** then in the Abbasid Caliphate. Jewish communities there were led by a dual-headed structure of the Exilarchs *(Rosh Galuta)* and the *Geonim*. The Exilarchs had authority over secular matters and relations with the sovereign. Meanwhile, the *Geonim* – plural of *Gaon*, which meant 'pride' and 'splendor' – were the presidents of the two great academies *(yeshivot)* of Sura and Pumbedita, which were the chief centers of Jewish learning.

---

144 As noted above, the Mishnah and the *Gemara* comprise the Talmud of which there are two versions: the Babylonian Talmud and the Jerusalem Talmud recording the discourses of the sages in the communities of Babylon and of the Land of Israel respectively.

145 For a list of Amoraim broken down by their respective generations and locales see the following *Wikipedia* entry: http://en.wikipedia.org/wiki/Template:Amoraim.

They were recognized as the highest spiritual and religious authorities and leaders, and effectively served as the supreme judges of the Jewish community worldwide.[146]

167. **The major collective creation of the *Geonim* was the Responsa Literature, in which they developed *halacha* by answering queries on Jewish faith and law.** These Responsas were book-long essays on Talmudic themes, often answering questions, which arrived from distant locations where no sufficient *talmudic* scholarship existed. Two important examples are the '*Siddur* of Amram Gaon,' addressed to the Jews of Spain in response to a question about the laws of prayer, and the "Epistle of Rav Sherira Gaon" *(Iggeret Rav Sherira Gaon)*, which sets out the history of the *Mishnah* and the Talmud in response to a question from the area of modern day Tunisia. This was largely a period of peace and prosperity for Jews, then under Moslem rule, and much of the work of the Geonim deals with issues of trade and commerce. In the latter part of the *Geonic* period, as the study of the Talmud expanded and academies *(yeshivot)* were established in other locations as well, the supremacy of the *Geonim* in Mesopotamia lessened. The dawn of the 2nd millennium saw growing political instability in Mesopotamia, the decline of the Babylonian Talmudic academies, the end of the Geonic Period and a shift in the Jewish world toward the Byzantine Empire and Christian Europe. With the Mongol conquest and the fall of Baghdad in 1258, the Jewish presence in Mesopotamia descended into a dark period.[147]

168. **The *Rishonim*, who were leading Rabbis during the 11th to the 15th centuries, represent the next era of rabbinical Judaism.** They operated in Southern France, Germany, Spain and Zion. They were the foremost scholars of the Bible, *Mishnah*, and Talmud, as well as commentators, philosophers, poets and grammarians. Some of the best known among them were the foremost biblical commentator, Rabbi Shlomo Itzhaki, known as 'Rashi,' and Rabbi Yehuda Halevi, a 12th century Spanish philosopher and poet devoted to Zion who wrote the Book of the Kuzari *(Sefer HaKuzari)*. However, most prominent among the Rishonim was Rabbi Moshe Ben Maimon, known as Rambam or Maimonides. His *Mishneh Torah,* which sought to detail all of the 613 commandments

---

146 See Johnson, *A History of the Jews*, p. 153: "From the fifth to the eleventh centuries, which is known as the age of *gaons* or *geonim*, scholars worked to produce collective rulings and compilations bearing the authority of academies…"

147 See Botticini and Eckstein, *The Chosen Few*, p.71-74 and 78-79 on the effect of the Mongol conquest.

and their proper observance, remains a cornerstone of Jewish legal thought, and his *Guide to the Perplexed* is one of the most influential philosophical creations of all time. Indeed, the epitaph on his grave reads, "From Moses to Moses there was none like Moses."

169. **The publication of the *Shulchan Arukh* (literally, 'Set Table') in 1563 by Rabbi Yosef Karo marked another milestone in the evolution of Jewish law, and the transition from the era of *Rishonim* to that of *Acharonim* (literally, 'last ones').** Acharonim refers to the leading rabbis and deciders *(poskim)* who lived in roughly the 16th century.[148] They were both Sephardic and Ashkenazi rabbis who operated across Europe, the Middle East and North Africa, as well as in Zion, particularly in the city of Safed *(Tsfat)*. This period continues until today.

170. **The *talmudic* process is upheld by designated institutions, primarily that of the *beit midrash*.** This institution has existed since the period of the 'pairs' *(zugot)* in the 2nd century BCE,[149] with the purpose of adapting Jewish thinking and law *(halacha)* to the ever-changing reality. It emerged in Yavne as the leading intellectual institution of the Jewish People following the destruction of Jerusalem, when all of Jewish society had to adapt. It institutionalized Jewish Flexigidity by creating a hybrid between the rigidity of Torah and traditions and the flexibility required for communal development.

171. **The most basic intellectual unit of the Jewish People and of the *talmudic* process is the study pair *(chevrutah)*.** Each study pair includes two people who regularly convene to engage in *talmud*. They work together through the ancient texts to understand the trail of wisdom blazed by the sages relating to an issue or a question *(she'e'la)* and to develop their own understanding of the matter at hand. One can imagine the Jewish People as incorporating countless study pairs within many *batei midrash*.

172. **This organization furthered the democratization of Jewish society building and of the development of *halacha*.** Everybody, regardless of background, is invited and expected to participate in an intellectually

---

148 The *Wikipedia* entry on Rishonim (http://en.wikipedia.org/wiki/rishonim) refers to the CODEX JUDAICA, Chronological Index of Jewish History, which argues that there was another trend of scholars between the *Rishonim* and the *Acharonim* from 1492 to 1648 with distinctive elements of scholarship, called "the consolidators" *(Kov'im)*.

149 See Binyamin Lau, *Sages Volume 1*, p. 164-169 (in Hebrew).

rigorous, transparent and competitive process of distilling new understandings from the ancient texts. Such broad participation in the *talmudic* process is made possible by the commitment of Jewish society to universal literacy and to the general education of the entire population, which began in the 1st century BCE.[150] Such engagement is not only a religious obligation, but also an act of citizenship and communal responsibility, which takes place every day in Jewish communities.

173. Thus, **in effect, the *beit midrash* became a society-building institution.** It is the place where Jews create societal knowledge and the source of the tremendous wealth of Jewish 'social technology,' i.e. of the great diversity of ways in which Jews were organized to serve their own needs.[151] It also inculcated a constantly renewing sense of social responsibility among a very broad base in the community. These institutions are thriving today more than ever before in orthodox and non-orthodox communities alike. In the State of Israel modern models of the *beit midrash* – such as Ein Prat, Elul, Alma, Binah and Kolot – have emerged to contend with contemporary issues of Israeli society.

174. **The Flexigidity of the *talmudic* process stems from its hybrid nature, which blends hard law with broader context, general frameworks with specific principles and precedents, conformity with innovation.**

175. **Rigidity of Jewish law stems not only from the canonized status of the ancient texts, but also from the obligation to conform to past generations**. Orthodox Jewish tradition preaches a rigid hierarchy of rulings, wherein every generation accepts the wisdom of its predecessors and their wisdom as a fixed foundation. Thus, according to Jewish orthodoxy, scholars in one era within the history of *halachic* development cannot legally challenge the rulings of previous-era scholars, roughly in the same manner that a lower legal instance cannot challenge the ruling of a higher legal instance.[152] Consequently, modern rabbis, who are *Acharonim*, cannot dispute the rulings of rabbis who are considered Rishonim, and came before them.[153] Hence,

---

150 See Botticini and Eckstein, *The Chosen Few*, p. 97-112.

151 On the idea of social technology see Eric D. Beinhocker, *The Origin of Wealth*, Harvard Business School Press, p. 15-16.

152 While Maimonides upheld the authority of the Talmud, his Mishne Torah faced harsh criticism for not giving the Talmudic sources of his conclusions.

153 A key issue in this regard is whether Rabbi Joseph Karo is a Rishon or an Acharon, and therefore whether his *Shulchan Aruch* can be disputed by an Acharon rabbi.

the evolution of Jewish law stems from a system that requires mastery of the wealth of ancient texts and deep acquaintance with the history of Jewish thought as a precondition for establishing law.

176. At the same time, **Judaism also embraces the need to innovate and establish legitimate ways for the development of Jewish law and society**. The 2nd century Talmudic sage Rabbi Joshua established that there is no *beit midrash* without innovation *(hidush)*.[154] Judaism legitimizes questioning and probing and students are encouraged to get to the root of their rabbis' teachings. These dynamics are essential for the on-going adaptation of society, which Judaism views as an inevitable and necessary process that must be regulated.

Thus, **Judaism's Flexigidity of law is founded upon a few pillars as shall be described below**:

177. *First*, **Judaism's Flexigidity of law stems from the rational tools of logic of the *talmudic* process in the *beit midrash*.** In the famous story, 'the Oven of Akhnai' *(Tanur Shel Akhnai)*,[155] the rabbis refuse to rule on the basis of proof by miracles, or, for that matter, charisma, maintaining for the majority the right to determine Jewish law based on a rational process of deliberation. This approach makes Jewish lawmaking an intellectual enterprise that can be governed by universal tools of logic in a transparent and accountable manner.

178. Furthermore, **Judaism has multiple approaches to guide the process of bringing Jewish law to bear on a specific issue** by inferring from the ancient texts the appropriate response to questions *(tshuvot)*. These sets of logical and rational tools are known as 'hermeneutic principles.'[156] One such system is attributed to Rabbi Ishmael, a 3rd generation Tanna (circa 90-135), who derived and distilled thirteen such principles *(midot she'nigzeret bahen HaTorah)*, building upon the prior work of Hillel the Elder. For example, they establish that a specific solution can emerge out of a general principle *(kal va'chomer)*.[157] Faithful Jews believe that these laws of reason are an integral part of the Oral Torah and were given by God

---

154 Babylonian Talmud Chagiga 3a

155 Bava Metzia 59b

156 Beginning of Sifra Leviticus. See also *Wikipedia* entry on Hermeneutic Systems: http://en.wikipedia.org/wiki/talmudic_hermeneutics.

157 See Rabbi Israel Meir Lau, *Foundations*, p. 41-44.

to Moses on Mount Sinai in order to facilitate the development of Jewish law and society. Rabbi Akiva created another hermeneutic system guided by the conviction that every word and sign in the Torah is essential and of deep meaning.[158] A third example is Jewish numerology *(gematria)*, which associates a number to every Hebrew letter and a numeric value to every Hebrew word, and therefore allows for finding additional meaning in the text.[159] **These rules represent the idea of Flexigidity of law in and of themselves, since, by their nature as logical rules, they are rigid, yet, collectively, they unleash tremendous flexibility for the Jewish People as a whole.**

179. *Second,* **the Midrashim are another source for Judaism's Flexigidity of law.** Midrashim are often free flowing, intuitive, creative and dynamic tales offering metaphors and giving context to the rigid law, helping to explain its complex ideas and thereby increasing its flexibility. They are divided into two general categories: *Midrash halacha* refers to exegesis that connect a specific *halacha* to its Biblical source, while *Midrash Aggadah* refers to rabbinic tales incorporating folklore, historical anecdotes, moral exhortations and practical advice in various spheres, from business to medicine.[160]

180. *Third,* **Judaism acknowledges the significance of the intellectual capacity to create *halacha* and to bridge existing traditions with emerging realities.** The Talmud distinguishes between two types of scholars and learners: a *Sinai* is one who has a tremendous ability to retain knowledge, as was passed down from the revelation at Sinai. An *Oker Harim* (literally, 'mountain mover') has an extraordinary capacity to create new wisdom that bridges the contradictions in the *halacha* as it is brought to bear on a question.[161] The Talmud debates which of them is more important for Judaism, and the answers vary, *inter alia*, according to context. Interestingly, Rashi says that one can be a 'mountain mover' even if they have imperfect knowledge.

---

158 See *Wikipedia* entry on Rabbi Akiva's hermeneutic system: http://en.wikipedia.org/wiki/ Akiva_ben_Joseph#Akiva.27s_hermeneutic_system.

159 See Rabbi Israel Meir Lau, *Foundations*, p. 45-47; Avot 3:23; *Wikipedia* entry on Gematria: http://en.wikipedia.org/wiki/Gematria.

160 As described in *Wikipedia* entry on Aggadah http://en.wikipedia.org/wiki/Aggadah.

161 See *Wikipedia* entry in Hebrew for סיני ועוקר הרים (Sinai ve Oker Harim).

181. *Fourth,* **Judaism's Flexigidity also stems from its tendency to establish frameworks and principles that incorporate a broad spectrum of human phenomena, helping Jews and humanity understand their past, present and future.** This tendency stems from the attempt to understand God's wishes on earth, and from the attribution of a divine logic and rational to His actions. In other words, as Jews try to gain deeper insight into God's wishes, they can build a better society to serve His wishes and be a light unto the nations. Examples for the Jewish quest to frame and understand the overarching logic and principles of the universe, humanity and Jewish society can be found in Ethics of the Fathers *(Pirkei Avot)*, which instructs the student of Torah to "Delve and delve into it, for all is in it;"[162] in the teaching of Hillel HaZaken that the entire Torah can be taught standing on one foot, distilled in the principle, "Don't do unto others as you would not have them do unto you;" and in Maimonides' thirteen principles of faith. This tendency may have underlay the works of the great Jewish secular thinkers, such as the philosopher Baruch Spinoza, Sigmund Freud and Albert Einstein. Their common denominator is their ability to deploy the force of rationalism and logic to the world's problems and produce a new and powerful framework for understanding human society and our world.[163]

182. *Fifth,* **consensus building is also essential for Judaism's Flexigid society.** During the era of Yavne and as long as a central religious authority existed, decisions were made based on majority rule.[164] Yet, while a regular majority was required for ordinary decision, special majorities were required for decisions that were critical for the community or for the fate of individuals, such as in criminal cases punishable by death and the declaration of war.[165] In the absence of power to enforce its

---

162 Pirkei Avot, 5:21

163 Johnson, *A History of the Jews*, p. 267 refers to the ability to "…construct a system of explanations and predictions of phenomena, which was both highly plausible and at the same time sufficiently imprecise and flexible to accommodate new – and often highly inconvenient – events when they occurred … of presenting … protean-type theory, with built-in capacity to absorb phenomenal by a process of osmosis…". Johnson writes about the risks of this tendency in the case of Nathan of Gaza (1643-1680) and Karl Marx.

164 See Binyamin Lau, *Sages Volume 2*, p. (in Hebrew). Johnson, *A History of the Jews*, p. 156-157: "One reason why Judaism clung together over the centuries was its adherence to majority decisions and the great severity with which it punished those who refused to submit to them once they were fairly reached."

165 See the debate concerning the "Oven of Akhnai" in Babylonian Talmud Bava Metzia 59b.

decisions, this 'democratic' process was essential for social cohesion, for maintaining the legitimacy of the *Sanhedrin* and, therefore, for obedience to its rulings. After the disbandment of the *Sanhedrin*, when religious authority was dispersed among communities, practice was able to become common law if, over a long period of time, it was broadly accepted by the community. When a practice became common law, rigidified by its broad endorsement, there were almost always Jewish groups who rejected it, clung to other rituals and preserved the engine of Flexigidity.

183. *Finally,* **Jewish intellectual evolution through the *talmudic* process has continued ceaselessly, punctuated by major projects of codification.** The application of law to reality breeds permanent discussions and new volumes of rabbinical rulings about Jewish life. Every once in a while, often centuries apart, a body of teachings and wisdom was distilled, formalized and codified and therefore rigidified to serve as a fixed point of reference for future generations. Key events of codification include the *Mishnah* by Rabbi Yehuda HaNasi in the 3rd century; the Responsas by Geonim between the 7th and 9th centuries; the Siddur by Rabbi Saadia Gaon in the 9th century; the Mishne Torah by Maimonides in the 12th century; and the Shulchan Aruch by Rabbi Yossef Karo in the 16th century. In this context, some would view the body of 'Hebrew law' of the State of Israel as a major effort of codification of Jewish law in modernity.

184. In a nutshell, **Judaism's Flexigidity of law is captured in the concept of PRDS (pronounced '*par'des*'), which is also an acronym**. The letter 'P' stands for the word '*pshat,*' which means literal, straightforward and face value understanding of the text; the letter 'R' stands for the word *remez* (a hint), which reads into the text clues to the resolution of dilemmas; the letter 'D' stands for the word '*drash,*' which allows for allegoric reading of the text, i.e. for explicating alternative and additional narratives altogether and for embracing homiletic ideas that are only suggested by allusion; and the letter 'S' stands for the word '*sod*' (secret) which opens the door to deeper insights and to hidden meaning in the text, e.g. to the world of Kabbalah and Jewish mysticism.

185. **One of the deepest divides in the Jewish world is about freedom of interpretation, and therefore societal innovation.** This division underlies the major rifts between the conservative and progressive forces in any generation.

186. **The roots of this tension preceded the Second Temple Era, but were brought to the fore following the destruction of the Temple, which required a deep realignment of Jewish society.** Rabbi Binyamin Lau describes how in that period, Ben-Zakai legitimized a very aggressive mode of religious and societal innovation, following the House of Hillel. It was described by the metaphors of a well *(be'er)* or spring *(ma'ayan)*,[166] and by the idea that innovation *(hidush)* is integral to the *beit midrash (ein beit midrash lelo hidush)*[167] and essential for the adaptation of the Jewish People. The challenge to these concepts came from the legacy of the House of Shammai, and from the ideology that the purpose of Jewish learnedness is mastery of past wisdom and its rigid application. That approach was described through the metaphor of a plastered cistern that doesn't lose a drop of water *(bor sud she'eino me'abed tipa)*, with tradition transmitted unaltered from one generation to another. Hence there is no freedom of innovation *(hidush)*.[168] This debate, which was declared to be settled in the favor of the House of Hillel during the Tannaitic period,[169] in accordance with Ben-Zakai, Rabban Gamliel II and Rabbi Akiva, continues to shape Jewish society today.

187. **This debate about freedom of interpretation continues.** Conservative factions tend to be more change averse. They are weary of any novel idea, committed to following traditions, and they accord authority to institute change only to towering figures that have mastered the world of *halacha*. Meanwhile, progressive factions are more open to embracing change earlier, allowing greater freedom to their communities to institute and experiment with change. In fact, one of the key differentiating factors among Jewish denominations in the USA – the Orthodox, Conservative, Reform and Reconstructionist movements – pertains to the authority to institute changes in laws, traditions and practices, and the threshold for doing so.

188. **The dialectic process, whereby a decision is made yet dissenting opinions are honored and preserved, is central to the entire structure of Jewish law and to Jewish Flexigidity.** Judaism accords respect to dissenting views regarding the condition of the community

---

166 See Binyamin Lau, *Sages Volume 2*, p. 38-55 (in Hebrew).

167 Babylonian Talmud Chagiga 3a

168 See Binyamin Lau, *Sages Volume 2*, p. 38-46 (in Hebrew).

169 See Binyamin Lau, *Sages Volume 1*, p. 196-199 and *Sages Volume 2*, p. 88-93 (in Hebrew).

and the appropriate responses to the challenges and opportunities it faces. The Talmud establishes that in certain conditions, different sides of a debate may nonetheless represent the wishes of God, captured by the famous saying that "both are the words of the living God" *("elu ve'elu divrei Elokim chaim")*.[170] This tradition has roots in the stories about the Houses of Hillel and Shammai, who had key disagreements between them, yet continued to intermarry their children.[171] Also, as mentioned earlier, the wisdom that Rabbi Yehudah HaNasi excluded from the *Mishnah*, known as the Braitot, remained an important non-authoritative source for rulings of rabbis in subsequent generations and were included in the Talmud. **Rabbi Jonathan Sacks calls these dynamics, "dignity of dissent."**[172]

189. **Social cohesion is a primary underlying logic of Judaism's 'dignity of dissent.'** The sages understood that social cohesion requires that views regarding the condition and future of society are, as much as possible, housed and debated within common institutions in a respectful, fair, transparent and accountable process. In such an environment, those whose view did not carry the day are more likely to remain a part of the community and continue to contribute to its development.

190. **This approach is also pragmatically essential for long-term security and prosperity.** A change of circumstances may affect the needs of the community. Hence, a view that is found to be more conducive for the wellbeing of the community under certain conditions may turn out to be ineffective in a different environment. Indeed, Judaism has creative ways to preserve and revisit dissenting views for use by future generations and different communities. This idea is captured by Rabbi Sacks who writes, "Judaism is the only religion whose key texts are anthologies of arguments."[173]

191. **For an argument to qualify as a legitimate dissenting view, it must be 'for the sake of heaven'** *(le'shem shamayim)*.[174] This criterion was traditionally understood to refer to the service of the wishes of God, but, in effect, it can also be measured by its service to the community. This principle establishes that an argument about the law, which is self-serving

---

170 Babylonian Talmud Eruvin 13b. See also Sacks, *Future Tense,* p. 195-198.

171 Babylonian Talmud Yevamot 1:4

172 See Sacks, *Future Tense,* p. 198-203.

173 Sacks, *Future Tense,* P. 183

174 Avot 5:17

in terms of power, money and status, compromises both the contender and the merit of the case, undermining the *talmudic* process. In Ethics of the Fathers *(Pirkei Avot)*, the dispute between Hillel and Shammai is contrasted with the confrontation between Moses and Korach and his clan *(Korach ve adato)*.[175] Hillel and Shammai spoke for the sake of heaven and kept the community unified. Their dispute was enshrined. Meanwhile, Korach and his clan, who pretended to be speaking for communal needs while being in fact self-serving, seeking power and wealth, were severely punished, serving as a reminder of, and a warning against, inappropriate ethical conduct and leadership in the Jewish public sphere. In other words, for an argument to qualify as being 'for the sake of heaven' and to be preserved in the repository of the Jewish People for future generations, it must be exclusively for the benefit of the community.[176] As Rabbi Sacks writes, "God gives his blessing to a multiplicity of perspectives and thus creates the phenomenon of non-zero-sum disagreements. Several views may be true, even if only one is authoritative as law."[177] **Judaism's approach in this regard is different from the common view in modern democracies, which assumes that public good is served through a political and economic process that balances the self-serving positions of protagonists who each selfishly seek to maximize their own political and economic interest.**

192. Therefore, **an argument that is perceived to cast doubt *(safek)* on the *Brith* is seen as illegitimate, and its service for the 'sake of heaven' may be contested.** For example, Elisha Ben-Abuya, a prominent 2nd century Tanna who turned away from Judaism, was ex-communicated and thereafter referred to as 'the other' *(acher)*. 16th century Baruch Spinoza, who articulated the narrative of secularism, was likewise ex-communicated. Twentieth-century Rabbi Mordechai Kaplan was ex-communicated by the Orthodox community on account of his naturalist theology in 1945. Nonetheless, their thought has had continued influence on Judaism: Ben-Abuya is still quoted repeatedly in the *Mishnah*, Spinoza's philosophies returned to Judaism with the *Haskalah* and Kaplan's legacy has had a marked impact on modern American Judaism.

---

175 Avot 5:17 on Numbers 17. See also Sacks, *Future Tense*, p. 196.

176 Avot 5:17

177 See Sacks, *Present Tense*, p. 197-198.

193. **The *talmudic* process is democratic and potentially taps the intellectual capacity of the Jewish People**. Into the days of the Great Assembly *(Knesset Gedolah)*, which was presumably active between 6th and 3rd century BCE, participation in Jewish lawmaking was effectively limited to a handful of people. The rise of the sages, first within the *Knesset Gedolah* and then with the *Sanhedrin*, allowed for broader participation of highly educated individuals. The formalization and institution of the hermeneutic principles in the era of Yavne, made the development of Jewish law a transparent and accountable process. With the growth of the beit midrash, it became accessible to the masses, allowing any educated Jew to participate in the process of determining Jewish law. Furthermore, it ensured that the process of lawmaking was fully intellectually meritocratic as clear guidelines for establishing the 'truth' were determined. With the broad general education that ensued, the intellectual capital of the Jewish People, effectively deployed towards the adaptation of its society was maximized.

194. **For a novel idea to have become a generally accepted Jewish practice and then law, it must have proved to have served the collective security and prosperity of the community, without compromising its core identity**. This 'proof' emerges through a painful, highly contentious and slow process that may last years, decades, generations or even centuries, as progressive forces adapt and implement it in spite of protests of conservative ones. Consistent proof of success would bring the more conservative factions to grudgingly gravitate in that direction, and eventually allow a change in practice.

195. Thus, **the force of Jewish Flexigidity is such that even the most conservative forces of Judaism go through transformations**. As mentioned, the general rule is that they gravitate grudgingly toward those innovations that increase the security and wellbeing of the community without compromising its identity. Their evolution is slow, often invisible to the impatient eye. But a broader view exposes the radical transformations that even the most conservative groups in Judaism undergo, rendering the view that they are stagnant and immobile unfounded. Though the scholarship of Maimonides in the 12th century was rejected by many of his generation, today it is integral to the Jewish religious canon. *Hasidim* in the 18th century confronted fierce resistance by the orthodoxy of the time (known as the *Mitnagdim* or the *Lita'im*) to become a mainstream mass movement among orthodox Jews. Rabbi Zvi Hirsch Kalischer (1795-1874), who was the

first orthodox rabbi to be also a Zionist, was criticized for calling for a mass return to Zion. Today, the largest ultra-orthodox *(Haredi)* Jewish community in the world lives in the State of Israel. The idea of mass public education for orthodox women initially faced fierce resistance and is now common practice in the Beth Jacob Seminaries. Finally, the ultra-orthodox *(Haredi)* community in Israel is different from that of the USA, and both of them have traveled a great distance since their days in Eastern Europe and elsewhere.

196. Furthermore, **in rare cases, this process of interpretation may lead to rabbis holding in abeyance explicit commandments of the Torah and long-held traditions that had become common law.** This lenience is explicated from the verse in the book of Psalms that the service of God may require withholding the application of the law *(et la'asot le'Hashem haferu toratecha).*[178] For orthodox Jews, it is mostly applied in unique, extreme and dire circumstances, when the entire existence of the Torah and the Jewish People may be at risk, or when a change of radical circumstances renders observance impossible. Examples include commandments that were withheld during the exile and until the return to Zion,[179] the shift from patrilineal to matrilineal descent as the test for membership in the Jewish People,[180] and the formulation of the Oral Torah in the *Mishnah* after centuries when writing it was strictly forbidden.[181] The so-called Prosbol of Hillel the Elder effectively circumvented a section of the Jubilee Law in the Torah, which called upon all debts to be written off *(shmita),* in order to prevent its stifling effect on trade.[182]

197. **Jewish law is the cement of Jewish society building, synonymous with Jewish religion, and its observance is an act of faith for most observant Jews.** The logic is straightforward: Judaism seeks to understand God's wishes in order to execute them precisely and create the model society that will be a light unto the nations. With the cessation

---

178 Babylonian Talmud Brachot 63a

179 Examples for commandments that have been circumvented during the exile and until the return to Zion include the full practice of the Jubilee year *(Yovel),* which will only exist when all twelve tribes return to Zion, and of the laws relating to the Temple.

180 This shift had taken place by the end of the First Temple Exile. See Ezra, Chapters 9, 10.

181 See Rabbi Israel Meir Lau, *Foundations,* p. 27.

182 See Binyamin Lau, *Sages Volume 1,* p. 171 on the manner in which rabbis in in Mishnah, Gitin 4:3 were able to circumvent an explicit directive of the Torah in Deuteronomy chapter 15.

of prophesy after the destruction of the First Temple, the understanding of God's expectations of Jews was then crystallized through an intellectual process of extracting law from seemingly mundane dilemmas based on past wisdom. Through this process, any such insight may over time turn into a law that will have to be religiously observed by observant Jews. Hence, the meta-story of faith stands out among the four meta-stories of Judaism because Jewish law embraces, co-opts, and, therefore, rigidifies values and practices that emanate from the other stories and prove to consistently serve the community. There are commandments and prayers that emphasize peoplehood by referring to the entire people of Israel *(klal ahm Israel)* and to mutual responsibility *(arevut)*; to nationhood, by referring to the sanctity of Zion, to repatriation and to reestablishing the House of David; and to being a light unto the nations by regarding the treatment of the poor, the needy and the sick.

198. *In conclusion,* **evolution of Jewish law and society has been the collective outcome of the process of settling the tension between rigid and ancient texts and traditions and the ever-changing reality and needs of the community.** This process continued during times of great prosperity, as well as in the harshest conditions of the concentration camps during the Shoah and in Soviet jails. In past centuries, Jewish law and society contended with issues such as global trade and commerce. In recent centuries since the industrial revolution, it responded to the use of electricity, communication technology and air travel. And, in very recent years, the *talmudic* process has been concerned with organ transplant, in vitro fertilization, cloning, stem cell research and treatment, the Internet, and space travel.

Flexigidity of Place: One Zion and Many Diasporas

> This section describes Judaism's Flexigidity of place between its rigid commitment to Zion and the ability of Jewish communities to exist and thrive anywhere on earth and within all societies. This worldwide web of communities is not only essential for Jewish resilience and survival, but also for its prosperity and leadership.

199. **The fifth pillar of Jewish Flexigidity is its relation to territory: While Jews are rigidly committed to the Land of Israel, to Zion, they can legitimately live a vibrant and full Jewish life around the world, wherever a Jewish community exists.**

200. **The loyalty to the Land of Israel is rooted in the story of nationhood, which speaks of the Jewish People as a nation *(umah)* that emanated from the specific territory of Zion.** Jews have kept uninterrupted presence in Zion and loyalty to it, and the desire to return and reestablish self-determination there has been permanent in the Jewish psyche. The story of nationhood determines values, practices, institutions, priorities and standards, which are described at length earlier in this book.

201. **However, the idea of life outside of the Land of Israel and of exilic existence appears in the Book of Genesis, and has been present in Judaism ever since.** Abraham and his family travel to the Promised Land, and are then twice forced to leave it and descend south to Egypt and Gerar until their eventual return.[183] Later, the People of Israel – descendants of the sons of Jacob – travelled to Egypt and, according to tradition, lived there for four centuries, preserving their names, language and costumes.[184] Of the exiles to Babylon, following the destruction of the First Temple, only some repatriated,[185] and henceforth the existence of a Diaspora has been a permanent feature of Jewish society.

---

183 See Genesis 12, Genesis 13 and Genesis 20.

184 See Genesis 47 about the descent of the People of Israel to Egypt. See also sources discussing the association between the survival of the People of Israel in Egypt and the preservation of their language, names and costumes: http://adderabbi.blogspot.co.il/2007/01/manufactured-midrash-name-speech-garb_12.html and http://dovbear.blogspot.co.il/2010/01/we-did-change-our-names-and-clothing-in.html.

185 Ezra 7:7

202. **The paradox underlying the Flexigidity of place is captured in the Jewish belief that the vision of the end of days of the return to Zion will be realized "soon in our time."** This yearning for the return to Zion did not stop Jews and Jewish communities from building institutions that reflected an understanding that exile may be long lasting. This has been the case until the emergence of Zionism in the 19th century and the establishment of the State of Israel in the 20th century.

203. **The return of the First Temple exile to Zion *(galut Bavel)* in 586 BCE *(shivat Zion)* ushered in the phenomenon of Diaspora Jewry,** which willfully lived under foreign sovereigns while relating to Jerusalem as a spiritual and religious center. While the largest and most flourishing Diaspora Jewish community of that time was in Mesopotamia, other prosperous communities developed around the Mediterranean Sea, in Central Asia and India.[186]

204. **As of that time, Judaism developed an extensive body of theory and practices that allowed for and legitimized life in the Diaspora.** It is believed that, living at a distance from Zion and Jerusalem, Jews in Babylon must have shifted their focus away from worship in the Temple and came to understand sanctity as emanating from the activities of Jewish life. They are believed to have studied Torah and other ancient texts in order to inform their life in a prolonged state of exile. This understanding allowed for religious Jewish life to develop wherever a Jewish community existed, and did not limit such life to Zion and Jerusalem. In that experience lay the seeds of community institutions such as the synagogue *(beit knesset)*, communal fund *(kuppah)* and committee *(va'ad)* that are generic, and have existed in a broad range of locations.

205. **Over time, while continuing to idealize life in Zion, Judaism came to include powerful narratives that eventually esteemed a prosperous Diaspora over immediate repatriation.** The prophet Jeremiah *(Yermiyahu)* was the first to acknowledge the possibility that forced exile not only will not spell the disappearance of the Jewish People but will rather help it correct its ways toward a return to Zion.[187] The Babylonian

---

186 See for example *Wikipedia* entry on the Cochin Jews: http://en.wikipedia.org/wiki/Cochin_Jews.

187 See also Johnson, *A History of the Jews*, p. 84: "Jeremiah was the first to perceive the possibility that powerlessness and goodness were somehow linked, and that alien rule could be preferable to self-rule."

Talmud equates life in Babylon to life in Zion.[188] During the 'Golden Era' in Spain Jews referred to life there in similar terms that were used to describe life in Jerusalem, and Vilna was reffered to as the 'Jerusalem of Lithuania.' In modern times, some ultra-conservative Jews reject Zionism and the active return to Zion and to the State of Israel, viewing such return as an attempt to hasten redemption *(ge'ulah)* and therefore as heresy. Many Jews who live in the USA today refuse to see themselves as being in the compromising condition of 'exile' *(galut)* and even reject the usage of the word Diaspora to describe their community.

206. **Some more progressive Jewish communities have even replaced Jewish practices that emphasized their ties to Zion with practices that stress their loyalty to their place of residence.** The Reform Movement of the 19th century nearly eliminated the place of Zion in its liturgy and rituals along with the role of the Hebrew language. Another example concerns prayers relating to agricultural and climate cycles of the Land of Israel by requesting rain in the winter and dew in the summer. In the Southern Hemisphere, in places such as Australia and South Africa where winter is between June and August and summer is between December and February, the traditional Jewish prayer does not make sense.[189] While most Jewish communities pray in the traditional way, effectively asking for rain in the Land of Israel, in other communities prayers were adjusted to reflect local conditions.[190]

207. Thus, **Judaism's Flexigidity of place is made possible by its duality regarding physical locations.** As mentioned earlier, while it is rigidly committed to Zion, it also allows for sustained vibrant Jewish life in the Diaspora. Therefore, Jews' collective attitude and loyalty to their place of residence in the Diaspora is also always qualified, as the Jewish psyche not only embodies a permanent association to Zion, but also a legacy of many, often successful, relocations.

---

188 Babylonian Talmud Ketubot 111a and Kiddushin 69b

189 See Avraham Infeld speaking to praying for rain at the "wrong time": http://www.youtube.com/watch?v=el0NB1c_Ec4.

190 Jews pray for the rain between fifteen days after Sukkoth and the first day of Pesach and pray for the dew between Pesach and after Sukkoth, which coincides with the seasons of the Land of Israel. In some Southern Hemisphere Jewish communities the prayer would be reversed or expanded to refer to both places.

208. **The Jewish People has seen thriving centers across the world,** including in the great cities of Mesopotamia, Alexandria[191] and along the Mediterranean shore of North Africa; in Central Asia; across Europe from the West to the East including Spain, France, Italy, England, Germany, Poland, Greece, Hungary, Russia, Belorussia, the Baltic countries and the Ukraine; Australia, South Africa and South America; and in Canada and the USA.

209. **The permanent motion of the center of gravity of the Jewish People is made possible by its organization as a global network of communities.** When an empire or a nation begins to decline, its local Jewish community suffers, as well. Initially, individuals and households begin to explore new opportunities and options for relocation, usually tapping into the Jewish network and connecting with Jewish communities in areas that seem to offer better prospects. In times of crisis and calamity, when suddenly a significant number of Jewish community hubs and nodes are compromised and even lost, mass relocation takes place. Then, what was a trickle in times of peace turns into a flood. Thus, the permanent motion of the center of gravity of the Jewish People is an outcome of millions of decisions by individuals and households that live within, and collectively comprise, the Jewish worldwide web.[192]

210. Hence, **Zionism's attempt to singularly focus Judaism and the Jewish People on life in Zion was ahistorical and doomed to fail.** Diaspora life has been a reality for the Jewish People since the Biblical age, and the existence of a Diaspora has been not only inherent to Jewish history, but also vital for Judaism's evolution. Zionism's call for all Jews to congregate in Zion and its de-legitimization of the Diaspora represents a departure from twenty seven centuries of Jewish history. The culture, values and practices that were developed in the Diaspora remain essential for the survival, security, prosperity and leadership of the Jewish People and therefore are unlikely to disappear. Optimally, Judaism should thrive not only individually in both the State of Israel and in the Diaspora, but also as one collective unit.

---

191 See Johnson, *A History of the Jews*, p. 132: "The Roman geographer Stravo said that the Jews were a power throughout the inhabited world. There were a million of them in Egypt alone. In Alexandria, perhaps the world's greatest city after Rome itself, they formed a majority in two out of five quarters. They were numerous in Cyrene and Berenice in Pergamum, Miletus, Sardis, in Phrygian Apamea, Cyprus, Antioch, Damascus, and Ephesus, and on both shores of the Black Sea. They had been in Rome for 200 years and now formed a substantial colony there and from Rome they had spread all over urban Italy, and then into Gaul and Spain and across the sea into north-west Africa."

192 See Barabási, *Linked*, p. 153-155, 287 and Ramo, *The Age of Unthinkable*, p. 236.

211. *In conclusion,* **Judaism's Flexigidity of place is critically important for Jewish survival, collective security and adaptability.** It underlies the ability of Jews to relocate themselves in its permanent search for security, prosperity and freedom of association. It has allowed the Jewish People to establish broad presence around the world as a collective, while preserving an unrelenting association to and presence in Zion. In modernity, it helps individual Jews and Jewish households to live across the planet while remaining deeply involved with the State of Israel.

Flexigidity of Language: Hebrew, Yiddish and Vernaculars

> This section describes Judaism's Flexigidity of language between its rigid commitment to Hebrew and its openness to the usage and mastery of other languages.

212. **The sixth pillar of Jewish Flexigidity is language. Judaism has a rigid commitment to Hebrew complemented by the full freedom to create and use other languages. Indeed, Jews have created over twenty different languages[193] and have repeatedly mastered the vernaculars of their places of residence.**

213. **The Hebrew language is believed to be endowed with inherent holiness,** being the very language used by God in the genesis of the world and in the Torah.

214. Therefore, **Jewish faith makes Hebrew literacy essential** by mandating the reading of the Torah and the prayer books. As the recitation of the Torah must be absolutely precise, proficiency in Hebrew reading and speaking is a necessary requirement for all Jews who observe this tradition. Furthermore, the process and ritual of Torah transcription ensures that the Hebrew language of the Bible would be near perfectly transmitted from one generation to another. Hence, a significant group of Jews has always been fully literate in Hebrew.

215. Also, **the unique structure of Hebrew is essential for unlocking the deep meaning of the Torah and the ancient texts.** It is based on root words *(shorashim)* that can be applied in many different ways to capture nuances, creating semantic fields of meaning and countless angles for interpretation. Traditionally held grammer *(tachbir)*, punctuation *(nikud)*

---

193 For more on Jewish languages see: http://www.jewish-languages.org/.

and pronunciation *(hagaya)*[194] add additional layers of insight, and much of this complexity cannot be conveyed in translation. This feature of Hebrew is of critical importance: faithful Jews believe that the Torah is the code for building a model society, which was given by God to Moses and through him to the Jewish People as a message for all humanity. Hence, as there is a direct connection between such mastery of Hebrew and the ability to obey the will of God.

216.   Meanwhile, **the structure of Hebrew allows for great flexibility in its development, is allows for its evolution and is essential for its eternity.** The revival of the usage of Hebrew as a spoken language in the early 20th century – inspired and led by individuals such as Eliezer Ben-Yehudah, Ahad Ha'Ahm and Haim Nachman Bialik – demonstrated its great agility. As new phenomena arise in technology, society and science, Hebrew is always able to adapt with new applications of its root words. Thus, for example, the three letter root *hashav*, which appears in the Bible and means to think *(lachhshov)*, has been applied in modern Hebrew to the words mathematics *(cheshbon)*, computer *(machshev)* and accountant *(ro'eh cheshbon)*.

217.   Yet, **Jews have also created hybrid languages such as Yiddish and Ladino.** For many centuries and until modern Zionism, Jewish tradition viewed Hebrew as a language exclusive for prayer and religious matters *(lashon hakodesh)*. Jews abstained from using Hebrew for mundane affairs. Hence, they communicated among themselves through unique dialects that combined the local language with Hebrew to capture the unique nuances of their culture. Twenty two such languages existed, known as the Languages of the Jews *(Leshonot HaYehudim)*.[195] Yiddish is the best known, blending primarily Hebrew and German. It was spoken in Eastern Europe and then in New York, preceding the emergence of modern English language by centuries. Ladino, combining Hebrew and Spanish, was spoken among communities where Spanish Jews settled following the expulsion from Spain, including in Turkey, the Balkans and even India.

---

194 See *Wikipedia* entry: http://en.wikipedia.org/wiki/mesoretic_text.

195 See *Wikipedia* entry on Jewish Languages: http://en.wikipedia.org/wiki/Jewish_ languages.

218. **Jews also mastered the vernacular of their places of residence, as well as the lingua franca of their time, producing some of the great philosophical and literary creations in these languages.** In ancient times, the lingua franca was Aramaic, which became the language of the Talmud. To this very day, some of the Jewish prayers, as well as the traditional wedding contract *(ketubah)*, are in this language. In the Medieval period, Maimonides wrote his philosophic works in Judeo-Arabic, as did some of the great Jewish poets of Spain. In the modern era, Heinrich Heine was one of the giants of German poetry, Romain Gary remains one of the great French authors, Leon Trotsky was an inspiring orator in Russian and English-speaking Jews have made a name for themselves in poetry, literature, art, cinema and culture.

219. *Finally,* in modernity, **Zionism made the idea of a Hebrew nation intrinsically linked to the usage of a Hebrew Language.** Following after Eliezer Ben-Yehuda, Ahad Ha'Ahm and others, it held that there cannot be a nation without a tongue. This position became a point of major contention with non-Zionist Jews and with the Reform Movement. In Israel today, command of Hebrew is seen by many Israelis as a requisite for being a part of society.

The Engines of Jewish Adaptability

> This section describes the forces that propel and calibrate Jewish adaptability, and shows how they emanate from tensions that are structured into and inherent to Judaism, never to be resolved. These tensions are between unity and adversity, inclusiveness and wealth creation, insularity and openness, idealism and realism, and powerlessness and security, as well as a consequence of the existence of multiple centers of flat meritocratic leadership.

Introduction

220. **'The invisible hand' was a breakthrough concept developed by Adam Smith to explain the workings of markets.** It revolutionized human understanding of how societies function and evolve by framing its invisible forces, which affect the conduct of all people anywhere to systematically produce similar outcomes manifested in prices and quantities.

221. **Jewish society, too, is shaped by invisible forces, which are permanently at play determining its collective outcome.** Their roots preceded the destruction of the Second Temple in the 1st century, but they were significantly shaped by that trauma. They have been evolving ever since with the progress of Jewish society, the social evolution of the non-Jewish world, and with the development of science and technology. Driven by these forces, millions of Jews all over the world who are mostly strangers to and very different from each other have nonetheless systematically produced outcomes that are remarkably similar.

222. **There are six such forces of adaptability, each representing a powerful and unresolvable tension within Jewish society, that ceaselessly spark societal innovation and progress.** These forces are: **a leadership structure that is 'flat' and fully intellectually meritocratic**, with no centralized power structure in the form of a 'government' or a 'president;' **a delicate balance among unity, adversity and diversity**, which encourages radical, progressive and innovative forces, as well as ultra-conservative ones, and allows the full spectrum between them to exist, while holding them together as one society; **an economic ethos of inclusive wealth creation** that legitimizes acquiring affluence, while setting obligations of social responsibility; a political ethos that balances **loyalty to a local sovereign with self-determination;** a religious ethos

that establishes **a clear vision of an ideal life, which is calibrated by reality**; and a delicate balance between **universalism and particularism, insularity and openness.**

223. **As if guided by an invisible hand, these tensions endlessly drive Jewish individuals, households and communities to grapple with the rigidities and flexibilities of Judaism, optimizing the pace of Jewish adaptation.** This interaction has allowed Judaism to respond to change, both opportunities and threats, as well as to rebuild in the aftermath of calamities. These dynamics are the subject of the following chapters.

Unity, Diversity and Adversity

This section is about the permanent tension among forces of unity and adversity in Judaism that breed Jewish diversity. Its *first part* names the 'centripetal' forces that pull Jews together, sustaining their unity as a people, religion and nation. The *second part* describes the 'centrifugal' structures, which incentivize Jews to radicalize their outlooks and to emphasize their differences. The *final part* describes how critical these dynamics are for Jewish Flexigidity.

224. **Jewish society balances forces of unity with dynamics that encourage internal adversity to produce a remarkably diverse society.** This is an outcome of a hybrid of strong 'centripetal' forces that 'pull' Jews toward each other and hold them together as one society, notwithstanding the powerful 'centrifugal' incentives, which set them apart. This unity often inspired non-Jews to view Jews as one cohesive society in spite of the fact that the Jewish People consistently one of the most diverse communities in humanity across the various geographies, polities and cultures that it dwelled among.

225. **A most powerful force of Jewish unity is the universal acceptance of matrilineal descent as the basis for membership in the Jewish People.** This is due to its technical nature, which produces unequivocal status in the vast majority of cases, and due to its disregard of ideology, faith, conduct and personal history of the parents or the child. By establishing that no Jew can exclude another Jew from the Jewish People, this law

creates a strong 'holding environment'[196] that can withstand astounding diversity of values, ideologies, communal structures, patterns of conduct and institutions at any given moment. It also allows for movement within the community and across generations: the child of a rabbi can lose faith *(lachzor be'she'ela)*, and the child of an atheist can repent *(tshuvah)*. There are many such examples in Jewish history. To name two: Gershon Shalom, one of the greatest scholars of the world of Kabbalah and Jewish mysticism, was the son of an assimilated family, and Baruch Spinoza had a traditional religious upbringing and education.

226. **The Torah, whose sanctity prevents any alteration in form and sound, is another anchor of unity.** The Torah is therefore identical for every Jew and Jewish community, anywhere and across time. When Jews speak about the Torah, they are referring to the same identical text, irrespective of their denominational affiliation. Conversely, one can only imagine the atomization of the Jewish People if every group could have changed the Torah and created its own holy text.

227. **The third force of Jewish unity is Jewish eschatology, i.e. the particular vision of the end of days *(achrit hayamim)*, which is embraced by Jews of faith.** By speaking to the four meta-stories, this vision integrates and unifies the hopes of traditionally devout Jews: It speaks of the aspiration for reuniting all Jews and their ingathering as a people in Zion to reestablish independence under the House of David; for the rebuilding of the Temple and renewing the work of the sacrifices; and for a time of global peaceful coexistence when all the peoples of the world will acknowledge the sovereignty of God, following the example of the Jewish People.[197]

228. **Another force of unity is comprised of the narratives, values, symbols and practices that promote and sanctify peace within the Jewish community and among its members.** The destruction of the Temple, which, according to Jewish tradition was a consequence of unfounded hatred *(sinat hinam),* has been a national trauma that generated a powerful narrative of and desire for unity among Jews. This desire is expressed in many prayers and practices, referring to the entirety of the people of Israel without qualification *(klal ahm Israel).*

---

196 See Heifetz, *Leadership Without Easy Answers*, p. 103-104. Heifetz defines 'holding environment' as "...any relationship in which one party has the power to hold the attention of another party and facilitate adaptive work".

197 Micha 4:2

229. **The four meta-stories, which create distinct and alternative gateways into Judaism, are another mechanism of Jewish unity.** Judaism does not offer its members a take-it-or-leave-it proposition about its meaning, but rather a menu of four frameworks. Each of these options offers a coherent story that is deeply rooted in traditions, texts, institutions, practices and spirit. Therefore, the ideological boundaries of the community are flexible and inclusive toward a range of legitimately Jewish outlooks.

230. *Finally,* **inherent to the unity of the Jewish People is its dignification of dissent.** Judaism encourages its members to express alternative views regarding the state of Jewish society and its necessary course of action. It provides not only the intellectual vehicles for the development and crystallization of such views, but also the platforms to present them before the community and the tools for effectuating them. This is critically important for keeping Jews actively engaged in the fate of the community.

231. However, **Judaism emphasizes the distinction between unity and uniformity.** Unity means a sense of togetherness and connectedness that transcends disagreements, which may sometimes be deep enough to qualify as divides. It implies the ability to compartmentalize differences while serving a common cause. In contrast, uniformity requires similarity of worldview, values and practices, based upon deep conformity and intolerance of dissent. The structure of Jewish society has continuously discouraged both conformity and uniformity, which are dangerous to the long-term security and prosperity of the community; notwithstanding the fact that certain communities do rigidly enforce conformity and uniformity within themselves.[198]

232. **Heated internal adversity and conflict are integral to Jewish society.** While the forces of unity hold all Jews together as a community, their differences set them apart. Tensions among Halacha, traditions, heritage, memory, and existing practices, on the one hand, and the ever-changing reality and needs of the community in affluence or distress, on the other hand, are inevitable and permanent.

---

198 Johnson, *A History of the Jews*, p. 199: "Judaism had too many external enemies to want to risk its internal harmony by imposing a uniformity no one really wanted. Indeed, one can see medieval Judaism as essentially a system designed to hold Jewish communities together in the face of many perils … above all the assault of two great imperialist religions."

233. Indeed, **the Jewish world is remarkably diverse, certainly in relation to its size and comprises an endless spectrum of economic, political, spiritual, religious and institutional structures**. For millennia it has included people living in Zion and in the Diaspora; in the largest metropolitan areas, as well as in the most remote and rural places; a range of religious and spiritual manifestations; in recent centuries, a wide variety of distinct denominations and a large secular contingency; and a variety of religious and non-religious institutions that make up each community.

234. **The diversity of the Jewish People is exacerbated by the extraordinary pressures on Jewish society to evolve at a fast pace due to its extensive engagement and interaction with humanity.** Like other societies, Jewish society, too, is exposed to the ongoing political, economic, ethical and technological change in the world, which disrupts its existing internal order. However, Jews present on the frontiers of humanity around the world intensely interact with other ideologies and societies through travel, trade, diplomacy, science and technology. Hence, the Jewish world is extraordinarily exposed to a permanent input of innovative ideas and powerful disturbance of the existing order. These disruptions are always met by welcoming and embracing progressive factions, as well as by hostile conservative forces, thus increasing the diversity of Jewish society.

235. Furthermore, **Judaism's internal and inherent dynamic of questioning (she'elot) and potential doubt (safek) are another powerful source of adversity.** The intellectual freedom inherent in Judaism encourages questioning of the dominant power, rejection of domineering cultures and defiance of preconceived notions. The broad participation in the intellectual process of *talmud* enhances this propensity and increases the ability of individuals to question the leadership of people in positions of authority.

236. **Occasionally, such doubt results in a challenge to Judaism's own premises.** It is such forces that breed a phenomenon of internal rebels who are brought up as Jews and whose life journey leads them to reject Judaism.[199] A few of them end up as chief antagonists from within Judaism, and even cross the line to become enemies of the Jewish faith and Jewish People, as well as, in recent decades, of the State of Israel. Isaiah's prophesy commonly misinterpreted to mean that the destroyers

---

199 See Sacks, *Future Tense*, p. 124-125.

of Judaism will come from within,[200] has been exemplified on several occasions throughout Jewish history: Hellenized Jews collaborated with the Greeks against the Maccabees; Elisha Ben-Abuya, who was the arch-heretic of the rabbinic age; Paul, who broke away from Judaism and established Christianity as a separate sect; Jewish converts to Catholicism who assisted the Spanish Inquisition; Jews among the Politburo of the Communist Party in the Soviet Union; and some of the leaders of the Boycotts Divestment and Sanctions Movement that single out Israel and deny the right of the Jewish People to self-determination and of the State of Israel to exist. In modern times, such people were framed as 'self-hating Jews.' In other words, **anti-Jewish Jews are an inevitable product of Jewish society.**

237. Yet, **Judaism does not seek to suppress conflict but rather to encourage, contain and regulate it.** This approach embodies the notion that conflict is essential for societal progress, and that differences in core values and ideals can rarely be negotiated and bargained to a middle-ground compromise. While tolerance, overlooking differences and whitewashing disagreements may create a more pleasant society, deep, polarizing debates in the service of the community are crucial. It therefore encourages fellow Jews to sharpen arguments as opposed to being complacently quiescent; to debate with others and get to the root of the conflict instead of engaging in shallow platitudes; to expose and polarize rather than remain ensconced in one's worldview.

238. **This logic is captured with the saying that arguments for the 'sake of heaven' are the 'words of the living God'** *(elu ve elu divrei Elokim chaim).*[201] The Jewish approach views members of the community, who stand strongly and fight wholeheartedly for their outlook regarding the service of God and the appropriate course of action for the community, as explicating the intentions of God. Such dynamics breeds heated debates, intense disputes, deep divides and even hostility, verbal abuse and occasional physical violence. As mentioned, Hillel and Shammai exemplified the most positive manifestation of this standard: in spite of their bitter disputes they remained respectful of and married their children

---

200 Isaiah 49:17 was originally meant as a blessing, meaning that the destroyers of the Jewish People will distance themselves from it, but it is commonly used as a curse that the destroyers of Judaism will come from within.

201 Babylonian Talmud Eruvin 13b

to each other.[202] They are contrasted with Korach and his clan *(Korach ve adato)*[203] who, in confronting Moses,[204] pretended to be speaking for communal needs while being self-serving. While tradition teaches that law was eventually decided by the House of Hillel because of they showed greater respect to their interlocutors, nonetheless the outlook of the House of Shammai remains present in Judaism to this day.[205]

239. **This entire structure reflects a deep understanding that a resilient society must contend with radical experiments, thereby challenging existing centers of power, institutions and conventions.** These constant changes in the external environment and the evolution of ideas mandate societal adaptation. In this process, a radical innovation, which may initially be rejected by the community, might well turn out to serve its long-term security and wellbeing and therefore, over time, become established custom and religious practice. Thus, Judaism must be united but not uniform, allowing for its own evolution and adaptation.

240. **A famous saying in Pirkei Avot establishes that it takes a tong (or 'plier') to make a tong** *(tzvat be'tzvat asuya).*[206] This is traditionally understood to mean that an element cannot be self-created, and therefore the first element must have been created by God in Genesis. Yet, it also captures the notion that only friction between two worldviews will develop both so long as the two are holding each other. One can imagine the Jewish world as countless pairs of pliers perpetually engaging each other, adversarial yet united, and, in so doing, crystallizing the optimal path for progress for the community.

241. Hence, **mutual respect is the ultimate relationship between two Jewish adversaries who are engaged in a debate for the 'sake of heaven.'** The ability to respectfully disagree is essential for Jewish longevity. **It is in fact a litmus test for a legitimate debate.**

---

202 Avot 5:17

203 Avot 5:17

204 Numbers 17

205 Babylonian Talmud, Eruvin 13b

206 Avot 5:6

Idealism and Realism: Divine and Mundane

> This section is about the tension between the ideal and the real and how they contribute to Jewish adaptability. The *first part* presents the various elements of the ideal framework of Judaism, while the *latter* looks at the different manners in which Judaism tailors itself to the requisites of reality in day-to-day life.

242. **The quest to lead an ideal life and to build a model society is central to Judaism. However, reality never allows for such idyllic existence to emerge, even among the most dedicated.**

243. **For Jews of faith, the Torah represents the code of God's expectations from individual Jews and their households, from their communities, from the Jewish People and nation and from humanity.** Brought together, these expectations define an ideal life and a model society.[207] The understanding of these expectations evolves, and their exploration takes place through a *talmudic* process of interpretation and application of the Torah.

244. **Jewish idealism is also shaped by each of the meta-stories on the collective and individual levels.** The story of being a 'Light Unto the Nations' envisions a Jewish society based on supreme ethics and uncompromising justice that informs and inspires humanity. The stories of peoplehood and nationhood envision the ingathering of all the Diasporas, including the ten tribes that were lost following the destruction of the Kingdom of Israel by the Assyrians, and the recreation of collective sovereign existence in Zion. The story of faith and covenant strives for a society of individuals and households that individually and collectively accept the sovereignty of God and follow His wishes. It longs for the rebuilding of the Temple in Jerusalem and for the resumption of the work of the sacrifices in the House of God.

245. **The Jewish vision of the 'end of days' *(achrit hayamim)* brings together the four stories into one coherent narrative, describing the ideal society.** This vision, as recounted in the Biblical books of Isaiah and Micha, speaks about the repatriation and re-congregation of the entire People of Israel on their land and of their repentance *(tshuva)*. The Temple will be rebuilt in Jerusalem and the work of the sacrifices will

---

207 Leviticus 19 provides a particular glimpse of the biblical conception of the ideal world.

be renewed, as all peoples of the earth join in accepting the sovereignty of God and acting according to His will. This would usher in an era of global peace and harmony: 'They shall beat their swords into plowshares and their spears into pruning hooks; nation shall not lift sword against nation, neither shall they learn war anymore.'[208] These beliefs are among the thirteen articles of faith of Judaism according to Maimonides.

246. *Finally*, **the notion of Jewish chosenness is a central theme in the context of Jewish idealism.** Jewish tradition holds that the Jewish People is the 'chosen people' and there have been extensive debates among the sages regarding the meaning of such chosenness. Rabbi Lau brings a debate between Rabbi Ishmael and Rabbi Akiva: while the former argued that chosenness is 'meritocratic,' depending on the performance of the People of Israel in the world of Torah and on the qualities of their society, the latter believed that it is inherent upon the relationship between Jews and God, like a genetic connection between parents and children. Hence, while some believe this chosenness entails certain rights, stature and immunities, others associate chosenness with the extraordinary burden to build a model society.[209]

247. **These ideals inspired many individuals and communities to seek a life of observance, service and self-sacrifice.** Jewish tradition has many stories of individuals who were wholeheartedly dedicated to performing the wishes of God. Many other Jews live a life journey of striving to come closer to these religious ideals.

248. **In different periods, different ideals inspired Jews to act and even transform their lives.** The ideal of nationhood inspired the Bar-Kochva Revolt in the 2nd century, and in modernity, many young people to abandon their Diaspora lives and settle in Zion. Some strove to build a Hebrew 'model society' in Zion, while other Jewish communities around the world are inspired by the ideal of *or la'goim* and *tikkun olam* in their community institutions, financial contributions and actions of mutual responsibility.

249. However, **these high ideals often clash with the requisites of ordinary life**. Most of Jewish society is not educated to the degree necessary for an ideal life of observance, and many lack the ethical and moral fabric

---

208 Isaiah 2:4

209 See in Binyamin Lau, *Sages Volume II*, p. 205-207 (in Hebrew).

required. There are also external conditions that often make it difficult for Jews to live up to the ideals of their society, such as personal safety, exile and economic hardships. And, in extreme conditions, observance of *mitzvoth* may create existential danger.

250. **Jewish society has developed the tools to regulate the tension between the ideal vision and the reality.** Within the world of Torah, it is the role of sages and rabbis to establish the conditions in which personal distress such as sickness, hunger and danger justify temporary compromises in observance of *Shabbat*, *kashrut* and other *mitzvoth*. They do so through the *talmudic* process of interpretation of texts and based on the wisdom of past ages.

251. **Throughout Jewish history, rabbis have struggled with the limits of accommodating to hardship and oppression under circumstances of tension between 'saving one's soul'** *(pikuach nefesh)* **and 'self-sacrifice'** *(mesirut nefesh* **or** *kiddush HaShem).* Rabbi Lau describes such debates among the sages during the 3rd century, when the Jewish community in Zion experienced harsh economic hardships under the Romans.[210] We also know of rabbinical rulings in the Nazi concentration camps, which allowed for the continuation of Jewish life in conditions of extreme scarcity. These rabbis established 'red lines' beyond which Jews should sacrifice their lives in order to preserve the central legacy of Judaism. This deliberation speaks in terms of when one should transgress so as not to die *(ya'avor u'bal yehareg* or *pikuach nefesh doche Shabbat)* and when circumstances merit the ultimate self-sacrifice *(yehareg u'bal ya'avor).*[211]

252. **Jewish realism is epitomized in its relation to the Diaspora: Jews were expected to develop their communities in spite of the belief that the vision of the 'end of days' would be realized 'soon in our time.'** The ideal condition was repatriation to Zion. The belief among faithful Jews was that this would happen soon, yet in an indefinite

---

210 See in Binyamin Lau, *Sages Volume II*, p. 345-354 (in Hebrew) the story of Rabbi Haninah ben Teradion who became a symbol of defiant self-sacrifice *(mesirut nefesh)* for *kiddush HaShem* in his overt rebellion against the decrees of the Roman Empire that sanctioned the world of Torah. In contrast, Rabbi Elazar ben Parta finds ways to preserve the observance of the Torah without sacrificing his life. Rabbi Yosi ben Kisma stands for greater accommodation of the Roman decrees, while passively yearning for the change of circumstances.

211 Babylonian Talmud Sanhedrin 74a

moment. Nonetheless, Jews and Jewish communities were expected to build lasting institutions that reflected an understanding that exile may be prolonged. This underlies the teaching of Rabban Yochanan Ben-Zakai that if one finds himself with a sapling in his hand when the messiah arrives, he should first plant the tree and then go greet the messiah.[212]

Flat Meritocratic Leadership

> This section is about the forces that drive Jewish leadership. *The first part* describes its five basic components: the religious authority *(rabbis)*, the political and administrative council *(nesi'ut)*, the court *(beit din)*, the ethical voice *(tzadik)* and the financier *(gvir)*. It also explores the interplay among them in a system of checks and balances. *The second part* describes the dynamics of competition among the multiple centers of leadership of the Jewish People, which create a critically essential mechanism for Jewish survival, security, prosperity and leadership.

253. **The flat and meritocratic leadership structure of the Jewish People is another powerful engine of Jewish adaptability.**

254. **The Jewish People does not have a central source of authority in the form of a 'parliament,' 'government' or 'president' that governs it.** Since the First Temple Exile and the emergence of Diaspora Judaism in 6th century BCE, no single entity had the power to issue a 'decree, 'verdict' or 'decision' that would govern the entire Jewish People and suppress deliberation about the state and the direction of the collective. Whereas this was true globally, it also often applied within large communities. On all levels, the contest among competing centers of power and leadership fervently continued.

255. **Throughout most of the Diaspora and most of Jewish history, leadership of Jewish communities was based on a balance of power and division of labor among five 'branches': the religious leadership *(rabbis)*, political and administrative authorities *(nesiut)*, a judiciary *(beit din)*, ethical and spiritual authorities *(tzadikim)* and the financiers *(gvirim)*.** The roots of this structure can be traced to the Bible. During the First Temple Era permanent tension existed among kings, priests and prophets, and during the Second Temple Era the fault line divided priests and sages. Meanwhile, in the Babylonian Diaspora, the

---

212 Avot de'Rabbi Natan B31

Jewish community adapted these institutions to life at a distance from Jerusalem and under a foreign sovereign. This model later informed the leadership in Yavneh following the destruction of the Second Temple. The architecture of Diaspora Jewry matured as of the 3rd century when Babylon emerged as the leading center of Jewish life for centuries to follow, and its evolution continues until today.

256. **The religious leadership of the Jewish People was consolidated into the hands of 'sages' *(chachamim)* and rabbis within the *beit midrash*.** As mentioned earlier, this political and societal transformation took place after the destruction of the Second Temple under the leadership of Ben-Zakai. Hitherto, the Sadducees, mostly comprised of priests *(cohanim)*, were the leading political faction. Their power, which stemmed from their traditional hereditary monopoly on the work of the Temple, was eliminated following its destruction. Thereafter, the Pharisees and the sages claimed the leadership of the Jewish People. Their legitimacy stemmed from piety, deep knowledge of *halacha* and tradition, and great intellectual prowess. They saw themselves as continuing the chain of transmission of the Torah, which began with Moses.[213] Henceforth, the role of priests was marginalized and limited to preserving the memory of the Temple *(zecher HaMikdash)*, with the promise that they would resume their sacred role upon the rebuilding of the Temple in Jerusalem in the end of days *(achrit hayamim)*.

257. **Ben-Zakai's revolution led to the rise of the 'rabbis' who became the religious leaders of the Jewish People.** They officiate at religious ceremonies, address questions of observance and provide spiritual support to their followers. Their authority may stem from their intellect and knowledge of tradition, strict observance and commitment to learning, righteousness, dedicated service to their entire community, their ability to counsel their followers and from being a force of unity. Historically, many rabbis were groomed since childhood for this role, having excelled as pious students and matured to leading a life dedicated to learning Torah, religious observance and service. In the modern day, while the qualifications for becoming rabbis and their role differ across denominations, the basic role of rabbis as described above has not changed.

---

213 Avot 1:1 lays out the chain of transmission of the Torah according to Rabbinic tradition, and describes the sages as the bearers of that tradition in their own days.

258. **Another branch of Jewish leadership has been the court system *(beit din)*, which is responsible for resolving disputes and establishing the law based on *halacha*.** Internal authority and legitimacy of the court and its judges *(dayanim)* was conditioned upon their stature as rabbis and pious students of Torah, upon the quality of their rulings and upon their righteousness and wisdom. Another source of authority for the court and its judges was often the local sovereign, when it empowered the court to adjudicate for the Jewish community in certain matters. Naturally, the power of the courts peaked wherever Jews were internally autonomous, isolated as a community and insulated from general society, such as in the ghettos of Europe. In open societies, where Jews are equally subjected to the laws of the land, the stature of the court is even more dependent on the esteem of its judges and the quality of its rulings, as its jurisdiction over Jews is voluntary.

259. **A third branch of leadership of Jewish communities is the political and administrative arm, historically referred to as the 'council' or 'presidency' *(va'ad or nesiut)*.** While in the Bible the *nasi* served as the head of a tribe,[214] in later periods this title referred to a leader of a Jewish community. A *nasi* served as the official representative of the Jewish community before the Assyrian, Greek and Roman sovereigns. He was vested with authority on certain matters of government such as taxation and carried the responsibility for the community's internal affairs. In Babylon, the office of the Head of the Diaspora *(Rosh Galuta)* had such responsibilities for centuries, and in Poland, the Council of Four Lands *(Va'ad Arba Ha'aratzot)* presided over the affairs of the Jewish community of Poland between the 16th and 18th centuries. In modern times, in free and open societies, the Federation system in the USA and the Board of Deputies in the UK may address collective needs such as education, food, security and burial services. They may also manage community assets such as the fund *(kuppah)*, the cemetery, community centers and schools where there is a clear advantage of scale.

260. ***Tzadikim*** ('righteous ones') are another component of Jewish leadership in the area of spirituality and ethics, serving as the social conscious of the community.** This phenomenon of righous individuals dates back to Biblical prophets like Samuel *(Shmuel)*, Isaiah *(Yeshayahu)* and Jeremiah *(Yirmiyahu)*, and has been integral to Jewish society ever since.[215] With the

---

214 Numbers, 1:16

215 Jonathan Sacks, *Future Tense*, p. 162: "Thus emerged the unique Biblical institution of the prophet, the man or woman empowered by God to speak truth to power."

rise of *Hasidic* Judaism, these people came to be knows as '*Tzadikim*.'The stature of a *tzadik* stems from unshakeable faith in God, a broad view of the needs of the People of Israel, learnedness, righteousness, absolute loyalty to truth, disregard of established authority and sometimes even mystical powers. They mostly avoided formal positions in the establishment of their time, and their power often rose when the authoritarian leadership of the People of Israel, of Jewish communities, of priests, judges and rabbis had a crisis of ethics, legitimacy and performance.

261. **Financiers *(gvirim)* make up the fifth branch of Diaspora Jewish leadership**. They are the major funders of the various institutions of the community, and therefore have a special status in it, often serving as brokers of power. Judaism expects every person and household to contribute to public causes. However, it acknowledges the special role played by large donors and has developed ways to encourage their generosity by allowing their participation in shaping community affairs.

262. In this context, **the community fund *(kuppah)* is a central institution**. The first example of such a community funded project was the building of the Tabernacle *(Mishkan)* nearly thirty five centuries ago,[216] and there are many other examples of such projects in Jewish history. The mission of the fund has been to mobilize resources in order to underwrite collective needs and community institutions, priorities and responsibilities such as education, charity, and even, in tough times, taxation. A large body of Jewish law regulates the raising of funds for the *Kupah*, their management and expenditure.

263. **These mutually reinforcing yet competing branches and circles of leadership have been present throughout the Jewish Diaspora and shaped the society of the Jewish community in Zion *(Yishuv)* before the creation of the State of Israel.** While these critical functions were always present in every Jewish society, the division of labor among them was often unclear and changed from one community to another. This was especially the case when certain individuals and institutions performed multiple roles, such as when one person served as a judge *(dayan)*, a rabbi, a philanthropist and an administrator for the community. It also existed in the *Yishuv*: the Jewish Agency was the administrative arm, which also managed the fund *(kuppah)*; Rabbi Abraham Isaac HaCohen Kook *(HaRav Kook)* served as the Chief Rabbi and the Head of the religious court *(beit din)*; A.D. Gordon and Berl Katzanelson served in the role

---

216 Numbers, 1:16

of the *'tzadikim'* of the Zionist movement; and the entire structure was underwritten by philanthropists, such as Montefiore, Rothschild, Hirsch and Wolfson from the Diaspora and by some local people of wealth.

264. **These institutions and offices of leadership evolved over time and according to local conditions**. The exilarch in Babylon had a different authority than his colleagues in the Jewish communities in Europe or the nasi in Zion under the Roman Empire. In modern times, while in the United Kingdom, the Chief Rabbi and the Head of the Board of Deputies are recognized by the British government and Crown as representatives of the community,[217] in the USA no such roles exists and the President of the USA engages an assembly of Jews he or she so chooses.

265. **This leadership structure is generally meritocratic, though Judaism continues to grapple with hereditary tendencies.**[218] Its leaders are usually those who have proven themselves to be ethical, hardworking, generous and smart. Maimonides established that the condition for a son to inherit his father's authority is being similar in 'fear of God,' i.e. in observance and faith.[219] In other words, bloodline is important, but fear of heaven is essential. Rabban Gamliel II was a descendant of Hillel and a skilled leader, and thus a perfect fit. This is notwithstanding the fact that in various Hassidic courts leadership is passed on from fathers to sons and sons-in-law and some Jewish communities were led by small oligarchies of families for multiple generations.[220]

---

217 See 'Board of Deputies of British Jews' in the website of the National Archives where it is said: "...the Board of Deputies retains the privilege of personal approach to the Sovereign on state occasions … it seeks to protect, to promote and to represent Anglo-Jewry." http://www.nationalarchives.gov.uk/a2a/records.aspx?cat=074-ACC3121_2&cid=0#0.

218 Johnson, *A History of the Jews*, P. 181: "In Babylonia, the gaon or head of each academy came from one of six families, and in Palestine he had to be descended from Hillel, Ezra the Scribe, or David himself. An outsider of colossal learning could be accepted, but this was rare … every member of the academy had a fixed seat in order of precedence, which was originally determined by birth. But he could be promoted or demoted, according to performance, and his stipend varied accordingly."

219 Rambam *Mishnah Torah*, Laws of Kings and Wars, Halacha 7: "The above applies if the knowledge and the fear of God of the son is equivalent to that of his ancestors. If his fear of God is equivalent to theirs but not his knowledge, he should be granted his father's position and given instruction. However, under no circumstance should a person who lacks the fear of God be appointed to any position in Israel, even though he possesses much knowledge."

220 See Johnson, *A History of the Jews*, p. 294 regarding such oligarchies among the Jews of Poland.

266. *Finally,* **permanent tensions existed among these branches of leadership and power, which created checks and balances within communities and the Jewish People at large.** In Babylon, the *Rosh Galuta* had inherent tensions with the rabbinical leadership of the *Geonim.*[221] The *Hasidiut* movement rose as a challenge of the spiritual *Tzadik* to the authority of the administrative and rabbinical leadership of its time.[222] And in the present-day USA, rabbis often challenge community institutions to take action on issues of morality and ethics.

267. As it were, **the State of Israel is the first case since antiquity where a significant number of Jews live outside of such an umbrella of Jewish leadership.** The sovereign government institutions of the State of Israel have dramatically altered the leadership of its Jewish community. While all of these structures of leadership continue to exist within Israel, they have been dramatically transformed and often made void by the context of sovereignty.

268. **The leadership of the Jewish People has historically been dispersed among multiple competing centers or 'hubs' of the Jewish worldwide web of communities, usually in key metropolitan areas.** Each hub houses a large Jewish population living in security and prosperity, as well as a cluster of community institutions, serving as the seat of the spiritual, intellectual, administrative and religious leaderships. At any given moment, there are several such 'hubs' across the world competing for influence, leadership and power. They engage in a brutally honest deliberation about the fate and future of the Jewish People, with each hub bringing forth an alternative view, shaped by the unique conditions of its existence. These lineages of contention include the Galilee in Zion and Sura and Pompedita in Babylon between the 3rd and 5th centuries; Cordova, Spain and Venice, Italy, during the Middle Ages; Vilnius, Lithuania and Berlin, Germany, in the 18th and 19th centuries. Today, Jerusalem, Tel Aviv and New York City stand out as hubs of Jewish life and leadership.

269. **The geographic spread of these hubs is crucial for Jewish diversity in that it crystallizes distinct outlooks.** Jewish communities have existed within a broad range of social, political and economic conditions and experiences, and are among the most progressive and traditional

---

221 See Gafni, *The Jews of Babylon in the Talmudic Era* (Hebrew), p. 98, 232-236.

222 See Johnson, *A History of the Jews*, p. 295-300.

outlooks of their time. In adapting to the surrounding and dominant culture, every community becomes a unique breeding ground for new ideas, demonstrable in its institutions, traditions and even *halacha*. Thus, Judaism had multiple outlooks stemming from and having been shaped by different human conditions in different geographies. That geographic anchoring was sometimes so distinct that Judaism associated certain outlooks with specific locations, such as the Babylonian and the Jerusalem Talmuds;[223] *Ashkenazim* and *Sephardim*, referring to streams of Judaism from central Europe and Spain respectively; *Lita'im* (literally, from Lithuania), referring to an ultra-orthodox stream of learned Judaism following the Gaon of Vilna *(HaGaon Me'Vilna)* and 'German Jews,' referring to a very progressive stream of Judaism, following the Reform Movement of 19th century Germany.[224] Meanwhile, Israeli sovereignty and control over Jerusalem and Judea and Samaria since 1967 bred a national-religious theology, which views Israel as the beginning of messianic redemption and sanctifies the physical ownership and settlement of the land. It is hard to imagine a similar worldview evolving in New York City.

270.   Yet, **the impact of each hub and every Jewish leader is limited and typically decreases with distance.** This is a natural outcome of the vast geographic spread of Jewish communities and the radical differences in the social, economic and political conditions of their existence. Hence, the relevance of rulings by rabbis in one area is often compromised by distance and may be ineffective and even irrelevant in another area. Furthermore, Judaism's internal forces of debate and inherent dynamics of adversity create a counterforce to every leader within and outside of their own community. While the Jews of Yemen widely embraced Maimonides, then living near modern day Cairo, as their religious authority, some of his contemporaries in Europe caused his works to be burnt.[225] Joseph Caro's authoritative compendium and manual of Jewish Law, the *Shulchan Aruch (literally: "A Set Table"),* which generally

---

223   See Rabbi Israel Meir Lau, *Foundations*, p. 36-40. Rabbi Lau explains how the different conditions in Zion and in Babylon affected the Jerusalem and the Babylonian Talmuds respectively in terms of their content and structure.

224   See for example Wikipedia entry on the 'German Reform Movement' at http:// en.wikipedia.org/wiki/German_Reform_movement_(Judaism).

225   Solomon of Montpellier and his pupil Yonah Gerondi incited burnings of the works of Maimonides in Montpellier and Paris respectively. Witnessing the burning of the Talmud in the same spot scarcely a decade later, Gerondi subsequently repented his actions and accepted the authority of Maimonides.

reflects the customs of *Sephardic* Jews, still required Moses Isserles' Mapah *(literally: "Table Cloth")* to make it applicable for Ashkenazi Jews.

271. **Fragmentation of authority and leadership has been a double-edged sword: it enhances Flexigidity but creates rifts within and among Jewish communities.** This internal tension among leaders and communities drives the permanent evolution of Jewish thought concerning law and society in tandem with changes in the external conditions. However, in some cases, dynamics of adversity may drive Jewish communities to a point of fundamental alienation, confrontation and even ruptures, as was the case with the Beothusians of the Mishnaic period and the Karaites of the Middle Ages. The modern ultra-orthodox community of *HaEda HaHaredit*, which is also extremely insular, may one day become a sect outside the normative fold of Judaism.

272. **The level of divisiveness among Jews emanates from the collective rabbinical temperament of an era.** Some rabbis and judges *(dayanim)* exercised their authority cognizant of the potential implications of their rulings on the cohesion of the community, while others caused deep rifts. Hillel the Elder, Rabban Gamliel II, the Lubavitcher Rebbe and Rabbi Kook are of the great unifiers of the Jewish People.

273. **One of the significant impacts of Judaism's leadership structure is inherent suspicion of individual genius.** Such suspicion is rooted in the Biblical warnings against false prophets.[226] Since the destruction of the Temple, it seems that Judaism favors slower and regulated processes of evolution to leaps and bounds inspired by charismatic leadership. This is a key message of the famous *midrash* on the Oven of Akhnai. Judaism puts even its giants, such as Maimonides, through the test of time and peer criticism. Traumatized by the devastating effects of *Shabbatayism* – named after the 17th century false messiah, Sabbatai Zevi, who eventually embraced Islam, and other false messiahs – Judaism is suspicious of epiphanies and revelations by individual geniuses, and places high barriers against their impact.

274. *In conclusion,* **this flat structure of meritocratic leadership propels Jewish adaptation in powerful ways.** *First,* **it feeds the Jewish People with a permanent stream of new ideas,** which emanate from Judaism's unmatched access to humanity and to the variety of human social,

---

226 Deuteronomy 13:1-5

economic and political conditions. Jews lived simultaneously in both the Babylonian and Roman empires, amidst the Islamic caliphate and the Christian church, and in the Soviet Union and the USA.

275. *Second,* **this structure prevents the stagnation that comes from the weight of hierarchical authority.** It ensures that there is always a Jewish voice and a source of leadership that persistently challenges the prevailing notion and dominating paradigm.

276. *Finally,* **this leadership structure encourages collective pragmatism toward security and prosperity.** Even if one community radicalizes and pulls Judaism to its limit, somewhere else in Jewish society there will be a community that embraces the other pole. When one community embraces one of the meta-stories of Judaism, there will always be other communities who will speak for the other stories. In this way the full spectrum of opinions and outlooks exist between them. Hence, the pretention of the State of Israel to represent all Jews is inconsistent with this legacy, and therefore unlikely to succeed. Thus, the collective outcome of the Jewish People is pragmatic in its gravitation toward greater security and prosperity.

Inclusive Wealth Creation

This section is about the balancing act that Judaism maintains between legitimizing wealth creation on the one hand, and obligating the sharing of wealth in support of both individual and collective needs, on the other hand. *The first part* explores different mechanisms that ensure that economic growth is inclusive through charity, preventing the segregation of the rich and encouraging other avenues of social mobility. *The second part* looks at mechanisms that have ensured the collective wellbeing of Jewish communities: broad education, a global presence and the offering of unique value to the societies within which they dwelled.

277. **The fourth engine of Jewish adaptation is its mechanisms that balance legitimization of and encouragement for wealth creation with strong social obligations to share wealth.**[227] It therefore creates an

---

227 The credit for pointing out the relationship between inclusiveness and wealth creation as one of the driving tensions of Judaism's adaptability goes to the concept to Rabbi Michael Paley, the Pearl and Ira Meyer Scholar in Residence at the Jewish Resource Center of UJA-Federation of New York.

effective vehicle of wealth redistribution and a powerful force for social cohesion, what Rabbi Jonathan Sacks refers to as a "microcosmic welfare state."[228]

278. **Creating and having wealth and living a life of comfort is a legitimate Jewish quest and activity, ascetic tendencies notwithstanding**. This outlook encouraged Jews to seek income, open businesses and travel distances. Handling and dealing with money was allowed, regulated and encouraged. The Bible details the affluence of Abraham, Isaac and Jacob, Joseph, and King Solomon. Rabban Gamliel II in the 1st century and Rabbi Yehuda HaNasi in the 3rd century were wealthy, as were the exilarchs in Babylon. In modern days, some heads of orthodox courts are rich, as well.[229] This acceptance of material wealth exists in Judaism alongside outlooks that associate purity with financial modesty and encourage freedom from material wants beyond essential needs.[230]

Meanwhile, Judaism establishes obligations and standards for redistribution of wealth within the community.

279. **The basic social and religious expectation is for Jews to help needy individuals**. The obligation toward the poor is significant: when harvesting crops one must leave the edge of one's field *(pe'ah)*, in addition to anything that was dropped *(leket)*[231] or left behind *(shi'checha)*[232]; and one must donate a tenth of the income to charity *(me'a'ser ani)*[233] two out of every seven years. In addition, the Bible establishes the obligation to cancel debts every fifty years and to return the land to its original owners,[234] effectively preventing the amassing of huge estates by a few individuals. Furthermore, Jewish holy days emphasize the collective and

---

228 Sacks, *Future Tense*, p. 37.

229 On the value of prosperity, see conversation between Rabbi Michael Paley and William Novak in "Kerem: Creative Explorations in Judaism", Jewish Study Center Press, Inc., Washington DC, 2012, volume no. 13 p. 40-43.

230 Prominent examples of asceticism in Judaism include Rabbi Zadok who fasted for forty years seeking to stave off the destruction of Jerusalem, Rabbi Shimon Bar Yochai who along with his son lived in a cave for twelve years, sustained by a carob tree and a stream, and Rav Zeira who fasted for a hundred days.

231 Leviticus 19:9 & 23:22

232 LeviticusDeuteronomy 24:19

233 Deuteronomy 14:28-29 & Deuteronomy 26:12-13

234 Leviticus 25:10

individual responsibility toward the poor and needy in the community and beyond. In addition, there is a significant body of Jewish law that regulates voluntary charity *(tzedaka)*,[235] and, most famously, Maimonides ranked the relative merits of eight different kinds of giving, the highest of which was to anonymously help someone make a decent living, and the lowest of which was to give unwillingly.[236] *Finally*, the *Aggadah* establishes equal moral standing between the wealthy and the poor, as the two are integrally associated by enabling each other to fulfill their respective roles in society.[237]

280. **Judaism further balances the wealth of individuals with that of communities and their institutions**. Members of the community are obligated to support its institutions. People of wealth *(gvirim)* are expected to donate primarily to the fund *(kuppah)* and to communal causes such as: education, food, security, burial, dowries for poor brides, and in ancient times, for the freeing of Jewish prisoners *(pidyon shvu'im)*. That obligation was social, as well as religious. Such 'community tax' is an explicit obligation, effectively expected even before charity to individuals *(tzedaka)*.[238]

281. **This process of giving is regulated by *halacha* and is deeply embedded in Jewish communities.** Judaism establishes criteria for determining

---

235 Johnson, *A History of the Jews*, p. 203: "...There were three trustees, solid citizens, for each kuppah ... they had power to seize goods from non-contributors ... there were carefully graded forms of welfare-provision, each with its own fund and administrators: clothes, schools for the poor, dowries for poor girls, Passover food and wine for the poor, orphans, the aged, the sick, burials of the poor, and prisoners and refugees ... A solvent Jew had to give to the kuppah once he had resided in the community a month; to the soup-kitchen fund after three, the clothing fund after six and the burial fund after nine."

236 Maimonides, *Misnhe Torah*, Laws of Gifts to the Poor, 10:7-14

237 See Noam Zion, *For the Love of God: Comparative Religious Motivations for Giving,* quoting the last Lubavitcher Rebbe, Reb Menachem Mendel Schneerson, *Sefer Shaarei Tzedakah*, 54-57: "As Maimonides ruled: "All who give the poor with a bad (angry/ begrudging/negative) face – even if one has given 1000 gold coins – has lost the merit" (Laws of Gifts to the Poor 10:4) .. Actually 'More than the householder has done for the poor [in being generous], the poor have done for the householder' (Leviticus Rabbah 34:8. Ruth Rabbah 5:9). For without the poor, the householder would have no opportunity to perform the mitzvah of tzedakah!"

238 See Johnson, *A History of the Jews*, p. 158: "...The obligation to pay communal taxes was religious, as well as social. Moreover, philanthropy was an obligation too, since the word zedakah meant both charity and righteousness. The Jewish welfare state in antiquity, the prototype of all others, was not voluntary; a man had to contribute to the common fund in proportion to his means, and this duty could be enforced by the courts."

the capacity to give financially and the expectation to do so. It details the processes of giving, for assessing needs and for the management of community funds. It also provides for honoring the donors, while limiting their influence on religious and judicial authorities, and condemns those who don't live up to their communal and moral obligations.

Judaism developed additional mechanisms to ensure that Jewish society is inclusive toward all of its members.

282. *First,* **Judaism expects wealthy Jews to support schools, communal institutions and Torah scholarship.** Moneymaking is often correlated with innovation and creativity with leading business people often extraordinarily attuned to new ideas. Yet, Judaism expects the wealth generated from such open-minded thinking and activity to be used in part to strengthen heritage, ensuring fair play in society between modernity and tradition, and leveraging the forces of flexibility to support societal rigidity.[239]

283. *Second,* **Judaism balances the human tendency to view wealth as a benchmark for success by creating alternative tracks for stature and social mobility, primarily through the world of Torah.** Literacy and Torah education were nearly universal, mandatory and, under ideal conditions, affordable and even free. As Jewish religious and spiritual leadership was largely meritocratic, all male Jews, the poor and rich alike, had an opportunity to become a prominent rabbi. This made the world of Torah a primary ladder for social mobility. Therefore, children of poor families who were pious students of Torah, could rise to prominence and leadership, be married off to wealthy families or reach a life of comfort by other means.[240] This powerful tool of wealth redistribution also ensured an influx of resources into the world of Torah. Thus, Jewish society balances the power of wealthy people with that of rabbis and lay leaders, praising intellectual achievements, righteousness and non-monetary giving of public service.

---

239 Johnson, *A History of the Jews,* p. 340: "...rich merchants married sages daughters; the brilliant yeshiva student was found a wealthy bride so he could study more. The system whereby sages and merchants ran the community in tandem thus redistributed rather than reinforced wealth."

240 Rabbi Akiva, for example, began learning at the age of forty after being a shepherd and became one of the greatest leaders of the Jewish People. He eventually inherited the wealth of his father in law, Kalba Saboa, of the wealthiest Jews of his time.

284. *Third,* **Judaism forces the interaction among people of varying affluence, preventing the segregation of the rich.** The powerful and rich of Jewish society are forced into direct visual contact and physical engagement with the general public through and within public institutions such as the cemetery, synagogue and *beit midrash*. This structure prevents the rich from isolating themselves from society and from the poor masses.

285. *In conclusion,* **Judaism has developed a social and economic system of inclusive wealth creation that is based on a hybrid of individual entrepreneurship and social responsibility**. Jewish law embodies the understanding that the financial success of individuals is a necessary yet insufficient condition for collective prosperity, and that a vast gap of income between the poor masses and the rich few breeds disunity. Judaism also views strong institutions as pillars of collective prosperity, and therefore incentivizes their support. It therefore encourages wealth creation, yet sets high expectations for and regulates its re-distribution.

286. Against this background, **Jews became leaders not only in all disciplines related to the works of society, but also of ideologies and movements ranging from communism and socialism to capitalism**. For many centuries, Jews explored ways to ensure collective and individual wealth creation in a manner that is ethical and socially responsible. This required nuanced observation of the forces that drive markets and societies, blending the prevailing reality with the interpretation of old texts in order to allow societal adaptation and the development of *halacha*. When academia in Europe opened up to Jews in the late 18th century, and with the subsequent emergence of new fields of academic research related to society, such as economics, psychology and sociology, Jews already had a millennia head start. Therefore, Jewish contribution in these fields has been unmatched on a proportional basis. Tellingly, nearly forty percent of Nobel Prize winners in the field of economics are Jews.

287. **Judaism also encourages the building of its collective wealth.** Prosperous communities of the Jewish People often collectively owned real estate properties and other sources of wealth. Such wellbeing is the product of a communal effort of individual community members and households and their institutions.

288. **The essential condition for a thriving Jewish community has been the auspices of a sovereign that ensured personal and communal safety, as well as cultural and religious freedoms.** Where such an

environment existed and a critical mass of Jews congregated, glorious legacies of intellectual, spiritual and often also of economic wellbeing followed. Meanwhile, loss of personal security and the compromise of economic, communal and religious freedoms would result in decline. Relative religious tolerance and political stability underlay the golden eras of Jews in places such as Babylon, Italy, Spain, Ukraine and Poland.[241] Intolerance and political instability led to the decline and even disappearance of these communities and many others.

289. **Collective prosperity of Jews had its roots in their universal education, necessary for the ability to read the Torah.** Since the 2nd century BCE, Jews have been unique in their attempts to and focus on trying to achieve near universal literacy among men.[242] Though this was typically the case in Hebrew, many of them were also literate in the lingua franca of their time and in the language of their place of residence. Many Jews, and most of their leaderships, also mastered mathematics and the science of time telling. Such prevalence of education only became common in developed societies in the 20th century.

290. **Beyond plain literacy, the Jewish intellectual mindset was also particularly conducive for identifying opportunities for wealth creation.** Since childhood, Jews were trained to read both the Written and the Oral Law, grapple with them, understand the hierarchy of legal systems, identify exceptions and extract flexibilities. Their training nurtured them to seek to understand the rationale of their local society. The combined effect of Jewish education often made Jews sensitive to the common law of the land, communicated through stories, jokes, context and environment. Thus, they would often be the first ones to identify new opportunities to create wealth within the framework of the law, often in path breaking ways.

291. **Jewish globalization has historically been another unique feature, essential for wealth creation.** While the universe of the non-Jewish population was often limited to their immediate geographic proximity, Jews have been surfing their global web of communities for many

---

241 On the myth of golden eras, see Wald, *Rise and Decline of Civilizations*, chapter 24, p. 169-173 (in Hebrew).

242 See Johnson, *A History of the Jews*, p. 106: "In their battle against Greek education, pious Jews began, from the end of the second century BC to develop a national system of education. To the old scribal schools were gradually added a network of local schools where, in theory at least, all Jewish boys were taught Torah."

centuries, being interconnected across political borders. Their internal value system, which emphasizes ethics in business dealings, hospitality and information sharing, was conducive to travel and trade. The elaborate mechanisms of Jewish law, courts and social enforcement, which were perhaps the only judicial system that operated across political boundaries until modernity, gave Jews a unique advantage in international trade and facilitated movement across vast distances. In a broken world of political disunity, particularly in Christian Europe, they were the global citizens who carried spices, money, technology, tradable goods, new ideas and, ultimately, progress. The *Geonim*, who led the large *yeshivot* in Babylon, issued answers *(tshuvot)* to questions *(she'elot)* from as far West as Spain, which would cross the ancient world with caravans of Jewish spice traders who travelled primarily across North Africa. In the Medieval period, Jews developed and carried monetary documents and became global financiers.[243] Later, as Western Civilization expanded its reach around the globe, so did the Jewish network of communities: the first Jewish settlers in America are thought to have traveled with Columbus himself[244] and Jews also settled the outskirts of the British Empire in places such as India, China, Singapore, Hong Kong, South Africa and Australia.[245] As of the 18th century, the phenomenon of Jewish families who operate across political borders emerged such as the Oppenheimers in the Austro-Hungarian Empire, the Rothschilds in France and England and the Khadouri and Sassoon Families in China, Singapore and Hong Kong. Nowadays, in the USA, most Jews are believed to have passports,

---

243 See Johnson, *A History of the Jews*, p. 283: "It was the unconscious collective instinct of the Jews both to depersonalize finance and to rationalize the general economic process ... as well as developing letters of credit, the Jews invented bearer-bonds, another impersonal way of moving money ... Next to the development of credit itself, the invention and still more the popularization of paper securities were probably the biggest single contribution the Jews made to the wealth-creation process .. here, too, the global perspective, which the Diaspora gave them, turned them into pioneers. For a race without a country, the world was a home."

244 Luis de Torres, Christopher Columbus's interpreter during his pioneering voyage to the Americas, is believed to have been Jewish. See also Johnson, *A History of the Jews*, p. 249: "Expelled Jews went to America as the earliest traders. They set up factories. In Saint Thomas, for instance, they became the first large scale plantation owners ... Jews and Marranos were particularly active in settling Brazil ... they controlled the trade in precious and semi-precious stones.."

245 For more information, see Wikipedia entries on the Jews of Australia (http://en.wikipedia. org/wiki/History_of_the_Jews_in_Australia), on the Jews of Hong Kong (http:// en.wikipedia.org/wiki/History_of_the_Jews_in_Hong_Kong), on the Jews of Singapore (http://en.wikipedia.org/wiki/History_of_the_Jews_in_Singapore).

in comparison to only thirty nine percent of all Americans,[246] and Israelis are disproportionally represented among the globetrotting backpacking community.

292. **The unique value that Jews brought to the peoples in whose midst they dwelled often served both their security and prosperity.** Jewish tradition holds that the famine in Egypt ended upon Jacob's arrival.[247] Jews often played critical economic roles as merchants, bankers and diplomats. For long periods this ensured political access and societal power. The Exilarch was highly respected under Babylonian and Muslim rule.[248] Maimonides was the personal physician of and advisor to the Sultan of Cairo. Sultan Beyazid II sent his ships to bring Jews from Spain to enrich his growing empire and famously said, "Ye call Ferdinand a wise king, he who makes his land poor and ours rich!"[249] And Jews were prominent financiers and political advisors on all sides of the First World War. Unfortunately, this economic success and frequent association with the powers that be often led to popular resentment against Jews that ultimately brought about their demise.

293. Indeed, **the ability of Jews to repeatedly prosper has been proven nearly without exception since the days of the Roman Empire.** This was the case in Alexandria until the 2nd century, in Spain between the 8th and 12th centuries, in Poland and Ukraine in the 16th and 17th centuries, in Germany in the 18th and 19th centuries, and in Western countries such as Australia, Canada and the USA following the Shoah.

294. *In conclusion,* **the economic mechanism of inclusive wealth creation propels Jewish adaptation in powerful ways.** *First,* it provides for sustaining the traditional world of Torah, without compromising the benefits and progress that stem from vibrant profit-seeking economic activity. *Second,* while it encourages individual Jews to accumulate wealth using the unique features of Jewish society, it also ensures the collective wellbeing of the community through its powerful mechanisms of redistribution that prioritize the needs of the collective. *Finally,* it encourages and facilitates

---

246 See http://travel.state.gov/passport/ppi/stats/stats_890.html re the number of Americans who carry passports.

247 See Rashi's commentary on Genesis 50:3, explaining why the Egyptian's wept over Jacob's death.

248 See Gafni, *The Jews of Babylon in the Talmudic Era,* p. 94-104.

249 See www.jewishencyclopedia.com/articles/14546-turkey.

the movement of Jews across their worldwide web of communities, thus constantly shifting the center of gravity of the Jewish People away from threats and hardship and toward prosperity and security.

Openness and Insularity

This section is about Judaism's balancing act between openness and insularity. It begins by reviewing the legacy and logic of Jewish particularism and then presents the forces that drive Judaism's openness to humanity. The section closes with a discussion of assimilation as an inevitable outcome of Judaism's outreach to humanity, as well as of the 'soft' and 'hard' tools Judaism developed to retain its members and ensure its continuity.

295. **Another force of Jewish adaptability is its dynamic tension between universalism and openness to the world and a desire to engage it, on the one hand, and particularism, seclusion and insularity, on the other.** This tension is found in the Bible and has been present throughout Jewish history. As Rabbi Sacks writes: "Judaism embraces both, denying neither."[250] He explains that the Bible plants the Jewish people, then called Hebrews and later Israelites, in the global context of humanity by beginning with eleven chapters that describe the origin of the world, presenting stories of universal meaning and a 'series of archetypes of humanity as a whole: Adam and Eve, Cain and Abel, Noah and the Flood, Babel and its builders ... not until chapter twelve do Abraham and Sarah appear on the scene, and from then on the entire narrative shifts its focus, from humanity as a whole to one man, one woman and their children.[251] **In other words, a blend of particularism and universalism is the fundamental and permanent condition of Judaism.**

296. *On the one hand,* **the Bible endows the People of Israel with a mission for humanity, which required deep engagement with the world.** The Israelites were to become the carriers of a universal message, which is to bring a blessing to 'all families of the earth,'[252] to be 'a light unto the nations'

---

250 Sacks, *Future Tense*, p. 74. See also Rabbi Israel Meir Lau, *Foundations*, p. 29 (in Hebrew), where Rabbi Lau explains that the Jewish perspective about the wisdom among non-Jews.

251 Sacks, *Future Tense*, p. 75. See also Wald, *Rise and Decline of Civilizations*, p. 207-210 (in Hebrew)

252 Genesis 12:3. See also Sacks, *Future Tense*, p. 75.

(or la'goim)[253] and to repair the world in the kingdom of God *(tikkun olam).*[254] That quest to affect humanity mandated extensive and intensive interaction with and gaining deep insight into the life of non-Jews.

297. Furthermore, **as a small people that has dwelled among much larger nations, the prosperity and security of Jewish society required interaction with powerful polities, cultures and faiths.** This relationship, dialogue and exchange among Jews and non-Jews occurred in areas as diverse as trade, finance, medicine, technology and diplomacy. Intellectual engagements, often in the form of debates, required deep acquaintance with foreign ideas, theology, philosophies and values, as well as with foreign languages, practices and conduct. This is known to have been the case throughout Jewish history and in the Diaspora since the First Temple exile. Judaism has interacted with the Babylonian, Hellenist, Arab and European cultures, as well as with Christianity and Islam. The 18th century saw the beginning of such engagement also with European academia and with universal ideologies such as socialism, communism and capitalism. As of the 20th century, such engagement has been nearly universal, including with Far East nations and religions such as Buddhism.[255]

298. *On the other hand,* **Judaism's message to humanity was traditionally carried by the Jewish People through its particular laws and society.**[256] The idea that Jewish law represents the divine code for a model society is echoed in the words of Moses, who said that it "will show God's wisdom and understanding to the nations"[257] and in the words of Isaiah who envisioned the People of Israel realizing their mission of being a light unto the nations by embodying God's laws in their society.

299. Thus, **the Israelites were to serve their universal mission from a permanent condition of otherness**: through a unique language, Hebrew; from a specific place, the Land of Israel, Zion; by means of their special laws, the *mitzvot*; and following a particular set of values and ethics.

---

253 Isaiah, 42:6

254 The term *Tikkun Olam* is used several times in the Mishnah, in the order Gitin, though in its earliest usage it did not have the same connotations as it commonly has today.

255 See Rodger Kamenetz, *The Jew and the Lotus*, talking about the interaction between Judaism and Buddhism.

256 See Sacks, *Future Tense*, p. 82-88.

257 Deuteronomy, 4:6

Unlike Christianity and Islam, which seek to convert all human beings to their way, Judaism does not proselytize. As Rabbi Sacks notes, it leads humanity through its difference and otherness, and, therefore, the Jewish mission is to 'teach all humanity the dignity of difference.'[258] He concludes: 'The God of Israel is the God of everyone, but the religion of Israel in not the religion of everyone.'[259]

300.   In addition, **the chosenness of the Jewish People has been another issue that separates Jews and their communities from non-Jews.** This notion views the Jewish People as being chosen by God *(haAhm haNivhar)* to serve as His emissary to humanity, and is therefore endowed with unique qualities *(ahm segula)*. This notion appears many times in the Bible and in multiple prayers, and has been an essential tenet in Judaism's self-perception. However, as mentioned, its meaning is contested and open for interpretation: some view the Jewish People as being endowed and burdened with a service to God and mission to humanity; others understand this chosenness to mean that the Jewish People has unique inherent societal qualities that make it different from other nations; and there are those who even hold the Jewish People to be ethnically and racially superior to non-Jews.[260] Naturally, these outlooks mandate the distinction and separation of the Jewish People from non-Jews, and its insulation inevitably causes alienation.

301.   Furthermore, **Judaism's internal and inherent dynamics of doubt *(safek)* encouraged the questioning of the dominant power.** The intellectual liberty inherent in Judaism encourages questioning of preconceived notions and rejection of domineering cultures. As Sacks notes, Judaism is inherently opposed to any dominant culture, faith and authority.[261]

---

258 Sacks, *Future Tense*, p. 80

259 Sacks, *Future Tense*, p. 74

260 See in Binyamin Lau, *Sages Volume II*, p. 205-207 (in Hebrew) about the debate between Rabbi Akiva and Rabbi Ishmael about the relationship among the People of Israel, the Torah and other nations. While Rabbi Akiva posits that the People of Israel was chosen by God, who therefore gave it the Torah. Hence, this is an unbreakable bond, like that which exists between father and son. In other words, the choseness of the People of Israel is inherent to its relationship with God. Meanwhile, Rabbi Ishmael likens the relationship between the People of Israel and God to that which exists between servants and their master, suggesting that such a relationship in conditioned upon the loyalty of the servant. In other words, should the People of Israel abandon the Torah, they would be like all other nations.

261 See Sacks, *Future Tense*, p. 76-88 on Anti-imperialism, The Counter-Platonic Narrative, The Unique and the Universal, and The Voice of the Other.

302. Thus, **Judaism's particular outlook places it on a course of inevitable friction and potential collision with any domineering culture and religion**. The Greek and Roman Empires clashed with the Jews when they sought to establish Hellenist values and practices as the norm of society. Christianity and Islam have historically aspired to claim the faith and soul of all human beings. Both also view the Land of Israel as holy, and were aggressive and even violent against the Jews throughout the world and for a long time, making Judaism's distinct and unyielding faith and social otherness their target and Jews their victims. Repeated confrontations – intellectual debates, persecutions, violence and bloodshed – were inevitable, as the Jewish outlook represented an affront to their aspirations for global domination.[262]

303. **Assimilation, through adoption of foreign outlooks, ideas, customs and practices and ultimately intermarriage, has been a permanent point of concern of Judaism.** A people that dispatches its members to the frontiers of knowledge, space and society acknowledges that some of them will be lost to the temptations of the outer world. In other words, assimilation is an inevitable outcome of the fundamental condition of Judaism, which engages with the world from a permanent condition of otherness. It is a logical yet painful outcome of an existential necessity, and thus the price of Jewish longevity. Indeed, many Jews willingly chose Hellenism, Christianity and communism, changed their language, names, customs, costumes, ethics and loyalties for practical and ideological reasons. As Jews are known to have constituted about ten percent of the Roman Empire in antiquity,[263] it would seem logical that the Jewish People should have numbered in the tens of millions by modernity. Indeed, some say that about a fifth of the present population of Spain carries Jewish blood.[264] Yet, at the turn of the 21st century, there are only an estimated

---

262 Examples include extensive interaction of Jewish philosophers with the Moslem Kalam, *The Kuzari* by Yehuda HaLevi and the debates between Jews and Christians in the Medieval period (see Johnson, *A History of the Jews*, p. 233).

263 Johnson, *A History of the Jews*, p. 171: "From being about eight million at the time of Christ, including 10 per cent of the Roman empire, they had fallen by the tenth century to between one million and one and a half million ... Jewish losses were proportionately much higher than the population as a whole ... these losses were only partly due to general economic and demographic factors. In all areas, and at all periods, Jews were being assimilated and blending into the surrounding populace. "

264 See this New York Times article citing a research which traces twenty percent of Spain's population to Jewish ancestry: http://www.nytimes.com/2008/12/05/science/05genes. html?_r=1&.

fourteen million Jews in the world.[265] Surely, many died in wars, were
forced to convert, succumbed to persecutions and mass exterminations.
But even before the Shoah there were still only an estimated fifteen
million Jews in the world.[266] Beyond those who were lost in body,
many others, perhaps even in greater numbers, chose to leave Judaism.
In addition to the disappearance of the ten tribes of the Kingdom of
Israel, Jewish history records assimilation among First Temple exiles,[267]
adoption of Hellenist culture from as early as the 3rd century BCE,[268] and
mass conversions to Christianity in Spain.[269] Assimilation remains one of
the most intensely discussed and hotly polarizing topics among Jews in
modern times.

304. **Judaism developed a variety of sophisticated societal tools, 'soft' and
'hard,' to battle the appeal of the dominant culture and decrease
assimilation.** These tools generate 'centripetal' forces that pull Jews back
in and keep them within Judaism's web of communities, thus balancing
the 'centrifugal' forces that push them out of their community and away
from their traditions.

305. **Some of these 'centripetal forces' are 'soft' and focus on nurturing an
eco-system, which keeps the community and all its members 'within
the fold.'** Historically, they include extensive and nearly universal
education among males; strict dietary laws;[270] unique languages such as
Yiddish and Ladino; match-making and early marriage; strong emphasis
on togetherness; a powerful narrative about shared legacy and destiny;

265 See Sergio Della Pergola, Jewish Policy Planning Institute, "Jewish Demographic
Policies", 2010: "The Jewish People comprises today just less than thirteen and a half
million individuals: 5.7 million in Israel and 7.7 million in the diaspora." (http://jppi.org.
il/uploads/Jewish_Demographic_Policies.pdf).

266 See United States Holocaust Memorial Museum's *Holocaust Encyclopedia* here: "In
1933, approximately 9.5 million Jews lived in Europe, comprising 1.7% of the total
European population. This number represented more than 60 percent of the world's
Jewish population at that time, estimated at 15.3 million."

267 Hence the phenomenon of intermarriage with foreign women opposed by Ezra the Scribe.
See Ezra 9 & 10.

268 The book of Maccabees chronicles not only the struggle with Greek culture and power,
embodied by King Antiochus IV Epiphanes and his army, but also within the People of
Israel between the Hellenizing Jews and the orthodoxy of its time.

269 Johnson, *A History of the Jews*, p. 223

270 Johnson, *A History of the Jews*, p. 134: "…circumcision did not prevent social intercourse.
The ancient Jewish laws of diet and cleanliness did."

and invocation of guilt. This struggle is permanently present in Jewish history. The Midrash attributes Jewish communal survival through four centuries of life and slavery in Egypt to such 'soft tools' as preserving their Hebrew names, language and costumes;[271] the modern *yeshiva* world developed as a reaction to Emancipation in the 18th century; the North American Jewish community spent many millions of dollars in the 1990s in attempts to preserve 'Jewish continuity;' and decreasing intermarriage and assimilation is central impetus behind the Birthright Israel project.

306. However, **in other times, when Judaism has faced a challenge to its entire outlook, it clung to its principles and values through self-sacrifice, force and violence.** Judaism embraced the ideal of sanctifying God *(kiddush HaShem)* through the sacrifice of self, which, in extreme cases, required enduring hardships and even martyrdom. Such was the story of Hanukah, when the Hasmoneans used brute force in their struggle against Hellenism, directed at both the Greek Empire and the Jewish Hellenists; it was the story of the Bar Kochva revolt, which Rabbi Akiva endorsed in response to the attempts of Caesar Hadrian *(Adrianus)* to enforce Hellenism as the universal religion of the Roman Empire; it was the story of those Jews who were willing to die at the hands of the Spanish Inquisition rather than convert to Catholicism; and it was the story of the so-called Prisoners of Zion, who defied the Soviet Union when it sought to eliminate the Judaism in its midst.

307. *Finally*, **Jewish society balances the extensive exposure to the world of some of its members with the insularity of its most conservative communities.** Jewish communities represent a spectrum between openness, progressiveness and universalism, on the one end, and insularity, conservatism, and particularism, on the other end. The opposite poles of this spectrum represent radically different, almost diametrically opposed worldviews. While the communal DNA of the former group changes quickly, and could be altered within one generation or less, the communal DNA of the ultra-conservative faction will be preserved nearly untouched and is very slow to change. The barriers that such ultra-conservative communities create in order to seal their members off from the world, as well as from other Jews who may have been affected by it,

---

271 See Genesis 47 about the descent of the People of Israel to Egypt. See also sources that discuss the association between the survival of the People of Israel in Egypt and the preservation of their language, names and costumes: http://adderabbi.blogspot.co.il/2007/01/manufactured-midrash-name-speech-garb_12.html and http://dovbear.blogspot.co.il/2010/01/we-did-change-our-names-and-clothing-in.html

encompass all aspects of life. In antiquity, such groups as the Essenes *(Isiyim)* took to the desert and rejected city life and other then modern practices. Today, such people avoid television, cellular phones, Internet and sometimes even public transportation, while strictly observing dietary and purity laws that ensure their exclusive congregation with similar-minded people.

308. **However, in some cases, extreme levels of insularity lead to a severing of such ultra-conservative communities from the Jewish People.** Layers of restrictions and deep resistance to communal change lead to seclusion not only from the non-Jewish world, but also from other Jews. Such communities would not eat with, live with and marry less observant Jews. In the absence of a critical mass of people, such factions are then doomed to becoming esoteric and eventually to disappear. While there will always be radical conservatism in Judaism, there is no guarantee that the ultra-orthodox groups of the Jewish People as we know them today will actually remain a part of Judaism in the future. The Essenes *(Isiyim)*, the Sadducees *(Tzdokim)* and the Karaites *(Karaim)* are three examples of conservative groups and rigid outlooks that used to be a part of Jewish society, failed to adapt and are no longer part of Judaism. Recently in Israel, a group of ultra-orthodox women began to cover themselves in dresses that are similar to the burkahs worn by Afghan Taliban women. Their radicalization gained them the condemnation even of ultra-orthodox rabbis, who found their ways distasteful and unbecoming. **Hence, the Jewish world loses members due to both extremes of progressiveness and of conservatism.**

Powerless Security

This section deals with the Flexigidity of the security of Judaism, Jewish communities and individual Jews. It begins by describing the two underlying reasons for the insecurity of the Jewish People: antisemitism, and the inherent otherness of Judaism. It then goes on to describe the mechanisms that Judaism developed to increase its security and to respond to its adversaries. The section ends with a discussion of the implications of the establishment of the State of Israel on the Flexigidity of Jewish security.

309. **The sixth engine of Jewish adaptability is the dynamics that Judaism developed to ensure its survival and the safety and security of Jewish communities and its members.** Since exiled by the Romans and with

few and rare exceptions,[272] Jews largely abdicated self-defense through use of force as a means to ensure their survival and the wellbeing of their communities. Instead, the Jewish People developed alternative mechanisms, rigidly uncompromising about religious and communal autonomy, yet flexible to a degree in accommodating its sovereigns. As Paul Johnson noted, 'At Yavne, the sword was forgotten, the pen ruled.'[273]

310. **The two unique underlying reasons for the insecurity of the Jewish People are antisemitism and the inherent otherness of Judaism.** This is notwithstanding the fact that, like other peoples, the Jewish People also experienced periods of instability and insecurity due to the permanent change in political, economic and social conditions.

311. **Judaism has been subjected to constant animosity for millennia, which in the late 19th century was termed antisemitism.**[274] The Book of Esther tells of Haman who incites King Ahasuerus *(Achashverosh)* of Persia against the Jews, using the arguments of their unique ways, which defer to a higher entity than the king.[275] In later periods, Jewish faith was attacked by Christianity, which accused Jews of failing to identify their own messiah and of being complicit in his death. Judaism was also challenged by Islam, which accused Jews of failing to accept Mohammed and the Koran. In later centuries primarily in Europe, Jewish societal otherness led to the demonization of Jews, who were framed at times interchangeably as: condescending, elitist, inferior, archaic, subversive and even as an active force of evil. In the 18th century, when Jews blended into general European society following their emancipation, hatred was redirected to their race, therefore condemning each and every individual, as well as the entire Jewish People. This outlook fed the Nazi 'Final Solution' to the so-called 'Jewish problem,' calling for the physical elimination of anyone who carried Jewish blood, tracing it three generations back, including entire Jewish communities and the entire Jewish People. Rabbi Jonathan Sacks writes that antisemitism has been 'less of a doctrine or set of beliefs than a series of contradictions ... Jews

---

272 Exceptions to this general state of affairs include: the Jewish rebellion under the Antonian dyansty in Cetisiphon, the case of the Jewish army against the Sassanid Empire in 425, the Jewish armed resistance to Islam in the Arabian Peninsula and Jews who fought against the Crusades in alliance with the Moslems.

273 Johnson, *A History of the Jews*, p. 149

274 The following framing follows closely Sacks, *Future Tense*, Chapter 5, p. 89-111.

275 Esther 3:8

were hated because they were rich and because they were poor; because they were capitalists and because they were communists; because they kept to themselves and because they infiltrated everywhere; because they held tenaciously to a superstitious faith and because they were rootless cosmopolitans who believed nothing.'[276] Indeed, even at the beginning of the 21st century, antisemitism exists around the world in all of its ancient and more modern forms.

312.   Furthermore, **in recent decades, antisemitism reoriented its focus against Jewish nationhood and peoplehood.** This so-called 'de-legitimization of Israel' – singling it out and negating its right to exist – singularly denies the right of the Jewish People to self-determination in its own State of Israel.[277] As Rabbi Sacks frames it: 'now the State of Israel has taken the role of the source of all trouble and evil in the world using its mythical power in world politics.'[278] This hatred is fed by an alliance that brings together the radical European left, continuing the communist legacy of demonizing Israel, and radical Islamists, both in Europe and the Middle East, many of whom embrace and preach demonic anti-Judaism and anti-Israel rhetoric. This 'red-green alliance' not only assaults the State of Israel, but also targets Jews for their presumed association with Israel and assumed support of its policies. Such an attack on Israel is ultimately an attack on all Jews.

313.   **The other underlying reason for the vulnerability of the Jewish People has been Judaism's inherent otherness, which inevitably challenges the dominant culture.** Unique laws and traditions regulate Jewish education of children and adults, lawmaking and courts, marital status, places of prayer and ritual, and communal institutions. In addition, different factions of Judaism tend to insulate themselves to varying degrees, even among the most open and welcoming societies. Put together and held separately, beyond a critical mass, all of these particular elements of Judaism can challenge a prevailing culture.

---

276 Sacks, *Future Tense*, p. 92

277 For a broad description of the phenomenon of de-legitimization of Israel see report by the Reut Institute, "Building a Political Firewall Against Israel's De-Legitimization", March 2010   (http://reut-institute.org/data/uploads/PDFVer/20100310%20Delegitimacy%20 Eng.pdf).

278 Sacks, *Future Tense*, p. 97

314. Furthermore, **Jews have historically had relationships and loyalties that transcended political borders.** The narrative of Jewish Peoplehood establishes unbreakable personal and collective bonds and relationships among all Jewish communities around the world irrespective of boundaries. In ancient times, we know of Jews who lived in Mesopotamia under Persian and Moslem rule, yet communicated extensively with Jewish communities within rival Greek, Roman and Byzantine Empires,[279] and during the First World War Jews all sides of the warring parties remained interconnected. In addition, the narrative of nationhood establishes links between Diaspora Jews and a distant land, Zion. And since 1948, the State of Israel has commanded the loyalty of many Jews around the world, who have mobilized to support it in countless ways.

315. Consequently, **Jews were repeatedly presumed to have and were accused of having multiple loyalties.** This became more prevalent since the emergence of the modern nation-state. Napoleon grappled with the priority of Jewish loyalties and whether Jews' initial loyalty was to France or to the fellow Jews.[280] The infamous Tsarist counterfeit of the Elders of Zion uses these loyalties to accuse the Jews of masterminding world politics and economics in their benefit. The Soviets held their 1952 Doctor's Plot trials against Jewish doctors, who were accused of being part of a global Jewish conspiracy against Bolshevism. Though vastly different, more recently, Stephen Walt and John Mearsheimer published a book that challenges the loyalty of the pro-Israel lobby, AIPAC, and its leaders to the USA, de-facto accusing them of placing Israel's interests before their own nation's.[281]

316. **Jewish collective and individual responses to the predicament of Jewish security have varied over time.** Judaism created flexible and sophisticated mechanisms to secure the standing of the Jewish community within the general society and to ensure its protection by the sovereign authorities.

---

279 On Jewish global traders as of the ninth century, see Botticini and Eckstein, *The Chosen Few*, p. 200-202.

280 In 1806, an assembly of Jewish notables was summoned by Napoleon to address twelve questions. Some of them focused on Jewish loyalty to French law and nation. For example: do the Jews born in France, and treated by the law as French citizens, acknowledge France as their country? Are they bound to defend it? Are they bound to obey the laws and follow the directions of the civil code? See Wikipedia entry on Grand Sanhedrin at http://en.wikipedia.org/wiki/Grand_Sanhedrin.

281 See John J. Mearsheimer and Stephen M. Walt, *The Israel Lobby and U.S. Foreign Policy*, Farrar, Straus and Giroux, New York, First Edition, 2007.

317. *First,* **Jews swore loyalty to the local sovereign, and observed the laws of the land** *(dinah de'malchutah dinah)* **to the extent that they did not impede on Jewish law and custom.** This happened even in places where the identity of state was anchored in Christianity or Islam, such as Morocco, Spain and England. Jews have gone to war in the service of their country against other nations who often also housed Jews. This has happened since antiquity. And the number of Jewish soldiers who served in the Allied Forces in World War II is over a million. Furthermore, Jewish individuals became distinguished military and political leaders in many nations, including the Soviet Union, the USA, Australia, France, the United Kingdom and Canada.[282]

318. *Second,* **Jews brought unique value to the peoples among whom they dwelled.** Many of them became prominent court physicians, business people, traders, scientists, chief financiers and leading thinkers. And, they did not shy away from acquiring political influence with some of them, such as Maimonides and Isaac Abrabanel, serving as chief advisors to sultans and kings. In modernity, many Jews play a prominent role in leading nations such as the USA, United Kingdom, France and Argentina.

319. **Another response of Jewish communities to the predicament of their security has been the adaptation of Jewish laws, institutions and customs to alleviate concerns about their loyalty.** Such sensitivity to the idiosyncrasies of local sovereigns was made possible by the decentralized process of Jewish lawmaking. In some cases, an adjustment was made, institutionalized for centuries within the Jewish community, and even received formal recognition from the state. Such was the case of the Exilarch in Babylon, the Board of Deputies and Chief Rabbinate in the United Kingdom, as well as with the Consistoire in France. In other cases, attempts to adapt Jewish customs failed and were rejected. Jewish Hellenists, who changed the working of the Temple to suit the Greeks, were defeated by the sword of the Maccabees. The Reform Movement in 19th century Germany attempted to accommodate the spirit of that era and to appease German nationalists. It eliminated Judaism's otherness in the form of association with non-German Jews and Zion, the use of the Hebrew language and the observance of *Shabbat* and dietary laws *(kashrut)*. Nonetheless, these measures made no difference to Germany's antisemites and to the Third Reich.

---

282 See *Wikipedia* entry on Jewish military history at http://en.wikipedia.org/wiki/Jewish_military_history.

320. *Finally,* **the ghetto is one of the institutions that historically epitomized the predicament of Jewish security in the Diaspora.** While the existence of quasi-autonomous Jewish quarters dates back to antiquity, the ghetto system emerged in Europe in different forms as of the 13th century, and crystallized in the early 16th century in the Ghetto of Venice. It represented a pact between the Jewish community and the local sovereign whereby in exchange for religious autonomy, self-government and security, typically within a walled space, Jewish communities committed to paying taxes and to loyalty.[283] The so-called ghetto system spread across Europe and survived until the emancipation of European Jews in the 18th century. Its logic was also manifested in different places across North Africa and the Middle East. The Jewish 'ghetto' in Morocco was called the Mellah and existed until the 20th century.

321. On the individual level, **many Jews concealed their Judaism or left the Jewish faith and people altogether in order to gain security, acceptance and economic benefits.** Some converted willingly or under coercion, while others simply hid their Jewishness. Jews became Hellenists and loyal Greek and Roman citizens. During the days of the Spanish Inquisition, those who converted to Catholicism became known as *Conversos*, while those who retained their Jewish identity and customs in secret were called *Merannos* ('concealed or coerced Jews,' *Anusim*). In 18th century Europe, Jewish parents would baptize their children to increase their opportunities,[284] and in modernity, when no baptism is required, some Jews simply conceal and suppress their identity to better capitalize on their opportunities.

322. **Some of the Jews who converted out of Judaism turned into enemies of the Jewish People and faith, and, in modernity, also of Zionism and of the State of Israel.** As mentioned earlier, Hellenizing Jews were bitter enemies of the Maccabees; a converted Jew led the Roman legion against the Jews of Alexandria and participated in the siege and destruction of

---

283 Johnson, *A History of the Jews*, p. 236: "...Jewish communities accepted oppression and second-class status, provided it had definite rules which were not constantly and arbitrarily changes without warning ... the ghetto offered security and even comfort of a kind. It made the observance of the law easier in many ways, by concentrating and isolating Jews...".

284 Johnson, *A History of the Jews*, p. 312: "Conversion to Christianity was one way in which Jews reacted to the age of emancipation ... Heinrich Heine (1797-1856), who had himself baptized the year after Karl Marx, referred to the act contemptuously as 'an entrance ticket to European society.' ... For a Jew, everywhere except in the United States, remaining a Jew was a material sacrifice.".

Jerusalem; *conversos* persecuted and prosecuted their fellow Jews during the period of the Spanish Inquisition; Bolshevik Jews were leaders in the campaign against Judaism in the Soviet Union; and some of the leaders of the Boycott Divestment and Sanctions movement, so-called BDS, that de-legitimizes Israel and seeks its disappearance are Jewish.

323. **Others, however, preserved their association with the Jewish People, remained loyal to it and even served it when an opportunity presented itself.** Benjamin Disraeli, who was baptized in childhood and became the Prime Minister of England, was a devoted supporter of Zionism, and Nicolas Sarkozy, a grandchild of a Jew, was a great friend of the State of Israel during his tenure as President of France.

324. Perhaps above all, **mobility has been the primary way for Jews to ensure their survival and collective security.** As mentioned earlier, the center of gravity of the Jewish People is in permanent motion, and Jews were repeatedly able to collectively relocate from locations of hostility, insecurity and poverty to places of acceptance, tolerance, opportunity and safety. Zion, Babylon, Spain, Poland, Germany, Russia, Morocco, Iraq and Iran have all been primary hubs of Jewish life, which declined with the deterioration of the conditions of Jews there. Hence the image of the 'wandering Jew.'

325. **Jews have developed sensitive ears and eyes to assess their stature in society, their prospects for prosperity and security, and whether the sovereign is committed and able to protect them and their institutions.** In their more subtle forms, casual remarks, jokes, art and music are often the 'canary in the mine.' Local and sporadic harassments and assaults on Jewish individuals and communities are warning signs, especially if they are not met with a harsh response by the political leadership and law enforcement authorities. They often foretell of great trouble that may eventually lead to yet another rushed relocation and exodus.

326. **Early concerns cause a trickle of people who are more sensitive, cautious, capable and daring**. In the past, they could either stay in spite of growing worries or leave to seek opportunity, tolerance and acceptance. Indeed, Jews were among the first to explore the new world and to settle in it, both in America and Australia. In modern times, Jews of communities in peril may take the safety measures of buying property in other countries and in Israel, acquiring foreign passports and sending their children to be educated abroad. Indeed, nowadays the Jewish world

is witnessing a continuous trickle of Jews out of countries like Venezuela, France and Belgium, where concerns are rising about the safety and future of the Jewish community, while the Jewries of Canada, the USA and Australia are growing.

327. **When the situation becomes untenable, Jews leave en masse.** The story of the exodus from Egypt of an entire community, which relocates virtually overnight due to oppression and intolerance, has been repeated many times in Jewish history. Over the past millennium, a mass departure of Jews occurred in France, England, Spain, the Ukraine, Russia, Algeria, Tunisia, Libya, Egypt, Syria, Lebanon, Iraq, Iran and Ethiopia. And, in the 1990s, more than one million Jews left the former Soviet Union within a four-year period.

328. **The otherness of Judaism tests the tolerance of sovereigns and compatriots, making Jews the harbinger of the humanism, progress, freedom, tolerance and prosperity of their societies.** In an environment of intolerance, Judaism and Jews became an easy target, repeatedly facing accusations of disloyalty, and being victimized and demonized. Their eventual mass departures deprived their former habitats of a highly skilled, industrious and loyal constituency, thereby paying a heavy price as a result. Meanwhile, where freedom and tolerance were inherent to the local culture, Jews were accepted, respected and protected, building flourishing communities and making great contributions to their societies. As Rabbi Sacks writes, 'Judaism is the voice of the other throughout history ... that is why the way a culture treats its Jews is the best indicator of its humanity or lack of it..'.[285] Since such an environment is inherently linked to economic development, it has been posited that the level of comfort of Jews is a powerful indicator for the prospects of prosperity of a nation. In other words, Jewish emigration is a sign of imminent decline, and immigration indicates coming prosperity.

329. As mentioned earlier, **shifts of Jewish demography are made possible by the architecture of the Jewish People as a network.** This organization as a worldwide web of communities has been vital in allowing Jewish individuals and households to relocate themselves around the world. Most Jewish households have a legacy of migration in their family stories, and family members who live overseas. Once they relocate, their new community often helps with orientation, employment, education and other needs. Thus, gravitational shifts of the Jewish People happen in a

---

285 Sacks, *Future Tense*, p. 82.

bottom-up manner. Every household takes its own decision about their path to prosperity and safety, as the ability to relocate is embedded both in Jewish families and in Jewish society.

330.   Furthermore, **the structure of the Jewish People as a worldwide web of communities also underlies its exceptional collective resilience.** As mentioned earlier, this flat architecture has been key to Judaism's survival, security and prosperity, and underlies the ability of Jews to transcend crises. Over the past two millennia, the Jewish People and its web of communities suffered massive setbacks, which led to dramatic shifts in its geographic spread. In fact, mass loss of a significant number of node communities in one area of Jewish society never paralyzed the Jewish People and was often followed by a rise to great political and economic power in another area shortly thereafter.

331.   **The State of Israel obviously represents a radical departure from the dynamics of powerless security of the Diaspora.** As of the 1880s, with the violent assaults on the Jews in the area of the Pale of the Settlement in Russia, Zionism concluded that the Diaspora model failed the Jews. Leon Pinsker argued that the Jewish People must self-liberate and repatriate to Zion. In the late 1890s, Herzl argued that only a sovereign state of the Jewish People, recognized by world powers and international law, could solve the Jewish predicament in Europe. Following the First World War, and particularly as of the Balfour Declaration of November 1917, the idea of a modern sovereign Jewish state began to take shape. As of the 1930s, a systematic effort of institution and capacity building toward statehood began. For many, the Shoah provided the ultimate proof of the necessity of Jewish sovereignty. The State of Israel was founded in 1948, ending nineteen centuries of forced exile and re-establishing Jewish reign in Zion. By the 1990s, virtually all Jews that so desired could freely immigrate to the State of the Jewish People.[286]

332.   Yet, **at the dawn of the 21st century, the simplistic truths of classical Zionism are challenged by reality.** Contending that the Diaspora model had failed the Jews, Zionism sought to eliminate the Diaspora and concentrate all Jews in the State of Israel. However, the Jewish community in Israel, comprising more than forty percent of world Jews, may soon become the only one under an existential threat. Meanwhile, Diaspora

---

286   On the spread of the Jewish network as an essential condition for the survival of the Jewish People and on the challenge of classical Zionism to this model, see Wald, *Rise and Decline of Civilizations*, chapter 26, p. 187-191 (in Hebrew).

Jewry has remarkably revived since the Shoah in all but demographic terms.[287] It is now as prosperous, secure and influential as ever before in tolerant and accepting societies. Furthermore, a new phenomenon of a nearly one million strong Diaspora of Israelis has emerged. Indeed, the notion that the USA or the State of Israel are the final destination of Jews and the end of their historical journey through humanity is Jewishly a-historical.

333. Thus, **at this moment in its history, the Jewish People has two models to assure its survival and security: the model of powerless security in the Diaspora and the model of powerful security in the State of Israel**. This condition calls upon Diaspora Jews to support Israel's survival, security, legitimacy and prosperity with their financial means and political influence. It also requires Israel to take into consideration the security and political needs of world Jewry in its own decisions and actions. In such a reality, **a vibrant Diaspora has clearly become an imperative for Zionism**.

---

287 "In 1933, approximately 9.5 million Jews lived in Europe ... more than 60 percent of the world's Jewish population at that time, estimated at 15.3 million." See United States Holocaust Memorial Museum's *Holocaust Encyclopedia* here. "The Jewish People comprises today just less than thirteen and a half million individuals: 5.7 million in Israel and 7.7 million in the diaspora." See Sergio Della Pergola, Jewish Policy Planning Institute, "Jewish Demographic Policies", 2010: (http://jppi.org.il/uploads/Jewish_Demographic_Policies.pdf).

The Workings of Jewish Flexigidity

This section provides a broad overview of the dynamics of Jewish adaptability based on the foundations that were laid earlier in this book. It attempts to describe the manner in which Judaism and Jewish society optimize the pace of societal adaptation through the interplay among many small units.

334. **The concept of Jewish Flexigidity attempts to capture in one word – and then to offer a framework – for understanding Jewish survival, resilience and prosperity, as well as Judaism's remarkable legacy of leadership.** Its underlying premise is that a small people that have not only survived for millennia but have also been at the frontier of humanity in so many spheres, must have mastered the art of societal adaptation.

335. **Evolution of societies and their adaptation is driven by fundamental crises of existing orders.** So-called 'fundamental gaps'[288] naturally emerge in every society between traditions, heritage, memories, existing practices and institutions, and the respective logics that they serve, on the one hand, and the ever-changing reality and evolving needs of the community in affluence or distress, on the other hand. Such gaps are inevitable, permanent and prevalent in any society, organization and corporation, and are mostly managed by the Flexigidity of the existing institutions. Invariably some powerful and consistent trends exacerbate certain tensions to a tipping point, where a society's capacity to adapt[289] can no longer accommodate the emerging reality. In such conditions, the community experiences escalating 'fundamental surprises' in the form of major setbacks such as an economic crisis, a war or mass civil protest. Such setbacks are inevitable, and become progressively more severe and frequent. Nassim Taleb calls them 'black swans.'[290] Such fundamental surprises grow increasingly threatening. Over time they not only create the societal ripeness for a fundamental change, but also catalyze collective

---

288 Dr. Zvi Lanir defines a 'fundamental surprise' as an event that exposes an entire system of ideas as irrelevant to reality, and therefore increasingly dysfunctional. See Lanir, in *The Fox Pocket Notebook*, chapter 2.

289 For a brief definition of adaptive capacity, see Heifetz, Grashaw and Linsky, *the Practice of Adaptive Leadership*, p. 10-12, and Heifetz, *Leadership Without Easy Answers*, p. 5.

290 For a brief definition, see Taleb, *The Black Swan*, p. 3-5.

'fundamental learning' or 'adaptation.'[291] Such learning – through many radical experimentations and the realignment of communal institutions – leads to the creation of new societal knowledge essential for prosperity and security in the emerging reality.

336. **Such transformations are set in motion by crises created by internal and external change.** In some cases, radical upheaval in the political, economic and technological conditions in the world at large either ends a period of security and prosperity, bringing about instability and poverty, or creates an opportunity for wellbeing and life without risk.[292] Yet some transformations are also driven entirely or in large part by internal crises and deep dissatisfaction with the performance of existing institutions due to their corruption, rigidity and ineffectiveness.

337. **The ability of societies to cope with such change varies.** Some cannot contain these pressures. They deteriorate into prolonged stagnation and decline and may even implode into a civil war, which may take decades to recover from. Few societies repeatedly fail to cope with change and turn into a permanent mess of insecurity and poverty, dismembered into small factions that fight each other without effective central authority, capacity to govern and community structures. The Balkans, Sierra Leone and Cambodia provided unfortunate examples of such collapse. Other societies successfully manage the process of 'constructive destruction' of old ideas, structures and institutions and the transition to new ones, which have a better prospect of ensuring collective prosperity and security. Such societies repeatedly and effectively cope with internal and external crises by adapting themselves, successfully sustaining security and prosperity amidst rapidly changing conditions. Examples include the United States and South Korea.

338. **Jewish society is no exception to these dynamics of change.** It, too, must cope with the evolution of the world around it and with its own internal dynamics of change. In most cases change can be accommodated within the existing structure, but in other cases it mandates a transformation.

---

291 Lanir and Heifetz define 'fundamental learning' and 'adaptation' respectively as evolution of such matters as values, priorities, patterns of conduct, incentives, structures, institutions, language and discourse in order to increase the security and prosperity of the community. See Lanir, in *The Fox Pocket Notebook*, chapter 7, and Heifetz, *Leadership Without East Answers*, p. 69.

292 On challenge and response as engines of rise and decline of nations, see Wald, *Rise and Decline of Civilizations*, chapter 21, p. 157-163 (in Hebrew).

339. **Clearly, Jewish society has been able to optimize its pace of collective adaptation over many centuries.** For most of this time, the Jewish People has been relatively prosperous and secure and in a permanent position of leadership. This is in spite of the dramatic changes around it, and the deep transformations that Jewish society has gone through internally. Judaism has been neither too fast to change so as to lose its togetherness nor too slow so as to become fossilized.

340. **This adaptation of Judaism has taken place as if guided by an invisible hand.** In more modern terms, Judaism optimizes the process of 'constructive destruction' of old ideas, structures and institutions and of transitioning into new ways which better address the needs of its communities. It balances the speed, curiosity, creativity, enthusiasm, and the often carelessness of its societal innovators with the slowness, introversion, rejectionism, skepticism and risk-aversion of its conservatives. While the formers leap from one new idea to another, the conservatives will only grudgingly gravitate in the direction of those innovations that prove to ensure greater long-term security and wellbeing for the community without compromising its identity. Judaism's enthusiasts and 'early adapters' blend in with and balance its skeptics and 'late comers,' its radicalism interplays with its conservatism, its progressive ideas grapple with ancient loyalties, the new mixes with the old as the flexible with the rigid in one societal whole. Ten major factors are at play here.

341. *First,* **Judaism's four meta-stories provide distinct frameworks for diagnosing the societal gaps that must be addressed, articulating a vision and designing a strategy.** As mentioned earlier, each story is coherent and is deeply rooted in Jewish traditions, texts, institutions, practices and spirit. Each of them creates a prism through which Jews can assess whether a certain development is 'good for the Jews.' The combination of these stories offers an additional layer of sophistication to the public discourse of Judaism and to the adaptability of the Jewish People.

342. *Second,* **the contours of Jewish society evolve, as well.** Judaism's Flexigidity of membership introduces flexibility in this regard through the freedom of individual ordained rabbis to perform conversions. This structure decentralizes and diversifies the interpretations and practices regarding the acceptance of new members into Jewish society. It thus allows every community to respond to the particular conditions of its

existence – be they religious acceptance or persecutions, prosperity or scarcity, security or lack thereof – by tweaking the requirements and processes of conversions over time and across geographies.

343. *Third,* **Jewish adaptability emerges out of a highly decentralized, bottom-up and collective dynamics among many thousands of units.** These dynamics are open to all Jewish individuals, households, institutions and communities, who can participate in an accessible, transparent and democratic manner. Each study-pair *(chevrutah)*, *minyan*, community, school and institution produces its own insights regarding the condition of Judaism and the most appropriate response to current challenges and opportunities facing the Jewish People. Each of them verifies facts, checks sources and challenges prevailing logic and rationale. This collective process of deliberation is based on universal education; acquaintance with a shared canon; accepted rules of debate, interpretation and lawmaking; and on accessible mechanisms of communication across the worldwide web of communities.

344. *Fourth,* **the 'flat' structure of Jewish leadership propels Jewish adaptation in powerful ways.** Each such unit of Jewish society is inspired to action or to inaction by its own leaders. In the absence of a center of political power and authority, such as a 'government' or a 'presidency' that operates in a top-down manner, Jewish leadership is in fact spread out across its worldwide network of communities.

345. *Fifth,* **Jewish adaptation benefits from unmatched access to humanity.** The global spread of the Jewish People exposes it to a very broad spectrum of human, social, economic and political conditions. This collective interface with varied geographies, cultures, philosophies and societies feeds Judaism with a very broad spectrum of inputs that fuel its evolution. Furthermore, Judaism also has the network that allows many communities to broadly engage in a discussion of the merits of such alternative outlooks. Thus, Judaism's vast geographic diversity is critically important for its survival

346. *Sixth,* **the approach of Judaism to society, aspiring for inclusive wealth creation, is critically significant for the adaptability of the Jewish People.** As mentioned earlier, it ensures a balance between the accumulation of affluence by individuals, the wellbeing of community institutions, social cohesion and justice and the underwriting of collective concerns such as Zion and the world of Torah. It is a system

that encourages its members to move across geographies, to use many languages and to engage with surrounding cultures in order to create economic opportunities and seize them. In doing so, Jewish business people and economically motivated immigrants carry new ideas across vast distances and constantly shift the center of gravity of the Jewish People toward ideas and places of security and prosperity. They synchronize the evolution of the economic foundations of Jewish society with its geographic spread, the progress of its institutions and structures and the key ideas that inspire it.

347. *Seventh,* **this architecture is immune to censorship and to any attempt to stifle a debate.** It ensures that there will always be a Jewish voice that persistently challenges the prevailing notion and dominant paradigm. That voice cannot be silenced nor can it be excluded. In fact, Judaism's meritocratic leadership structure guarantees that debates for the betterment of the community are consistently thoughtful, rich, insightful and passionate.

348. *Eighth,* **Judaism is resistant to false prophets, big ideologies, epiphanies, miracles and revelations** even of individual geniuses and giants. Its decentralized society and leadership structure encourages questioning through the thoughtful, slower and regulated process of *talmudic* deliberation. The four meta-stories of Judaism are so deeply engrained that none of them can eliminate the others, therefore structurally preventing collective enchantment with an appealing zeitgeist.

349. *Ninth,* **the architecture of Jewish society encourages collective pragmatism that ultimately encourages security and prosperity.** Even if one community goes radical and pulls Judaism to an ideological extreme, somewhere else in the network there will be a community that embraces the other ideological pole, and the full spectrum of outlooks will exist between them. Therefore, the collective outcome is necessarily pragmatic.

350. *Finally,* **the process of establishing *halacha* is the keystone of Jewish adaptability, consequently optimizing the pace of Judaism's societal progress.** It embraces only those customs that have proven over long periods of time to serve the security and wellbeing of the community ultimately turning them into law. Meanwhile, Jewish society allows for experiments, some radical, to transpire in its midst. Its established institutions are hindered in their ability to ban such experiments and to

expel their leaders and constituents from its tent, primarily due to the coalescing power of the law of matrilineal descent.

351. **In this context, the tension and balance between adversity and unity become crucially important for Jewish adaptability.** In fact, Jews may represent the ultimate risk-hedging civilization. While Jewish communities are spread over all continents and dozens of countries and range in practice and structure between ultra-conservatism and radical experimentation, Jews are nonetheless bound by the unity of their network. While innovation is essential for dealing with change, there is uncertainty as to which novelty will prove effective or, alternatively, take a section of the Jewish community over the edge and into the abyss. This is why it is also critically important for Jews to have a faction that remains steadfast to old traditions.

352. **This systemic structure is the source of confidence for the Jewish People in times of peril and dramatic change.** Its organization as a worldwide web of communities that are interconnected by shared values and 'protocols' of text, language, calendar, ceremonies and clear lines of spiritual authority cemented as religious obligations is outstandingly resilient. Jewish history has shown that while Jews may have repeatedly experienced severe setbacks, they nevertheless reemerged powerful and prosperous. In other words, while some or many Jews may be suffering, their legacy engenders confidence that the Jewish People will not only survive but will eventually thrive again.

The Crescendo of Flexigidity in the 20th Century

> This section describes the dramatic transformations of the Jewish People since the 1880s, which culminated in the Shoah, the rise of USA Jewry and the establishment of the State of Israel.

353. **Jewish Flexigidity and adaptability were tested to their limits in the 20th century.** In the 1880s, seventy percent of world Jews, numbering about nine million,[293] lived in central and eastern Europe, many in harsh conditions in the *shtetls* of the Pale of the Settlement *(Tchum Hamoshav)*. The rest lived mostly in Western Europe and in Moslem countries across North Africa and the Middle East. Today, a little more than a century later and following decades of persecutions culminating in the Shoah, the entire demographic center of gravity of the Jewish People was relocated to the USA and to Zion. While the State of Israel is secure and prosperous, embodying Jewish sovereignty and the right of the Jewish People to self-determination, the North American Jewish community has become perhaps the most powerful Diaspora Jewish community in history. This was a century in which the Jewish People was irreversibly transformed.

354. **At the dawn of the 20th century, Judaism in Central and Eastern Europe – primarily in Shtetl townships and in the Pale of Settlement – was in a state of severe crisis.**

355. **The *shtetls* were the primary form of Jewish life that existed in the areas of modern Eastern Poland, Ukraine, Belorussia and the Baltic countries.** They emerged around the 13th century, when Jews escaped Western Europe to safety under the Polish Kingdom, and were closely interconnected through travel, trade, familial ties and a shared language, Yiddish. In the Shtetl townships Jews were a sizeable minority and even, in many cases, the majority, living in a vibrant religious, communal and cultural environment.

356. **The 1648 Khmelnitsky pogroms in Ukraine ushered in the decline of *Shtetl* Jewish life.** These pogroms led to the death of perhaps as many as one hundred thousand Jews and to the destruction of many Jewish communities, encouraging the migration of Jews back to Western Europe. Furthermore, the pogroms marked the beginning of a long

---

293 See Wikipedia Entry: Historical Jewish Population Comparison at http://en.wikipedia.org/wiki/Historical_Jewish_population_comparisons.

period of political instability, when sovereignty in this region of Europe changed hands among Russia, Poland, Ukraine and other nations. Jews were the primary victims of this turmoil, suffering continual insecurity and poverty, as well as frequent restrictions, persecutions and violence.

357. **In 1791, Russia established the Pale of Settlement** *(Tchum HaMoshav)*, **which exacerbated the crisis of Eastern European Jewry.** This was the space within which the Jews had to reside, covering areas within present day East Poland, Ukraine, Belarus and the Baltic countries.[294] Its purpose was to geographically contain and economically exploit Jews through countless restrictions on their professions, property ownership, land acquisition and travel, as well as through a brutal twenty-five yearlong military service. Furthermore, the contours of the Pale of Settlement were repeatedly altered and reduced, thus causing forced relocations of entire communities and a permanent condition of poverty and internal refugeeism among Jews. The crisis of Jews in Russia reached unprecedented levels following the assassination of Czar Alexander II in March 1881. The ensuing pogroms, some allegedly state sponsored, lasted for three years, and the <u>May Laws</u> introduced by Czar <u>Alexander III</u> in 1882 dramatically worsened the condition of Jewish life there. In 1903, the Russian secret police forged the *Protocols of the Elders of Zion*, portraying Jews as enemies from within who are masterminding global politics and economics in order to justify their persecutions. These developments led to a gradual decline of *Shtetl* life until its ultimate demise at the hands of the Nazis.

358. Meanwhile, **in Western Europe as of the late 1890s, Judaism was facing a crisis of a different nature with the emerging failure of the emancipation of European Jewry.**

359. **The French Revolution of 1789, inspired by the so-called European Enlightenment, brought tremendous promise to Jews.** Roughly at the same time that Russia restricted Jews to the Pale of Settlement, in Central and Western Europe – primarily in France, the Austro-Hungarian Empire, Germany and Italy – the European Enlightenment movement brought unprecedented opportunities and freedoms to Jews. However, in exchange for their equal standing in society, Jews were expected to abandon their particularities – including their costumes, language,

---

294 For a map of the shifting boundaries of the Pale of Settlement see: http://commons. wikimedia.org/wiki/File:Map_showing_the_percentage_of_Jews_in_the_Pale_of_Settlement_and_Congress_Poland,_The_Jewish_Encyclopedia_(1905).jpg.

education and religious traditions, as well as their notions of peoplehood and nationhood that transcended political borders – and to embrace the ethos of their nations. As the French Count Clermot-Tonnerre famously said, "We must refuse everything to Jews as a nation, and accord everything to Jews as individuals."

360. **The Jewish Enlightenment Movement** *(Haskalah)* **embraced these opportunities, emphasizing the need to acquire secular education and to integrate Jews into the general society.** It called for significant reforms in the observance of religious traditions. This approach inspired Judaism's Reform Movement, which sought to modernize Jewish religious practices and communal life. Moses Mendelssohn (1729-1786) predated and inspired this new outlook: A pious German Jew, he was both a leader of the Jewish community and a highly regarded intellectual of his time. The ethos of the *Haskalah* Movement was captured by Judah Leib Gordon (1830-1892), a *maskil* from Vilnius, who wrote: "…be a man abroad and a Jew in your tent, a brother to your countrymen and servant to your king."[295] Indeed, many Jews accepted this challenge – turning their backs on particular Jewish traditions, mobilizing to serve in the militaries of their nations and even joining local nationalist associations.

361. However, **despite the European Enlightenment Movement, antisemitism in European societies persisted, grew and mutated in opposition to the integration of Jews.** The emancipation of Jews, which allowed them to blend unnoticed into society, prompted a new form of antisemitism that no longer focused on their religion, but rather on their 'race.' This subjected every Jew to suspicion and rejection due to their 'racial inferiority.' Furthermore, the crisis in the Pale of Settlement continuously instigated migration of Jews from the East to the West. These so-called 'Eastern Jews' stood out in modern Western European cities by their norms of dress and customs, and their presence fed their demonization by antisemites. Finally, the loyalty of Jews to fellow Jews across borders, especially when there was political hostility, was seen as subversive and disloyal. This tension exploded in France during the 1894-1906 Dreyfus Affair and would shape German politics until World War II. Hence, while Jewish *Maskilim* increasingly integrated with and blended into general society, with many of them eventually intermarrying with non-Jews and assimilating altogether, anti-Jewish forces in Europe continued to rise, and the tacit deal of emancipation did not materialize

---

295 Yehuda Leib Gordon, "Awake My People", 1863. See also Johnson, *A History of the Jews*, p. 303.

362. **Jewish society in Europe of the late 19th century was vulnerable and fragile both internally and externally.** The Jewry of the Pale of Settlement suffered ferocious external attacks, which must have led many to question the legitimacy and wisdom of their leadership and institutions that were inevitably seen as impotent and incapable of addressing the plight of the community. Meanwhile, in Central and Western Europe, emancipation and *Haskalah* met with growing antisemitism and with internal resistance due to intermarriage and assimilation. At the same time, the perceived promise of the USA and other nations for a new world of opportunity, acceptance, tolerance and economic prosperity were increasingly appealing to many Jews, and new ideologies began to percolate among young Jews. In short, the Jewish world of that era was on the verge of dramatic fundamental change, with every young Jewish man and woman and every Jewish household facing critical life decisions among multiple diverse choices.

363. **In Central and Eastern Europe, traditional Judaism remained vibrant, yet generally divided into two major groups: the *Litaim*, also known as the *Mitnagdim*, and the *Hasidim*.** Litaim (literally, 'those of Lithuania') refers to a stream in Judaism that is characterized by utter lifelong dedication to the study of Torah and Talmud and to a life of strict observance, where Torah scholarship is the primary measure for social stature. It was centered in the areas of historic Lithuania – nowadays covering East Poland, Belorussia and Latvia – and was inspired by the Vilna Gaon (1720–1797) and Rabbi Chaim Volozhin. Meanwhile, the *Hasidut* movement (literally, 'piety' or 'loving-kindness') refers a stream of Judaism inspired by Rabbi Israel ben Eliezer (1698–1760), also known as the Baal Shem Tov. His outlook emphasized the spiritual and religious experience of the individual through prayer *(tefilah)* and intent *(kavanah)*, viewing the religious leaders of the community not merely as sages *(chachamim)* and rulers in matters of *Halacha (poskim)*, but also as righteous people *(tzadikim)* who served as a medium between the community and the higher sanctity of God, carrying the title of Rebbe or *Admor*. Furthermore, *Hasidut*, which spread primarily in the areas of Romania, Hungary, Ukraine and East Russia, adopted slightly different prayers and dietary laws that created separations among Jewish communities. The Litaim initially saw the *Hasidut* movement as a cardinal threat to Judaism in the aftermath of the traumas of Shabbatyism, and bitterly opposed them, becoming known as *Mitnagdim* (literally, 'those that are opposed'). The main feuds between the two movements took place from the 1770s to the early 1800s. In subsequent decades, they

grew closer, as major *Hasidic* courts also emphasized deep learnedness and strict legal observance, while some communities of *Litaim* embraced ideas of *Hasidut*. By the late 19th century, the two movements were brought together by the threat of Jewish Emancipation and the *Haskalah* Movement, which challenged both of them, albeit in different ways.[296]

364. **Migration out of Europe, primarily to the USA, was another option, which many Jews embraced as of the 1880s.** Political tolerance and economic opportunities inspired many Jews to seek new life across the ocean where acceptance did not require compromising their unique identity. Over a sixty year period, from the 1880s to 1940, millions of Jews would embrace this proposition, and the Jewish population in the USA would grow twenty-fold to almost five million,[297] many of them settling in the New York City area. Many other Jews immigrated to Latin America, primarily Argentina, Canada, South Africa and Australia. Over time, USA Jewry built rich and powerful communities with vibrant institutions that not only addressed local needs, but also reached out to Jewish communities in need around the world and extended vital support to the Zionist enterprise.

365. **Zionism was the third option available to Jews at that time.** It called for Jewish repatriation to Zion and for the reestablishment of Jewish life there as a remedy for the predicament of the Diaspora. Leon Pinsker's 1882 *Auto-Emancipation* laid out this vision in principle and details, the first formal association of Zionists, *Hovevei Zion*, emerged in Eastern Europe in the 1880s. Herzl's 1896 vision of a state for the Jewish People, *The Jewish State*, was received with great fervor, and popular support for Zionism became widespread among European Jewry. However, only few actually repatriated to Zion, totaling less than eighty thousand over a thirty-year period until 1914, and six hundred thousand until 1948. Zionist ideology transcended the call for mere relocation to Zion, and sought to transform the entire existence of individual Jews and households into Hebrew men, women and families, overhauling community life and creating a new culture with a revived ancient language.

---

296 See Johnson, *A History of the Jews*, p. 296-300 for general description of the development of *Hasidut* and the opposition led by the Vilna Gaon *(Mitnagdim)*.

297 See http://www.jewishvirtuallibrary.org/jsource/US-Israel/usjewpop1.html citing figures from the American Jewish Year Book.

366. *Finally*, **many Jews were inspired by and attracted to the Marxist, socialist and communist movements, which called for a revolution in the existing order of their societies.** These Jews believed that only a transformation of the entire society would *inter alia* address the Jewish conundrum, which was viewed as inseparable from the general distress in society. They believed that Jews are just as oppressed by the ruling classes as other disempowered groups. Therefore, the plight of the Jews would only be alleviated when the fundamental condition in society was reformed. Some Jewish Marxists and communists would disassociate themselves altogether from Judaism and the Jewish People, and a few would eventually lead the persecutions against fellow Jews, the Zionist movement and the State of Israel. Others would merge their Jewishness with their socialist outlook to establish the secular Bund Movement and the so-called *Yiddishism* that celebrated the unique Jewish cultural heritage within European society, particularly in Central Europe. Another faction ended up in Zion. They grappled with the hierarchy between Jewish peoplehood and Hebrew nationhood, on the one hand, and the communist ideal of a global class struggle, on the other hand. For some, this dilemma would continue until the crimes of Stalin against the Jews and millions of others were exposed in 1956.

367. Thus, **in that period, young Jews in Central and Eastern Europe had six major choices**: *first option* was to continue life in the *Shtetl* the way it had been for centuries; *second option* was to embrace modernity and the tacit deal of emancipation by becoming a *maskil* in seeking secular education, wearing modern cloths and containing Jewish identity to the private sphere; *third option* was to join the Marxists, communists and socialists, thus turning away from the Jewish faith and sometimes even turning against the Jewish People; *fourth option* was immigrating, primarily to the USA, but also to Latin America, South Africa and Australia; *fifth option* was to become a Zionist and seek a future in Zion; and another option, embraced by many, was conversion to Christianity.

368. Indeed, **by the early 1900s many Jewish families were split, often bitterly, among Zionists, communists, those who immigrated to the new world, and those who stayed behind with their parents in the *Shtetl*.** This dramatic period was immortalized by Shalom Aleichem's famous story *Tevya the Milkman*, which was adapted into the play *Fiddler on the Roof*, telling the story of a pious Jewish milkman named Tevya whose one daughter marries a Christian and another marries a communist while Tevya and the rest of his family are forced out of the Shtetl and choose to live in America.

369. **The first half of the 20th century saw the condition of European Jewry sink to a historic low. In the East, the 1917 communist revolution in Russia ushered in a new period of persecutions.** Theoretically, communism should have been favorable to the Jews, as its atheism was supposed to be agnostic to Judaism, and its leadership was populated by many Jews. Nonetheless, hatred of Jews penetrated and eventually dominated this movement, as well. Rather quickly, Jews and Jewish communities were systematically targeted, unfolding a seventy-yearlong assault on Judaism, Jewish communal life and institutions, and, as of the 1950s, also on the State of Israel. It began initially in the Soviet Union, but after World War II this became policy everywhere behind the Iron Curtain in Central European countries such as Poland, Hungary, Romania, Bulgaria and Czechoslovakia. Soviet Bloc countries accused Jews of disloyalty, capitalism and of so-called 'counter revolutionary tendencies,' and boycotted the State of Israel as a colonist power that was the source of all evil in the Middle East. This period of oppression would only end with the demise of communism in 1989, which led to an exodus of more than one million Jews from the former Soviet Union in fewer than five years, mostly to Israel, Germany and the USA.

370. **The most devastating blow to European Jewry came from Nazi Germany and its fascist accomplices.** Between 1933 and 1945, centuries-old hatred toward Jews in Europe and the evolution of antisemitism into a racist ideology reached its inevitable conclusion: that Jews, and people with any Jewish blood, had no right to live. During World War II, Nazi Germany and its accomplices designed, built and operated an industrial complex of concentration, labor and extermination camps across an area that stretched from Russia to the Western border of France and from Norway to Tunisia. Six million Jews would die. The one-thousand-year-old, three-and-a-half-million strong Polish Jewry and half-a-million strong flourishing German Jewry were all decimated. So were, with few exceptions and to varying degrees, the Jewries of Norway, Denmark, the Baltic Countries, The Netherlands, Belgium, France, Italy, Greece, Romania, Hungary, the Czech Republic, Slovakia, Ukraine, Belorussia, East Russia and Tunisia. Of those who survived, an estimated two million were caught under the boots of communism behind the Iron Curtain for another four and a half decades, while most others became displaced. They would end up primarily in the USA and in Israel, but also in Latin America, South Africa, Canada and Australia.

371. **From the ashes of the Shoah, the Jewish People has experienced six decades of dramatic and continuous rise in its overall political power, prosperity and security.** Most Jewish communities and Jews, who used to live in poverty and under oppression, are now free and significantly better off, as most Diaspora Jews live among the most developed nations in religious freedom. The Jewish community in the USA became perhaps the most politically and economically prosperous and powerful in the history of Jewish Diaspora. It houses a flourishing Jewish life of unprecedented diversity. The Jewish national movement proved among the most successful in the 20th century, and the State of Israel has become strong, secure and developed, housing a new vibrant Hebrew civilization that did not exist a century ago. The traditional world of Torah, which was decimated by the Nazis in Central and Eastern Europe, reemerged primarily in the USA and Israel and is now thriving as never before. In other words, practically all individuals, households and communities of the Jewish People are better off now than they were sixty years ago and, perhaps, for millennia.

Part III
The Zionist Disruption
to Jewish Flexigidity

<u>1860s-1948: Emergence of a Hebrew Hub in Zion</u>

This section of the book describes the impact of Zionism on Jewish Flexigidity. Its first part addresses the near century-long transition of the Jewish community in Zion from being a dormant and minute corner of the Jewish world in the 1840s to being a vibrant hub of that network, unique in its Hebrew character, by 1948, when the State of Israel was established. During this period, many of the fundamental elements of Jewish Flexigidity of the Diaspora were adjusted in Zion by a Hebrew society to create a life of autonomy in preparation for the coming sovereignty. The second part describes how the Flexigidity of Zionism peaked by 1967, epitomized by the stunning victory in the Six-Day War, and how it declined in the decades that followed.

From Slow Awakening to Adaptability on Steroids[298]

372. **The proto-Zionist idea of the 1800s was radical: solving the plight of Diaspora Jews by relocation to Zion.** In the 1840s, the Jewish settlement in Zion was a small, poor and dormant corner of the Jewish worldwide web of communities. It numbered about seven thousand, a small minority among the Arab majority, and amounted to less than one percent of world Jewry.[299] The deep changes that occurred in European Jewish society as of the 18th century with the emergence of *Hasidut* and *Haskalah* had little impact on that Jewish community. Orthodox Jews associated mass return to Zion primarily with messianic times, while *Maskilim* embraced the promise of acceptance and opportunity in Europe. Immediate collective repatriation could not have been a more radical idea to many.

373. **Like prior Jewish transformations, modern Zionism emerged as an outcome of internal and external crises.** European Jewry of the 19th

---

298 General research of this section was significantly helped by the following *Wikipedia* entries in English and their corresponding entries in Hebrew: Old Yishuv, New Yishuv, First Aliyah, Second Aliyah, Third Aliyah, Fourth Aliyah, Fifth Aliyah, Moses Montefiore, Yehudah Chai El-Kalai, Zvi Hirsch Kalisher, Moses Hess, Leon Pinsker, Herzl, Ahad Ha'Ahm, Rothschild, A.D Gordon, Rabbi Abraham Isaac Kook, Ze'ev Jabotinsky, Berl Katzanelson, David Ben-Gurion, Haganah, Hibat Zion, Biluim, Hovevei Zion, Rishon LeZion, Zikhron Ya'akov and Zionism. All relevant claims within these entries were subsequently cross verified with other sources.

299 See Wikipedia entry Old Yishuv http://en.wikipedia.org/wiki/Old_Yishuv and Wikipedia entry in Hebrew הישוב הישן here.

century was in transition caused primarily by the plight in the Pale of Settlement in the East and by growing disillusionment with emancipation in the West. Against this backdrop, the wave of nationalism and national movements in Europe motivated a handful of Jewish leaders to reframe their understanding of Judaism and to reawaken the ancient story of Jewish nationhood, largely suppressed since the Bar Kochva rebellion. The decline of the Ottoman Empire created a historic opportunity to realize these ambitions in Zion.

374. Against this backdrop, **the Heralds of Zionism** *(Mevasrei HaTziyonut)* **began their activities in the 1860s.** They envisioned mass repatriation of Jews to Zion, and contemplated different ideas about purchasing land and settling in it, as well as about the institutions necessary to advance their ideals. In the early 1860s, the German-French socialist Moses Hess (1812-1875) called for a Jewish state in his book *Rome and Jerusalem*, and orthodox rabbi Zvi Hirsch Kalischer (1795-1874) called for repatriation on religious grounds. In Eastern Europe, a number of associations for the settlement of Zion were established, while one of the most influential leaders of British Jewry, Sir Moses Montefiore (1784-1885), underwrote the construction of the first Jewish neighborhoods outside the walled Old City of Jerusalem. In 1879, Eliezer Ben-Yehuda (1858-1922) called for reinstituting Hebrew as the everyday language of the Jews, after it had been fossilized and largely restricted to prayer and ritual life for centuries. Similar radical ideas were also espoused by a small but growing number of prominent non-Jews in Germany, the USA, England and Australia. Thus, when the concept of 'Zionism' was coined in 1890, it described a national movement that had already been in motion for a few decades.

375. **Auto-emancipation became the organizing idea of Zionism in the 1880s, inspiring immigration, land acquisition and settlement in Zion.** It was framed by Leon Pinsker (1821-1891) in 1882 in his seminal work by that name. Pinsker rejected the notion that emancipation in Europe could address the plight of its Jews. He called for immediate repatriation to Zion and for establishing a Jewish state where all Jews would be able to rebuild "their honor." Pinsker believed that the world would only recognize the Jews as a nation when the Jewish People would return to its land. Small groups of Jews were inspired by this vision to raise money, buy land, relocate to Zion and establish the first modern Jewish settlements there as of 1882. **This approach came to be known as 'Practical Zionism'** *(Tziyonut Maasit).*

376. In addition, **by the early 1880s the Zionist movement began to emerge as a comprehensive and collective effort of Diaspora Jewry**. Dozens of Zionist associations were established in Russia and Romania bringing together *Hovevei Zion* (literally, 'Those who are Lovers of Zion') within a movement by the name of *Hibat Zion* (literally, 'Love of Zion'). In 1884, 36 delegates of the *Hovevei Zion* associations met in Kattowitz, Germany, to establish the leadership of the nascent movement and its initial institutions. This was the first international Zionist conference. And, in 1885, Baron Edmond James de-Rothschild of Paris (1845-1934) began a legacy of Diaspora philanthropic activity in support of the Zionist movement.

377. **In 1896, Theodore Benjamin Ze'ev Herzl (1860-1904) assumed the leadership of the Zionist movement and placed its cause on the agenda of leading nations and Jewish communities around the world**. Herzl's experience as a journalist covering the Dreyfus Affair in 1894 led him to conclude that emancipation had failed. He felt grave urgency to resolve the 'Jewish problem' in Europe by removing the Jews from Europe into a state of their own. His book *Der Judenstaat*, literally 'The State of the Jews,' published in 1896, lays out his vision and articulates the rationale of Zionism. He then launched a relentless diplomatic campaign among the highest political authorities of his time and established the Zionist Congress and other institutions to promote his vision. Within a remarkably short period of time, Herzl's ideas spread throughout the Jewish world and he succeeded in placing the Jewish question on the world agenda. He attracted both support and opposition: while Zionists aligned with him, the *Maskilim* and the orthodox rejected his cause. Herzl died in 1904 at the age of forty four, having dedicated the last eight years of his life to the Jewish People. None of his descendants survived the turmoil in Europe that he so feared. Per his will, his remains were taken by the State of the Jews in 1949 for final burial in Jerusalem on a mountaintop named in his honor, 'Mount Herzl.'

378. *In conclusion*, **by the early 1900s, Zionism faced many challenges**. During the twenty three years of the first wave of immigration, the so-called *First Aliyah*, from 1882 to 1905, thirty thousand immigrants in total came to Zion, mostly from Europe, but also from Morocco, Persia, Yemen and Bukhara, now in Uzbekistan. They were a meager minority compared to those who immigrated to America or stayed in Europe. They established thirty-four agricultural settlements between the border with Lebanon to the Northern Negev, which were fragile and small, faced legal, practical and financial challenges and were attacked ideologically by other Jewish factions.

379. **The *Second Aliyah*, between 1905 and 1914, would transform Zionism through its quest to develop a new Hebrew society.** By that time, the idea of a Jewish State had already taken root in the hearts and minds of many Jews, and a Jewish national movement had come to life. Over forty thousand immigrants would come to settle Zion, mostly from the Russian Empire and Romania, as well as from Yemen.

380. **A minority among them brought a revolutionary worldview blending secularism, nationalism and socialism.** They sought to establish communal agricultural settlements, which would transform Jewish individual, community and collective life. They envisioned a society of Hebrew persons *(Adam Ivri)*, who spoke Hebrew, worked their own land and defended themselves. Thus, while Herzl wanted to replicate European life in Zion, they wanted to build a unique egalitarian Hebrew society.

381. **The First World War, which broke out in 1914, placed the Zionist movement in a crisis.** The Jewish world became split between the fighting parties: 'The Allies,' Britain, France and Russia, later joined by the USA, on one side, against the Central Powers of the Austro-Hungarian and German Empires, later joined by the Ottoman Empire, on the other side. The Jewish settlement in Zion, numbering nearly 80,000 under Ottoman rule, suffered hardships, restrictions, forced conscription and even deportation of the Tel Aviv population to Egypt. By the end of the war, the Zionist movement had mobilized in support of the British Empire and marginally participated in its efforts to conquer the Holy Land.

382. **The 1917 Balfour Declaration, recognizing the right of the Jewish People to a national home *(bait leumi)* in the land of Israel, and the end of the First World War ushered in a period of dramatic development for Zionism.** The establishment of the British Mandate in 1919 transformed the political environment in Zion. At that time, still numerically insignificant, Zion's Zionists were yet to represent a breakaway from the legacy of Diaspora Jewry or a rupture in its evolution. However, they had been brewing a revolution by developing a comprehensive set of concepts, blending modern societal ideals with traditional Judaism, conducting multiple radical experiments and demonstrating fast learning and remarkable adaptability toward a vision of full communal autonomy and coming sovereignty.

383. **Several waves of immigration would shape this Hebrew society during the following three decades to become a vibrant and diverse hub of the worldwide web of Jewish communities.** *The Third Aliyah* of thirty five thousand immigrants between 1917 and 1924, primarily from Russia, Poland and Romania, was comprised of predominantly urban immigrants, who settled in Jerusalem, Haifa and Tel Aviv. A minority of young pioneers merged nationalist and socialist ideals to develop innovative institutions and agricultural communities in order to prepare Zion for the mass-repatriation of the Jews. The *Fourth Aliyah* between 1924 and 1929 is credited with fostering the emergence of a class of small business entrepreneurs. About eighty thousand immigrants, mostly from Poland, USSR, Romania, Lithuania, Yemen and Iraq brought rapid urban development mainly to Tel Aviv. This *Aliyah* ended with the deep recession of 1926-1927 and with the Arab riots of 1929. It expanded the outlook found within Zionism from its sixty-year long near-myopic focus on agriculture to include urban and industrial development, as well as settlement with private capital. *The Fifth Aliyah* – numbering two hundred and eighty thousand legal and illegal immigrants over a ten-year period until World War II in 1939 – transformed the Hebrew society and leapfrogged Zionism. Sixty thousand German Jews, so-called 'Yekes,' who were often urban, highly educated and skilled, well-to-do, and religiously and politically moderate, led to the development of a strong middle-class and industrial sector. The Jewish population doubled and grew to thirty percent of the overall population. Its industrial capacity leapt, reaching twice the per capita production and income of the Arab population. All urban Jewish communities grew, and Tel Aviv turned into a European-style city with cafés and shops. These immigrants also established one hundred new settlements, including along the borders of Mandatory Palestine, thus doubling the number of Hebrew communities. This was a period of dramatic development for Hebrew medicine, academia, education, culture, music, theatre, research, agriculture and industry. All waves of immigration were motivated by a mixture of Zionist ideology, the relative peace and quiet under the British Mandate, rising antisemitism and political and economic persecution in Europe and the USSR, and due to restrictions on immigration also to the USA.

384. Thus**, just prior to Jewish statehood in 1948, the Jewish community in Zion had become an important global Jewish hub**. It was sizable, numbering over six hundred thousand, home to five percent of world Jews in the aftermath of the Shoah. It was highly diverse in terms of origin, albeit most came from Eastern and Central Europe. It had the

full spectrum of religious observances between a very orthodox faction, a staunchly secular group and many who were traditional. It may have been the most diverse Jewish community in the world, with a unique creation: the Hebrew civilization.

385. **David Ben-Gurion (1886-1973), who began to emerge as the foremost Zionist leader as of the early 1930s, was arguably to Zionism and to the future State of Israel what Rabban Yochanan Ben-Zakai was for post-destruction Judaism.** His ideology, vision and politics shaped the institutions of the *Yishuv,* the state-in-the-making, as well as those of the State of Israel. His intellectual creation, exceptional in its breadth and depth, was compounded by a unique political capacity to mobilize, build coalitions and determinately execute, as well as by superb diplomatic capabilities to envision and create, lasting strategic alliances with Britain, France and then the USA. His political career, initially as a leader of a workers' party, and later at the helm of the Zionist movement, lasted sixty years. He led in turn the worker's factions, the *Histadrut* and the Jewish Agency. He then served as the Prime Minister of the State of Israel for thirteen years. He was unrelenting in his belief in the imminence of Hebrew statehood and in the glory of the State of Israel, a devoted socialist in his outlook, and a ruthless pragmatist about realizing these visions. Ben-Gurion was eventually recognized by *Time Magazine* as one of the most influential figures of the 20th century.

Zionism's Talmud, Flexigidity of Mission and Structure

386. **The ideology of Zionism and the practicalities of state-building presented a monumental challenge to society, eliciting an intense *talmudic* process.** The scope of issues, their newness and complexity were daunting, equivalent to those which followed the destruction of the Second Temple. Herzl intuitively understood this challenge when he envisioned a Temple which will be built to accommodate modernity. Traditional sources of *halacha* on community-building may have been elaborate, but the context of doing so in Zion was transformative. There were little or no accepted authorities on issues such as diplomacy, politics, land acquisition, settlement and use of force. In the absence of 'questions' on such matters during the millennia of the Diaspora, no Jewish law evolved addressing these issues. Furthermore, accepted process was lacking, too. It was unclear who had authority to legislate and decide: a local representative body of the *Yishuv*, the Zionist Congress representing all Zionists worldwide, a rabbinical council or some other body that was

yet to be formed. Individuals of the highest intellectual caliber, such as Pinsker, Herzl, Ahad Ha'Ahm, A.D Gordon, Rabbi Abraham Isaac Kook, David Ben-Gurion, Berl Katzanelson and Ze'ev Jabotinsky led this collective effort, and were its leaders.

387. **The meta-stories of Judaism framed the debates on the nature and purpose of Zionism and on the meaning of modern Jewish sovereignty.** Inspired by the legacy of the meta-story of nationhood, Zionism grappled with determining the borders of the land based on biblical sources or on pragmatic political considerations, with the nature of the relations with the Arabs and with the philosophy and practice of use of military force. The meta-story of peoplehood underlay the debates on the responsibilities of the *Yishuv* toward the different communities of the Diaspora. The meta-story of faith generated issues regarding the character of public education, the role of rabbis in society, the place of *Halacha* in the work of the legislature and judiciary, and the observance of *Shabbat*, *kashrut* and other customs in the public sphere. The ideal of being a light unto the nations underlay the debates regarding social justice and the place of non-Jews in the Hebrew society, and inspired the quest for building a model society in Zion.

388. Thus, **Zionism inherited from Judaism its Flexigidity of mission, by integrating the ideals of peoplehood, nationhood, faith and *or la'goim* within its narrative.** Naturally, Zionism is the modern manifestation of the narrative of nationhood. The story of peoplehood is embodied in Zionism's quest to address the condition of the entire Jewish People through society and nation building, and to place itself in the broad context of shared Jewish history and destiny. The narrative of being a light unto the nations inspired the Hebrew polity to seek to establish a model modern society that carries a message to humanity through its humanism, development, ethics, prosperity and equality. And, the narrative of faith and covenant emphasizes Zionism's religious and cultural identity, often framing modern Zionism within the broader religious vision of the mass return to Zion. The four meta-stories – the tensions among them and among the factions that upheld them – can be traced across Zionism and throughout its history.

389. **Zionism's Flexigidity of mission has been critical to its success, unity and vitality, by validating diverse sources of inspiration and alternative frameworks for adaptation.** The four meta-stories broadly expanded the range of legitimate Zionist views and behaviors: secular

and religious, socialist and capitalist, urban and agricultural. Thus, Zionism's proposition to its followers was a menu of opportunities for meaningful communal, spiritual, intellectual, religious and ethical life. Indeed, a very diverse group of people associated with Zionism. The system of settlements, which encouraged small groups to self-organize, allowed for a multitude of communal variations housing a broad diversity of worldviews. Furthermore, each story offered a distinct framework for understanding the challenges facing Zionism and for designing appropriate responses. Inevitable and irreconcilable tensions among the four stories in security, economics and social development and geopolitics led to pragmatic solutions and to many societal innovations that often emanated from a hybrid of two or more stories. For example, the quest to establish a national home for the Jewish People, on the one hand, and the socialist ideals of a just society, on the other hand, inspired the *Histadrut* to be both a labor union and an executive arm for realizing the national project.

390. **By the 1920s and 1930s the ideological foundations of Zionism were consolidated into a balancing act among nine big ideas,** which came out of the meta-stories of the Jewish People. These pillars were the ideals of: (1) sovereignty, ownership and control of Zion; (2) political self-determination; (3) security and self-defense; (4) economic self-determination toward prosperity; (5) humanism, liberalism and democracy; (6) the quest for creating a model society; (7) seeking a Jewish majority; (8) developing a Jewish public sphere; and (9) leadership of the Jewish world.

391. **These ideals are inconsistent and in tension with each other.** Allowing one of them to dominate would compromise others and distort the moral, social and political equilibrium of Zionism. For example, democracy and Jewishness are in tension in countless ways in the public sphere, especially in the presence of a significant non-Jewish minority. Also, controlling all of the Biblical Land of Israel may undermine Jewish democracy, majority and identity.

392. Therefore, **Zionism, like Judaism, balances and synergizes its founding ideals.** It allows multiple groups to develop within its society, each with its own ideology. Whenever possible, its relatively flat structure of communities and leadership favored practical steps and local understandings to decisive ideological choices that would alienate major factions. For example, Zionism accepted the existence

of 'streams' in education *(zramim)*, which reflect various worldviews in the Hebrew society, including the ultra-orthodox and Arab streams that are non-Zionist, and avoided forcing one narrative upon all of them. As mentioned, Zionism mostly engaged in painful societal decisions only when it had to. This was the case following the 1947 United Nations Partition Decision, which forced Zionism into accepting the idea of a territorial compromise of ancestral lands in order to establish a Jewish national home with international legitimacy.

393. Hence, **Zionism has been inoculated against the appeal and dangers of big ideologies, and has been doggedly pragmatic.** This is anchored not only in the Jewish tendency to ask questions and to challenge prevailing norms, but also in Judaism's internal dynamics that generate collective pragmatism. Neither communism, socialism or capitalism, nor the world of *halacha* or secularism ever succeeded to dominate the Zionist public sphere. The Greater *Yisrael* ideology and the idea of Jewish supremacy of the far right wing, and the ideology of 'Canaanism' of the far left wing, could never be mainstream. Indeed, radicals had a place in Zionism's political system, but only at its outskirts.

394. Therefore, **the ideological debates of Zionism resulted in arrangements that reflected permanently evolving compromises**. For example, in certain areas that are particularly secular or house non-Jews, there is traffic and commerce on *Shabbat*, while in others there is neither. While the vast majority of bus lines have mixed seating, in specific ones the custom is for men and women to sit in designated areas. Furthermore, many ideological factions built their own communities and settlements, where they designed a unique code of conduct to suit their outlook.

395. **These dynamics led to a dramatic incline in the flexibility of Zionism's structure.** The settlements of the first Aliyah were modeled after Diaspora communities with similar anchor institutions, such as synagogues, courts *(beit din)*, committees *(va'ad)* and rabbinates *(rabbanut)*. The *Second Aliyah* and *Third Aliyah* conducted radical experimentations with this model. Inspired by ideals of equality and democracy, they created multiple new forms of association, both agricultural and urban. By 1948, the *Yishuv* had more than thirty different categories of settlements – such as *kibbutz*, *moshav*, *kfar* and *moshava* – in more than three hundred locations. These settlements made up a network of resilient and prosperous communities, closely intertwined not only internally but also with the Diaspora, a Hebrew extension of the Jewish worldwide web of communities.

396. Yet, **the vision of statehood required the establishment of representative national institutions and a new structure of Jewish leadership and authority.** In 1920, Knesset Israel came into being as the national general representative institution of the Jewish community in Zion, boycotted only by the very ultra-orthodox community. The Knesset Israel appointed an executive arm called the National Committee *(HaVa'ad HaLeumi)*. Both were recognized by the British High Commissioner as the official representative bodies of the *Yishuv*, marginalizing the rabbis and the religious court system of the *Old Yishuv (HaYishuv HaYashan)*. Indeed, the Hebrew community in Mandatory Palestine needed to prepare for eventual statehood and sovereignty by consolidating authority over internal and external affairs. As the process toward statehood matured, particularly following World War II, increasing centralization of power and disciplining of political and military lines became essential. This was the underlying reason for the clash between the National Institutions of the Yishuv *(HaMosadot HaLeumyim)*, under the leadership of David Ben-Gurion, and the Revisionists groups, the *Irgun (Etzel)* and *Lechi*, on the right, and with the communists, on the left. The institutions of the *Yishuv* would eventually serve as the foundations for the Parliament and government of the State of Israel.

397. **This representative structure of the national institutions was essential for preserving the unity of the *Yishuv*.** The civil in-fighting prior to the destruction of the Second Temple created a national trauma. That trauma, and the absence of a formal coalescing authority in the Diaspora, inspired Judaism to ensure that its leading institutions would be representative. Following this legacy, the *Yishuv* secured the legitimacy of its own institutions – primarily Knesset Israel – by ensuring broad representation. Hence, Knesset Israel was a diverse representative body, elected based on the principle of proportional representation that granted each faction power based on the popular support it received. Even the defense force, the *Haganah,* was led by a representative body of different parties, notwithstanding the split of the Revisionist party in 1931.

Rigidity of Place and Language

398. **In the areas of place and language, Zionism largely embraced rigidity, by calling upon all Jews to come to Zion and be a part of the Hebrew culture.** The predicament of the Jews, particularly in Europe, led to attempts to address their crisis in multiple locations including in North America and Argentina. Herzl explored the possibility of creating an

immediate shelter for European Jewry in different sites *(miklat le'laila)*, most famously in Uganda. However, in 1905 the Zionist Congress rejected this idea, and Zionism singularly committed to building a homeland for the Jewish People in Zion. In the decades that followed, Zionism would come to reject Diaspora life *(galutiyut)* altogether.

399. **A similar process took place regarding language: After decades of debate, in around 1900, Zionism not only embraced Hebrew as its sole language, but also sought to disseminate it in the Diaspora as part of the revival of the Jewish People.** This vision led to establishing Hebrew associations around the world, to building Hebrew communities such as Rehovot and Tel Aviv, and to promoting Hebrew literacy, literature and culture.

400. However, **in spite of Zionism's best efforts, the Flexigid nature of Judaism in relation to place and language proved tenacious.** All the while that the *Yishuv* was developing, the majority of Jews preferred to remain in the Diaspora. Some, such as the ultra-orthodox *Haredim* and the classic Reform Movement, rejected Zionism and its call for mass-repatriation altogether. Following Israel's independence in 1948, all barriers on Jewish immigration to Zion were lifted and strong incentives for them to do so were put in place. Zionism would had the power and resources to support and even actively seek the dismantling of Jewish communities around the world, as indeed happened in places such as North Africa, Iraq, Russia and Ethiopia.

401. Yet, **Judaism's Flexigidity of place and language persist into the 21st century.** Despite efforts of the State of Israel to the contrary, the Jewish Diaspora is vibrant and – in a development that would have been inconceivable to the early Zionist ideologues – a large Diaspora of Israelis has emerged. Furthermore, while in Israel a growing number of people speak Hebrew as their mother tongue without mastering any other Jewish language or vernacular, in the Diaspora, a very significant number of Jews, particularly in the USA, do not speak Hebrew at all. Thus, **while Judaism has proven unwilling to break with its Flexigidity of place, in the area of language, Flexigidity is waning.**

A Hybrid of Openness and Insularity, Idealism and Realism

402. **The permanent tensions in Judaism between universalism and particularism and between openness and insularity were central to shaping Zionism.** Many of Zionism's founders were *Maskilim* who envisioned a Jewish polity that would be modern and deeply engaged with the world. Meanwhile, religious Zionists tended to be more focused on the particularist aspects of the Jewish state, and therefore more prone to being insular. Thus, both universalism and particularism, openness to and insularity from the world were integral to Zionism since its inception, shaping its identity, institutions and course and being essential for its success.

403. **Zionism housed both idealism and crude pragmatism.** Its approach to nationhood and state-building was often messianic and religious by character. It aspired to realize a vision, which was initially highly improbable. However, its implementation was pragmatic. Zionism's claim to Zion stemmed from the Torah, but it pragmatically withdrew its demand for ancestral territories in Trans-Jordan, and accepted the Partition Plans of the Peel Commission in 1936 and then of the United Nations General Assembly in 1947. It embraced socialism but legitimized entrepreneurship, working with Jewish Diaspora capital, in particular from the USA. It collaborated with and confronted the British simultaneously, and it signed the Transfer Agreement *(Heskem Ha'ha'avara)* with Nazi Germany in 1933 to facilitate the *aliyah* of German Jewry. Its pragmatism was captured by the slogan 'another dounam, another goat' *(od dunam od ez)*.

Economic Self-Determination Toward Inclusive Growth

404. **Economic self-determination, prosperity and wellbeing have been integral to the aspirations of the Jewish national movement.** Zionism sought to create a new category of landowning and self-sustaining Jews, the Hebrews, and to address the deep poverty and allegedly unhealthy social and economic structure of Jewish communities, particularly in Eastern Europe but also in Arab countries.

405. **Zionism took after Judaism in balancing wealth-creation with strong social obligations.** These tendencies emanated from its forefathers: Moses Montefiore was a successful businessman and Moses Hess was a socialist. They are echoed in the works of Herzl, Ben-Gurion and others.

The five waves of immigration included all shades of economic and social ideology, from free marketeers to communists. The Hebrew society of the *Yishuv* comprised of small business owners, large industrialists, a service economy, a strong bureaucracy, socialist communities and a class of craftsman in both agricultural and urban settings. They built a web of institutions that addressed collective needs in areas such as healthcare, welfare, sports and education.

406. Meanwhile, **as of the Second Aliyah, the socialist worldview ascended to the leadership of the Hebrew society and became synonymous with it.** It is doubtful that this cohort was ever a majority. Yet, their ideological motivation, organization, institutions and leaders – primarily David Ben-Gurion and Berl Katzanelson (1887-1944) – granted them the mantle of leadership. They designed a unique and pragmatic hybrid of socialism, capitalism and nationalism, committing their workers' movement to serving national objectives beyond their sectorial needs. The *Histadrut* labor union viewed itself as the executive arm of the entire Zionist movement in settlement, immigration, defense and state-building as of the late 1930s and as late as the first decade of the State of Israel.

407. **By the establishment of the State of Israel, in 1948, the *Yishuv* had become a prosperous community, with the societal infrastructure for achieving its ultimate goal of full political and economic self-determination.** It was an exceptionally egalitarian and cohesive society, where both socialist and capitalist worldviews co-existed. Wealth-creation was legitimate, yet checked by high obligations for societal responsibility through philanthropy and taxation. It had developed all aspects of infrastructures and utilities essential for statehood such as water and electricity companies, sea ports, an airliner and a shipping company. The industrious Hebrew community, less than one third of the population under the British Mandate, became the economic engine of the entire polity, including the Arab population.

The Foundation of a Jewish Majority

408. **Another pillar of Zionism has been the establishment and preservation of a Jewish majority within the Hebrew polity.** David Ben-Gurion framed the fundamental ailment of the Diaspora as being a non-sovereign minority. Therefore, he called for the creation of a Jewish sovereign majority in Zion, which was essential for the Hebrew society he envisioned. His logic stipulated that such a polity can be Jewish

and democratic only if Jews were a majority. Otherwise, protecting the Jewishness of the Hebrew polity would mandate granting Jews immunities and privileges in spite of their being a minority. Such a political regime would necessarily be a non-democratic one, and therefore inevitably illegitimate in the eyes of the Jewish People and the world.

409. Thus, **as of the 1930s with the ascent of Ben-Gurion to leadership, the quest for establishing a sovereign Jewish majority became central to Zionism.** Initially, this was to be achieved by mass repatriation and strategic acquisition of territories in different areas of Zion. In 1937, when the idea of partition of the land was first raised by the Peel Commission and accepted by the Zionist leadership, the *Yishuv* already numbered a few hundred thousand Jews, concentrated in distinct geographic areas. Henceforth, the acceptance of the need to forgo sovereignty over some ancestral lands in order to ensure a Jewish majority became a central theme in Zionist discourse. It underlay Israel's acceptance of the November 1947 United Nations General Assembly Resolution 181 that enshrined the principle of two-states-for-two-peoples by declaring a 'Jewish state' and an 'Arab state' in the territories of the British Mandate. In the 1947-1949 War which followed, Arab-Palestinian society imploded and many departed to Lebanon, Syria, Jordan and Gaza. The newly established State of Israel would not allow their return.

From Powerlessness to a Military Power

410. **One of the key areas where Zionism would part ways from the traditions of the Diaspora, demonstrating remarkable adaptability, would be in defense and military affairs.** In a slow process that lasted nearly a century as of the 1880s, Jews would transition from absolute powerlessness to being arguably the per-capita most militarily powerful nation in the world. This astounding transformation involved innovative philosophy, institutions, structures, patterns of conduct and radical experimentation.

411. **The starting point could not be lower: throughout centuries of Diaspora life, the mechanisms of safety and security of Jewish communities and their members were shaped by powerlessness**. The defense and protection of Jews and their communities were entirely dependent upon the goodwill of the local sovereign. The *First Aliyah* continued to embrace this outlook, by outsourcing its security to the local Ottoman authorities and to neighboring Arab communities. These

arrangements were persistently maintained in spite of the fact that the first settlements suffered from on-going insecurity.

412. **Self-defense became an ideological tenet of the *Second Aliyah*.** The outlook of its members was shaped by the trauma of the pogroms in Russia, as well as by their long-term view toward Jewish statehood, which mandated a nucleus of a Hebrew defense force. As of 1907, they established associations for self-protection, the most important of which was *HaShomer* (literally, 'The Guardian').

413. **The *Third Aliyah* laid the foundations for a national defense organization,** the *Haganah* (literally, 'Defense'), which was established in 1920. The formative moment of transition from localized guardianship to national defense came in April 1921, when an Arab mob attacked Hebrew settlements. Thereafter, the defense forces of the Jewish community evolved from one round of violence to another, in 1921, 1929 and 1936-39.

414. **Over time, the *Yishuv* began to develop a more activist and offensive military outlook.** The Arab riots of 1929 represent the beginning of this transformation: hitherto, the Hebrew National Institutions embraced an approach of 'constraint' *(havlagah)*, which was exclusively defensive and localized. Its objective was to sustain British political support for Hebrew statehood. The 1929 riots led to an outcry for a more aggressive and offensive approach against the Arab population and even against the British. This debate would lead, in 1931, to a split in the *Haganah* and to the establishment of the *Irgun Tzva'i Leumi* (literally: National Military Organization, also known by the acronym *Etzel*) under the leadership of Ze'ev Jabotinsky.

415. **The Arab revolt of 1936-39 *(HaMered HaAravi HaGadol)* was the first 'total' confrontation between the *Yishuv* and the Arab community, which ended with an Arab defeat and with the framing of the so-called Two-State Solution.** The Arabs sought to establish an Arab state in Mandatory Palestine, to stifle the Hebrew community and to cancel the plans to establish a Hebrew state. Their tactics combined a systematic campaign of terrorism and guerilla warfare, economic boycott and political action against the Hebrew community and the British. Meanwhile, the *Yishuv* sought to reaffirm the British commitment to a Jewish national home by collaborating with the British against Arab aggressions and by exercising caution in use of military force. Consequently, in May 1937,

the British Peel Commission suggested, for the first time, the partition of Mandatory Palestine into Jewish and Arab states based on a demographic logic and on the principle of two-states-for-two-peoples, thus enshrining the idea of Jewish statehood. Eventually, this confrontation ended with an Arab political, economic and military debacle, and with the Jews continuing to pursue immigration, land acquisition and settlement.

416. Thus, **Jewish acceptance and Arab rejection of the logic of partition as of 1936 should have been expected.** For Zionism, the partition decision represented a historical achievement that was founded upon nearly a century of collective effort against tremendous adversity. For the Arabs it represented a political and diplomatic defeat.

417. **World War II provided another boost to the Hebrew defense forces.** While the Arab leadership, under Haj Amin Al-Husseini (1897-1974), endorsed the Nazis, the *Yishuv* mobilized its own military capabilities to support the Allied Forces and specifically the British in their effort to liberate Europe. Thus, the *Yishuv* not only lived up to its mission of serving the cause of the entire Jewish People, but also acquired invaluable military expertise. Meanwhile, the Warsaw Ghetto Rebellion notwithstanding, the Jews of Europe were framed as being led 'as sheep to the slaughter' *(ke'tzon la'tevach)* with no one to protect them from their awful fate. Furthermore, the Zionist Movement was accused of indifference to the plight of European Jewry, with the exception of those who were associated with it. However, henceforth, the powerful narrative of 'never again' emerged, further legitimizing the necessity of a national home for the Jewish People as a safe haven for all Jews and the build-up of a military force capable of defeating all of its adversaries.

418. **Zionism's attitude toward the Arab population in Zion was framed by Judaism's four meta-narratives.** In Zionism's early outlook, Jewish nationhood and the ideal of *or la'goim* were complementary because of the progress and human development that a Jewish polity was supposed to bring to the local Arab population, which was seen as under-developed. However, as early as the late 1890s, Ahad Ha'Ahm feared an inevitable confrontation with the Arab population. His vision of 'Cultural Zionism' called for the Hebrew community in Zion to become a qualitative cultural beacon for world Jews. That vision did not require mass repatriation and significant land acquisition, and was partially designed to avert such

an otherwise inevitable clash with the Arabs.[300] Nevertheless, by the early 1920s, the assertive expansion of the Hebrew settlement as part of the Jewish national revival helped crystallize the national identity of the Arab population, as well. One approach of Zionism on the left, inspired by Marxist and socialist ideals, aimed for coexistence between Jews and Arabs, who were both allegedly 'oppressed,' albeit in different ways. While a small minority believed in co-existence within a unified democratic society of Jews and Arabs, the majority, led by David Ben-Gurion, accepted that ensuring a Jewish majority would require partition of the land. The more nationalist group, led by Ze'ev Jabotinsky, rejected the notion that the Arab population would ever accept the Hebrew society in their midst. They opposed any territorial compromise and believed in the erection of an 'Iron Wall' *(Kir HaBarzel)*, i.e. in militarily frustrating all Arab efforts to destroy the Hebrew community until they accepted it. David Ben-Gurion's outlook would eventually mix the two: embracing the political logic of partition and the security logic of the Iron Wall.

1948: A Sovereign Hebrew Hub of the Jewish Worldwide Web

419. **The establishment of the State of Israel in 1948 and the War of Independence represented the culmination of nearly one hundred years of monumental Jewish effort.** On November 29, 1947 the United Nations General Assembly accepted a decision to partition the territory of the British Mandate into two states, granting Jews fifty two percent of that land, while declaring Jerusalem as a Corpus Separatum to be governed by the United Nations Trusteeship Council. The State of Israel was officially established on May 14, 1948, upon the departure of the British High Commissioner, while already being engulfed within the flames of war. In the first phase of the fighting – between the UN decision in November 1947 and the proclamation of Israel in May 14, 1948 – local Arab mobs attacked the communities of the *Yishuv*. Initial significant Arab successes turned into decisive setbacks and the Arab-Palestinian leadership collapsed. By the end of the war the majority of the Arab population would become refugees in Lebanon, Syria, Jordan and Gaza. On May 15, 1948, five Arab armies attacked the nascent State of Israel with the declared intention to destroy it and to decimate its Jewish community. Yet again, initial advances turned into a humiliating defeat for all but the Jordanian forces. The war ended in March 1949 with

---

300 See in "A Truth from Eretz Israel", in *All the Writings of Ahad Ha'Ahm*, The Jerusalem Publishing House, 1953. His article *"Lo Zu HaDerech"* ('This is not the way'), appeared in HaMelitz, 1889.

an astounding military victory and the conquest of an additional twenty six percent of the land, including most of the Negev and the Galilee. The casualties of the Yishuv were heavy, with over six thousand dead, amounting to one percent of the population. Yet, during the nearly sixteen months of fighting, the *Haganah* matured from being a well-organized militia into an army, bolstered by thousands of overseas volunteers, many of them experienced Jewish veterans of World War II.

420. **At that time, the *Yishuv* was already a remarkably successful, innovative and inspiring Hebrew hub of the Jewish worldwide web.** Within seventy years, Jews were able to establish their economic, societal and political self-determination, having overhauled and adapted the values, institutions and patterns of conduct of Diaspora life. The Hebrew society was made up of many diverse settlements and communities, including *kibbutzim*, hundreds of agricultural settlements, cities and townships and the growing metropolis of Tel Aviv. It was also made up of a myriad of Zionist organizations, most notably the Jewish Agency, the *Haganah* and the *Histadrut*. It had revived the Hebrew language and created a new category of Jews who owned land, were self-sufficient and defended themselves, the Hebrews. It was a resilient and prosperous community, having demonstrated remarkable growth and adaptability in the face of deep political and economic upheaval. Zion now served as a seat of Jewish spiritual, intellectual, administrative and religious leadership, enshrined with the Flexigid mission of the Jewish People.

421. **Israel's Declaration of Independence and its symbols integrated and institutionalized the four meta-stories of Judaism into the modern polity.** The language of the declaration, the emblem of the state and the anthem are all rooted in the narrative of Jewish nationhood. The declaration speaks of past sovereignty, forced exile, uninterrupted loyalty to Zion and eventual repatriation. At the heart of the emblem of the State of Israel is the *Menorah* depicted as it was engraved on the Arch of Titus in Rome, where it is being taken away by Roman soldiers following the destruction of the Temple. The anthem speaks of the ancient hope of the Jewish People to return to Zion and to live freely in it. Yet, Israel's Declaration of Independence also invokes the covenant between God and the People of Israel, by framing the modern State of Israel in the context of the age-old dream of redemption and of the ingathering of the exiles, as well as by placing trust in the "Rock of Israel" *(Tzur Israel)*. It embraced the narrative of peoplehood by framing the State of Israel in the context of the dreams and destiny of the entire Jewish People, and

committed the nascent and small state to its service. And, it pledges to contribute to the advancements of all inhabitants of the land and of the entire Middle East.

422. **Israel emerged from its War of Independence as a remarkably inspiring success story,** realizing Herzl's 1897 premonition that a State of the Jewish People would be established within fifty years. Three years after the Shoah, when millions of Jews were helplessly fed into the crematoriums, it represented a new type of a Jewish person: proud, confident, defiant, capable, pioneering, self-reliant and successful. The Hebrew community in Zion was perhaps the most vibrant and diverse in the world, second only to New York City. Its outlook inspired millions of Jews to study Hebrew, to join Zionist associations, to support Israel politically, to contribute money and, ultimately, to immigrate to it, to *make aliyah.* In this respect, Ahad Ha'Ahm's vision was effectuated: Israel was born as a spiritual beacon for the Jewish world.

1948-2010: Peak and Crisis of Israel's Flexigid Society

This section describes the manner in which the successes of the State of Israel over the first two decades of its existence until 1967 embodied tremendous adaptability, which it inherited from the Flexigid structure of the *Yishuv* and the Diaspora. It then outlines the ways in which Israel became rigid, abandoning key elements of the Flexigidity of its society, which underlay its remarkable achievements.

1948-1967: The Peak of Zionism's Flexigidity

423. **Within a twenty-year period until 1967, Israeli society broke away from Diaspora traditions.** Until the early 1900s, the *Yishuv* did not represent a breakaway from the legacy of the Diaspora. Yet, by 1948, it had already developed its own distinct institutions, structures, language, symbols, heroes and villains that were unique in the Jewish world. Israel's breakaway from Diaspora traditions accelerated following the proclamation of its independence. Thereafter, Israel needed to establish effective governance over its territory, to absorb mass immigration and to contend with a minority that hitherto had been a bitter enemy. During the following years – as Israel grew in population and strength, and the center of gravity of the Jewish world shifted in its direction – the Hebrew society in Zion began to emerge as a new category in the Jewish world.

424. **During this period and in spite of powerful adversity, Israel became a regional military superpower, frustrating Arab hopes and aspirations to physically destroy it.** The 1947-1949 victory was overwhelming. In the 1950s, Israel became integral to the Western block, building nuclear capabilities, establishing its technological edge and arming itself with the most modern weapons. 1967 saw a stunning military victory achieved within six days against a coalition of Egypt, Syria and Jordan and a takeover of the Sinai Peninsula, the Gaza Strip, the West Bank and the Golan Heights. Jews could now visit the Old City of Jerusalem and pray at the Wailing Wall *(Kotel)* to which they had been denied access by the Jordanians. In Hebron, Jews were now able to visit the Tomb of the Patriarchs *(Me'arat HaMachpela)* – which, according to Jewish tradition, was purchased by Abraham – for the first time since the 14th century. And, Sinai oil fields granted Israel access to energy. Shortly thereafter, a close alliance with the USA emerged, and Israel became a leading force in the struggle against the Soviet Block.

By 1967, Israel secured its physical existence by frustrating Arab hopes, intentions and actions to destroy it through the use of force. The self-perceived David had turned into a Goliath in the eyes of many. Zionism sought to revolutionize the life of Jews and Jewish communities through settlement *(hityashvut)*, labor *(avodah)* and defense *(shmira)*. The 1967 victory represented the ultimate validation of this outlook, which elevated the stature of every Jew around the world. Israeli society experienced a period of exhilaration, prosperity and confidence.

425. At the same time, **Israel's population grew five-fold from 1948 to 1970 with the ingathering of immigrants from nearly one hundred countries.** Upon its establishment in 1948, Jews in Israel numbered six hundred thousand. Within two years, the population doubled. By 1970 it reached three million. In some cases, entire Jewries repatriated, such as from Yemen and Iraq, while in the case of Moroccan and Romanian Jewries, the majority emigrated either to Israel or to other countries. Smaller numbers came from developed nations such as Australia, Canada, Europe and the USA. Thus, the demographic center of gravity of the Jewish People steadily shifted in Israel's direction.

426. **This was also a period of explosive economic development**. The first few years of unemployment, shortage and low foreign currency reserves – known as the Austerity Period *(Tkufat HaTzena)* – ended following the signing of the 1952 Reparation Agreement with Germany. Thereafter, Israel experienced an episode of sustained high real growth that continued until 1972, averaging five and a half percent per capita, making Israel one of the fastest developing nations and one of the most remarkable development stories of the 20th century.

427. Furthermore, **the 1967 victory unleashed a new wave of Jewish religious fervor.** For many, that victory validated the framing of the establishment of the State of Israel following the Shoah as possibly hinting at the beginning of 'redemption' *(ge'ulah)*. The unification of Jerusalem by Israel and the reinstitution of Jewish sovereignty over the Old City of Jerusalem, other holy sites and the ancestral lands of Judea and Samaria, were now seen as events of messianic proportions. A powerful coalition of factions, led by the national religious outlook, embarked upon a giant effort of settling the newly seized territories, particularly Judea and Samaria, with an aim toward establishing an unbreakable grip of these territories.

428. **Israel's successes turned the meta-story of nationhood into the dominant story of the Jewish People, and Zionism's attitude became domineering.** By 1967, Zionism ascended to become the leading ideology of the Jewish People, overshadowing the narratives of peoplehood, faith and *or la'goim*. Zionism framed the Jewish nation-state as the ultimate remedy for the troubles of Jews in the Diaspora, claiming the exclusive loyalty of Israelis and of Diaspora Jewry. Indeed, many acquiesced to Zionism's dominance.

429. **Yet, as of 1967, the State of Israel began to face the effects of its remarkable successes: rigidity, corruption of leadership, crisis and the need for adaptation.** The revolutionary phase of the creation of Israel nearly exhausted itself causing major disruptive developments. It fundamentally altered the condition of Judaism, creating many opportunities yet also complicated challenges.

430. **Some of these disruptive developments were essential and integral to Zionism, and therefore inevitable.** For example, the ingathering of the Diasporas, the establishment of sovereignty and becoming a majority in Zion stemmed directly from the Zionist ideology and were central to it. They represented the essence of the historic panacea that Zionism sought to achieve in Judaism and in Diaspora society. As it did.

431. However, **the reality of Jewish sovereignty, the establishment of a bureaucratic government apparatus and the 1967 victory created additional consequences for Judaism.** Primarily, Israel was now in control not only of an Arab minority within so-called Israel proper, but also of a few millions of non-citizens, primarily Palestinians in Gaza and the West Bank, who were seen as 'occupied.' In effect, Israel became overstretched geographically; its economic structure would prove to be overly centralized and rigid; its Zionist ideology came to be overconfidently dominant; its relationship to the Jewish world was now constrained by growing arrogance toward and ignorance of the Jewish Diaspora; and its political system would prove underwhelming. In the immediate aftermath of the 1967 victory, few, like David Ben-Gurion, could foresee the looming and inevitable economic, societal, political, and leadership crisis, which would take decades to resolve.

Mamlachtiyut: The Novelty of Being a Sovereign Majority

432. **Statehood and sovereignty were a novelty for Judaism and Zionism, requiring deep societal adaptation, primarily in two areas: consolidating the power to govern in the hands of a central authority and co-citizenship with the Arab minority.** A new outlook and a massive body of law on issues such as security, military and foreign affairs, economics and education had to be created. The technical legal act, through which the State of Israel adopted the laws of the British Mandatory Government, ushered in decades of Knesset legislation. Over time, an extensive body of Hebrew law was created to address the unique condition of a Jewish nation-state. The highly representative structure of the Knesset gave all factions and voices of Israeli society the right and ability to participate in this process.

433. **The monumental effort of establishing the constitutional and legislative foundations of Jewish statehood was framed by David Ben-Gurion's outlook and vision for Israeli society known as** *Mamlachtiyut (*literally, 'statism'*).*[301] This philosophy envisioned a balance between the strength of the central authority of the Government of Israel, on the one hand, and the liberty of various factions in Israeli society to preserve their unique voice and character, on the other hand. It attempted to turn the many communities, ideologies and factions – not only of the *Yishuv* but also among the immigrants – into a dynamic society led by a cohesive political body with an effective executive.

434. **Initially, this outlook required a concentration and consolidation of power into the hands of the Government of Israel.** As a result of the decentralized structure of the *Yishuv*, this process met fierce resistance by many. Zionist leaders, primarily from the right and the left wings of the political spectrum, became Ben-Gurion's antagonists, fighting for their respective power, influence, independence and legacy. A number of societal fault lines embodied this transformation: *First*, the Knesset and the government needed to take over the responsibility for key civilian areas such as immigration absorption, health care, employment and settlement from party forums, the *Histadrut* and the Jewish Agency. *Second*, the government needed to establish its monopoly over the use of force, and the security establishment needed to be de-politicized. This process unfolded in a few dramatic episodes of politics and even

---

301 See Nir Kedar, *Mamlakhtiyut: David Ben-Gurion Political-Civic Ideas*, Ben-Gurion University Press & Yad Ben-Zvi, 2009.

violence. Most famous among them were the sinking of the weapon ship, *Altalena,* and the dismantling of the Palmach in 1948. *Third,* in 1953 the party-affiliated education system was replaced with a state-sponsored mandatory education system divided into 'streams' *(zramim)* for the secular Jews *(Mamlachti),* modern orthodox Jews *(Mamlachti-Dati),* ultra-orthodox Jews *(HaZerem HaHaredi)* and for Arabs.

435. **The other deep societal challenge faced by Zion's Jews was their transformation into a ruling majority and their relationship with the Arab minority in Israel's midst.** The mass exit of nearly half of the Palestinian-Arab population in 1947-48 and the Jewish immigration that followed irreversibly changed the demographic makeup of the land. Jews now became a sovereign majority in a democracy, which was in control of a significant minority numbering hundreds of thousands of Palestinians. Since Jewish law developed primarily when Jews were a minority, little in it could serve as a relevant source. In fact, the philosophy and practice of this relationship had to be developed and implemented literally overnight beginning during the flames of war.

436. **Ben-Gurion's *mamlachtiyut* provided the framework for the relationship between the state of Israel and its Arab minority, as well.** This outlook framed the Arab citizens as equal rights Israelis within the unitary framework of the national institutions. It therefore called for their full participation in the political process on the local and national levels, similar to all other Israeli citizens. At the same time, it also rejected demands for an elected body that would collectively represent the Arab population as a group before the Government of Israel. Meanwhile, it allowed for Arab individual and collective particularism, such as by using the Arab language in official documents and publications, by recognizing a designated stream of the education system that teaches a particular curriculum in Arabic, and by preserving the stature of the Moslem courts. Hence, Arab parliamentarians served in all Knessets since 1949, even while their communities were managed by a military governorate *(Mimshal Tzva'yi),* which was only dismantled in 1966. Arab citizens have also led their own municipalities and non-governmental organizations and have served in different branches of the government and the judiciary.

437. Nonetheless, **the relationship between the State of Israel and its Arab citizens remains tenuous due to obvious, permanent and inevitable philosophical and practical tensions.** The fundamentals of

the State of Israel – its ethos, law, anthem, symbols, language, national holidays and relationship to world Jewry – embody its Jewishness. At the same time, Israel is a liberal democracy, which functions through its sovereign legislative and executive institutions. This structure creates inherent tensions among the fundamental identity of the State of Israel as the nation-state of the Jewish People, which is also a democracy, and the reality that nearly twenty percent of Israel's population is Arab. That minority population is expected to be loyal to both ethos, that of Israel's Jewishness and of its democracy. In such an environment, Arabs are structurally vulnerable to repeated questioning of their loyalty to the state, even when they function legally and within its sovereign institutions. Furthermore, these tensions are exacerbated by the gap in economic development between Jews and Arabs, which dates back to the days of the British Mandate, and by the exemption of Israeli Arabs from mandatory military and national service. In other words, the relations between the State of Israel and its Arab minority will remain a key challenge for Zionism and the State of Israel in the coming decades. Therefore, they are also a challenge to Judaism.

Disequilibrium of Territory, Demography and Identity

438. **Another disruption to Jewish Flexigidity has been the ideological disequilibrium of Zionism and the overstretch of the State of Israel created by the victory in 1967.** Henceforth, fundamental values dear to many in Diaspora Jewry were no longer consistent with Israel's reality and policies.

439. **Until 1967, Israel was ideologically cohesive and equilibrated among its central ethos, yet physically vulnerable**, particularly at its 'narrow waist' of seventeen kilometers in the area of Netanya. It was a democracy with a very significant Jewish majority. Therefore, the Jewishness of its public sphere was beyond question.

440. **The 1967 war led to confidence in Israel's physical survival, yet also to deep ideological disunity.** The effect of that war was not only a geographic expansion of Israel's territory that made Israelis feel secure, but also the frustration of Arab belief in their ability to destroy it. At the same time, when Israel came to control the West Bank and Gaza with their significant Palestinian population, its founding values were pitted against each other. Israel's Jewishness, territory, demography and democracy were no longer consistent, and the most fundamental

and unique character of Zionism – the existence of a sovereign Jewish majority – was threatened.

441. **Following that war, Israel became overstretched ideologically, militarily and financially.** Ideologically, as mentioned, its founding values were no longer consistent with each other and with reality. Militarily, the Israel Defense Forces was stationed along extended borders, which represented an unacceptable reality to its enemies and therefore inevitably led to future confrontations. Financially, supporting such military capabilities and alignment would become unbearable for Israel's economy.

442. **That overstretch made Israel vulnerable when challenged by pragmatic Arab leadership.** As long as Arab countries remained absolutist and rejectionist, seeking Israel's total destruction, Israel easily mobilized internal forces, demonstrated cohesion and enjoyed broad international legitimacy and support. When Arab leadership accepted Israel's existence and came forward with reasonable initiatives and propositions, Israel's internal cohesion and international support were compromised. The case of Egypt's President Anwar Al Sadat illustrates this point. When President Sadat secretly offered Israel in 1972 a political agreement that would include Israeli withdrawal in Sinai, his offers were disregarded. Yet, similar ideas were accepted by Israel in 1974. In between, the 1973 Yom Kippur War – initiated by Egypt – tamed Israel's hubris and placed the USA as a broker between the parties. Israel's eventual decisive military victory notwithstanding, this war is framed in Israel as a 'trauma' and in Egypt as a 'victory.'

443. Thus, **following the 1973 War, Israel faced three possible courses of development.** *One course of development* was to hold fast to the ancestral territories of Judea, Samaria, Sinai and the Golan and to protect Judaism's supremacy in Israel, while controlling a very large non-Jewish minority. The inevitable impact of this approach would have been a loss of Israel's international legitimacy, disenchantment by many Diaspora Jews and internal disunity. *A second possible course of development* was to hold on to these territories and to Israel's democratic values by granting equal rights to their residents, at the risk of losing Israel's Jewish character, when Jews are no longer a significant majority. *The third option* was to withdraw from the newly liberated and acquired territories or from parts thereof, in order to ensure that Israel's Jewish character and democracy remain consistent with a solid demographic reality.

444. **The meta-stories of Judaism did not offer clear guidance for this predicament**. The story of nationhood, while calling for seizing control over the entire Land of Israel, also emphasizes the quintessential importance of preserving the Jewish majority in the State of Israel. The story of Peoplehood also carries a dialectic message in this regard: while supporting Israel's territorial concessions in order to increase cohesion with liberal Diaspora Jews, it also challenges Israel's right to make such historical compromises in Zion on behalf of the entire Jewish People. Finally, while there are powerful religious voices that call for clinging to the ancestral lands of Judea and Samaria, others invoke Jewish laws and traditions to call for a territorial compromise of these territories in favor of security, peace and the human rights of the Palestinian population of the West Bank and Gaza.

445. Therefore, **the 1967 War ushered in a prolonged period of heated debate, which has been the central fault line of Israeli politics and society**. One faction framed a withdrawal from the 'occupied territories' – whether unilaterally and unconditionally or pending upon an agreement that ensures 'security' and 'peace' – as an existential interest for Israel. Another faction envisioned Israel's eternal control over Judea, Samaria, East Jerusalem, Gaza, the Golan and Sinai. It sought physical settlement there, integration of their economies with Israel's and an extension of Israel's sovereignty and legal jurisdiction over them. During the protests against the withdrawal from Sinai in 1982, the demonstrations against the Oslo Accords between 1993 and 1995, the assassination of Prime Minister Yitzhak Rabin in 1995, and the protest against the withdrawal from Gaza in 2005 these tensions reached boiling points.

446. Nonetheless, **as of the 1970s, Zionism and the State of Israel embarked upon a process of a territorial contraction in order to restore Zionism's equilibrium and decrease Israel's overstretch**. After a rather short debate, the forces of Jewish adaptability powerfully pushed Israel to downsize. To date, there have been three crescendos in this political struggle over the legacy of the 1967 War: *First*, between 1979 and 1982 following the Camp David Accords with Egypt that led to Israel's full withdrawal from Sinai; *Second*, between 1993 and 2001, during the era of the Oslo Process and in lieu of the withdrawals within the West Bank and Gaza and the establishment of a Palestinian Authority led by the Palestine Liberation Organization (PLO); *Third*, in 2004-2005 with Israel's so-called Unilateral Disengagement from Gaza, which included the dismantling of Israel's civilian and military presence there.

In the case of Sinai, following the trauma of 1973, military and economic considerations were central in legitimizing Israel's withdrawal. In the case of Gaza and the West Bank, the underlying logic of the withdrawals was primarily demographic, aiming to save and serve the vision of an independent self-governing, democratic and demographically Jewish state of Israel, which is a legitimate member of the family of nations. In fact, every Israeli Premier since Yitzhak Rabin in 1974 has engaged in this process, even those presumably elected to serve the opposite agenda.

447. **The 1979 Peace Accord with Egypt was a historical achievement for Israel and for Zionism.** Israel withdrew from Sinai in exchange for 'peace.' The Israeli-Egyptian border was the first to be bilaterally agreed upon and internationally endorsed, thus establishing a cornerstone of Israel's fundamental legitimacy according to international law. That agreement ushered in decades of coexistence between the two nations, and allowed Israel to significantly shrink its military and divert resources to more pressing civilian needs. Henceforth, the largest and most significant Arab nation not only recognized Israel and coexisted with it with little friction, but also was at times a strategic ally.

448. **The Oslo Process, the Peace Treaty with Jordan and the Unilateral Withdrawal from Gaza were additional milestones in restoring the equilibrium of Zionism and decreasing its own overstretch.** The cornerstone of the 1993-1995 Oslo Accords was an exchange of letters between PLO Chairman Yasser Arafat and Israel's Prime Minister Yitzhak Rabin, which included mutual recognition. The bi-lateral agreements between Israel and the PLO effectuated a framework for Palestinian state-building through an interim self-governing Palestinian Authority. Henceforth, Israel no longer needed to manage the daily affairs of the Palestinians in Gaza and the West Bank through a Civil Administration. The 1994 Peace Treaty with Jordan further enhanced Israel's fundamental legitimacy, making its border with Jordan bilaterally agreed upon and internationally endorsed, as well. The political assassination of Prime Minister Yitzhak Rabin in 1995 was a major setback in that process. The 2005 Unilateral Disengagement from Gaza rid Israel altogether of its control over close to the one and a half million Palestinians living there. Henceforth, a de-facto independent Palestinian statelet was established in Gaza, yet, unfortunately, that area was soon taken over by Hamas and became hostile territory.

449. At present, **the equilibrium among Zionism's ideals will be determined by the fate of Israel's control over the Palestinian population in the West Bank.** The 1999-2001 Camp David Process attempted to achieve a Permanent Status Agreement with the Palestinians. That agreement should have brought into being a Palestinian state and ended Israel's control over the Palestinian population. That effort failed. Nonetheless, the underlying logic of restoring the equilibrium of Zionism remained powerful, driving Prime Minister Sharon to withdraw from Gaza and to dismantle three settlements in the West Bank. As of 2006, the Olmert Government engaged in serious negotiations with the Palestinian leadership. And, in 2009, Prime Minister Netanyahu of the right-wing Likud party accepted the principle of 'two states for two peoples,' while other leaders in Israel began to entertain the idea of unilateral withdrawal from the West Bank and recognition of the Palestinian Authority as a state there.

450. Meanwhile, **some Arab and international groups that seek Israel's implosion work against ending Israel's control of the Palestinians in order to maintain the present overstretch.** They worked to undermine any agreement that may allow for Israel's withdrawal from or within the West Bank. Their hope is to enhance Israel's overstretch, rejecting any notion of ending the conflict with Israel and of recognizing its right to exist. Therefore, they oppose the 'two-state solution,' which would require recognition of the State of Israel alongside a Palestinian state.

451. **Their alternative political vision calls for a 'one-state solution.'** It envisions a single political unit of Jews and Arabs, where Jews will eventually become a minority and the Jewishness of Israel will be eliminated. To that end, some of them even call for the voluntary dismantling of the Palestinian Authority in order to further overstretch Israel by increasing the economic, diplomatic and ethical burden on it.

452. **In recent years there has been a confluence of political objectives between the de-legitimizers of Israel and Zionism's right-wing.** While espousing diametrically opposed visions of the final outcome, both do not want Israel to end the control over the Palestinian population. This confluence deepens Zionism's quagmire and prolongs its ideological disequilibrium.

National Security: The Predicament Continues

453. **Israel is a regional superpower, representing an absolute departure from the Diaspora model of powerless security.** The Israeli military and defense establishment are remarkable by any standard, all the more so considering Israel's size. The Israel Defense Forces, particularly its air force and intelligence branch, are of the finest in the world, and Israel allegedly possesses nuclear military capabilities. It is one of the few nations that put satellites into orbit, and its civilian defense industries are global leaders. In addition, Israel is a close and intimate ally of the world's greatest superpower, the USA, and maintains outstanding relations with most other world powers. In short, the Jewish People has never had such military might at its disposal.

454. Nonetheless, **the State of Israel is yet to eliminate the existential threat that it faces.** Zionism came to address the perceived perpetual security predicament of Diaspora Jewry and the inherent lack of safety for Jews and Jewish communities. It aspired to do so through a fundamental transformation of Jews from being the 'objects' of history to being its 'subjects,' i.e. from being powerless to possessing and using force to defend themselves and their communities. Indeed, over recent decades Israel has been able to defend itself and to protect its citizenry. Nonetheless, at the beginning of the 21st century, Israel remains a nation whose right to exist is fundamentally challenged and it continues to face daunting physical, political and legal obstacles.

455. *First,* **the challenge of military security and physical survival remains central to Zionism.** The 1936-1939, 1947-1949 and the 1967 Arab attempts to terminate the Zionist project failed. However, Israel has faced a continual need to sustain a powerful military and defense establishment and to use it repeatedly in order to defend itself and its citizens. Major events in this respect include the 1967-1970 War of Attrition along the Suez Canal; the 1973 Yom Kippur War against a concerted attack by Egypt and Syria; the 1982 Lebanon War to secure Israel's Northern communities from Palestinian terrorism, which turned into an eighteen-year-long bleeding presence in Lebanon against the powerful Iran-supported guerrilla army of Hezbollah; the Palestinian terrorism of the 1970s and 1980s; the 1987-1990 first Palestinian popular uprising *(Intifa'adah)*; the 1991 First Gulf War, when missiles were fired on Tel Aviv from Iraq; the Second Palestinian Uprising *(Intifa'adah)* of 2001-2003, during which a Palestinian campaign of terrorism was

waged against Israeli civilians; and Israel's major operations against Hamas in Gaza as of 2007. Additionally, over the years, Israel has conducted thousands of military operations, most of which remain secret. Nonetheless, at present, Israel remains the focal point of radical Islamic fundamentalism, and the Islamic Republic of Iran, Israel's primal foe sworn to its destruction, aspires to regional hegemony and may soon possess military nuclear capabilities. Except for South Korea, it is the only free and democratic society that is under permanent existential threat. In recent years, both Prime Minister Sharon and Prime Minister Netanyahu have invoked the legacy of the 1938 Munich Agreement and the pre-Shoah vulnerability in describing Israel's condition.

456. *Second,* **Israel's political existence is challenged in spite of great strides that were made in this regard.** Since its inception, Zionism has sought explicit international recognition of the right of the Jewish People to self-determination in its own nation-state. The State of Israel inherited that expectation, and further aspired for explicit and tacit de-jure and de-facto Palestinian, Arab, and international recognition of its right to exist and in its boundaries. That goal was realized to varying degrees along the borders with Egypt and Jordan through peace treaties and with Lebanon and Gaza, unilaterally, in 1979, 1994, 2000 and 2005, respectively. However, the right of the Jewish People to self-determination in its own state continues to face broad opposition in the Middle East and beyond.

457. Specifically, **in recent years Israel has been facing attempts to bring about its political implosion through a systematic and systemic assault on its political model known as the 'de-legitimization of Israel.'** Inspired by the collapse of great military powers such as the Soviet Union and South Africa, a network of nations and non-governmental organizations envisions Israel's disappearance as well, in spite of its military might. They work to de-legitimize Israel's right to exist as a state that embodies the right of the Jewish People for self-determination. They reject any notion of explicit or tacit recognition of Israel and of ending the conflict with it. And, they continuously work to single Israel out, demonize and boycott it. Furthermore, many seek to undermine the so-called 'two-state solution' in order to deny Israel the recognition that such a solution would entail, and strive to prolong Israel's control of the Palestinian population in the West Bank, which they view as an asset for their campaign. Some of them even call for voluntary dismantling of the Palestinian Authority in order to exacerbate Israel's overstretch.

458. *Third,* **Israel's alliances with key powers of the Middle East are historically unstable.** In 1978, Israel lost its primary regional ally in Iran, which instead became a sworn enemy. In the 1990s, Israel became a strategic ally of Turkey, though that relationship deteriorated with the rise of an Islamic government there as of 2003. In 2011, with the so-called 'Arab Spring,' the Mubarak regime in Egypt collapsed, shaking the peace accord between the countries. At a certain period in 2012, when Egypt was taken over for a short while by the Islamic Brotherhood, it seemed as if Israel may be in tension and confrontation with the three great powers of the Middle East: Turkey, Egypt and Iran. Luckily, while that scenario has not materialized to date, it highlights the great challenges that Israel continues to face in its region.

459. *Fourth,* **Israel's civilians are the most threatened among developed nations.** A primary objective of Israel's government has been to turn Israel into a space that is safe for its citizens, tourists and investors so that they may conduct themselves in oblivion to its broader national security concerns. Indeed, to date, Israel has succeeded in doing so, with few and brief exceptions such as during the Second Palestinian uprising in 2001-2002 and during the Second Lebanon War in 2006. However, Hezbollah and Hamas have been amassing sophisticated capabilities to disrupt Israel's civilian space. While Israel has been gearing to protect itself through defensive systems, deterrence and surgical offensive capabilities, in recent years, its civilian population was repeatedly targeted and remains highly threatened.

460. *Finally,* **Israel's effect on the security and wellbeing of Jews in the Diaspora holds a mixed record.** Zionism aspired to increase the safety of Jews around the world. Initially, its outlook was myopic, expecting them to permanently resolve the predicament of their personal security by relocation to Israel. Indeed, as mentioned, millions of Jews repatriated, primarily from Europe, North Africa and across the Middle East. Furthermore, while the security of Jews around the world remains primarily dependent upon their local governments, Israel, through its security establishment, has been doing a lot to help protect Diaspora Jewish communities primarily from terrorism. Nonetheless, Diaspora Jews have been occasionally targeted because of Israel, both politically and through terrorism and violence.

461. *In conclusion*, **Israel's national security continues to face daunting challenges.** Israel's successes have been remarkable, and, at the beginning of the 21st century it is stronger than ever before. Yet, key pillars of its national security outlook – primarily its physical existence, the safety of its citizens and its fundamental legitimacy – remain threatened in a rapidly changing and emerging environment.

Ingathering of Diasporas and Narrowing Exposure to Humanity

462. **The ingathering of the Diasporas into the State of Israel has dramatically affected Jewish Flexigidity.** In 1950, the Knesset passed the Law of Return *(Hok HaShvut)*, which granted all Jews the right to settle in Israel and gain citizenship. The law was amended in 1972 to also offer immediate citizenship to those who have a Jewish grandparent, as well as to their spouses and underage children. Immigration that followed transformed the State of Israel and Diaspora Jewry: while Israel's population grew nearly six-fold in twenty years and twelve-fold in sixty years, dozens of Diasporas were disintegrated and even dismantled altogether. Due to the compounded effect of World War II, the Shoah and the upheaval of 1948-1967 surrounding Israel's establishment, the geographic spread of the Jewish People was profoundly transformed.

463. **This transformation decreased the breadth and diversity of the Jewish network.** Eighty percent of the Jews of the world are currently located in the USA and the State of Israel. The vast majority of the rest of Diaspora Jews – with the notable exceptions of Russia, France and Argentina – are now concentrated in a few English-speaking nations, primarily Canada, United Kingdom and Australia. Hence, Judaism's exposure to humanity and to societies around the world – to different cultures, philosophies, outlooks, languages and customs – decreased, and therefore, its systemic resilience, as well.

464. As mentioned earlier, **the prosperity and security of the Jewish People in the Diaspora required extensive and intensive interaction with many polities, cultures and faiths.** This dialogue occurred in areas as diverse as trade, finance, medicine, technology, philosophy and diplomacy. It underlay Judaism's acquaintance with foreign languages, practices and conducts, and the worldwide web of relationships that the Jewish People already had at the beginning of the 20th century.

465.   Furthermore, **the leadership of the Zionist Movement was exceptionally disposed toward international affairs**. Many Zionist leaders were cosmopolitan, particularly who that were brought up in Central Europe in educated families of *Maskilim*. They often mastered several languages and were well-traveled across Europe, where they had family members and long-standing associations. Herzl, Chaim Weitzman, David Ben-Gurion, Golda Meir and Abba Eban embodied this model and were master statesmen.

466.   **This leadership was particularly fit to serve Zionism during a period of great global instability, which required maneuvering regional and international politics and the building of shifting alliances.** Key events included the breakdown of the Ottoman Empire, the First World War, the creation of the Soviet Union, the turbulent 1920s, the establishment of the League of Nations and other global institutions, the rise of Fascism, World War II and the immediate post-war era. During the 1950s and 1960s, in the bi-polar environment of the Cold War, the State of Israel cast its lot with the West and developed strategic alliances with France, Germany and then with the USA.

467.   **The universal outlook of the founding leaders of Israel also underlay its prominence in the area of international development.** Inspired by the vision of being a light unto the nations, and as a response to its regional isolation following its establishment, Israel reached out to developing African, Asian and Latin American nations. It developed extensive relationships with them and became a leading nation in international assistance on a per-capita basis during the 1960s. Unfortunately, following the 1973 War and the energy crisis that followed, many of these countries severed their diplomatic relations with Israel under Arab pressure, although extensive business and economic ties continued.

468.   **The turning point for Israel's international outlook was the 1967-1973 period, when the Arab-Israeli conflict became a focal point of global tension, and Israel became the subject of diplomatic hostility and de-legitimization.** At that time, under Arab and Soviet pressure, all Non-Aligned and Eastern Bloc nations discontinued their relations with Israel. In the United Nations and other international organizations, Israel was often singularly blamed for the Arab-Israeli conflict, suffering countless condemnations of its policies and practices. This was in spite of Arab rejection of Israel's very existence and comparatively draconian mass-oppressions in nearby countries. A low point was the 1975 United

Nations General Assembly Resolution 3379, which determined that "Zionism is a form of racism and racial discrimination." In 1991, this resolution would become the only United Nations resolution ever to be revoked. Furthermore, as mentioned, Israel was systematically delegitimized, and the view of Jews as a people and the legitimacy of their association to Zion were rejected. This de-legitimization continues to take place not only in Arab countries that are enemies of Israel, but also in Egypt, Jordan and the Palestinian Authority who signed peace treaties with Israel and among certain liberal circles in Europe.

469. Over time and in response, **many Israelis embraced a discourse of disenchantment with and distrust toward the world and its international institutions.** The ancient prophecy that the Jewish People shall dwell alone *(ahm le'badad ishkon)*[302] was seen as being realized. Israeli leaders and citizens downplayed the significance of the international community, further distancing Israel from the world through their outlook and conduct. The budget of the Government of Israel for foreign relations decreased and Israel never resumed its leadership position in international development.

470. Furthermore, **the factions of Israeli society that celebrated the particularism of Judaism and Israel grew in number and political influence.** The national religious group that emphasizes the nationalist tendencies, and the ultra-orthodox group that embraces the particularism of Judaism, grew demographically. Consequently, their influence on Israeli society and politics increased, as well, pushing Israeli mindset and practices toward greater insularity.

471. Nonetheless, **Israel continues to maintain a robust global outlook.** Being a de-facto geopolitical island, such outreach to the world is essential for its national security, diplomatic relations, international standing and economic development. Many Israeli manufacturers must export in order to thrive, because the Israeli economy is too small. Many Israeli individuals seek significant personal and professional experiences in foreign countries in business, academia and the arts, which cannot be attained in Israel. In fact, Israel leads the world in exporting talent, and the globetrotting community of Israelis is outstanding in size.

472. **That outlook is heavily concentrated in the USA.** This has been in large part an outcome of Israel's relative international isolation. It is

---

302 Numbers 23:9

also a consequence of Israel's shared strategic interests and values with the USA, as well as of the influence and mobilization of the Jewish community there and its powerful pro-Israel lobby, AIPAC. While fewer Israelis have meaningful ties with European society, many of Israel's political, military, business, academic, civil-service and civil-society leaders were educated in American universities and spent formative periods there. And, nearly a quarter of Israel's diplomats are stationed across North America. All of the above notwithstanding, in recent years, focus is also shifting to other rising nations, primarily China and India.

473. *In conclusion*, **at the beginning of the 21st century, openness and insularity, universalism and particularism continue to shape Israel's outlook.** Israel houses very insular voices, which are happy to disengage from an international community that they view as biased against and hostile to Israel. Israel also houses a significant and prominent community of global citizens who are disproportionally represented among international corporations and organizations, and among the global academic, art and business communities. Many Israelis are engaged with a global effort to improve the condition of human development around the world within the vision of *tikkun olam*, and the Israeli community in the area of innovation, science and technology is a global leader.

From Meritocratic to Political Leadership

474. **One of the most fundamental departures of the State of Israel from the Flexigid legacy of the Diaspora has been in the area of leadership.** The leadership of Diaspora communities has been mostly meritocratic and based upon intellectual, administrative and diplomatic skills, emerging in self-organized, self-governed and self-reliant communities. Every community was made up of multiple institutions that were led by lay leaders and professionals. No central authority could control all communities into a monolithic mold. Individual communities too were often decentralized, with multiple voices of leadership. Furthermore, the impact of every leader in the Jewish Diaspora decreased with distance, and the collective evolution of the Jewish People was shaped through the interplay between multiple leaders and centers of leadership. Naturally, **the establishment of the State of Israel and the institution of its government apparatus represented a radical departure from this largely meritocratic leadership structure of the Diaspora into a heavily politicized and centralized structure of government.**

475. *First,* **inspired by the vision of** *Mamlachtiyut,* **the government sought to centralize power and control into its hand and away from communities, party forums and non-governmental organizations.**[303] In the early 1950s, Israel's newly instituted government was suddenly responsible for providing education, welfare, employment and healthcare to the residents of the *Yishuv,* as well as to hundreds of thousands of new immigrants. It had to build hundreds of additional community centers *(matnasim),* early childhood centers *(tipot halav),* schools and other community institutions, appointing their management and underwriting their budgets.

476. Consequently, **the civic leadership and philanthropists who traditionally led Diaspora Jewish communities and the** *Yishuv* **were relieved of their communal responsibilities and sidelined by the government.** As national budgets could suddenly underwrite entire bureaucracies, accountability no longer flowed 'downwards' to the community but 'upwards' to politicians and bureaucrats. Hence, the needs of the community no longer guided decisions, but rather political considerations and partisan favoritism. As Rabbi Sacks writes: "The result was … weakening the very institutions that had been the source of Jewish strength in the past: communities, charities, voluntary associations and community based schools."[304]

477. *Second,* **the philosophy of the 'melting pot'** *(kur hituch)* **further dismembered the traditional community-based structure of Diaspora Jewry in Israel.** This ideal called for the new immigrants to be co-opted into the Hebrew society and turned into Hebrew persons. This concept denied the legitimacy of the authentic communal identity of the immigrants and prevented them from reestablishing their communities in Israel.

478. *Third,* **mass immigration during Israel's first years diluted the community-based web structure of the** *Yishuv.* Within a year of its proclamation, the population of the State of Israel was doubled, mostly by refugees from Europe and by immigrants from places such as Iraq and Yemen. Veteran communities of the *Yishuv* were expected to participate in accommodating the newcomers and in turning them into 'Israelis.' In some cases, communities grew several-fold within only a few years. These communities and their institutions could not absorb so many ad-

---

303 See Sacks, *Future Tense,* p. 174 on the threat of '*Mamlachtiyut*' to the societal structure of Judaism.

304 Sacks, *Future Tense,* p. 169

hoc assemblies of poor and dislocated families and individuals from many nations and cultures in such a short period of time. They were irreversibly changed.

479. *Finally,* **in 1985 the Government of Israel withdrew from and privatized Israel's network of community institutions.** The economic and budgetary crisis of the early 1980s not only forced the Government of Israel to contract by more than forty percent, but also ushered in a new outlook, which was imported primarily from the USA.[305] It held that a market system provides the ultimate remedy to society's ills, dwarfing the role of public and communal institutions. It therefore called for privatization of national assets. In a process that lasted about twenty-five years, key services and sectors were sold to the private sector or subjected to narrow criteria of cost-effectiveness and budgetary balance. Within this process, the Government of Israel shed the responsibility for community institutions that were turned into service providing platforms and seen primarily through budgetary for-profit lens.

480. Hence, **Israeli society was no longer organized as a network of communities, and the institutions that had served as its building blocks were depleted of their mission, resources, leadership and vision.** By the 1990s, the basic societal unit of Israel's society was no longer the 'community' but rather the individual household, and the organizing framework became the municipal government. Lay leadership became sidelined and marginalized by politicians and bureaucrats, and institutions within the community were no longer accountable to its citizenry. In fact, Israel represents the first case in Jewish history where a significant number of committed Jews do not live within a community.

Furthermore, **the structure of Israel's government also affected the dynamics of leadership within Israel's Jewish society.**

481. *First,* **the organization of Israeli society as a 'contractual democracy' compromises the Flexigid dynamics of adaptability among the network of communities and small units.**[306] In such a system, power is

---

305 See Sacks, *Future Tense*, p. 174 on the "…adoption of Thatcherism and Reaganomics and reliance on the market rather than the state. The result was the growth of consumerism and what J. K. Galbraith called private affluence and public poverty. Neither of these is the covenantal way…"

306 See Wikipedia entry on Consociationalism at: http://en.wikipedia.org/wiki/Consociationalism.

often divided based on political agreements among different parties that represent distinct constituencies and interest groups. Mapai's *Histadrut* and healthcare providers embodied this notion in the past, while nowadays the *Haredim* and the national-religious factions have assumed a similar role. These groups de-facto control entire societal apparatuses such as schools, welfare services, corporations and even security, often viewing their sectorial needs as synonymous with and even superior to those of the collective and the state. Israel's political and electoral system rewards their focused and disciplined political conduct with disproportional power and influence over the rest of the society, which sways resources in their favor and distorts the natural dynamics of Jewish adaptability, which are based upon the interplay among many small units.

482. *Second,* **Israel's elected officials became more distant from their communities.** During the first decades of Israel's existence, parties had local branches, leadership and activists in every community. Party forums allowed for authentic grassroots participation in the political process. Over time, power shifted in the direction of party barons who controlled agenda, appointments and policies. Grassroots participation became ineffectual and therefore declined. Some political parties experimented with the model of party primaries, which was imported from the USA. But that system, too, favored powerful organized groups, and had its own shortcomings. In the nineteenth Knesset, elected in 2013, this reached a point where two thirds of the Members of Knesset were effectively appointed by the party leader who commands their exclusive loyalty and accountability.

483. *In conclusion,* **the traditional structure of communal leadership of the Flexigid society has been dismantled in Israel.** The Diaspora model that created direct and authentic connection and dialogue among communal leaders and their constituents practically disappeared from Israel. Communities no longer own and shape their institutions, which are controlled by politicians through government entities, distant from their constituents and minimally accountable to them. The legacy of meritocratic leadership, whose legitimacy directly stems from communities and their institutions, became rare in Israeli society.

484. Thus, **over time, a mismatch emerged between the nature of Diaspora leadership and that of Israel's.** In the Diaspora, successful community leaders typically rise to power meritocratically based on a track record of service, commitment and dedication to and generosity toward the

community. They are usually highly experienced, have a record of communal leadership and often serve extended tenures. This grants key Diaspora institutions with the stability essential for management and leadership. By contrast, Israel's political elite is highly politicized and sectorial, nonprofessional and has powerful incentives for short-sightedness.

485. **In spite of the above, Israeli society created alternative tracks for meritocratic leadership.** *First,* mayors became a central force in shaping Israeli society. They are more directly responsive to the needs of the population than members of Knesset and are accountable to local communities. They not only have set terms in office of five years, but also good prospects of getting re-elected for additional tenures. *Second,* non-profits and philanthropies assume a growing role in Israeli society based on their individual respective skills. *Third,* some corporations within the Israeli business community have committed to serving societal needs within and through their business models. In other words, the void created by the decline of Israel's government is gradually being filled by other sources of leadership in Israeli society.

Non-Inclusive Economy and Society

486. **The non-inclusiveness of Israel's society represents another major departure of Israel from the legacy of Jewish Flexigidity.** It not only weakens the fabric of Israel's society but also compromises Israel's ability to tap into its talent when confronting the formidable challenges that it faces.

487. **Universal access to education and a transparent system of mobility through the world of Torah were the key vehicles for turning Diaspora Jewish society into a highly inclusive one.** While wealth-creation was encouraged, high obligations were established for sharing wealth with the community by contributing to its institutions, schools, charity, the world of Torah and to the Jewish community in Zion.

488. **The society and economics of the *Yishuv,* and of the State of Israel in its earlier decades, were inspired by this Diaspora legacy of inclusiveness.** The Hebrew community blended socialist ideas, social values of mutual responsibility and a 'big government' that routinely intervened in, designed and guided the economy with capitalist worldviews, an emerging market economy and a vibrant entrepreneurial

class. Israel produced one of the most remarkable episodes of economic growth in modern era, which lasted for twenty-two years until 1972. And, all this while, Israel remained among the most egalitarian societies among developed nations.

489. **Between 1973 and 1985, Israel sunk into a 'lost decade' of economic stagnation and decline.** The defense budget skyrocketed in the aftermath of the 1973 Yom Kippur War and during the global energy crisis that ensued. Government policies failed to address the crisis, and Israel transitioned from single digit annual inflation to hyper-inflation, from a balanced budget to a huge deficit, and from a balance of payment to dangerously depleting foreign reserves.

490. **The Economic Stability Program of 1985 *(Tochnit Hayitzuv Hakalkalit)*, was a turning point in Israel's economic and societal development, ushering in a new era of capitalism.** Significant cuts in government expenditures and subsidies, privatization, mass exposure of the economy to foreign competition and huge structural changes unfolded. For example, the banking system collapsed, was then nationalized and subsequently privatized over a twenty-five-year period. In 1994, the *Histadrut* was finally dismantled: its corporations were sold and it began to focus solely on its role as a labor union. And during the 1990s, both the *kibbutzim* and *moshavim* movements were bailed out by the government in exchange for their restructuring, during which many of them lost their egalitarian nature to become suburban communities of family-owned homes and properties.

491. **The Economic Stability Program turned out to be a remarkable macro-economic success.** In fact, all of its major objectives were achieved: inflation was successfully eradicated, fiscal discipline was restored, debt was decreased to average OECD levels, the New Israeli Shekel became a strong currency and Israeli industry successfully competed in international markets. The immigration of roughly one million *olim* from the former Soviet Union to Israel between 1989 and 1994 gave the Israeli economy an invaluable impetus toward an period of rapid growth.

492. However, **while the economy grew, the benefits of growth did not trickle down, and the quality of life for most Israelis even deteriorated in key areas such as housing, education and job security.** In other words, Israel's growth has been non-inclusive, and its benefits were not

shared by society. It was driven by a very small and entrepreneurial risk-taking sector of technology, which naturally and legitimately also reaped significant fruits. Additionally, the collateral benefits of this growth were sapped by small, politically empowered sectors such as the large labor unions, the defense establishment and the settlement movement. Meanwhile, the 'average' Israeli – who works in a small business, holds a government job or works for a large corporation, who lives in suburban Israel or in the Negev and Galilee – did not participate as much, did not contribute as much and did not benefit as much. Even the Israel Defense Forces, once the great equalizer of Israeli society, became an institution that enhances social gaps. In other words, **the informal covenant between the government and the citizens that growth will 'trickle down' did not materialize.**

493. **The privatization of key societal infrastructures has been another chief reason for the crisis in the quality of life of Israelis.** Until the 1980s, the *Histadrut* and various government agencies provided for the essential quality of life components such as education, culture and sports. This was done through institutions such as community centers *(matnasim)*, early childhood centers *(tipot halav)*, sports framework and youth movements. As of 1985, many of these societal infrastructures lost their core allocations and were forced to balance their budgets. Services that could not be 'sold' were no longer viable and were discontinued. Thus, the middle-class and the weaker echelons of society suffered from dwindling public goods and services in quantity and quality.

494. Furthermore, **many failed privatization efforts resulted in the skyrocketing cost of living** *(yoker hamichya)*. The objective of having a smaller government was achieved through budget cuts and by selling government-owned entities to the private sector. However, major privatization projects failed to establish an efficient market, and the monopolies and cartels of the government and the *Histadrut* were in fact replaced by new privately owned oligopolies. Their owners – nicknamed 'tycoons' – gained monopolistic positions, primarily in markets of basic products and services such as food, pensions and communications. A massive reallocation of wealth took place from the general public to a small number of business groups and families, who extracted extraordinary profits by their ability to maneuver regulations and limit competition.

495. **Consequently, since 1985 and over a twenty-five-year period, Israeli society has become one of the most polarized among developed nations**. A small group benefited from a cycle of affluence, where productivity and income grew exponentially, guaranteeing good education, safety and access to technology. Compounded by intra-connections and political access, this group had many opportunities to create even more wealth. Meanwhile, a growing section of the population had stagnating and even declining income in real terms that had to underwrite a rising cost of living. Their education, access to technology and opportunities were compromised, and therefore their long-term wellbeing, as well. With the privatization of community institutions across Israel, stronger populations in wealthier municipalities had better services while the people living in weaker areas often had much less. Hence, most Israelis needed to do much more with unchanging means. Societal gaps widened dramatically: poverty and vulnerability expanded, including among dual-income families; a small, globalized and powerful group enjoyed disproportional access to resources, opportunities, privileges and immunities; and the wellbeing of the middle class eroded.

496. **Children are the silent victims of this reality**: The combination of growing financial challenges among many households and the erosion of public services compromises their education, skills, health and future assets. Consequently, their ability to participate and compete in the labor market of the 21st century and to provide for their future families are undermined. Unfortunately, Israel increasingly transitioned from a society where children of poor backgrounds had a fair opportunity to succeed – evidenced in Israel's current leadership – into a society where the social stature of parents determines the prospects of their children. The long-term implications hereof are not only declining human capital within Israel, but also erosion of solidarity with and loyalty to the State of Israel and its institutions.

497. **Additional reasons propel Israel's crisis of inclusiveness.** Some of them are 'institutional' in the sense that they are rooted in the basic structure of Israel's society, economy and government. Others are global in the sense that they affect other developed nations, as well.

498. *First,* **two sectors of Israel's society – the religious orthodox *(Haredim)* and the Arabs – are disproportionally represented among Israel's poor.** They do not equally participate in the labor market nor are they as productive on average. Their access to education and skill-building

is limited and their families are relatively large. This reality continues a legacy of poverty from the times of the *Shtetl* and from the days of the Ottoman Empire and the British Mandate. Therefore, their relative poverty is a fundamental condition that is hard to transform.

499. *Second,* **Israel's demographic growth at an annual rate of 1.8% makes Israel the only developed country with a fast-growing population.** Most of this population growth emerges from the socio-economically weak stratum of society, namely the Jewish ultra-orthodox *(Haredim)* and Arab citizens, in particular the *Bedouin.* However, the average Israeli educated middle-class family is also larger on average as compared to similar families in other developed nations. By definition, the larger the family, the lower the income per capita, and the more difficult it is to accumulate wealth from one generation to the next.

500. *Third,* **the *Histadrut,* and especially its powerful unions, are a major driver of Israel's societal crisis.** They increase labor-market inflexibility and therefore decrease productivity, shortchanging non-unionized workers and perpetuating monopolies that increase the cost of living and harm services. In recent years, two classes of workers have emerged in Israel, often within the same establishment: unionized ones, whose rights and benefits are generous, and non-unionized workers *(ovdei kablan)* who are vulnerable and underpaid.

501. *Fourth,* **the declining capacity of the Government of Israel to govern compromises its ability to address such complex societal challenges in a rapidly changing environment.** Political dynamics of dogmatism, credit claiming and struggles over turf are counterproductive when dealing with such matters. Rarely does a single government agency have the necessary mandate and capacity to design and implement an effective approach and response. In other words, most often, designing effective laws and policies vis-à-vis such complex and dynamic challenges requires multiple agencies to sustain collaboration in a substantive manner. They must transcend the focused pressures of special interest groups and uphold the general interest of the 'unorganized' general public and small-business owners. This is a threshold that most modern governments in developed nations do not meet. Unfortunately, Israel is no exception.

502. *Fifth,* **Israel's government system of contractual democracy exacerbates this crisis.** Few constituencies – such as the settlers, the ultra-orthodox, the agricultural sector, the large labor unions and the

defense establishment – gained disproportionate influence. They exercise focused and disciplined political power to shift resources from the general public to their own constituencies.

503.   *Sixth,* **the redirection of Israel's creative spirit from society-building to technology and business diverts focus and talent from societal challenges.** For nearly seventy-five years, Zionism was a world leader in the societal innovation of its communities, institutions and structures. This thrust lost momentum in the 1970s, and much of Israel's entrepreneurial energy was redirected during the 1980s to the hi-tech industry. The export-oriented technology sector became the engine of Israel's economic growth and a key vehicle for economic mobility. It gained Israel world fame under the banner of 'The Start-Up Nation.' However, the difference between societal innovation and technological innovation is that while the former is authentically local, cannot be relocated and benefits society, the latter can be relocated, as indeed often happened, benefits only a few people and often represents a mindset of short-term gains. The Israeli ideal, which used to be associated with settlement, community building and service, became to establish and sell a start-up company. Few thousands of new millionaires emerged, often with little or no conception of societal responsibility.

504.   *Finally,* **globalization powerfully and consistently exacerbates Israel's societal challenge of inclusiveness.** Globalization, which generously benefits the 'global class' and marginalizes unskilled labor, amplifies societal gaps. It exerts harsh pressures on individuals and businesses to continuously update their professional and personal skills. Many find these demands unbearable, and gradually become unskilled laborers and even unemployable.

505.   Consequently, **while Israel disengaged from the inclusive model of Diaspora society, it failed to develop an alternative societal vision.** The legacy of Jewish communitarianism of the *Yishuv* became a societal shell, depleted of resources, substance, leadership and purpose. Until the mid-1980s, the Government of Israel had direct and indirect control over community institutions and the services they provided. Henceforth, shrinking government budgets and weak services, unsuccessful privatization projects and regulatory failures have eroded this system. For a large section of Israel's population, such mechanisms of inclusiveness no longer even exist. The network of cohesive communities of the *Yishuv* was dismantled into a host of individuals and households that have to

fend for themselves. No alternative promising vision for Israeli society has been offered.

506. **This reality led to a crisis of trust in the government and in the entire market system, which reached a boiling point in 2011 with the mass social protests.** The informal covenant that growth will trickle down and benefit the entire population did not materialize. Gradually, the public became aware of massive regulatory failures, incompetence of anti-trust agencies and of the vulnerability of the legislative process to the influence of large corporations and powerful sectors. Eventually, the widespread societal frustrations erupted in the form of mass nationwide protests in 2011 fueled by the rising costs of housing, food, healthcare and parenting. Fundamental trust in the national institutions and in the market system had eroded. These sentiments led to a massive political reshuffle in the 2013 elections with forty percent of Members of Knesset replaced. However, in the absence of a new societal vision, the inclusive legacy of the Flexigid society remains a distant vision.

Politization of Religion

507. **The formal association of religion and Jewishness with sovereign power and authority is another area where Jewish Flexigidity was challenged by the State of Israel.** This breach with the Flexigid society occurred in four separate yet related arenas: legislation of the Knesset in matters that were previously governed by the 'invisible hand' of Jewish society; the ability of orthodox factions to dominate in matters relating to Israel's Jewishness; the displacement of the traditional community-based rabbis in favor of an apparatus of central and local rabbinates; and, consequently, the disenchantment with and disengagement from Judaism by many Israelis.

508. **The Jewishness of the Hebrew public sphere has been a subject of political debate since Zionism's inception.** The so-called 'Heralds of Zionism' *(Mevasrei HaTziyonut)* ranged in their outlook from secularism to religious orthodoxy, and, decades later, Herzl and Ahad Ha'Ahm disagreed about the place of Jewish religion in the public domain. The Hebrew community of the *Yishuv* comprised of a diverse mix of religious observances ranging from orthodoxy to staunch secularism, and matters of religiosity were intensely contested. In 1947, David Ben-Gurion and the senior *Haredi* rabbis formulated the so-called "Status Quo" in order to unify the *Yishuv* in the face of the coming war. They

affirmed the Jewish character of the future state in relation to *Shabbat* and *kashrut*, formalized the authority of rabbinical courts over matters of civil status of marriage and divorce, and enshrined the autonomy of the *Haredi* education system. These understandings became the basis for the relations between religion and state in Israel.

509. **Upon the establishment of the State of Israel, its government took the power to legislate and regulate on matters of Jewish life, which had hitherto been resolved by the workings of Judaism's 'invisible hand'.** The Knesset, the government and the courts began to shape the Jewishness of society in a top-down manner. In doing so, they compromised the dynamics of Flexigidity, which had emerged from the interplay among multiple diverse units. Factions, groups and communities no longer had to inspire and convince each other by engagement and deliberation. Those that could muster the political power were henceforth able to use it in order to enforce their outlook on others. The shadowy corridors of legislative halls, where lobbyists, legislators and bureaucrats interact, came to replace the open public sphere as the primary arena where the identity of society was supposedly determined.

510. In such an environment, **orthodox factions came to dominate and domineer Israeli society in most matters relating to Israel's Jewishness and religious assets.** Together, the so-called *Haredim* and national religious *(datiyim leumiyim)*, have been able to use their political power to take care of their own communities, often at the expense of the general public. They have also been able to force their view regarding matters such as the observance of *Shabbat*, *kashrut* and other customs in the public sphere even in secular areas, to control the local rabbinates and other religious services that govern civil matters for the entire population such as marriage, divorce and burial, and to manage access to and worship in Jewish holy sites such as the Wailing Wall *(Kotel)*. As such, key services, such as transportation, were shut down on Jewish holy days even within non-observant communities. They have also been able to exclude progressive Jews from practicing Judaism in holy sites according to their own ways and to deny formal recognition of their rabbis.

511. **The issue of membership and conversion embodies these dynamics and has been the subject of heated political and societal feuding.** Upon the establishment of the State of Israel, such membership in the Jewish People became a matter of Israeli law since it carried with it a package of legal rights and obligations in areas such as immigration,

citizenship, personal status, military service and settlement in lands that belong to the Jewish People. This debate regards both conversions within Israel and in the Diaspora.

512. **Within Israel, the orthodox factions have been able to dominate the definition of who's a Jew and conversions.** The exclusive authority of Israel's rabbinate, which is controlled by orthodox factions, to officiate conversions established the strict condition of religious observance *(torah ve mitzvoth)* as the benchmark for joining the Jewish People *(giyur ka'halacha)*. It also enabled them to disregard conversions performed by non-orthodox rabbis in Israel and abroad regardless of their requirements and even if they met the standard of strict religious observance. This condition is particularly compromising for those who were converted into Judaism overseas by a non-orthodox rabbi and their children, should they want to be married in Israel. It is also compromising for non-Jewish immigrants in Israel who would like to join the Jewish People but are not religiously observant. This issue repeatedly erupts in cases of fallen IDF soldiers who lived as Israelis and Jews, but whose Judaism is posthumously challenged by orthodox authorities when determining their military burial arrangements. Though they may not have gone through such *giyur ka'halacha*, for many non-orthodox Israelis they were 'converted by fire,' their service qualifying them as having joined the Jewish nation and people.[307] Finally, this condition compromises non-Jews who are not religious yet would like to join the Jewish People as citizens of the Jewish state. They may be soldiers, labor immigrants or refugees, as well as their Israeli-born and raised children. In Israel, the sole path available to them for becoming Jews is an orthodox conversion process requiring strict religious observance. This is true even for those who have proven their commitment to the State of Israel and the Jewish People by performing distinct service in culture, art, morality, security and diplomacy.

513. **Another critical contention has been over the 1950 Law of Return** *(Hok HaShvut)*, which established the rights of Jews to immigrate to Israel *(olim)*. The 1970 amendment to the law determined a 'Jew' to be a child of a Jewish mother or any person who converted into Judaism

---

307 See for example the case of an infantry soldier who died in service before his conversion process was completed. Nonetheless, he was given a Jewish burial in a military cemetery. See Ynet article, "Golani Soldier Gets Jewish Burial Despite Incomplete Conversion," Ynet, March 28, 2010, at http://www.ynetnews.com/articles/0,7340,L-3869405,00.html.

and is not a member of another religion.[308] Since the enactment of this law, *Haredi* parties have demanded that only conversions by orthodox rabbis in the Diaspora be recognized for the purpose of the law. However, repeated attempts to amend the Law of Return in that exclusionary spirit have been frustrated, in part due to mobilization of the Diaspora.

514.   Furthermore, **another break from the Flexigidity of Jewish society has been in the structure of rabbinical authority in Israel.** Rabbinical leadership in the Diaspora is by and large meritocratic, responsive to the needs of the community and permanently competitive. Every community has a rabbi that offers spiritual inspiration and guidance to its members and whose influence depends on learnedness, charisma, esteem and relevance. Thus, the legitimacy of rabbis emerges bottom-up from their communities, establishing a permanently evolving network of small units, which is essential for Jewish Flexigidity. Meanwhile, in Israel, rabbis have been appointed top-down by a rabbinic council with the authority to affect the lives of people who live within the geographic area to which they were assigned. In many cases, particularly in all non-observant sectors, their outlook was more orthodox and sometimes even anti-Zionist, alien to that of the residents who they were supposed to serve, yet to whom they were not accountable. Therefore, many city rabbis in Israel are disconnected from the population they were supposed to lead. The rabbinate became a deeply politicized and often corrupted institution, permeated by ethical, intellectual and spiritual mediocrity, whose communal legitimacy has become deeply compromised.

515.   Meanwhile, **the position of a 'community rabbi' whose incentives are to serve a self-selecting constituency has been largely lost.** While orthodox Jews sought inspiration and religious guidance from towering *Halachic* figures, non-orthodox and secular people amassed disgust, disrespect and resentment toward orthodox rabbis and the ethics they represented. Many communities no longer embraced a rabbinical authority that could bring to bear Jewish tradition on local needs and

---

308   Article 4b of the Law of Return. Thus, this law differs from *halacha* by excluding Jews who converted into other religions, while allowing non-Jewish children and grandchildren of Jews, along with their spouses, the right to immigrate to Israel.

See the famous 1962 Supreme Court case of Rufeisen vs. Minister of the Interior, ((1962) 16 PD 2428), also known as the "Brother Daniel Case". In that instance, Rufeisen was a Jewish child who had been hidden during the Shoah and subsequently converted to Catholicism and became a practicing friar. He was denied citizenship based up upon the Law of Return. Rufeisen was, however, allowed to gain citizenship through other channels.

dilemmas. Many non-orthodox Jews came to reject the world of Judaism altogether, as it was represented to them through the overpowering presence of the orthodox rabbinate. Nonetheless, in recent years this critical function has begun to reemerge in Israeli society.

516.   *Finally*, **the politization of religion in Israel deepened the crisis of Jewish identity among a large constituency, which is deeply committed to the Jewish People, yet Jewishly ignorant and alien to Jewish traditions and institutions.** A variety of sources – some secular and others religious – inspired and shaped the identity of the Hebrew society to contain a spectrum of outlooks from staunch secularism to religious orthodoxy. David Ben-Gurion, for example, is known to have been an outspoken secular who did not observe *kashrut* nor *Shabbat*, yet was deeply informed and knowledgeable about Judaism. However, after decades of state intervention in religious matters, overpowering by the orthodox factions and a disconnect between rabbinic authorities and Israeli society, secular Zionism has become largely synonymous with ignorance of Judaism. In Israel emerged the first-ever large constituency of Jews who are passionately Jewish yet Jewishly ignorant.

Under-performing Government: An Eroding Keystone

517.   **The unique condition of the State of Israel within the context of Jewish history requires its legislature, executive and judiciary to be outstanding.** They must successfully deal with the ordinary challenges of modern governance and with the permanent adversity and exceptional volatility that Israel faces. They must also rise to be a new structure of Jewish leadership and governance, which, while anchored in the reality of Jewish sovereignty that is in control of a non-Jewish minority, nonetheless strengthens the mechanisms of Jewish survival, security, prosperity and leadership.

518.   However, **Israel's political system increasingly suffers from politicking and skewed incentives.** The first twenty-five years under the reign of Mapai saw relative political stability and a highly effective government that led to a golden era of security and growth. The political culture ensured a correlation between the skills and experience of politicians and their spheres of responsibility. However, the emergence of a two-party system following the 1977 elections led to a decline in the capacity of the Government of Israel to govern effectively. Over time, Israel's electoral system, government and politics came to emphasize politicking and

public appearance over executive and legislative capacities. Highlighting this trend, in recent governments, only a minority of ministers manage portfolios in which they have in-depth acquaintance with the subject matter of their responsibility.

519. Thus, **over time, a mismatch emerged between Israel's challenges and the weakness of its government structure and institutions**. Israel faces daunting societal challenges. They require a top-down governmental capacity to design policies in a broad, substantive and long-term manner and to effectively implement them. They also require agility, openness and the capacity to experiment with new ideas and structures on the national, regional, municipal and communal levels. Meanwhile, Israel's electoral system generates powerful incentives for the opposite: short-term, sectarian and populist conduct, as well as for rigidity, inefficiency and prolonged processes. Indeed, Israeli governance has been underperforming relative to other developed countries and the quality of life in Israel is ranked at the bottom of the ladder among developed nations.[309]

520. Furthermore, **to date and from the perspective of Jewish Flexigidity, the record of Israel's government has been poor.** As mentioned, the de-centralized and meritocratic leadership structure of the Diaspora that has proven itself for centuries has been replaced in Israel with an establishment that is highly centralized, political and bureaucratic. Such a system is not only governed by powerful skewed incentives, but also lacks the impetus to take a broad view of the past, present and future of Jewish society. Sadly, within only a few decades, the societal architecture of a network of communities, which has been so critical for Jewish Flexigidity, was dismantled in Israel without an alternative vision for an inclusive society in its stead. **This disappointing reality stands in contrast to the presumption of many Israelis for Israel and its government to lead, guide and represent the entire Jewish world.**

---

309 See the 2013 Better Life Index (http://www.oecdbetterlifeindex.org/) of the Organization for Economic Cooperation and Development (OECD), which ranked Israel 25th out of 36 mostly developed nations included in the rankings. Israel ranked particularly low not only on housing, income and job security, but also in areas where Jewish communities have been outstanding such as on community support, civic engagement and education.

Rigidity of Mission: Domineering Outlook and Negation of Diaspora

521. **Zionism and the story of nationhood developed a domineering outlook during the first few decades of Israel's modern independence.** While these ideological tendencies existed in Zionism since its inception, they flourished following the astonishing successes of Israel's earlier years, particularly between 1948 and 1967. Zionist ideology framed that endeavor as the culmination of two millennia of Jewish history, which included forced exile, a legacy of hardship in the Diaspora, uninterrupted loyalty to and presence in Zion, national revival and eventual repatriation with international recognition. It held the Government of Israel exclusively responsible for this endeavor and, therefore, also at times, the representative of the entire Jewish People.

522. **Over time, Zionism developed a robust narrative, which co-opted Judaism's other meta-stories.** It viewed the establishment of a state for the Jewish People as the ultimate rationale of Judaism and the entire Jewish People in our time, and as their defining collective effort. It encompassed the story of peoplehood by framing the State of Israel as a remedy for the plight of all Jews, by committing it to the service of world Jewry and by pledging it to be a safe haven even for those Jews who did not choose to live in it. Additionally, Zionism not only claimed to build a model society in the State of Israel, but also framed Israel as the most effective platform for serving the mission of *or la'goim*. Finally, it framed itself as the realization of the millennia-long religious yearning for the return to Zion.

523. **Many Zionists thus held that the identity of any Jew can be fully realized in Israel by virtue of their Israeliness.** They argued that simply by living in Israel, a Jewish person can serve the ideals of nationhood and peoplehood and be a part of a society that strives to be a light unto the nations. Many also claimed that simply living in Zion and serving the State of Israel fulfill key Jewish religious commandments, an outlook which applies even to secular Jews who do not observe *Halacha*.

524. **This outlook negated the Diaspora and legitimized a systematic attempt to dismantle it through *aliyah*.** Decades of persecution in Russia and antisemitism in Western Europe culminating in the Shoah were seen as undeniable proof of the inevitable fate of the Diaspora. Thus, Zionism ideologically diminished the importance of Diaspora Jewish traditions with an attitude that was often condescending. It

associated the Diaspora with assimilation or with a traditional way of life rooted in the condition of exile, both of which were held to be undesired and compromising for the Jewish People. The Zionist 'blood for money' narrative emphasized the sacrifices and risks of Israelis on behalf of all Jews.[310] Thus, it narrowed the role of the Diaspora to providing financial and political support to Israel without question and reservation. It also called upon all Jews to make *aliyah* sending 'aliyah emissaries' *(shlichei aliyah)* to Jewish communities around the world. As late as 2005, the message of Prime Minister Ariel Sharon to Jewish communities in France and the USA was: come home to Israel.[311]

525. Meanwhile, and as should have been expected, **the Flexigidity of mission of the Jewish People persisted as the other meta-stories fought the domineering outlook of Zionism.** As Zionism grappled to integrate the four meta-stories of Judaism under the framework of Jewish nationhood, the inherent tensions among the stories were sharpened. As their internal logic is structurally irreconcilable, Zionism's myopic focus on the narrative of nationhood increased tensions within the Diaspora Jewish world.

526. **The story of religion and faith saw a major resurgence following the Shoah, with mixed attitudes toward Zionism.** Orthodox communities thrive both in Israel and the Diaspora. In Israel, the national-religious orthodox constituency is deeply committed to the ideal of Jewish statehood, and in the Diaspora, as well, orthodox communities are often staunchly supportive of Israel. Other orthodox communities, both in Israel and the Diaspora, reject the idea of the State of Israel and refuse to partake in its building, viewing Zionism as hastening redemption *(ge'ulah)* and therefore as heresy. Some, like the *Neturei Karta* faction, actively work against Israel, siding with its enemies.

527. **The narrative of *or la'goim* also galvanized the support and attention of many Jews, often in defiance of Zionism.** Large constituencies of Jews dedicate time, energy and resources to participating in and to supporting organizations that commit to improving the human condition in the world. Many of them view *tikkun olam* rather than Zionism to be the organizing rationale and ultimate purpose of Judaism in modernity. While many of them serve that ideal within Jewish social service

---

310 See Matti Golan, *Blood for Money*, Kinneret Zmora Betan Dvir, 1992 (in Hebrew).

311 See speech by Prime Minister Sharon in the Herzliya Conference on December 18th, 2003: "Aliyah is the central goal of the State of Israel."

initiatives and institutions, others do so in non-Jewish settings, in some cases refusing to associate their actions and contributions with the Jewish People altogether. Furthermore, within the idyllic framework of *or la'goim*, some Jews hold the State of Israel to the highest standards of morality and are inclined to criticize its performance and policies. Few even conclude that Israel's conduct fundamentally undermines its right to exist, becoming themselves anti-Zionists.

528. **The narrative of peoplehood also re-emerged in defiance of Zionism's attempt to claim exclusive centrality for the State of Israel.** This interpretation of peoplehood emphasizes the equal legitimacy of Jewish communities around the world, viewing Israel as one of multiple Jewish centers. It therefore challenges Zionism's view of Israel as the undisputed focus of attention and efforts of the entire Jewish world, and is often hostile to its efforts to encourage *aliyah* from prosperous Jewish communities. The flagship program of this approach has been the Birthright Israel Project, which grants every Jewish child a free ten-day trip to Israel in order to strengthen Jewish identity and communities in the Diaspora, rather than encourage *aliyah* to Israel. Indeed, the support of the State of Israel for this project represented a turning point from Zionism's exclusionary outlook toward the Diaspora.

529. *Finally,* **Zionism's negation of the Diaspora has also been challenged by powerful trends within Israeli society and the Jewish world.** These trends have undermined the view of the Diaspora as it was framed by the classical Zionist outlook.

530. *First,* **Diaspora Jewry is unprecedentedly vibrant and prosperous.** Zionism viewed the Shoah as the kiss-of-death for Diaspora Jewry. However, as mentioned earlier, Diaspora Jewry is more prosperous, secure and vital today than ever before. That reality fundamentally challenges the outlook of Zionism that Jews have no future outside of the State of Israel.

531. *Second,* **a permanent and vibrant Diaspora of Israelis has emerged.** From Zionism's perspective, the concept of an 'Israeli Diaspora' is an oxymoron: there was either Israel or a Jewish Diaspora. Zionism did not have a concept for a large constituency of native Israelis who then chose the Diaspora to live there as Israelis and Jews. This ideological void was translated into a discombobulated policy: until recently, Israeli diplomatic missions engaged Jewish communities as partners and counterparts but

ignored the communities of Israelis within their geographic assignment. Furthermore, while Diaspora Jews were expected to support Israel, Diaspora Israelis were spared of such anticipation, as they were supposed to soon repatriate. Furthermore, that attitude impacted the relationship between the traditional establishment of Diaspora Jewish communities and the Israelis in their midst: both showed relative disinterest in and even arrogance toward each other.

532. *Third,* **Israel became a relatively secure and prosperous nation**. This condition eroded the necessity for and logic of the Diaspora's financial contributions to Israel. An expectation for synergy, mutuality and partnership emerged on the Diaspora side in its stead, stemming from the view of Israel and Diaspora Jewish communities as equals.

533. *Fourth,* **a more nuanced and critical engagement with Israel emerged among Diaspora Jews.** Israel's predicament with regards to the control of the Palestinian population has driven a wedge through Diaspora Jewry. Many of them, on both sides of the political spectrum, no longer grant unconditional political support to the Israeli government. Few, particularly on the left, have even waived their support for Israel altogether.

534. *Finally,* **the power to shape the relationship has been decentralized**. In the past, the Government of Israel and a few large institutions such as the Jewish Agency and the umbrella organization of the Jewish Federations of North America and United Israel Appeal *(Keren HaYesod)* had the power to shape and drive the relationship between Israel and Diaspora Jewry in a top-down manner. In recent years, those institutions have declined in their capacity to serve this mission and countless peer-to-peer and community-to-community connections have instead emerged, effectively driving Israel-Diaspora relations in a bottom-up manner. The Internet, social networking platforms and other technologies that facilitate direct personal engagement further accelerate this trend.

535. *In conclusion,* **Zionism's outlook failed to conquer the public sphere of the Jewish People**. As it became more domineering, the other meta-stories of the Jewish People evolved, as well, remaining relevant to the hearts and minds of many Jews both in Israel and the Diaspora. The Flexigidity of mission of the Jewish People remains vibrant.

The Rise and Decline of the Flexigidity of Zionism

536. **Zionism became one of the most successful national movements of the 20th century.** It realized its ambitious vision of establishing a state for the Jewish People and a polity where Jews are the sovereign majority. En route, it rose from the ashes of the Shoah and frustrated its ideological, diplomatic and military enemies. Forty percent of world Jews live in Israel and half of all Jewish babies are Israelis. Zionism's astounding success in military, economics, diplomacy, state and society building, technology and other fields continue to inspire many.

537. **Zionism prides itself on its revolutionary foundation and character.** It sought to transform the Jewish People and nation, Jewish communities and the life of individual Jews. Indeed, the reality of a sovereign Jewish majority has been transformational, and the Israeli Jewish *Sabra* is seen by many as a new kind of a Jewish person in mindset, values, culture and way of life. Israel's communities are different from those the Jewish communities of the Diaspora and Israel's leadership faces entirely different challenges from its Diaspora counterparts. Meanwhile, the stature and role of the Jewish People among the family of nations has been transformed as well from being a passive to an active force.

538. However, **Zionism has also evolved out of Diaspora Jewish society, adapting its legacy to the realities and challenges of a sovereign state.** It needed to develop conceptual frameworks that would prove effective in areas as diverse as security and military affairs, social and economic development, law and diplomacy, and to continuously update them. In fact, Zionism and the State of Israel were shaped by the interaction between the concepts and mechanisms of Jewish existence in the Diaspora and the challenges of the reality in Zion. Just as Israel and Zionism affected the Diaspora, so too has the Diaspora been a shaping force in Israel. Furthermore, as decades go by, powerful forces are curbing many of the revolutionary aspects of Zionism, reconnecting with the wisdom of Diaspora Jewry and with the essential foundations of the longevity and success of the Jewish People.

539. Indeed, **Zionism has been blessed by a leadership that was able to seize upon a unique historical chain of events.** A few critical decisions driven by individual leaders have made a huge difference, and the ability to read the geopolitical map with clarity and act with determination and courage will continue to be essential for Israel's prosperity and security.

Join the conversation www.flexigidity.com

540. Yet, **Zionism's successes have also been an outcome of its remarkable Flexigidity, which it inherited from Diaspora Judaism.** Zionism has been rigidly uncompromising on its cores values such as its commitment to Zion, democracy, Jewishness and security. Meanwhile, it has demonstrated remarkable flexibility, creativity and agility working through the tectonic shifts of the 20th century and the astounding societal and security challenges it faced. It integrated the four meta-stories of Judaism under the framework of Jewish nationhood and preserved a balancing act and equilibrium among their formative ideas.

541. **That prism of Flexigidity highlights the structure of society as the most powerful determinant of Zionism's past successes.** Flexigidity of mission, the architecture of the *Yishuv* as a web of many interconnected small units and its flat structure of leadership, and the *talmudic* process in the Hebrew public sphere were vitally important for Zionism's success.

542. Yet, **that same prism of Flexigidity also exposes the risk that Israel may become a disruptive force for the entire Jewish People.** Most Israelis do not live within the framework of a functioning community whose authentic meritocratic leadership is directly accountable to them. Furthermore, Israeli society is non-inclusive, with growing societal gaps, where households fend for themselves in the absence of a vibrant community. The traditional *talmudic* process of law-making, which was evolutionary, community-based and intellectually meritocratic, was replaced by politicized debates in the Knesset and by a superficial shouting media. Mass-immigration to Israel shrunk the world-wide-web of communities in the Diaspora and significantly decreased its diversity. And, Zionism's myopic and exclusionary focus on the story of nationhood led to a growing rift between Israel and much of Diaspora Jewry. Finally, powerful trends within Israel turn it inwards, nationalist and insular. While some of these fundamental changes were essential and integral to the Zionist project, others were consequential, unintentional and even unnecessarily excessive. As Rabbi Sacks writes: "...though Israel managed remarkably the transition from powerlessness to power, it did so at the cost of weakening the very institutions that had been the source of Jewish strength in the past: communities, charities, voluntary associations and community based schools. Even religion became a branch of the state. So, while the state grew strong, society grew weak. ... in place of a single national community, there was an endless proliferation of local communities ... each had its own political party or

parties. Every battle was fought in the political arena."[312] In other words, **the legacy of Jewish Flexigidity is in crisis in Israel**.

543. **Israel's demographic success makes the crisis of Flexigidity of its own society a challenge to the Flexigidity of the entire Jewish People.** More than fifty percent of world Jews will soon live in Israel in an environment that is largely ignorant of and does not participate in the Flexigid dynamics of the Jewish People. In the past, Zionism's negation of the Diaspora did not entail offsetting global Jewish Flexigidity because the vast majority of Jews lived in the Diaspora. However, when a significant majority of Jews will live in Israel, the Jewish People may reach a tipping point where Zionism and Israel will have severely compromised the secret of Jewish invincibility.

544. Meanwhile, **Israel's existence is not wholly secure and it continues to face daunting challenges.** Like other nations, Israel, too, faces the growing pressures of global political, technological and economic volatility. However, Israel also uniquely faces permanent adversity to its very existence. What is more, while Israel ascends to first-world prosperity, internal divides are deepening, and as it becomes more rigid and nationalist in its outlook, the rift with much of the Jewish world is growing. History teaches that all nations inevitably decline. Israel is particularly vulnerable to such dynamics.

545. **Israel's evident failure to develop an outstanding philosophy and structure of governance exacerbates concerns about its longevity.** Its public sphere suffers from the ills of superficiality, sectarianism, shortsightedness and populism. Its politicians have little or no incentives to consider the broad view of Judaism and the Jewish People. Thus, when Zionism and Israel turn their back on the secrets of Jewish survival, security, prosperity and leadership in the Diaspora, they do so without even debating an alternative model that is not only uniquely Jewish and Israeli but also exceptionally resilient and prosperous.

546. **This is why, from the perspective of Jewish Flexigidity, it is fortunate that Zionism's proposition that all Jewish eggs be placed in Israel has not been realized.** The dynamics of Jewish Flexigidity made such aspiration an impossibility to begin with. Judaism's dynamics of doubt and internal debate would have never allowed one outlook to dominate the Jewish world. Yet, from this perspective of Flexigidity, Zionism's

---

312 Sacks, *Future Tense*, p. 170.

aspiration to solve the predicament of Diaspora life by collective repatriation to a sovereign state may have inadvertently created an even bigger dilemma for Judaism. The State of Israel may still reach a point where it fundamentally disrupts the Flexigid mechanisms of Jewish survival, prosperity and leadership.

547. **The ability of Judaism and the Jewish People to sustain a small and prosperous nation that faces permanent adversity is questionable.** These concerns are ancient. Dr. Micha Goodman points out that Rabbi Yehuda HaLevi, in his book, the *Kuzari (Sefer HaKuzari)*, successfully answers all the questions of the Khazar King except two: why don't the Jews return to the Land of Israel and would they act differently from other nations when they regain power there.[313] With a legacy of three past failures, destructions and exiles, and a reality of mediocre governance, these questions still loom over Zionism and the State of Israel.

548. Therefore, **the engagement with the art and science of society-building and governance is essential for Israel's future, blending the unique Jewish societal knowledge with modern notions.** Zionism came to solve the predicament of Diaspora Jewry. It successfully transformed key elements of Jewish society, creating both great opportunities and considerable threats, dramatically affecting the entire Jewish world. Thus the balancing act between old and new, tradition and innovation, rigidity and flexibility is among the greatest challenges for 21st century Zionism.

549. Furthermore, **the opportunities to propel Israel to new levels of wellbeing and to address its challenges may actually stem from the legacy of Diaspora Judaism.** Key ideas of the Jewish Flexigid society can be adapted and even recreated as powerful platforms and engines of security and prosperity in modern Israel. Community institutions of the Diaspora may be adjusted to address contemporary needs. The worldwide network of Jewish communities may provide invaluable contribution to Israel's international standing. The ideal of *tikkun olam* may create new horizons to Judaism and Israel's presence in and contribution to humanity. And, the Diaspora model of meritocratic intellectual leadership may be amended to groom authentic Israeli equivalents.

550. Therefore, **the revitalization of Israel's Flexigidity is of critical significance not only for Israel's own future but also for the future of the Jewish People.** In an era of fundamental change both within Israeli

---

313 See Dr. Micha Goodman, *Kuzari Dream*, p. 197-202, 302-304.

society, as well as in its geopolitical surroundings, Israel's adaptability will determine its ability to thrive. Furthermore, as Israel claims to be the state of the Jewish People and will soon house a significant majority of Jews, the Government of Israel will need to expand its view of its leadership role in the Jewish world, serving all Jews including those who may not conform to its world view. Neither Israel's government nor its Parliament are currently structured to fill this role.

551. Yet, **confidence in Zionism's and Israel's future still stems from the legacy of Jewish Flexigidity.** Zionism has been a dynamic national movement that has evolved and adapted to dramatic changes, while being rooted in Jewish traditions. It has generated new ideas, institutions, structures and priorities in order to seize the opportunities and contend with threats. **Zionism has been a verb, not a noun. Zionism of the 21st century must remain so.**

Part IV
Re-Vitalizing Israel's Flexigidity: From State Building to Society Building

Flexigidity Top-Down by the Government of Israel

This section outlines the adjustments necessary within Israel in order to revitalize the Flexigidity of Israeli society. Its first part focuses on actions to be taken by the government and the Knesset top-down using tools of legislation, regulation, policies and budgets. The second part focuses on areas where civil society can make a significant grassroots bottom-up difference, primarily by developing a web of communities that are prosperous, inclusive and resilient.

552. **The existence of a sovereign government that shapes the Flexigidity of its society makes Israel unique in comparison to any other Jewish community.** Such government apparatus operates primarily through the work of the central government and its agencies, local municipalities, the Knesset and the courts, where only a few thousand people are effectively driving legislation, regulation, budgeting, adjudication and policy-making. For example, the powerful Budget Department of the Ministry of Finance and the Attorney General Office in the Ministry of Justice significantly affect the Flexigidity of Israeli society through their decisions in the areas of their professional responsibility. These entities do not exist in the ecosystem of Diaspora Jewry.

553. **The nature of governmental decision making stands in contrast to the legacy and dynamics of the Flexigid society.** Government decisions are all too often led by politicians who serve specific economic and political interests and by civil service professionals, guided by narrow professional mandates. They are shaped by deals of give-and-get that are driven by unrelated considerations. Broad based public involvement in this process is limited and rare in most cases, and takes place primarily through non-profits, advocacy, media outlets and lobby groups. Meanwhile, communities, which are the building blocks of the Flexigid society, are often absent or excluded from this process. And, there is no formal mechanism for involving Diaspora Jewry even on matters that concern its own wellbeing.

554. Meanwhile, **Israel's Flexigidity and that of Diaspora Jewry must become a matter of Israel's governmental responsibility and concern.** As Israel becomes the largest and most powerful Jewish entity in the world, its decisions influence the overall Flexigidity of the entire Jewish People. Therefore, its ability to take a broad view of Jewish society and the incentives to do so are crucially important for its capacity to successfully shape its society and to lead the Jewish world.

Join the conversation www.flexigidity.com

Following hereinafter are some of the key areas where the action of Israel's government will have a profound effect on Jewish Flexigidity.

Israel's National Security and the Unity of the Jewish People

555. **Zionism's outlook determinately expects the Jewish world to unify in support of Israel and its government.** It holds that Israel's mission is to serve all Jews, thus subsuming the meta-stories of peoplehood, faith and covenant, and of *or la'goim* within the framework of Jewish nationhood. This is the foundation of Zionism's expectation from the Jewish world, both institutions and individuals, to extend unconditional political and financial support to the State of Israel, in general, and to its ruling government.

556. Indeed, **the national security of the State of Israel has been a collective effort of the Jewish People.** While the bulk of the work and sacrifice was done in Israel, critical and invaluable diplomatic, political and financial support came from Diaspora Jewry. This legacy goes back to the early days of Zionism and continues today with organizations such as United Israel Appeal *(Keren HaYesod)*, Jewish Federations of North America and America Israel Public Affairs Committee (AIPAC).

557. However, **Judaism's Flexigidity of mission renders such unified Jewish support for Israel and Zionism conditional and unlikely.** As discussed earlier, Judaism not only sustains its other meta-stories in defiance of Zionism's domineering outlook, but also makes anti-Zionist forces inevitable and as integral to Judaism as Zionism itself.

558. Therefore, **the unity of the Jewish People is heavily dependent on Israel's overall societal performance.** When Israel's nationhood credibly integrates the narratives of faith, peoplehood and *or la'goim* and enhances them, support for Zionism among Diaspora Jewry increases. When Israel's societal performance challenges these stories, support for Israel dwindles, as many Jews must choose between Israel and other values that are central to them. When Israel is corrupt, discriminatory and incompetent, Jews around the world distance themselves from it. When it contributes to humanity and stands for justice, the Jews of the world unite behind it.

559. **National security conduct is the key area that determines the collective attitude of world Jews toward Israel.** Until 1967, with the memory of the Shoah still fresh and traumatic, Israel had the unified and unwavering support of the Jewish world, few exceptions notwithstanding. Thereafter, especially as of the 1980s, collective Jewish support for Israel could not be taken for granted, and fluctuated over the years. The Jewish People unites behind Israel when its extended hand for peace is rejected and when it is forced into fighting for its survival against all odds and does so morally. Conversely, Jews in the Diaspora distance themselves from Israel when its military conduct is unethical and politically questionable. The Jewish world united in support of Israel following the 1976 Entebbe Raid in Uganda, when Israel freed hostages taken by Palestinian terrorists, and criticized Israel during the 1982 Lebanon War. More recently, Israel's military campaigns in Lebanon and Gaza, the settlement effort in the West Bank, and the perception that it does not wish to end its control over the Palestinian population, are leading to a growing rift among many Jews and Jewish communities. So much so that in many Jewish institutions Israel is no longer a unifying force, but rather a contentious issue.

560. **This is particularly true as Jews and Jewish communities may be increasingly viewed under the pretext of Israel.** Israel's actions and realities, achievements and failures will increasingly affect the stature of Diaspora Jewish communities within their own societies. While Israel's success may favorably reflect upon Diaspora Jews, the de-legitimization of Israel, being a recent mutation of antisemitism,[314] will thrive on Israel's ethical inconsistencies and even failures, targeting Jews on those grounds. This condition therefore challenges Israel to a higher standard of ethics and morality.

561. Thus, **the logic of Flexigidity calls upon Israel's national security leaders to expand their view and to take into account the unity of the Jewish People as a matter of great significance.** Israel's national security will remain complex and challenging. It will continue to require military and diplomatic determination, agility and courage, as well as the mobilization of Israeli society and external support. Thus, this needed perspective and consideration of the Jewish world adds another layer of responsibility upon the already burdened shoulders of Israel's leaders when they come to determine policy. The significance hereof transcends practicality of political and financial support. Decisions on matters such as military activities, preemptive action, relations with the Palestinians

---

314 See Rabbi Sacks, *Future Sense*, concerning the mutation of antisemitism.

and international development policies must be shaped also with the Jewish world in mind.

Ending Control of the Palestinian Population

562. **The 1967 Six-Day War placed Zionism in a state of unsustainable disequilibrium and overstretch.** As described earlier, that war exacerbated the inherent tensions among the Zionist ideals of sovereignty, ownership and control over the ancestral Land of Israel; its values of humanism and democracy; the ideal of Jewishness and Hebrew society; and the quest to preserve a Jewish majority. Furthermore, in 1967 Israel also became overstretched financially, strategically and militarily. Therefore, Zionism and Israel withdrew from Sinai and then from Gaza, and engaged in a political process with the Palestinians in a prolonged effort to restore equilibrium to their core values.

563. **The final phase of restoring this equilibrium in Judea and Samaria is also the most difficult from the Jewish, Zionist and Israeli perspectives.** First, locations in the West Bank such as Beit El, Hebron and Efrat are the Biblical cradle of Jewish civilization. Second, there is a real security threat of radical Islamic and Arab groups using the West Bank as a launching pad for attacks on Israel's economic and civilian centers, should Israel withdraw from these territories. Third, some anti-Israel groups and forces are also working against ending Israel's control of the Palestinians because they would like to preserve Israel's overstretch. They yearn for Israel's ultimate implosion within a large political entity where Jews become a small majority and even a minority. Therefore, the staunch opposition to any such withdrawal in Israel and the Jewish world is reinforced by external forces that do not want to see such withdrawal either.

564. Furthermore, **the meta-stories of Judaism do not provide clear guidance, as they support both Israel's continued control of Judea and Samaria, as well as its withdrawal from these territories**. The logic of religion and faith, basing upon religious texts, can support continued sovereignty there, as well as a territorial compromise in favor of peace. The logic of peoplehood supports withdrawal in order to preserve the unity of the Jewish People, but also challenges the right of the State of Israel to compromise ancestral lands. The logic of nationhood supports continued sovereignty and control over these territories, as well as withdrawal in order to protect the Jewishness of the State of Israel.

Join the conversation www.flexigidity.com

Finally, those who embrace the narrative of *or la'goim* are also split: most cannot fathom a Jewish state that controls a Palestinian population against its will, but few speak for the challenge of Israeli-Palestinian and Jewish, Christian and Moslem co-existence in one society.

565. **From the perspective of Jewish Flexigidity, Israel's predicament in the West Bank is threatening to the unity of Jewish communities and of the Jewish People as a whole.** In the present reality, the Palestinian population in the West Bank is neither independent to exercise its right to self-determination nor is it offered the chance to be integrated into Israeli society. And, Palestinian civilians there – whose lives are controlled by Israel's Ministry of Defense Civil Administration – do not enjoy the same rights as the Israelis who live in these territories, the so-called 'settlers.' This condition pits two of Judaism's meta-stories – that of nationhood and that of *or la'goim* – against each other. It therefore threatens the Flexigid Jewish society, as the traditional dynamics of unity and adversity within many communities and among them are unable to contain that tension and contradiction.

566. Furthermore, **the situation in the West Bank may compromise Israel's political model as the State of the Jewish People.** On the one hand, integration of the West Bank Palestinians into Israel's political system within the framework of the so-called 'One-State Solution' will inevitably dilute Israel's Jewish character. Such a large Palestinian constituency does not share the societal DNA of Jewish Flexigidity, yet will still have a stake in shaping its future. This scenario would make Israel less appealing to many Diaspora Jews. On the other hand, failure to end the control over the Palestinian people will inevitably lead to Israel's isolation and delegitimization in the world, causing a chasm within large sections of Jewish Diaspora. In such a scenario, Israel would increasingly disenchant many Jews. Some of them may become skeptical about the logic of the State of Israel, critical of it and even negate it, not just because of Israel's 'human rights record' but also because of its effect on world Jewry. Israel would then be supported by a smaller faction of world Jews. Its claim of being the State of the Jewish People may then be discredited.

567. Thus, **from the perspective of Jewish Flexigidity, ending the control over the Palestinian population in the West Bank is essential in spite of its increasingly unfavorable circumstances.** Israel's benefits from a future Israeli-Palestinian agreement continue to decrease. Until 2001, the framework of such a negotiated deal would have been 'land for peace,'

bringing about an 'end of conflict' and 'finality of claims.' Then, in the face of continued Arab and Moslem animosity toward Israel, the contours of such a contract became 'land for security, 'possibly within an interim arrangement. If present trends persist, even guarantees for security may not be achievable, and Israel may face the existential need to end its presence in the West Bank through unilateral realignment.

Integration of and Equality for Israel's Arab Citizens

568. **The 1948 War placed Israel – and the Jewish People, dating back to Biblical times – in a hitherto unprecedented situation where a Jewish majority controls a significant non-Jewish minority.** Upon its establishment and after the War of Independence in 1949, Israel controlled over 150,000 Arabs citizens who were Christian and Moslem, representing about ten percent of the population.[315] Their community had been recently defeated in a fateful conflict, in which some eighty percent of their brethren departed to Arab territories and were never allowed to return. Their ethos was foreign and often hostile to Zionism and Judaism, and, for most of them, the State of Israel represented the defeat of their society. It has been at least two millennia since the Jewish People had to contend with such issues, if ever. Jewish law is elaborate on the treatment of individual non-Jews who dwell among Jews. Yet, it was non-existent with regard to co-existence within the same society with a non-Jewish minority, whose collective identity may even be adversarial.

569. **Initially, this condition did not fundamentally upset the equilibrium among Zionism's ideals.** With an overwhelming Jewish majority and under such political circumstances, Israel could not only be both Jewish and democratic, but the Military Governorate of the Arab population was initially seen as both necessary and legitimate. The fact that this community could elect its representatives to the Knesset as of the first 1949 elections, alleviated some of the tension between Israel's claim and aspiration to be democratic and the de-facto condition of its Arab minority. As of 1966, the Military Governorate was dismantled altogether. Henceforth, Israel's Arab citizens were supposed to enjoy equal rights in the State of the Jewish People.

---

315 According to United Nations Special Committee on Palestine (UNSCOP), in September 1947 there were approximately 1,900,000 people living in Mandatory Palestine, 68% of whom were Arabs and 32% were Jews. According to the Israeli Bureau of Statistics, by 1949 the Arab population in Israel numbered 159,100. See "Statistical Abstract of Israel, No. 55," 2004 and "Statistical Abstract of Israel 2007: Population by district, sub-district and religion".

570. However, **the integration and equality of the Arab population remains an ethical and practical challenge for Israel.** In 2013, an estimated eighteen percent of Israel's population was Arab, and seventy percent of this constituency was born and raised as citizens of Israel. While the level of socio-economic development of Arab communities in Israel rose dramatically since 1949, the lag behind Jewish communities, which began with the first Hebrew settlements, remains. While the laws of Israel and the rulings of the courts provide for full equality, in many instances, discrimination against Arab communities and citizens still persists in the allocation of government resources and in the limited opportunities available to them in the private sector. As such, issues relating to the place of Arab citizens in the State of Israel is a topic of frequent public discourse and significant concern.

Furthermore, **relations with the Arab population in Israel have far-reaching consequence for Jewish Flexigidity both in Israel and in the Jewish Diaspora.**

571. *First,* **shaping the place of non-Jews and specifically of Arabs in the Hebrew and Zionist society requires a *talmudic* process.** While there are multiple resident and citizen populations of a variety of nationalities and religions in Israel, the most significant by far is the Arab one. Their membership in Israeli society demands the creation of a modern and relevant body of laws and regulations that are rooted in past sources, yet relevant to a modern society. This *talmudic* process must address the place of non-Jews in the nation-state of the Jewish People, where Jewishness permeates the public sphere through the ethos, calendar, national anthem and emblem and the Hebrew language. It must balance equal opportunities and affirmative action, collective and individual identities, loyalty to the state and freedom of association and action, and the Jewish unitary character of the state with the particular identities of its non-Jewish communities. That this process has taken place, to date, primarily in the institutions of Israel's government, Parliament and judiciary, and not within civil society in the traditional Flexigid manner, may be highly compromising.

572. *Second,* **the equality and integration of Israel's Arab citizens is of significant importance for the unity of the Jewish People.** Many Jews judge Israel through the prism of the meta-story of *or la'goim,* closely observing its treatment of its minority populations. Should Israel fail to treat its minorities properly, the chasm with large segments of the Jewish Diaspora will deepen, while demonstrable successes in this regard will

create a new source of pride and unity among Jews. While the former condition pits the meta-stories of nationhood and *or la'goim* against each other and increases disunity among Jewish communities, the latter possibility stands to synergizes them and enhance Jewish cohesion.

Decentralizing Rabbinic Power

573. **The nature and structure of Israel's rabbinic leadership is crucially important for Jewish Flexigidity both in Israel and in the Diaspora.** This is one area where the Flexigidity of Israeli Jewry, soon to be the largest Jewish community in the world, has been significantly and unnecessarily compromised by the establishment of the State of Israel. That distortion was made possible by an electoral system that allows orthodox factions to overreach beyond their own communities through the legislation of the Knesset and the policies and budgets of the government.

574. As mentioned, **in Israel, the dynamics of Flexigidity have been distorted by the orthodox de jure and de facto monopoly over Israel's religious assets, formally marginalizing non-orthodox perspectives.** This point relates primarily to the orthodox control of the rabbinate and other essential religious services. It affects the lives of Israelis in areas such as dietary laws *(kashrut)*, observance of *Halacha* in the public sphere, marriage and divorce, adoptions, burial and conversions. It also affects access to and worship in holy sites, most contentiously at the Wailing Wall *(Kotel)*. Additionally, the orthodox establishment was granted the ability to repudiate rabbis who were not orthodoxly ordained. Granting Jewish orthodoxy such power and influence would have not been possible in the Diaspora. Thus, Israelis – the majority of whom are non-orthodox – are subject to the most stringent interpretation on matters of their civil status, which usually does not conform with their own personal outlook.

575. **Jewish Flexigidity in Israel was also compromised by the disempowerment of the community-rabbis in favor of Israel's central and local rabbinates.** As mentioned, the Diaspora model of rabbinical leadership, which is meritocratic, responsive to the needs of the community and permanently competitive, was nearly lost in Israel. In its place, rabbis have been appointed top-down by a rabbinic council to serve people to whom they may be strangers and even alien. Recent legislation of 2013 notwithstanding, that structure remains politicized, often corrupted and its communal legitimacy deeply compromised.

576. Thus, **the perspective of Jewish Flexigidity calls for a restructuring of rabbinic leadership in Israeli society, giving the power back to the communities, to households and to individuals.** In other words, Flexigidity of Israeli society will increase once state-sponsored rabbinic authority in Israel becomes accountable to the general public, to communities and to the people. Israel's Flexigidity would grow if communities would be allowed to choose their own rabbis, deciding who will teach them and learn with them, serve them, determine *Halacha* for them and be accountable to them; if a much bigger and more representative body of people would elect Israel's Chief Rabbis; if every family, couple and person could choose the rabbis who adjudicate their personal matters; and if multiple denominations would manage religious assets. **As Rabbi Sacks writes, "Judaism must be de-politicized and put back where it belongs, in civil society, far removed from all structures of power. That is the challenge of Judaism in the State of Israel in our time."**[316]

Governance that Serves Societal Pragmatism

577. **Collective pragmatism has been one of the key characteristics of Jewish society and an outcome of the dynamics of Jewish Flexigidity.** As described earlier, that outcome emerges out of the interplay between the decisions and actions of many small units of communities and households, many of whom may espouse radical outlooks. The absence of one authority that controls the life of all Jews has been an essential condition in this respect.

578. **The establishment of the State of Israel dramatically altered this societal mechanism through the creation of institutions of central authority.** The concentration of power in the hands of a government has been essential to the Zionist revolution in Jewish life. This government acts in areas where Israel's Jewish majority manifests its sovereignty, such as security, foreign affairs and various internal matters. The concentration of power into the hands of that government, particularly during Israel's earlier decades, circumvented the Flexigid interplay among Israel's community units.

579. Therefore, **Israel's electoral system and governmental structure of checks and balances are critically important for the collective pragmatism of the Jewish world.** The incentives that drive the work

---

316   Sacks, *Future Tense*, p. 178.

of Israel's legislature, the Knesset, and the government will determine whether the State of Israel is collectively pragmatic. The overall performance of Israel will have profound implications for the performance of the entire Jewish People, considering the growth of Israeli Jewry and the centrality of Israel to world Jewry. A pragmatic Israel will enhance and harmonize with the pragmatism of the entire Jewish People, while a radical and dogmatic Israel may polarize and radicalize large sections of Jewish Diaspora.

In order to serve the collective pragmatism of Israeli society, Israel's governance and electoral system must meet a few criteria:

580. *First,* **the Knesset and government must empower Israel's community-units as the foundational building block of society.** This can happen through laws and policies that encourage the development of local communities and their institutions and encourage their professionals and civic leadership to assume responsibility for shaping their destiny. As mentioned earlier, a societal architecture of a network of smaller community-units has been the foundation of Jewish Flexigidity.

581. *Second,* **the electoral system should encourage different sectors to deliberate and collaborate on the grassroots level.** Israel needs to nurture an electoral system that incentivizes Arabs and Jews, secular and religious across Israel to engage with each other in order to seek common ground. Such a political system is more likely to produce policies and laws that stem from a broad view of society and of the Jewish world. Unfortunately, at present, Israel's electoral system encourages the creation of sectorial parties, be they Arab, *Haredi* or national religious. Thus, many Israelis are exposed to a political discourse that is excessively and unnecessarily sectorial and radical, with weak incentives for collaboration, respect and mutual understanding.

582. *Third,* **the electoral system should encourage politicians to develop a broad view of society and be accountable to multiple factions, voices, constituencies and geographies.** Theoretically, the foundation of Israel's electoral system – which has Israel as a single electoral district – encourages politicians to develop a broad view of society. That system pushes parties to address people from the entire country and across all ages and life conditions. However, that same electoral system does not incentivize voting for large parties, and therefore its political spectrum comprises of multiple smaller sectorial entities. This condition

encourages segmentation and sectorial conduct, particularly when certain groups, such as the ultra-orthodox, national religious and Arabs, preserve their independent institutions to serve their specific constituencies.

583. *Fourth,* **the electoral system can encourage the creation of centrist coalitions that work 'across the aisle.'** At present, Israel's electoral system tends to encourage the largest party to initially attempt to build a political block with more radical factions in order to ensure the necessary majority in the Knesset. A slightly different electoral system could encourage the winning party to anchor its coalition in an alliance with the other large party across the aisle and toward the center. Naturally, the former structure encourages more radical and dogmatic politics while the latter one would tend to produce more pragmatic outcomes.

584. *Finally,* **they must create incentives for Israeli politicians to consider world Jewry.** Israel has taken responsibility for and committed to serving the entire Jewish world. Nonetheless, the non-ideological incentives for Israeli politicians to incorporate world Jewry into their considerations are weak. While this constituency does not vote in Israel, it does in effect participate in Israeli society and politics through political contributions and financial support to key non-governmental organizations. In this respect, Israel's present electoral system, in which the entire country is a single voting district, not only creates an incentive for politicians to think about world Jewry but also allows them greater liberty to focus on that topic in the Knesset.

Israel's 'Melting Pot' and the Ultra-Orthodox

585. **Another disruption to the Flexigidity of Israel's society has been the emergence of a large ultra-orthodox community that is excessively insular.** This phenomenon stems from the outgrowth of a large constituency of *Haredi* men who dedicate years and even decades to exclusive learning and teaching of Torah *(torato umanuto)*, exempted from military service and without acquiring modern professional skills.

586. **In the Diaspora, the forces of society and economics contained this phenomenon of *torato umanuto* to a small scale, which the community could viably support.** Jewish tradition and culture expected even the smartest students of Torah to earn a living and support their families, and, indeed, nearly all of the leading rabbis mentioned in the Talmud had professions. Only a small and dedicated intellectual elite actually

devoted their entire lives exclusively to the study and teaching of Torah and to establishing *Halacha* as rabbis and judges *(dayanim)*.

587. **In Israel, the availability of government budgets allowed for a disproportionally large community of fulltime learners to emerge.** This community largely lives in separate cities and neighborhoods and has its own network of schools, welfare organizations and communal institutions. In general, it has been exempted from military service and does not join the modern labor market. That reality is made possible by Knesset legislation and by government policies and budgets. It also stems from the electoral system, which most often grants this community disproportional political power.

588. **This model is financially, politically and socially unsustainable.** As the *Haredi* community continues to grow at exceptionally high rates, their virtual lack of contribution to the military burden becomes more readily apparent and polarizing and the extensive financial support of their institutions becomes fiscally untenable.

589. **Such integration of the *Haredi* community into Israel's labor market and military service is essential for other reasons, as well.** The logic of Flexigidity understands the interaction among multiple voices and facets to be vital for healthy societal dynamics. Military service and the labor market are the two great 'melting pots' of Israeli society, where Israelis of all walks of life interact, co-exist and create. The Haredim are painfully missing in these environments.

590. *Finally,* **this process may also broaden the base of Zionism in Israeli society.** Many modern *Haredim* are de-facto open to engaging with the fundamental idea of Zionism, which views the State of Israel as representing the collective right of the Jewish People to self-determination. Some of their leaders have already assumed ministerial positions within Israel's government that hold responsibility for all Israelis. In recent years, a representative of the Sephardic Haredi party, Shas, was even a member of the security and foreign affairs cabinet, and in 2010, that party joined the World Zionist Organization. Indeed, inclusion of *Haredim* within the broader Zionist discourse and engaging them in the collective efforts of Israel's state and society-building is a central frontier for Zionism in the coming decades.

Flexigidity Bottom-Up: Leadership
<u>For a Network of Prosperous & Resilient Communities</u>

This part of the book focuses on areas where civil society can make a significant grassroots bottom-up difference to the overall Flexigidity of Israeli society and the Jewish world, primarily by developing a web of communities that are prosperous, inclusive and resilient.

591. **Israeli Jewry is unique in its intimate physical concentration.** In Israel, more than forty percent of world Jews live in a space that is relatively small, excluding the area of the Negev desert, roughly half the size of the state of New Jersey. By way of comparison, in the USA a similar number of Jews are spread across a continent. Furthermore, Israeli Jews are highly interconnected due to geographic proximity, the mandatory and broad military service and the higher education system.

592. **Israel's civil society is vibrant, with a legacy that stems from the early decades of Zionism and from the Jewish Diaspora.** The *Yishuv* was made up of a network of communities organized around a web of institutions and led by civic leaders. As described earlier, this environment allowed for many societal innovations led by a vibrant community of societal entrepreneurs. That energy of creativity persevered, and is now evident not only in Israel's high-tech world, but also across Israeli society.

593. Meanwhile, **the lingering crisis in the capacity of the Government of Israel to govern expands the societal space for non-governmental leadership.** As mentioned earlier, that crisis is the outcome of internal deficiencies, as well as of global trends of a rapidly increasing pace of change that challenges the capacity of all governments to govern effectively the world over. Indeed, in recent years, the societal space created by Israel's weakened and shrinking national government is being filled by mayors and local authorities, nonprofit organizations and philanthropies. They assume a greater responsibility for key societal issues that hitherto used to be managed by the central government from Jerusalem.

594. Consequently, **Israel's civil society will play a critical and probably growing role in shaping Israel's future and overall Flexigidity, and will therefore also have great influence on the Jewish world.** As the Government of Israel, like other governments of developed nations,

declines in its capacity to address the acute needs of the population, societal entrepreneurs will increasingly inspire and drive multiple efforts of learning and adaptation. They will do so primarily by working on the local and community levels within thousands of institutions such as schools, community centers and synagogues in a bottom-up manner.

Following hereinafter are some of the key areas where Israel's civil society can and will have a profound effect on Israel's Flexigidity.

Broadening the Mission of Israeli Society: Nationhood, Faith, Tikkun Olam and Peoplehood

595. **Zionism and Israel's attempt to narrow the mission of Israel and world Jewry to nationhood was doomed to frustration.** As mentioned earlier, Zionism framed state-building as the organizing collective logic for the entire Jewish People, and treated Judaism's other meta-stories of faith, peoplehood and *or la'goim* from a domineering and instrumental perspective. However, the other meta-stories of Judaism are tenaciously rooted in Jewish culture and tradition, and would not be dominated. The outcome was an alienation of many Diaspora Jews from Israel.

596. Therefore, **Israel must re-vitalize its Flexigidity of mission by making the ideals of *or la'goim*, peoplehood and faith central and integral to it**. Indeed, in recent years, Israel has begun to gravitate in this direction, and the emerging synthesis of missions can become a foundation for a more vibrant relationship between Israel and world Jewry, which will bring significant value to both.

597. *First,* **Israel can become a primary platform for serving the ideal of peoplehood.** This was the inspiration for the Taglit-Birthright project, which was the first case in which the Government of Israel significantly supported an effort whose logic was to strengthen Diaspora Jewish communities. In the future, Israel must continue to support and strengthen Jewish communities around the world with financial resources, teachers and social workers, as well as security know-how and assistance. Israel should also establish itself as the central repository of Jewish artifacts, traditions, music, texts and rituals, primarily of communities that have declined and disappeared such as in Eastern and Central Europe and across the Islamic world. Institutions such as the Museum of the Jewish People, formerly called the Diaspora Museum *(Beit HaTfutzot); Yad VaShem*, Israel's center for Holocaust research, documentation, education

and commemoration; and the National Library of Israel are global Jewish institutions that enrich and are enriched by Diaspora communities. Thus, they are vital to this mission of Israel.

598.   *Second,* **Israel should embrace an audacious goal of making a distinctly Jewish and Israeli contribution to humanity, in partnership with the Jewish world.** Israel – through governmental and non-governmental activities – is already engaged with acute needs of human development in Africa and elsewhere in the developing world. However, this contribution should be deliberate, on a national scale, large and highly leveraged. The benefit that emanates from it must be credibly associated with Israel and the Jewish People. This would not only serve the vision and value of being an *or la'goim* and of *tikkun olam*, but also help build the legitimacy of the State of Israel and improve its moral and political standing in the international community. In addition, such activities will strengthen Jewish Peoplehood by bringing Diaspora Jews and Israelis together. In fact, this is a challenge that the Jewish People is uniquely aligned to meet given its global presences and disproportional representation at the forefront of research, technology, organizations and actions toward improving the human condition around the world. Finally, since trillions of dollars will be spent addressing these challenges, there is significant promise for Israel's economic development should it lead on such global challenges of humanity.

599.   In this context, **the stature and status of the Arab minority in Israel, and particularly of the Bedouin community, is of paramount importance.** Without offering this community a credible and accessible path for development, progress and integration, Israel's leadership on issues of *tikkun olam* will be clouded.

600.   *Third,* **Israel must continue to develop itself as the world's largest center of Torah, Judaism and Jewish learning.** An unprecedented number of Israeli *Haredim* commit their lives to *Torah* and *Halacha*, and the orthodox national religious community is also dedicated to intensive and extensive study of Torah. Even among non-orthodox groups, there are many who command great knowledge in the ancient and modern religious texts and traditions. Organizations like the Hartman Institute, Beit Morasha, the Secular Yeshiva, Pardes, Binah, Elul, Kolot, Alma and the Ein Prat Academy are initiatives that make the world of Torah accessible to many Israelis, helping to turn Israel into the largest center of Jewish learning in history. Open public spaces in city squares, community

centers, beaches and parks are increasingly used for modern engagement with Judaism. As a growing number of Israelis embrace their Jewish heritage, Israel's public sphere is filled with spiritual innovation. In the past, so-called 'progressive Judaism' was imported from the USA to an Israeli society, which was polarized between seemingly dogmatic and deeply entrenched 'secular' and 'orthodox' constituencies. However, if present trends persist, Israel will become a primary source of Jewish creativity, enriching world Jewry with its own distinct cultural, religious and societal creation.

601. **All of these areas are led by civil society, notwithstanding the critical role of government policies and funding.** Societal entrepreneurs are those that initiate the institutions, projects and programs that drive these agendas. They are the ones that often offer a vision, design the strategies and go through the essential phases of experimentation until new models are crystallized and consolidated. Only then, the government may support and scale such activities with funding and policy.

602. **Broadening of Israel's mission is urgent due to the growing rifts between Israel and Diaspora communities.** These rifts stem from gaps of expectations between Israelis and Diaspora Jews. While the story of nationhood is naturally more dominant in Israel, the narratives of peoplehood and *or la'goim* are more prevalent in the Diaspora, particularly among the younger generation. These different perspectives often cause tension and friction, which can be decreased if Israeli society credibly broadens the view of its mission. Otherwise, the rift between Israel and the Jewish world may grow to be unbridgeable.

Network of Communities, Meritocratic Leadership and Inclusive Growth

603. **Revitalizing Israel's network of communities to be led by meritocratic leadership is essential for inclusive growth and vice versa.** In fact, these seemingly separate visions – of being a network of communities and of generating inclusive growth – are, in reality, a systemic whole, which must lay at the core of Israel's Flexigid society. The interplay among many communities and their authentic local leaderships can be the driver re-empowering the 'invisible hand' of Israel's adaptability in the 21st century.

604. **A revitalization of Israel's network of prosperous and resilient communities is an essential condition for Israel's Flexigidity**. As described earlier, Jewish Flexigidity stems from the interplay among many small and interconnected community-units, which are permanently competing and interacting. Sadly, the evolution of the State of Israel compromised that network of communities, which existed in the *Yishuv* and was rooted in the legacy of the Diaspora. Consequently, Israel's overall Flexigidity declined. It must now be reenergized in order to enhance the capacity of Israeli society to be resilient, cohesive and prosperous.

605. In this context, **the legacy of the Diaspora, which teaches that every vibrant community must have a set of institutions at its core, is acutely relevant to Israel**. In the Diaspora, these building blocks included, *inter alia*, a school, a council *(nesiut or va'ad)*, a ritual bath *(mikveh)* and a fund *(kuppah)*. In Israel's communities, these institutions will necessarily need to be adapted to the context of sovereignty and to the existence of a government that collects taxes and regulates and underwrites key services. Schools and sports teams, early childhood centers *(tipot halav)*, youth centers *(merkazei noar)*, community centers *(matnasim)*, public spaces, and places for art, culture and music – **thousands of institutions altogether – stand to be the building blocks of Israel's Flexigid network of communities**.

606. **Such a structure creates a societal space for a significant local and meritocratic leadership**. These thousands of institutions can allow tens of thousands of civic grassroots leaders to assume responsibility and lead. Should Israel transition into a society of closely networked communities, made up of vibrant communal platforms, a large cadre of authentic local civic leaders, Jewish and non-Jewish, can emerge and participate in shaping the future of Israeli society through their own communities. They will thus revitalize Israel's Flexigidity and bolster the Jewish world.

607. **De-centralizing power as concerns community matters and allowing local diversity is essential for this societal vision and structure**. Every community, through its civic leadership and professionals, should have the freedom to take ownership of its institutions and establish its own unique patterns with regards to programing, content and priorities. Meanwhile, the Knesset, the Government of Israel and local authorities should provide budgetary security and legislative and regulatory foundations in order to ensure sound financial management, accountability and transparency. Hence, while community platforms should share multiple commonalities, each should also be distinct, unique and local.

608. **Such significant, vibrant, nationwide and grassroots meritocratic leadership is at the core of the Flexigidity of society.** The Diaspora legacy teaches that the evolution and adaptability of society is an outcome of the interplay among multiple centers of leadership that compete over the assessment and possible course of development. Tens of thousands of leaders anchored in thousands of institutions would necessarily enrich Israeli society and revitalize its Flexigidity.

609. **Israel's inclusive prosperity is dependent upon its communities and their institutions.** Inclusiveness requires that economic growth be driven by, benefit and improve the quality of life of a large section of the population, the so-called middle class. What is more, the logic of inclusiveness mandates that the weaker echelons of society and the geographic periphery grow faster than the national average and narrow the gaps that have emerged in recent years. In this respect, vibrant community platforms – dedicated to education, vocational training, healthcare, home economics, security and safety, accessible to all citizens and supportive of local small businesses – are not only essential for adult citizens to realize their capabilities and to accumulate human capital, but also for ensuring equal opportunity for children and wellbeing of senior citizens. **Hence, vibrant community institutions are an important driver of quality of life of individuals and households, and an effective platform for building human and social capital.**

610. **Such inclusive growth is essential for Israel's Flexigidity.** In the Diaspora, universal education within the world of Torah ensured broad participation in society, maximizing its intellectual potential, creating a vehicle for mobility and legitimizing communal institutions. Similarly, in Israel, inclusive growth is the condition for expanding participation in social and economic development and for tapping into the full intellectual and productive potential of society. It is therefore also essential for social mobility, for the reality of equal opportunity and for a sense of fairness that legitimizes communal and national institutions.

611. In this respect, **the Israel Defense Forces is of critical importance to the vision of inclusive growth.** The IDF is the largest human development operation in Israel, potentially offering soldiers formative experiences of skill and character building. In some of its areas such as leadership, technology and logistics, military training is so valuable that it is unrivaled by any other setting. In fact, many associate Israel's broad military service with the great successes of its technology and

business sectors.[317] In the past, the IDF used to be an equal opportunity system and a vehicle for inclusiveness. In recent years and for a variety of reasons, the mandatory military service has become an economically polarizing environment. A small minority of soldiers, particularly in the elite units and in the technological branches, receive invaluable training and professional skills that launch their careers. Others, who serve in ordinary field units, in supporting frameworks and in the headquarters, generally experience an environment that does not necessarily advance their human capital. Furthermore, about half of the women and nearly forty percent of men, particularly Arabs and *Haredim*, are currently exempted from service. While this may create a sense of injustice among many who do serve, it also denies those who do not serve the personal and professional benefits of military service. **Hence, placing Israel on a path of inclusive growth requires a new approach with regards to the mandatory military service, balancing broad conscription, equal opportunity for human development during the service and general economic productivity in society.**

612. Yet, **Israel's vision must go beyond mere inclusive growth to leaping the quality of life of its residents in order to close the gaps with the most developed nations and retain its talented young professionals.**[318] This means that Israel's economy must grow faster than the long-term average growth of other developed nations, as it successfully did between 1951 and 1972. Such a leap is not a luxury but rather a necessity for Israel in order to retain its human capital. The disparity between Israel's excellent human capital and the mediocre quality of life it offers in comparison to other developed societies has turned Israel into a leading exporter of human capital. If this disparity continues to grow, Israel may be vulnerable to 'brain drain', which refers to emigration of a critical mass of its qualified and educated citizens, eroding the professional and academic backbone of its society.

613. **There is no 'recipe' for leapfrogging a nation and each country that leapt has shaped its unique economic and social path** according to its own history, social structure, system of government and unique assets

---

317 See Dan Senor and Saul Singer, *Start-Up Nation*, Chapter 2, Battlefield Entrepreneurs, p. 41-54.

318 A 'leapfrog' is a rare and unique societal phenomenon, which occurs when average annual real GDP growth exceeds 3.5% for at least eight years, as was the case in Israel between 1951 and 1972, when Israel enjoyed average annual real growth of 5.5%. See Hausmann R., Pritchett L., Rodrik D., "Growth Accelerations", NBER Working Papers Series, Harvard University, 2004.

and burdens. Such a leap results from a 'perfect storm' of successful economic policy; societal, political and ideological ripeness; leadership; and powerful global trends. It is a meta-economic phenomenon, involving the entire society. Therefore, general economic theory is insufficient to understand it and sound economic policy alone cannot generate it.

614. **Inclusive growth based on a network of prosperous and resilient communities and led by meritocratic civic leadership must become a shared and unifying vision of Israeli society.** As mentioned earlier, inclusiveness, a cornerstone of Jewish Flexigidity in the Diaspora, was compromised in Israel, depleting its capacity to evolve and its resilience. Furthermore, global trends, and particularly the change in the nature and pace of change, affect all modern societies, Israel included. They increase social gaps and decrease social cohesion, in spite of any governmental efforts to the contrary. In such an environment, the legacy of Flexigidity suggests that each community in Israel must be aligned to support the development of its own human capital and economy. This allignment can be achieved through civically led community platforms interconnected and synergized to enhance local prosperity, inclusiveness and resilience, and, consequently, quality of life. Such a structure stands to create a whole that is greater than the sum of its parts.

615. Furthermore, **such an Israeli society will expand and deepen the relationship with the Jewish world.** It will more closely resemble the way Jews have been organized in the Diaspora, and therefore will ease the direct connections among communities. Thus, the worldwide network of Jewish communities may potentially be 'expanded' to include Israel's communities. By engaging them directly in areas of similar interest, the number of relationships across the Jewish world can increase significantly. In such an environment, the power and capacity to generate such societal impact will have been disseminated to countless new participants. Their ability to build thousands of new direct peer-to-peer and community-to-community connections will enrich them and boost overall Israeli and Jewish Flexigidity.

616. Thus, **a vision for the future resilience and prosperity of Israel's society can stem from the unique foundations of Flexigidity.** In this context, several such foundations stand out. *First,* the traditional structure of a network of small community-units can inspire the organization of Israel's society in the 21st century. *Second,* the legacy of Jewish communitarism is a distinct and invaluable asset of Israel, and its modern Hebrew manifestation can be central to the quality of life of Israel's Jewry. *Third,* the Jewish

legacy of life-long learning is critically relevant in the 21st century when professional and technical skills must be permanently replenished.

617. **This vision will require a decade or more to be effectuated.** Israel's last transition, which lasted two decades beginning in 1985, was preceded by a 'lost decade' of societal stagnation and slow decline. This envisioned transformation, too, will take significant time to emerge, requiring leadership and sustained societal learning and creativity by government, civil society, unions, the corporate and business sector and academia.

618. **'Adaptive capacity' for successfully coping with such accelerated change will be essential.** Heifetz defines such capacity as "the resilience of people and the capacity of systems to engage in problem-defining and problem-solving work in the midst of adaptive pressures and the resulting disequilibrium."[319] Indeed, in a rapidly changing world, most people will need to continuously learn to do new things in different ways, and most major industries and small businesses will have to evolve in order to stay relevant through the dynamics of 'constructive destruction.' The ability to do so collectively and individually will determine Israel's ability to navigate the pace of change. Societal failure to collectively adapt, compounded by the increasing benefits of a privileged few, may eventually destabilize Israel's economy, society and political system.

619. *Finally,* **the lingering crisis in the capacity of Israel's government to govern creates the societal space for such a vision to emerge and attract powerful forces of leadership.** Business leaders, mayors and municipal governments, philanthropists and nonprofits are increasingly assuming responsibility and leading in areas that used to be controlled and managed by the central government. Furthermore, hundreds of communities of young people are self-organizing and relocating to struggling neighborhoods in order to improve quality of life there. What is now needed is a network of resilient, cohesive and prosperous communities to emerge, where community institutions will play a critical role in increasing local prosperity and resilience and reducing vulnerability and poverty. Hence, from this perspective, **Israel's crisis of governance may be a blessing in disguise, allowing for the revitalization of Israel's society to be organized as a network of prosperous and resilient communities led by a vibrant civic leadership.**

---

319 See Heifetz, Grashow and Linsky, *The Practice of Adaptive Leadership*, p. 10-11, 303.

Flexigidity of Law: The Challenge of Israel's Talmudic Project

620. **Zionism has faced daunting challenges that required it to perpetually evolve its outlook by blending Jewish sources with modern ideas.** This burden of creating new societal knowledge is rapidly increasing due to the accelerating pace of technological, societal and political change, which mandates constant innovation of new ideas at unprecedented pace. These dynamics exacerbate the pressures on Israel's leadership to nurture the connection between its modern society with its Jewish roots.

621. However, **the number of people who are intellectually engaged with the future of Israeli society from a learned Jewish perspective is insufficient.** As mentioned earlier, one the most significant unintended consequences of Zionism has been the prevalent ignorance of Judaism among secular Zionists. Indeed, Israel's secular Jewry is often passionately Jewish and committed to the Jewish People, yet largely unacquainted with Jewish texts, traditions, history and legacy. Furthermore, while Israel houses the largest ever community of learners of Torah, only a small minority among them is dedicated to the application of this wisdom to the needs of modern statehood relating to security, economics and society. And, many of those that do so espouse a national-religious outlook that places Israel within a particular religious perspective of coming 'redemption' *(ge'ulah)* and the deriving focus on redeeming of the land *(ge'ulat haaretz)* through defense and settlement. Thus, only a few organizations and people are enriching the public sphere with an approach that blends Jewish sources with a 'secular' academic approach to such matters.

622. Thus, **revitalizing the Flexigid society requires a network of *batei midrash* dedicated to such *talmudic* discussion of Israel's future.** Such institutions should be based on a number of principles, stemming from the tradition of Diaspora Judaism, yet adjusted to Israel's unique conditions.

623. *First,* **their purpose should be to create a wealth of societal knowledge regarding contemporary challenges facing Israeli society by engaging Jewish tradition and Halacha enriched by modern academic learning.** Such knowledge must be created on both national and local levels regarding general and particular challenges. It must address the full spectrum of issues ranging from security and foreign affairs, to economics, social matters, law enforcement and relations with the Arab minority. It must transcend big picture matters to specific dilemmas using the technique of 'questions' and 'answers.' For example, Jewish law and tradition could be brought to bear on all matters of welfare such as treatment of people with disabilities, public housing, pensions, labor relations, unemployment benefits and affirmative action, as well as treatment of immigrant laborer and asylum seekers, enriching public discourse and governmental decision making.

624. *Second,* **many of these *Batei Midrash* should be anchored in and serve local communities.** To date, the tendency has been to develop *Batei Midrash* that deal with the broad challenges facing Israeli society. However, the logic of Flexigidity and the legacy of a network of communities call for many of these *Batei Midrash* to be anchored in local communities and to deal with their specific needs, thus creating multiple centers of intellectual engagement and leadership on challenges that face Israeli society.

625. *Third,* **some *Batei Midrash* may become platforms for engagement and societal knowledge-creation with Israel's non-Jewish citizens, particularly Christian and Moslem Arabs.** They can become a space where the rules of engagement among multiple religions are based on the respective religious legacies and sources, and on a shared effort to intellectually explore contemporary societal issues, through the lens of tradition and religion. Any societal innovation that emerges, which can be anchored in the legacies of multiple religions, will necessarily bear more legitimatcy and be more resilient.

626. *Finally,* **such *Batei Midrash* can enrich Israel's leadership with an intellectually meritocratic cadre that is deeply anchored in the legacy of Judaism.** Such institutions will create new gateways for participating in shaping Israel's future and its society through an intellectual engagement that is based on Judaism's universal systems of logic. Among secular Israelis it may enrich the acquaintance with Jewish traditions and sources, as well as, hopefully, increase the respect towards Jewish orthodoxy.

Among the orthodox, it can deepen the acquaintance with matters and dilemmas of modern statehood, legitimize national institutions, and create a setting where they can interact with other Israelis.

627. **The critical significance of such Israeli *talmudic* process for the Flexigidity of Israel's society is evident.** It will increase the number of gateways and frameworks for assessing Israel's condition and designing the course of its development. It will create multiple competing and complimentary centers of leadership. It will expand the cadre of leaders who rise based on intellectual meritocracy. It will be anchored in the communities. It will increase interconnectedness and mutual respect among Israelis. And, it may come to lie at the heart of the light that Israel has to offer to the family of nations.

Flexigidity of Place: A Vibrant Diaspora as a Zionist Imperative

628. **The worldwide spread of the network of Jewish communities has been key to Jewish Flexigidity and to the survival of Judaism.** It 'hedged Judaism's bets' on any single culture, polity and economy, and broadened its exposure to the diverse philosophies, languages and outlooks of the world. It made Judaism resilient, agile and impossible to vanquish. This has been the ultimate survival mechanism of the Jewish People, compensating for its inherent weakness as a powerless minority.

629. **Zionism achieved significant success in dismantling this Jewish worldwide web.** Its transformative vision was for Jews to become a sovereign majority in Zion. It called upon all Jews to repatriate and concentrate there, negating Diaspora exilic existence *(galutiyut)*, thus de-facto calling for depleting the Diaspora and ultimately dismantling it altogether. Great strides were made toward realizing this vision with mass immigration of thousands of Jewish communities and millions of Jews to Israel. Nowadays, nearly half of the Jews in the world live in a secure and prosperous State of Israel, whose Jewish population is growing consistently. This represents a remarkable demographic, political and ideological success for Zionism.

630. **However, the logic of Flexigidity challenges the wisdom of Zionism on this point.** It views the present reality of the vast majority of the Jews of the world being concentrated in just two economic, political and cultural baskets as compromising the overall resilience of the Jewish People. It questions the official vision and policy of the State of Israel

that would like to see Jews concentrated in just one location: Israel. As described earlier, it fears that theoretical scenario of repatriation of all Jews to Israel in order to solve the 'Jewish predicament' in the Diaspora may create an equally significant challenge of vulnerability for Judaism. This is particularly true when the State of Israel and Israeli Jewry face unique existential threats, and when, thus far, Israel's government fails to qualify as inspiring.

631. Furthermore, as mentioned earlier, **the facts on the ground challenge Zionism's vision of being the exclusive home for world Jewry.** Jewish Diaspora is as vibrant, secure and prosperous as it has ever been. And, a new phenomenon of a Diaspora of Israelis – hundreds of thousands of immigrants to the USA, Germany, Canada, Australia and other places – has emerged in recent decades and seems to be permanent for the foreseeable future.

632. Thus, **Zionism and the State of Israel must embrace the notion that a vibrant Diaspora is a Zionist imperative.** It is not only essential for the long-term survival and prosperity of the Jewish People, but also carries great significance for Israel. The unique voice of the Jewish Diaspora has been important for Israeli society in multiple areas. Hence, Zionism's determined call for *aliyah* should be morphed into supporting lifecycles of commitment to Israel and movement between Israel and the Jewish world.

633. **The strengthening of Diaspora Jewry must become a high priority for the State of Israel.** Government policies and budgets can address critical needs of the Diaspora, be they in the areas of security, education, culture and language. The Taglit Birthright Project, designed to bolster Diaspora Jewry, was an important milestone in this regard, and additional steps have been taken in that direction for example by the Jewish Agency for Israel. But Zionism is yet to articulate and embrace such a comprehensive approach that informs policies, priorities, budgets and institutions, particularly by the Government of Israel.

634. Furthermore, **Zionism's Flexigidity of mission, which raises both flags of nationhood and peoplehood, mandates a partnership between Israel and the Diaspora.** From the religious and cultural perspective, the centrality of Zion cannot be contested in Judaism. However, in many other areas all Jewish communities stand on equal footing. This means that mutual expectations must be anchored in real needs. Therefore, the mindset, which sets an expectation from the allegedly 'rich Diaspora' to

extend financial support to a 'poorer Israel' as if it were a 'Jewish tax,' is no longer as relevant when Israel ascends to first world prosperity. Therefore, future relationship must be based on a shared vision and an agenda that inspires millions of Jews not only to view Israel as central to their identity and wellbeing, but also as a priority of their generosity. Such an agenda can include supporting weak Jewish communities around the world, servicing the value of *tikkun olam* by making a distinctly Jewish and Israeli contribution to humanity, society building in Israel, Hebrew literacy and exploration of Jewish culture, rituals and traditions.

635. **A point of particular significance in this regard is the rebuilding and strengthening of Jewish communities in places outside of the State of Israel and the USA.** As explained earlier, these communities – such as in Eastern Europe, Latin America, China and India – are extraordinarily significant to Jewish diversity, richness and resilience. Revitalization of a five-thousand strong Jewish community in any of these places is far more important to Jewish Flexigidity than an additional similar size community in New York City.

636. **Another such point of importance relates to the view of the Diaspora of Israelis as inevitable and inherent to world Jewry.** The traditional approach of Zionism has been condescending toward Israelis who live overseas. As opposed to immigrants to Israel who 'elevate themselves' *(olim)* by repatriating to Zion, those who leave Israel are seen as 'going down' *(yordim)*. Prime Minister Yitzhak Rabin even referred to them as a 'drop-out weaklings' *(nefolet shel nemushot)*. As mentioned earlier, this constituency represents an oxymoron for classical Zionism, which related to either Diaspora Jews or Hebrews and Israelis. Nonetheless, the Diaspora of Israelis – who emigrated from Israel, yet view themselves as Hebrews and Israelis – is a permanent and growing phenomenon within the Jewish People, numbering hundreds of thousands at the very least.[320]

637. **This mindset of classical Zionism constrained Israel's ability to effectively engage Diaspora Israelis.** Its policies and practices focused on calling upon them to repatriate and on offering them primarily consular services. In other words, Zionism and the State of Israel refused to acknowledge that many Israelis emigrated from Israel, to view them as de-facto ex-pats and to shape policies accordingly.

---

320 See the website of the Knesset estimating the number of Israelis who live outside of Israel to range from 225,000 to 750,000. See http://www.knesset.gov.il/mmm/data/pdf/m03082.pdf.

638. **The logic of Flexigidity offers an alternative view focusing on the reintegration of Israeli ex-pats into the local Jewish community.** It views the on-going movement of Jews among communities as an inherent feature of the Jewish People, essential not only for Judaism's collective prosperity but also for Israel's. It celebrates the ability of Jews throughout history to plug-and-play Jewishly across the worldwide web of communities not just as a matter of religion, but also of continuity and quality of life. Unfortunately, non-orthodox Israelis have often lost that ability, feeling estranged from the institutions of the community within which they live, suffering the inevitable consequences of vulnerability and excessive assimilation. Therefore, **the logic of Flexigidity calls upon the State of Israel to partner with local Jewish institutions in reintegrating Israeli ex-pats into the Diaspora communities.**

Broadening the Band of Engagement with Humanity

639. **In the Flexigid society of the Jewish Diaspora, engagement with the world was a collective societal effort.** Every community and many individuals organically sustained their own relations with non-Jewish communities and polities. In the spirit of peoplehood, they often spoke for other Jews. These dynamics happened in trade, diplomacy, philosophy and academia. In its early phases and until the establishment of the State of Israel, Zionism's engagement with the world was also built upon multiple local Zionist associations that promoted its ideals within their local settings.

640. **The State of Israel represents a departure from this model, narrowing the band of society that is responsible for external affairs.** Its sovereign government concentrated the power to design and execute Israel's international affairs primarily in the Office of the Prime Minister and in the Ministry of Foreign Affairs. Additional government agencies were also empowered to develop relations in areas such as trade, finance, sports, business and health care. Therefore, far fewer Jews, Jewish communities and institutions within Israeli society are present at the frontier of Judaism's engagement with the world.

641. **The bi-polar geopolitical environment of the second half of the 20th century may have been conducive for such concentration of diplomacy in the hands of government.** Indeed, governments were the key players in the world that emerged following World War II, when the international community was divided primarily between two blocks, one

led by the Soviet Union and the other by the USA. In such a setting – when Israel was part of the Western block closely aligned with the USA and in conflict with the Arab world, which was supported by the Soviets – civil society was marginalized from Israel's international affairs.

642. However, **the international political system that is emerging at the beginning of the 21st century is increasingly atomized, gravitating away from Israel's traditional strongholds.** The universe of international affairs is now shaped by numerous small units of local and global corporations, universities and not-for-profits, as well as by individuals, nations and international organizations. While Israel's allies in the USA and Europe are immersed in an economic and political crisis, other powers, such as China, India, Brazil and Russia, are rising. While among the former, Jews are disproportionally powerful and influential, among the latter there is no numerically significant Jewish population. Furthermore, the so-called 'Arab Spring' seems to have led to the breakdown of Arab central governments and to the rise of Arab civil society as a significant player. And, the de-legitimization of Israel is itself led by a global network comprised primarily of not-for-profit organizations and individuals. The compounded impact of these trends on Israel's international standing is inevitably transformative, even if its effects are not yet fully revealed.

643. **This environment requires Israel to develop extensive, deeper and more meaningful relations with other societies and many more players** The past emphasis on relationships among governments and leaders can no longer address Israel's global needs and must be broadened. Israel must simultaneously increase the breadth and depth of its engagement with the world and its different societies, primarily by addressing acute development needs of individuals and communities.

644. Therefore, **Israel's external relations must become a shared responsibility of society, no longer exclusively led by traditional government institutions.** In other words, the gap between Israel's needs in the international arena and its governmental capacities is unbridgeable. Official representatives of the Government of Israel and the diplomats of the Ministry of Foreign Affairs do not have the resources to sustain, deepen and expand Israel's global presence. Thus, Israel's global standing must become a shared responsibility of Israeli society. The band of Israel's interface with the world can be dramatically broadened through the synergized efforts of the governmental and non-governmental sectors.

Key in this respect are non-governmental institutions within Israel, such as universities, hospitals, museums and think tanks, which can become platforms for deep and substantive external relations with the world.

645. In this respect, **a collective effort by Israeli society and government and by the Jewish world in the area of *tikkun olam* can become a keystone to Israel's future international standing.** Such a partnership – aiming to make a distinctly Israeli and Jewish contribution to improving the quality of life of many millions of disadvantaged people around the world – will significantly expand Israel's engagement with humanity, strengthen its moral standing and fundamental legitimacy and even support its economic development.

646. *Finally*, **Israel's ability to realign its global presence not only stems from its legacy of Jewish Flexigidity but will also help revitalize it.** It emanates from Judaism's balancing act between the universal and the particular, from the architecture of the Jewish world as a worldwide web of interconnected communities, from a history of past relations with and life among many societies, and from the meta-story of *or la'goim* and its interplay with the other stories of nationhood, peoplehood and faith. Such an outlook of engagement with the world and contribution to the world will not only enrich the mission of the State of Israel but also re-expand Judaism's interaction with humanity.

Questing a Model Society

647. **The ideal of a being a model society *(or la'goim)* has been at the foundation of Zionism since its inception and has enriched its vision for decades.** As described earlier, leaders such as Ahad Ha'Ahm, Herzl and A.D. Gordon made it central to their vision of Zionism. David Ben-Gurion also understood this vision to be essential for the future State of Israel, and therefore made it a centerpiece of his Zionist vision. Other leaders of Zionism emphasized alternative, additional and complementary aspects of the Hebrew model society. It helped shape the vision of the *kibbutzim* movement, was eventually enshrined in Israel's Declaration of Independence, underlay Israel's commitment to the growth of developing countries and inspired the Government of Israel and many Israelis to extend a helping hand in cases of humanitarian crisis around the world.

648. **The 21st century manifestation of aspiring to be *or la'goim* is as relevant to the future of Israel's Flexigid society as ever before.** Israeli sovereignty has dramatically transformed the context for serving such an ideal. On the one hand, its political system creates a disincentive for politicians to budget such efforts, particularly as Israeli society is struggling with its own challenges of poverty and vulnerability. On the other hand, the accumulated capacities of the State of Israel, compounded by the prosperity of Diaspora Jewry, create unprecedented opportunity for serving this ideal. Seizing this opportunity to create a distinctly Jewish and Israeli contribution to humanity is of vital significance to Israel's future for multiple reasons.

649. *First,* **a credible quest to be *or la'goim* associates the vision of the State of Israel with the ancient mission of the Jewish People and is essential for its Flexigidity of mission.** This connection at the very fundamental level of society is essential for the togetherness of the Jewish world. It inspires Israelis to contribute to humanity and plays a crucial role in the desire of Diaspora Jews to engage, collaborate and partner with Israel and Israelis.

650. *Second,* **it elevates the debate regarding the vision and character of Israeli society and mobilizes talent and leadership.** In the area of economics, it enriches the traditional deliberation common in modern societies about notions of justice and fairness, and informs the debate on the treatment of non-Jewish residents and citizens *(gher toshav)* in Israel. In the area of security, it strengthens moral considerations relating to the use of military force, and legitimizes the activities of the Government of Israel in times of humanitarian crises around the world.

651. *Third,* **it creates a surplus of fundamental legitimacy for Israel.** While the systemic and systematic de-legitimization of Israel erodes its fundamental legitimacy, Israel's credible quest to be a model society adds to its acceptance. Ideally, at some point, Israel can reach a point where its contribution to humanity is so remarkable that it comes to be viewed by many as indispensable.[321]

652. *Finally,* **this ideal of being a model society highlights some of the key notions of Flexigidity in Israel.** Israel would be admired should it succeed in generating inclusive growth based on a network of communities that are

---

321 The credit for the concept 'indispensability' as a national security goal for Israel goes to my colleague, Roy Keidar.

led by meritocratic civic leadership; introducing intellectual meritocracy into its public sphere; integrating its Arab minority; and becoming a leading force in addressing humanity's acute challenges.

Pioneering Society-Building

653. **The ideal of pioneering** *(halutziyut)* **establishes an expectation for personal responsibility, action and sacrifice in the service of the Zionist vision.** This ideal has inspired and mobilized many individuals and small groups as of the 1880s, and continues to do so today. It legitimizes individual actions in a de-centralized manner so long as they serve Zionism's broader outlook. It was embodied by David Ben-Gurion, who upheld it in his vision of Israeli society and retired from Premiership to *Sde Boker*, a young kibbutz in the heart of the Negev.

654. **The ideal of pioneering was critical to Zionism because it bridged its far-sighted visions with the often challenging reality through individual and communal action.** Building a Hebrew civilization, the ingathering of the Diasporas and ultimately establishing a state for the Jewish People were utterly imaginary in the eyes of many as late as the 1930s. In the same way, Israel becoming a model society feels unattainable to many today. Yet, the ideal of pioneering inspires many to take individual action and make their own contribution to this big vision. The legacy of actions by tens of thousands of people and communities that ultimately created the foundations for Jewish statehood continues to inspire many Israelis to believe that all the ills of their society can be repaired. It implies that countless inputs and actions by many can lead to a whole that is far greater than the sum of its parts.

655. **The fervor, devotion and willingness of pioneers to sacrifice stems from an outlook that places their actions in the broad context of Jewish history and destiny and within the framework of the stories of peoplehood, nationhood and faith.** Throughout Zionism's history, such inspired and pioneering individuals have been disproportionally engaged in defense, education, civil service and community building, challenging the materialism and perceived hedonism as seen by many Zionists in the coffee shops and salons of Tel Aviv.

656. Thus, **the meaning of** *halutziyut* **evolved over time to meet contemporary challenges of the Hebrew society and the State of Israel.** Being a 'pioneer' *(halutz)* and participating in the realization

of the Zionist vision *(hagshama)* were ideals of the Zionist movement in the pre-state days. Special camps and sites for preparation *(havot hachshara)* toward *hagshama* were founded in the late 19th century all over the Diaspora by Zionist youth movements. They trained participants in agricultural work, taught them Hebrew, Jewish history and Judaism, and prepared them for their responsibilities of self-defense. By 1948, thousands of graduates of these camps had become *halutzim,* i.e. 'immigrants' *(olim)*, 'settlers' *mityashvim)* and 'defenders' *(meginim)*. After 1948, pioneering continued to refer to settlement in the remote and unpopulated areas of the newly established state, to military service and to absorption of the mass immigration. As of the 1970s – against the backdrop of the crisis in the Zionist Labor Movement, the *kibbutzim* and the *moshavim* – the discourse of pioneering was taken over by the Settlement Movement. This now meant building communities and living in Sinai, the Golan, Judea, Samaria and Gaza. By the 1990s, *halutziyut* also came to encompass the assumption of responsibility for Israel's societal periphery, in development towns and poverty-stricken areas, by communities such as the so-called 'city kibbutz.' Hence, if in the early 1900s this ideal inspired young people to sit on a stool and milk a cow, in the early 2000s it inspires high-tech entrepreneurs upon acquisition to insist on maintaining the research and development of their companies in Israel.

657. **Pioneering is as relevant and necessary as ever for the Flexigid society**. The vision of Israeli society organized as a network of communities and communal institutions may sound far-fetched. Yet, the legacy of pioneering allows for collective movement in that direction, with the hope that ultimately, beyond a tipping point, that vision will become a reality. If past pioneers dedicated themselves to settlement and defense, future ones may be community-builders in community centers, self-appointed diplomats and founders of *batei midrash* for an Israeli *talmud*.

Israeli Flexigidity: The Art and Structure of an Adaptable Society

658. **The world is currently going through a dramatic revolution in the nature of change, which increases pressures on all human societies to adapt.**[322] The everlasting process and challenge of economic, social, political and technological evolution and adaptation has been known to human societies and to Judaism for millennia. However, in recent

---

322 This section significantly builds upon the works and teachings of Prof. Ron Heifetz and Dr. Zvi Lanir.

decades, the pace, frequency and scope of change have increased exponentially. The so-called 'flat world revolution' has brought billions of new people onto the global playing field based on infrastructures and technologies that allow them to interact, collaborate and exchange ideas at ever growing speed and efficiency. This process has been framed and captured by concepts such as 'the flat world,' 'the age of unthinkable,' 'the permanent revolution' and 'black swans'.[323]

659. **Consequently, the need for 'fundamental learning' – for creating new knowledge and for adaptation – is growing.** Every innovation – conceptual, institutional and technological – has a decreasing life expectancy before a new one emerges and sweeps the carpet of relevancy, effectiveness and efficiency from under its feet. Hence, as the pace and frequency of revolutions increase, the longevity of a successful new idea decreases. With every such paradigm shift, individuals, organizations, institutions and businesses, as well as peoples and nations, must create new knowledge in order to ensure their prosperity and security, and to adapt their values, priorities, patterns of conduct, institutions and incentives.

660. **Continued failure in the test of fundamental learning results in irrelevancy**, which may express itself in many ways: an individual may become unemployed and then unemployable; a business may lose market share or face a lawsuit; a nonprofit may lose donors and support; and nations may decline and even implode into a civil war, or ultimately even cease to exist. This is true in social issues and economics, in the business, government and non-government sectors, and on the local, national and international levels.

661. **Societal innovation is limited in its ability to alleviate these pressures for fundamental learning.** *First*, only few innovations breed sustainable long-term security and prosperity. The rest either do not provide even a significant short-term benefit, offer a trade-off between short-term gains and long-term losses or do not prove to be resilient beyond initial success. *Second*, many long-term consequences in complex systems are unintended and, therefore, cannot be foreseen even by the most brilliant minds. Occasionally, initiatives may even cause a backlash that will have

---

323 See Nassim Nicholas Taleb, *The Black Swan: The Impact of the Highly Improbable*; Thomas L. Friedman, *The World Is Flat: The Globalized World in the Twenty First Century*; Joshua Cooper Ramo, *The Age of Unthinkable: Why the New World Order Constantly Surprises US and What We Can Do About It.*

a reverse effect from that which was originally hoped for. *Finally*, while many naturally embrace innovation over tradition, sometimes the old ideas are the most relevant.

662.   Furthermore, **there is the predicament of success.** Any new innovation stems from a compromising reality and begins with an experiment. Successful innovations then become 'best practices' that are consolidated into institutions, habits and patterns of conduct. Flexibility is lost. Rigidity emerges. The serving elite of the first phase often ages, tires and retires. A new generation rises that enjoys success and tries to protect it, replacing risk-taking with risk-aversion and turning forces of change into protectors of status quo. Thereafter, rigidity and stagnation often lead to ineffectiveness, irrelevancy and ultimately to decline. Hence, paradoxically, as the only constant is change, the seeds of decline are always sown the moment success is attained.

663.   **The ability of communities to respond effectively to the challenge of adaptation varies.** Some successfully adapt to ensure renewed security and prosperity, which may sometimes even qualify as renaissance. They are evidently rising and their future is brighter, more prosperous and affluent than their present. Most muddle through. Others stagnate, prove unable to change altogether and eventually suffer harsh consequences that may even amount to collapse and decimation. The underlying cause for this is the extent to which they are relevant to the challenges and opportunities they face. Relevancy propels growth. Irrelevancy leads to growing insecurity and fewer resources.

664.   **Governments and political systems of developed nations have proved ill-structured and ill-equipped to meet the challenges of a rapidly evolving world.** The 'change in the nature of change' exposes the inherent weaknesses of political and bureaucratic systems, which lack the incentives to take a substantive, systemic, broad and long-term view of the issues at hand. Furthermore, government elites have limited collective access to knowledge, experiences and wisdom. The failure of the societal contract of recent decades, as it regards to the trickle down of growth, has led to a breakdown of trust in politicians among nearly all developed nations.

665. **In such an environment of turmoil, leadership is being increasingly exercised without formal authority.** Ron Heifetz defines leadership as the activity of mobilizing people to face the necessary adaptation in order to ensure the security and prosperity of their community. Such activity can take place from a position of authority by a minister, a rabbi and a school principal or from someone without authority. Yet, as the world is changing at such an accelerated pace, there is a growing mismatch between the structure of institutions and the mandates that their authority figures hold and the emerging reality. Consequently and inevitably, more leadership will necessarily be exercised without authority, primarily from civil society. This highlights the paradox of leadership in our time: while there is greater flexibility and more opportunities for creative and innovative action by leaders, the required adaptation and the pressures on leaders are growing exponentially, as well.

666. **Israeli society is at the 'bleeding edge' of this challenge.** It uniquely faces permanent adversity and exceptional volatility in the Middle East and around the world creating unmatched pressures for fundamental learning and adaptation. At the same time, as its government and political system continuously fail to address the deep societal concerns of Israeli society, a deep breakdown of trust permeates among Israelis.

667. Furthermore, **Israel is subject to and a victim of its own success.** Zionism's initial ideology, from the 1860s to the 1950s was revolutionary, seeking to transform Jewish society and to create a new polity in the Middle East. Indeed, the first fifty years of the 20th century were an era of radical and extensive societal experimentation and 'adaptability on steroids,' which peaked between 1948 and 1967. At its summit, Israel became so successful and powerful that it could no longer grow territorially and militarily. An overstretched Israel suddenly faced unprecedented adversity. It took five years for the peak of 1967 to begin to collapse in a series of adjustments that included the 1973 Yom Kippur War, the 1982 First Lebanon War, the collapse of the economic order in 1983-85 and the First Palestinian Uprising in late 1987. These events eventually led to a withdrawal from Sinai, a new economic outlook, the Oslo Peace Process, and the withdrawal from Lebanon and Gaza. Thus, the 1967 Six-Day War, which may mark the peak of Israel's success, may also mark the turning point of when Israel became a status quo protecting society.

668. **At that moment of supreme success, Zionism failed to update its societal approach in a way that was integral to its Jewish heritage and relevant to its future.** Israel's intellectual and pioneering energies focused on the management and protection of its territorial acquisitions, while two of the most costly endeavors of Israeli society since 1973 have been the settlement of the West Bank and the military. Society building was neglected, together with education, infrastructure, welfare and personal safety. Societal innovation subsided, the originality of the Hebrew civilization eroded, and the void that emerged was filled by general theories about economics and society, free-market and competition that were imported primarily from the USA without any Jewish roots and attributes. Thus, the Flexigidity of Israeli society, with its underlying ethics of inclusiveness and intellectual meritocracy, were compromised –and at a dire cost.

669. **This is why Israel's adaptability must be revitalized bottom-up and not just top-down.** Legislation, policies and budgets are essential yet insufficient. Israel's government is structurally constrained in its ability to lead Israel into prosperity in the 21st century, even if the electoral system is successfully reformed and bold decisions are taken and implemented. The pace of change in the world simply compromises the ability of central authorities to govern effectively. Meanwhile, the full potential of Israel's civil society is yet untapped.

670. **Being organized as a network of communities that are led by meritocratic civic leadership is the essential condition for Israel's 21st century renaissance.** The general public always possesses a great wealth of relevant information, knowledge and insights about its needs and potential solutions, which may stem from old traditions and from innovations happening in any corner of Israeli geography and society. Yet, that knowledge is scattered. The continuous process of its timely extraction and crystallization will necessarily involve trial and error, conceptual innovation, use of technologies and institution-building. Such broad societal evolution, tapping into the full potential of society, can only materialize through a network of vibrant, empowered and interconnected communities that are made up of thousands of institutions. In other words, **the adaptability of Israeli society and its future security and prosperity will stem from its architecture. This is the legacy of Jewish history and this is the vision for Israel.**

The Great Paradoxes of Jewish Flexigidity

This section describes the great paradoxes of Jewish Flexigidity: *The first paradox* is that Jewish society produces remarkable collective pragmatism out of the interplay among many radicals. *The second paradox* is that Judaism and the Jewish People may be in a state of rare vulnerability in spite of the fact that they may have never been more powerful, prosperous and influential in the world. *The third paradox* is that while Jewish Flexigidity has proven to be self-sustaining, even in the most difficult periods, there is also in an acute need for Flexigid leadership, due to societal developments both in Israel and the USA that erode it.

The Paradox of Collective Pragmatism Emerging from Many Radicals

671. **One of the great paradoxes of Jewish society stems from collective pragmatism, which emerges in spite of the particular radicalism prevalent in its midst.** The Jewish People has repeatedly produced a collectively pragmatic outcome. Jews congregated in countries that were generally prosperous and secure and literally shifted their geographic 'centers of gravity' multiple times. They were repeatedly able to accumulate exceptional wealth and political influence while preserving the autonomy of their core institutions and retaining their unique identity, effectively adapting countless times. At the same time, the Jewish public sphere is often comprised of many radical voices. Some of them are path-breaking innovators in the areas of ethics, spirituality, society, technology and politics. Others are staunch conservatives, clinging to ancient customs and habits. The interplay and the interaction between them is a unique phenomenon of Jewish society.

672. As mentioned earlier, **small and diverse communities are the building blocks of Jewish society**. While they share common, essential components, no two Jewish communities are identical, differing in their values, priorities, structures and institutions, and, therefore, lifestyles. Every node-community is relatively small, with even the largest modern synagogue only bringing together a few thousand families. In other words, the architecture of the Jewish People is conducive for and comprised of many small units. [324]

---

324 See Nassim Nicholas Taleb, *Antifragile: Things that Gain from Disorder*, p. 65-66, 69-71.

673. **All community-units of Jewish society are independent and autonomous, yet directly and indirectly interconnected and interdependent.** Such ties exist through personal relationships, associations, legacies and values. They allow for shared learning, the transmission of new traditions and collective adaptation. At the same time, every unit has the freedom to adapt the values, priorities and conduct of its own institutions to the needs of its members and to its specific local context. Thus, inevitably, some communities will develop a particular and even radical outlook.

674. **The leadership of the Jewish People is similarly dispersed.** Many centers compete for influence, leadership and power through brutally honest deliberations over the state of the Jewish People and the future of their community. Such debates occur within each community and among them. Yet, the impact of every leader and idea is limited and decreases with distance due to the vast geographic spread of the Jewish People and the radically different social, economic and political conditions of its communities. No single leader was able to sway all Diaspora Jews without opposition, not even Maimonides.

675. **Polarization, deep disagreement and even conflict are essential for the societal progress of Judaism.** Each member of the community is encouraged to sharpen their argument, stand strongly and fight wholeheartedly for their outlook. Moral standing for this stems from the duty to explicate the intentions of God while striving for the betterment of the community. Such dynamics breed heated debates, intense dispute, deep divides, as well as hostility, abuse and occasionally even internal violence. Judaism nonetheless prefers getting to the root of the conflict by exposing and polarizing the opposing worldviews to a cozy feeling of false togetherness based on shallow platitudes. Furthermore, Judaism understands that differences in core beliefs can ultimately breed new and essential ideas, and therefore chooses to regulate conflict, rather than suppress it.

676. **This entire structure reflects a deep understanding that a resilient society must contend with radical experiments and ideas in its midst.** Naturally, such experiments challenge the existing centers of power, institutions and conventions. Therefore they antagonize and provoke aggressive responses that may become abusive and violent. However, Judaism establishes powerful mechanisms to protect such voices and to keep them within the community. Its profound insight was that societal

adaptation and the evolution of ideas, together with constant changes in the external environment, may turn today's fringe into tomorrow's mainstream. Judaism is designed to be united but not uniform.

677. **Essential to this structure and dynamic are the forces of Jewish unity that pull Jews toward each other.** They ensure that most of these voices and perspectives will remain a part of the same society and continue to communicate with each other through the Jewish network. The inherent respect in Judaism for dissenting views that are 'for the sake of heaven' *(le'shem shamayim),*[325] i.e. for the service of the community, is critically important in this context. Many factions, particularly within the extremes of the Jewish spectrum, do not engage each other directly. Nonetheless, their views do get across through the worldwide web of communities because they are much closer to each other in this network than they might realize or admit. In rare cases, the innovation cannot be contained by Jewish society and the confrontation leads to a split or to harsh measures of ex-communication. Such was the case with the Baytusim of the Mishnaic Period and the Karaites of the post-Talmudic era, Elisha Ben Abuya and Baruch Spinoza, who ultimately were no longer considered part of Jewish society.

678. Ultimately, **for a new idea to become a generally accepted Jewish practice and sometimes even taking on the force of law, it must prove to serve the collective security and prosperity of the community, without compromising its core identity.** This 'proof' emerges through a painful, highly contentious and slow process that may last decades at a minimum, while the progressive forces adapt and implement it in spite of protests by the orthodox ones. Consistent, demonstrable success brings the more orthodox world to grudgingly gravitate towards allowing a change in its practices. The corollary of Jewish law and society with Jewish religion and faith rigidifies and eternalizes those few experiments that prove to consistently serve the security, prosperity and identity of the community. This process may take decades, generations and centuries to unfold, but eventually it affects even the most traditional groups in Judaism, whose pace of adaptation is slower than meets the eye. These dynamics of Flexigidity are permanently unfolding.

679. Thus, **the collective pragmatic performance and adaptability of Jewish society stems from its individual community-unit.** As every community-unit evolves it challenges the other interconnected

---

325 Avot 5:17 on Numbers 17. See also Sacks, *Future Tense*, p. 196.

community-units to embrace or reject that change, or to adapt it to their own context. Yet, Judaism's internal forces of debate and inherent dynamics of adversity create a counterforce to every innovation. This is why the potential chaos that may emerge out of the interplay among so many units with individual discretion rarely materializes. Every change in any one unit is calibrated by the responses of many other peer communities.

680. **These dynamics of evolution generate sophisticated risk-hedging of societal mechanisms that optimize the pace of Judaism's collective adaptation.** Innovation is essential for dealing with change, yet some novelties will prove invaluable over time, while others can be ill-conceived and even disastrous. Judaism 'hedges' these risks in that some of its factions engage with change while others are insulated from it, clinging steadfastly to old traditions. Therefore, Judaism is a permanently evolving hybrid of old and new, innovation and tradition. Its pace of progress and 'constructive destruction' of existing ideas, practices and institutions is optimized by its 'invisible hand.' The more radical the initial change, the more aggressively it will be challenged by others. Consequently, over time, radical innovations may be tamed, adjusted, adapted and potentially institutionalized, while simultaneously letting go of traditions that no longer serve the needs of the community. These mechanisms ensure that even epiphanies and revelations by individual geniuses go through the decentralized process that generates Judaism's collective pragmatism.

The Paradox of Security, Resilience, Prosperity and Vulnerability

681. **Another great paradox of our time is between Jewish power, influence and affluence, on the one hand, and the rare vulnerability of the Jewish People, on the other hand.** Paradoxically, both stem from the concentration of Jews in Israel and the USA. This is perhaps the inevitable cycle of Jewish history where prosperity and security encourage immigration, which in turn leads to concentration, which results in vulnerability.

682. **Jewish power, prosperity and influence at the beginning of the 21st century are at a historic high,** following nearly seven decades of dramatic and continuous rise since the Shoah. The Jewish national movement has been among the most successful in the 20th century, and Israel is strong, secure and developed. Meanwhile, most Diaspora Jews live in prosperous

and free nations within respected and influential communities, and USA Jewry may be the most politically and economically powerful Diaspora Jewish community in history. Few Jews are oppressed, and only a handful of communities are discriminated against. The world of Torah and Jewish life are flourishing and an unprecedented number of people dedicate themselves to Judaism. In conclusion, the vast majority of individuals, households and communities of the Jewish People are better off today than they were seventy years ago or ever before.

683. **But, geopolitical changes raise the concern that the power and influence of the Jewish People may be peaking,** as an outcome of a confluence of a few dramatic and powerful dynamics:

684. *First,* **the State of Israel raises concerns about its own longevity.** As described earlier, in spite of dramatic successes, Israel's national security remains mired in an unending control of the Palestinian population and by hostility to its very existence, while a radical Islamic regime may soon have access to a nuclear weapon. Two Israeli prime ministers in the past decade invoked pre-Shoah memories to describe the risks facing Israel. Concurrently, Israeli society suffers from some of the ills that are prevalent among other developed nations. In other words, Israel has yet to produce an approach to governance that is uniquely Jewish yet outstandingly effective in diplomacy, security and economics, meeting the expectation of being a model society.

685. *Second,* **the USA may be declining.** It is Israel's primary strategic ally and the home of eighty percent of Diaspora Jewry. Therefore, its military and diplomatic stature and its economic wellbeing have a profound impact on the future of the Jews. Hence, the weakness of USA governance and its deep and multi-generational economic and societal crisis of a looming debt and massive deficits are dark clouds on the horizon of the Jewish People.

686. *Third,* **globalization is eroding the unique value and edge of the Jewish People, which has traditionally been the foundation of its economic wellbeing.** Global interconnectedness through social media and telecommunication compromises a unique advantage for the Jewish People that stems from its global network of communities. Universal education is increasingly common and is no longer a distinctly Jewish characteristic. Many nations and peoples now have flourishing Diasporas, and some, like the Chinese, Lebanese and Korean, have reached global presence.

687. *Finally,* **the dynamics of Flexigidity, which ensured Jewish survival, security, prosperity and leadership, are being extensively and rapidly compromised.** As described earlier, many among Israel's Jewry no longer live within the framework of a community and participate in the dynamics of Jewish Flexigidity. In the Diaspora, the community structure is being challenged, as well. Thus, a high number of Jews no longer carry forward the DNA that ensured Jewish longevity.

688. *In conclusion,* **while this is a golden era of unprecedented security and prosperity for Jews, it is also a period of grave concern and emerging vulnerability.** Jewish Flexigidity is being altered and, perhaps, compromised by external developments and internal trends.

The Paradox of an Acute Need for Flexigid Leadership Now

689. **Another great paradox is between the proven resilience and adaptability of Jewish society, on the one hand, and the acute need for Flexigid leadership, on the other hand.**

690. **The framework of Flexigidity should engender confidence in the Jewish future.** Jewish society has demonstrated its ability to survive, prosper and to repeatedly offer leadership to humanity, outliving many great empires. That legacy implies that the Jewish People has the inherent capacity to adapt and evolve, and that Jews can be certain that Judaism will exist deep into the future.

691. Furthermore, **the dynamics of Jewish Flexigidity continue to propel an exceptional number of Jewish individuals and organizations to lead by experimenting with breakthrough concepts.** Such leadership, innovation and creativity stem from the permanent, structured and inherent tensions of Jewish society described earlier, such as between unity and adversity, idealism and realism, and openness and insularity. They are broadly evident in Israel and in the Diaspora. They inspire confidence that new ideas and structures will continue to emerge and be experimented with, and, if proven to serve the prosperity and security of the community, will eventually be institutionalized and scaled.

692. However, **some of the transformations that occurred over the past decades are unprecedented in their depth, radicalism and scope.** These changes compound the dramatic revolutions that occurred primarily in Europe during the 19th and early 20th centuries. So much so that the vast majority of Jewish households and communities have been profoundly impacted by them.

693. In general, **Israeli society has become 'rigid' by dismantling its architecture as a network of communities.** It concentrated many responsibilities that used to be handled at the community level into the hands of a central government. That structure is more rigid, politicized and insulated. Hence, many of the dynamics of Jewish Flexigidity were compromised in and by the State of Israel, and some of them barely exist in Israeli society. Consequently, the majority of Israeli Jews, who represent forty percent of world Jewry, no longer carry forward the DNA of the Jewish Flexigid society.

694. **Meanwhile, Diaspora Jewry, particularly in the USA, has moved in the direction of 'Flexibility.'** It has abandoned many of the elements that balanced the de-centralizing tendencies of the Jewish ecosystem such as the allegiance to Zion, mastery of Hebrew, connection to the world of Torah and the centrality of community institutions. This is captured by the statistics that fifty percent of Jewish young adult marry non-Jews without a desire to continue Jewish life within their households, and forty percent of USA Jews define themselves as 'just Jewish,' which often means that they have lost any meaningful association with Judaism and the Jewish People through community, Torah, tradition, Zion and Hebrew. Here too, many Diaspora Jews no longer carry forward the DNA of the Flexigid society.

695. Thus, **the longevity of Jewish Flexigidity should not be taken for granted, as the ecosystem that supported it may be going out of balance and become dramatically weakened.** The pace and scope of change both in Israel and the Diaspora are of historical magnitude. A large number of Jews are changing their societal DNA simultaneously at an unprecedented speed. This post-Shoah period of such geographic, economic, technological and societal transformation can only be equated to the aftermath of the destruction of the Temple. Then too, Jewish longevity should not have been taken for granted.

696. **Meanwhile, Jewish leaderships in Israel and in the Diaspora are growing apart.** The societal DNA in both locations is increasingly different. On the Israeli side, many of its politicians may have more in common with parliamentarians in other democratic countries than with the leaders of Diaspora Jewish communities. In the Diaspora, fewer leaders have a deep association with a State of Israel that is no longer so dependent on their collective mobilization. It is becoming increasingly more difficult for leaders in Israel to incorporate the perspective of Diaspora into their actions, and vice versa.

697. Therefore, **the Jewish People is in dire need of leaders and acts of leadership that stem from a holistic and broad view of Judaism, Jewish society and history, qualifying as 'Flexigid leadership.'**

Part V
Flexigid Leadership

The Challenge of Leadership in the Flexigid Society

This section explores the issue of leadership in the Jewish Flexigid society. Its first part defines 'Flexigid leadership' and distinguishes it from other types of leadership, making the point that it always engages with adaptive challenges. It then provides a short introduction to the theory of 'adaptive leadership' and establishes that such leadership would primarily stem from people who have no formal authority. The final part offers a few guidelines for 'Flexigid leadership,' i.e. for leadership interventions that are designed to enhance the Flexigidity of the Jewish People and to restore its vitality.

Flexigid Leadership Defined and Differentiated

698. **Jewish Flexigid leadership is necessarily inspired by a holistic, broad, historic and systemic view of Jewish society and focused on its fundamental elements**. It aims to serve the security and prosperity of the entire community, placing its particular focus within the broader context of Jewish history, legacy and destiny. Such leadership engages issues such as law, membership, community institutions, mission, language, place, unity, prosperity and security. In contrast, leadership that caters to any single faction within Jewish society, embodying a zero-sum approach where one sector gains at the expense of another, cannot qualify as Flexigid leadership.

699. **Flexigid leadership may also emanate from gravitating back to old traditions and from institutional and ideological innovations**. Chabad frames its actions within a broad view of Jewish history and society, allowing Jewish masses around the world to reconnect with old traditions. Meanwhile, the progressive movements that call for an egalitarian approach between men and women in Jewish practices also place their leadership within the broader context of Jewish history and society. Both examples view their interventions as essential. Both qualify as initiatives of Flexigid leadership.

700. **Towering individuals have played a central role in Jewish adaptability**. The leadership of such individuals stems from challenging existing structures, priorities and practices, from setting personal examples, from utmost dedication and from their ability to build lasting institutions. Inspiring examples of such individuals who led historical transformations of the Jewish world already mentioned in this book

include Rabban Yochanan Ben-Zakai, the Ba'al Shem Tov, the Vilna Gaon, Moses Mendelsohn, Herzl, Berl Katzanelson and David Ben-Gurion.

701. **Yet, Flexigid leadership can emanate from any place in society:** from conservative and progressive factions and from any denomination; from people in positions of authority operating as professionals in various Jewish institutions; from people acting without formal authority; from towering figures and from ordinary community rabbis and civic leaders; from men and women, the learned and novices of any age; from Israel, the USA and any other geographic location; from existing institutions and from the fringes of the Jewish community.

702. **All Flexigid leadership is necessarily 'adaptive leadership'** as defined by Ron Heifetz. Such leadership is about engaging with a challenge to the longevity, security and prosperity of the Jewish community and Jewish People. Most often, it is unprecedented and requires societal learning and adaptation. Such a challenge emerges due to societal, political and technological changes, undermining the status-quo, forcing the prevailing mindset, outlook and patterns of conduct to adapt, pressuring existing institutions and structures to be reformed, and necessitating new language and discourse to emerge.

703. Meanwhile, **not all adaptive leadership in the Jewish People amounts to Flexigid leadership**, particularly when it solely serves one faction and provides a situational or temporary remedy. For example, when the *kibbutzim* were created in the early 20th century in order to experiment with model modern Jewish society, they were seeking to offer Flexigid leadership. When, in the 1980s they were reformed, this adaptive leadership no longer qualified as Flexigid leadership for the Jewish People. It was mostly about their own survival and interests.

The General Challenge of Adaptive Leadership

704. According to Ron Heifetz's definition, **leadership is work that serves adaptation that is essential for the community.**[326] Hence, the work of a 'leader' must begin with a diagnosis of a gap between the prevailing mindset, institutions and habits, on the one hand, and the emerging reality,

---

326 On the definition of leadership and its characteristics, see Heifetz, *Leadership Without Easy Answers*, p. 11-66, and specifically p. 19-27. See also Heifetz, Grashow and Linsky, *The Practice of Adaptive Leadership*, p. 23-28.

on the other hand, which necessitates a realignment of the community in order to ensure its prosperity and security. Then, the leader must craft a strategy to help the community evolve by adapting its values, priorities, patterns of conduct, institutions and incentives. He or she must then take action to effectuate change. Failure of the community to adapt results in irrelevancy, which may come in the shape of economic decline, internal strife and insecurity.

705. **An adaptive challenge requires societal learning both as regards the nature of the challenge and the response.** Heifetz distinguishes such challenges from 'technical problems' whose nature is well-known, and, therefore, books and experts already exist to provide a 'fix.' Meanwhile, in the case of adaptive challenges, no manuals or authority figures can provide a resolution to the crisis, which requires creating new knowledge and adaptation.[327]

706. **Essential to such societal learning is broad experimentation and innovation.** Leaders must establish the capacity to launch experiments, assess their effectiveness and learn from them. The long-term consequences of such experiments are often unintended and therefore unpredictable. Few may succeed to increase the prosperity and security of the community. Some would eventually prove to be disastrous. Most will require tweaking and even overhauling to prove worthy.

707. Thus, **the essence of leadership in such an environment is orchestrating knowledge-creation regarding the challenges that face society and driving essential adaptation.** As Heifetz teaches, the art of adaptive leadership requires the ability to diagnose the condition of the community and of the leader, to make tough decisions, to take risks and to manage conflict and tensions.

708. **Such leadership occurs in an environment of extreme complexity and uncertainty,** where there is no direct link between 'cause' and 'effect,' 'action' and 'consequence,' and where the societal whole is different from the sum of all actions and inputs. Therefore, no one actually has direct and explicit authority and control over the 'system,' the challenges it faces and the stakeholders that will ultimately shape its course. In other words, adaptive leadership is, by its nature, risky and uncertain.

---

327 On the distinction between technical problems and adaptive challenges, see Heifetz, *Leadership Without Easy Answers,* p. 73-76. On adaptive challenges see also p. 30-35. See also Heifetz, Grashow and Linsky, *The Practice of Adaptive Leadership,* p. 19-23.

709. Furthermore, **a leader can rarely intervene in a similar eco-system twice.** By nature, a permanently dynamic society can never be identical at any two moments. Furthermore, acts of leadership in the first intervention may have already changed society. While knowledge of society is vital and general guidelines for leadership exist, every condition is particular, cannot repeat itself and requires adaptation. With rare exceptions, **the system is always unique and acts of adaptive leadership are necessarily pioneering.**

710. **The need for such adaptive leadership is mounting in modern society, as the pace of change is rising.** Frequency and scale of revolutionary scientific and technological innovations are growing, pressuring communities to adapt. Such dynamics also affect every individual, organization, institution and business, as well as every people and nation.

711. Heifetz highlights that **leadership is inherently different when exercised from a position of authority as opposed to without authority.**[328] **People in positions of authority are bound by a tacit and explicit covenant that limits their freedom to lead.** That covenant exists between every 'authority figure' and the stakeholders that gave her power. It mandates that the 'authority figure' protects the status quo and benefits the stakeholders in exchange for status, salary and perks. Such an authority figure is supposed to assign roles, resolve conflicts, protect the community and provide for its needs. Leadership from their perspective is to be exercised on others, but not on the stakeholders themselves.[329]

712. Therefore, **there is inherent tension between holding authority and exercising adaptive leadership.** While authority figures are appointed in order to protect the status quo of their stakeholders, leadership thus defined is about changing the status quo. This is why leadership from a position of authority is a perilous endeavor, as the harshest opposition would often come from the stakeholders themselves, typically those who appointed the authority figure and may now feel betrayed by their agent and appointee.

---

328 Heifetz, in *Leadership Without Easy Answers*, discusses leadership with authority in part II, p. 67-180 and leadership without authority in part III, p. 181-232. Specifically, see pages 67, 71-76, 84-88, 101-110, 113-122, 125-129, 138-144, 159-170, 173-177, 183-189, 205-208, 217-231.

329 On leadership from a position of authority, see Heifetz, *Leadership Without East Answers*, p. 67-150. On leadership with authority in adaptive situations, see p. 125-143.

713. Meanwhile, **adaptive leadership without authority results from the actions of people who do not have a formal mandate to lead.** They take action in order to accelerate societal learning and adaptation with an aim of protecting and increasing the prosperity and security of the community. Their actions often challenge the prevailing order and those that are dependent on and benefit from it. Therefore, people who lead without authority inevitably meet resistance, directed against their vision and targeted against them personally. This is why Heifetz warns that the work of leadership, and particularly that which is done without authority, is always dangerous.

714. **The necessity for leadership without authority is rising in increasingly dynamic societies.** Structures and institutions, where authority figures reside and operate, were designed in the past to address the challenges of their time. They inevitably evolve, yet are rarely able to do so effectively over time. Meanwhile, the ever-growing pace of change in the world creates bigger and more frequent gaps between institutions and reality. Therefore, as the mandates of authority figures are in a permanent deficit of relevancy, the significance of leadership without authority is rising in society.

The Qualities of Flexigid Jewish Leadership

> This final section of the book articulates some guidelines for leadership that is designed to revitalize the Flexigidity of the Jewish People. Such leadership must be placed within the broad context of Jewish history and society, be authentic and respectful of adversity, be anchored in extensive diagnostics while still relating to a vision, taking action and building community institutions.

715. **Flexigid leadership – through countless individual acts and innovations – drives the evolution of Jewish society and ensures its survival, security, prosperity and leadership.** It is mostly associated with towering individuals who left a lasting mark on Judaism that echoed for decades, generations, centuries and even millennia. However, the collective evolution of Jewish society is ultimately made possible through the Flexigid leadership of innumerable civic leaders and professionals at any given moment, whose efforts and actions were not enshrined in collective Jewish history.

716. **Flexigid leaders and acts of Flexigid leadership in Judaism share a number of characteristics.** These characteristics emerge in the legacies of Biblical, rabbinic and modern figures such as Moses, King David, the prophet Deborah, Rabban Yochanan Ben-Zakai, Maimonides, Rabbi Saadia Gaon, the Vilna Gaon, the Lubavitcher Rebbe, Herzl, Ahad Ha'Ahm and David Ben-Gurion. **In an era of acute need for such Flexigid leadership, it is essential to understand its qualities.**

Speaking to the Broader Context of Jewish Society and History

717. **Flexigid leadership places itself in a broad context of Jewish history, addressing acute societal needs.** It connects the past and present of the Jewish People with a desired future. Prime examples include Rabbi Yehuda HaNasi who sought to protect the Oral Torah in the aftermath of the Bar-Kochva rebellion by formulating the *Mishnah* and the Heralds of Zionism who aimed to address the crisis of Jewish society in the Diaspora following centuries of exile by mass-repatriation to Zion.

718. **Such leadership envisions a societal whole that is greater than the sum of all activities taken by the leaders and their followers.** It seeks a transformation that will come into being out of the accumulation of

numerous 'technical actions' by many people across society. Such a 'systemic effect' is 'non-linear' in the sense that there is no direct correlation between the activities of leaders and the countless actions of people that they inspired, on the one hand, and the resulting reality that will emerge, on the other hand. Therefore, the followers are often expected to obey and adhere even if the bigger vision is unknown, unclear and uncertain to them *(na'a'se ve'nishma)* When Ezra the Scribe commanded that the Torah be routinely read in public in 6th century BCE, the purpose was to enshrine it in Jewish society. When the ideology of Zionism called upon its followers to settle the land and to build agricultural communities, the overall purpose was to resolve the crisis of Judaism in Europe and to repair the exilic condition. Hence, in different times, places and contexts, different actions may have been required, but there was always a link between such activities and the broader vision of Jewish security and prosperity.

719. *Finally,* **narratives are also essential for such Flexigid leadership.** They bring together in a coherent story all the above elements: the broader context of Jewish past, present and future; a challenge facing Jewish society; the vision, mission, purpose, strategy and activities of the leader; and the actions required from the inspired masses.

Vision and Fundamentals

720. **A compelling vision, which is audacious and attainable, is essential for Flexigid leadership.** Such a vision must outline a reality in which the given crisis facing society is remedied through a transformation. It must describe a new order and a different trade-off among values and priorities that will allow society to effectively confront the challenges it faces and seize its opportunities.

721. **Such a vision must be informed by the Flexigidity of mission of the Jewish People.** As mentioned earlier, Judaism offers four alternative frameworks regarding its mission, vision, purpose, legacy and destiny: peoplehood, nationhood, *or la'goim* and faith. Jewish Flexigid leadership must be anchored in one of the four meta-stories, or in a combination thereof. Each of these stories may produce different actions in different contexts, and a similar action may fit into more than one narrative. The story of nationhood may alternatively inspire settlement in Judea and Samaria or the evacuation of such settlements. And, a project such as Taglit-Birthright may be inspired by both the logic of nationhood and

that of peoplehood. Indeed, the towering leaders of the Jewish People integrated multiple meta-stories into their narratives and visions.

722. Therefore, **Jewish Flexigid leadership is necessarily about the fundamental elements of Jewish society** such as law, membership, community, mission, language, place, unity, prosperity and security. It must address core underlying issues in order to offer a fundamental remedy to the challenges facing society. It must envision different institutions, new ways of getting things done, and a new language and discourse. It necessarily requires painful departures from existing norms and practices in order to create the space for societal innovation.

723. **Publicly articulating such a vision may be constructive for or obstructive to societal progress.** In certain cases, it may help galvanize and coalesce diverse groups. In other cases, when there is unity of tactical action, explicitly articulating such a vision may undermine societal progress. Nonetheless, Flexigid leadership requires a compelling vision whether it is publically communicated or not.

724. In other words, Flexigid leadership does not just happen by accident. **Flexigid leadership is deliberate.**

Diagnosis and Strategy

725. **Flexigid leadership is a thoughtful undertaking based on a thorough analysis** that bridges the existing reality, societal gap that must be addressed and the aspired vision. It is almost always heavily under-resourced as a result of the way its audacious goals are framed within the broader context of society as a whole and the full scope of Jewish history and destiny.

726. **In describing the societal gap that is to be addressed, the brewing crisis between the existing order and the emerging reality must be exposed.** This requires identifying the areas where the prevailing mindset, existing structures and institutions, language and discourse, and patterns of conduct are no longer effective and should therefore be adapted.

727. **Its tacit underlying assumption is the notion that there are 'no broken systems.'** This notion suggests that all entities – be they families, organizations, nations and societies – are perfectly aligned to produce the outcomes they produce, even if they appear dysfunctional to some

members and to outside observers. Thus, there is logic to every societal system, from which generalizations can be made and articulated.

728. **This process of diagnosing such a dynamic system must be ongoing as society is ever-changing.** There is permanent motion among its different elements. At any given moment, some of the traditional forces and structures are deeply entrenched and powerful, slowly eroding or 'on the edge of chaos.' Furthermore, leaders transform the systems into which they intervene, as any act of leadership in and of itself impacts society. Therefore, there can rarely be two identical interventions. Thus, **accurate societal diagnostics is essential for successful Flexigid leadership.**

729. *Finally*, **Flexigid leaders must articulate a strategy that bridges between the emerging crisis, the scarce resources and the vision.** That strategy must be comprised of principles and guidelines that engender confidence that the vision is attainable, informing broad participation and action. It must envision the dynamics of scaling where initial, local and experimental beginnings become common practice. It must identify the necessary resources and guide their mobilization. With such a strategy, a leader must act as a catalyst that brands the vision; presents it to the many stakeholders; establishes, documents and models cases of success; informs and educates people in positions of authority, leadership and influence; and builds essential partnerships.

Boots on the Ground: Community, Institution and Capacity Building

730. As mentioned earlier, **communities are the building blocks of Jewish society, and institutions are the building blocks of communities.** Their development must be at the heart and focus of Flexigid leadership.

731. **The life-cycle of institutions from birth to death is integral to the evolution of Jewish society.** Jewish history is full of examples of institutions that emerged, rose to prominence and served a critically important societal role in specific periods and contexts. Some dominated, became rigid, lost relevancy, declined and eventually disappeared. Some were destroyed never to reemerge after the changed circumstances. Examples include the Great Assembly *(Knesset Gedola)*, the Yavne Academy and the great academies *(Yeshivot)* of Mesopotamia, and the Council of Four Lands *(Va'ad Arba Haaratzot)*. In the 21st century, organizations such as the Zionist Congress, the World Zionist

Organization, the Jewish Agency for Israel and the Jewish Federation system in the USA are challenged to adapt by a world that increasingly favors flexibility and agility over rigidity, and the wisdom of crowds over that of committees.

732. Therefore, **essential and integral to lasting Jewish Flexigid leadership is affecting existing institutions and building new ones.** Such Flexigid leadership is rarely just about articulating an idea, initiative or a specific program, but also about the developing the institutions and capacities that will carry it forward, theoretically in perpetuity. Indeed, many of the towering figures of Jewish history were relentless institution-builders. Rabban Yochanan Ben-Zakai built the academy in Yavne, Rabbi Akiva had forty thousand students, Rabbi Saadia Gaon led the Jewish academies in Babylon and Herzl initiated key institutions of the Zionist movement.

733. **Developing the capacity of institutions to adapt is a central challenge for Flexigid leadership.** Effectively dealing with a specific challenge in a particular context and location may be commendable yet is insufficient. Leaders that made a lasting impact on Jewish society were able to build institutions that were adaptive, with an inherent ability to evolve, survive and thrive while addressing different challenges in different contexts and over a long period of time. Their philosophy was accurately Flexigid, anchored in rigid foundations yet flexible to remain relevant. This often entailed allowing the emergence of many small units in a bottom-up fashion that were bound together by a great vision, yet were free to reflect local conditions. The greatest institutions of Jewish society and history – synagogues, *Yeshivot*, the councils and the Chabad network – embody this delicate balance.

734. *Finally*, **effectuating significant change in the Jewish worldwide web of communities requires impacting the 'hubs'** as they have disproportionate influence over the entire Jewish network, or large sections thereof. Most Flexigid Jewish leaders naturally gravitated to the great Jewish communities of their time, mostly in large bustling metropolitan areas. They worked within their leading institutions and were able to affect the Jewish world through the vibrant interconnectedness of their community with other leading hubs near and far.

Authenticity and Partnering Across Society

735. **A vision of a Jewish Flexigid leader must be inclusive toward most, if not all of Jewish society.** As mentioned earlier, such leadership addresses a fundamental gap that concerns the entire Jewish society, or large sections thereof, with a broad view of Jewish past, present and future. By definition, it transcends any specific faction and is beyond situational, temporal and local concerns and considerations. Therefore, such a vision is necessarily inclusive in that it concerns itself with the needs of many Jews, Jewish communities and their institutions. It must be about 'expanding the pie' for all and not about catering to any single faction or issue at the expense of another.

736. **Effectuating such a vision requires leadership by a committed and serving elite**, comprised of people who hold positions of authority, leadership and influence and use their power for a greater good. A vision that informs Flexigid leadership necessarily establishes foundations for collaboration across societal lines as it speaks to a broad spectrum of society. It necessarily falls beyond the capacity of any single leader to effectuate it single-handedly. It requires the commitment of and action by an entire group of people in positions of influence, authority and leadership from all sectors of society that are mobilized in order to realize that vision.

737. **The individual identity of Jewish leaders determines their freedom of association.** As mentioned earlier, Jewish Flexigid leadership can emanate from anywhere in its society. Yet, the identity of leaders profoundly impacts their scope of leadership: the kind of positions they can credibly take; the associations they can naturally create; the rivalries they will inevitably face and the divides they must bridge. Flexigid leadership by a Jewish, Zionist, Israeli, secular businessperson is different from that of someone in the USA who belongs to the Conservative movement and works as a principal of a Jewish day school. So, too, Flexigid leadership by an orthodox Jew in Estonia will need to reflect the reality of his community

738. Therefore, **Flexigid leadership requires authenticity**. Statements about values, priorities and issues – be it about a place of residence in Israel or the Diaspora or about denominational association, for example – are important yet insufficient. Authenticity emerges from a life's journey of struggles and choices that validate the position one wants to lead from and serves to legitimize their vision and action.

739. Therefore, **Flexigid leaders must have the capacities to engage partners across the Jewish society.** They need to 'negotiate' and 'deliberate' with a multi-faceted group of people and organizations. They must be able to work beyond their natural constituency, gain the trust of and collaborate and partner with factions that have different values, priorities and patterns. Shared interests may be important, but they are also contextual and insufficient for sustaining resilient and long-lasting partnerships. By doing so, they transcend the existing delineations within society and create a new reality of transformative alignments and coalitions.

Respect for Adversity and Dignity of Dissent

740. As shown earlier, **the Jewish world progresses pragmatically through the engagement, friction and even confrontation among strong individuals and groups.** This is based on the notion that conflict is essential for societal progress, and therefore it must be encouraged yet regulated, but not suppressed. Thus, Judaism encourages its members to sharpen their arguments and not dilute them; to debate their fellow Jews and get to the root of the conflict over engaging in shallow platitudes; to expose and polarize the opposing worldviews and not to cover them. Such dynamics breeds heated debates, intense disputes, deep divides and even hostility, verbal abuse and physical violence. The societal logic is to get to the bottom of the question: "What will best serve the security and wellbeing of the community and preserve its identity?" Such forceful and regulated engagement among leaders has been essential for Jewish survival, security, prosperity and leadership.

741. **This societal structure sends a conflicting message to leaders: while they are encouraged to fight wholeheartedly for their outlook, they are also reminded of their interdependence on their counterparts.** Like any other society, in the Jewish People there is no leadership without opposition and occasional verbal abuse, physical violence, marginalization and even excommunication. At the same time, Jewish society is deeply interconnected. The full spectrum between progressive and conservative factions plays a vital role in optimizing its pace of adaptation to ensure collective survival, security, prosperity and leadership. As Flexigid leadership is inherently about taking a broad view of history and society, Flexigid leaders can only on rare occasions legitimately disregard another Flexigid leader.

Join the conversation www.flexigidity.com

742. Therefore, **the ultimate relationship between two Jewish adversaries who are working to better the condition of the community is one of mutual respect and gratitude.**[330] Jewish Flexigid leaders who are protagonists must acknowledge their interdependence and interconnectedness, as well as that they are all stakeholders in the future of society, jointly shaping its course through their adversity. These notions should increase the dignity of dissent among Flexigid leaders and tame the animosity of their conflicts and the fierceness of their engagements. In other words, mere tolerance does not qualify. As mentioned earlier, Judaism holds those who fight for their worldview in order to serve the wellbeing of the community as serving God *(le'shem shamayim)* and explicating His intentions *(Eleh Ve'Eleh Divrei Elokim Chaim)*.

743. **The Talmud equates such respectful adversity with the struggle between Hillel and Shammai.** The two great sages contested each other's opinions, yet treated one another with great respect and kept the community together by marrying their children. The Talmud also establishes that eventually law was made according to the House of Hillel, whose students treated their interlocutors with extra respect by teaching the opinion of the House of Shammai before their own. **Such an attitude is as essential today as two thousand years ago**.

---

330 See Bronfman and Zasloff, *Hope, Not Fear*, p. 77 for a different take on the idea of mutual respect. Bronfman and Zasloff write: "Some call for tolerance, but I prefer the words "mutual respect.." Credit also goes to David Suissa of Los Angeles for crystallizing this insight.

Epilogue

Flexigidity is a simple concept designed to allow for deeper and better understanding of Jewish survival, resilience, prosperity and leadership. It highlights the critical significance of Judaism's inherent, structural and unbridgeable tensions between old and new, tradition and innovation, rigidity and flexibility. It exposes the forces that drive Jews apart while keeping them together, optimizing the pace of Jewish adaptability in the face of an ever-changing political, technological and economic reality, and it shows how the conservative and the progressive factions of Judaism are interconnected and interdependent. It frames the architecture of the Jewish People as a network of small units – communities and their institutions – as the most important foundation of Jewish longevity.

From that perspective it is evident why the Jewish People may be at a crossroads of historic magnitude. At a time of unprecedented power and prosperity, Jews may be in a rare position of vulnerability, being over-concentrated in Israel and the USA, where their societal DNA is being changed dramatically. In other words, the long-term security of the entire Jewish People is possibly being compromised precisely at the historical peak of Jewish influence and affluence. In this context, Zionists and Israelis should be particularly concerned: while Israel seeks to ensure its longevity and security, and to serve the broader cause of the Jewish People, it is also rapidly compromising some of the essential ingredients of Jewish Flexigidity.

The paradox of that concern is inescapable. If the idea of Flexigidity implies that Judaism is eternal in human terms, both resilient and adaptable, why should one worry? After all, it mandates that Jewish society is self-correcting by optimizing its own pace of societal evolution through the endless interplay among its countless small units. In simpler words, Judaism will successfully thrive even through the current wave of unprecedented change.

The answer is that Jewish adaptability also stems from the sense of urgency among many Jews. Evolution of Jewish society is propelled by leaders who are permanently driven by a sense of an imminent threat and possible catastrophe, as well as by a 'can-do' legacy and attitude. Hence, the collective adaptive capacity of the Jewish People, which renders it exceptionally resilient, stems from the permanent sense of concern among many individual Jews. In other words, Jews are collectively resilient, yet individually insecure.

This book should make a powerful and unshakeable argument that a wealth of

Join the conversation www.flexigidity.com

new societal knowledge must be created in order to cope with the new realities of the 21st century. While much in Jewish history may generate relevant insights, nothing there provides a blueprint for action and a manual for building the capacities and institutions that will ensure survival and prosperity in the emerging realities of the coming century.

That is the reason why Flexigid leadership is vitally essential at this point in time. Such leadership must stem from countless people and organizations that commit themselves to a leadership that is planted in a broad view of Jewish history and inspired by a holistic and systemic view of Judaism and Jewish society. To have a long-lasting effect, such leaders must address the fundamental societal elements such as law, membership, community, mission, language and place based on a broad understanding of Jewish history and society. And, they must engage in the labor of capacity and institution-building.

Furthermore, as they use the framework of Flexigidity toward their own leadership, they should also contribute to its development through their own experiences and insights. The era when one person provided such a comprehensive framework addressing any and all issues while others subscribed and used it or criticized and rejected it, is both unrealistic and unnecessary. In fact, it is an outlook that is alien to the legacy of the *talmudic* process and the Talmud itself. The Flexigidity Project has been inspired by this insight. As modern tools of communication allow for engaging many participants in such deliberation, the shared comprehension of Jewish society must be the outcome of a collective effort.

The Flexigidity Project grew out of my work and personal experiences, and as a response to my need for an organizing framework to guide my actions. I am not an academic, nor am I a passive observer, but rather a participant in the collective undertaking of the Jewish People. I do not think of this book as offering a 'historical perspective' or a 'prophetic voice.' Inspired by Kurt Lewin's famous saying that "there is nothing more practical than a good theory," I intend to use the Flexigidity framework in my own work and hope that it will be found useful by many others.

In 2004, I founded the Reut Institute to respond to my sense of urgency concerning the Jewish People and the State of Israel. Together with my colleagues and with the support of friends around the world, we built Reut over the years as an institution that seeks to provide Flexigid leadership in areas of the security and prosperity of Israel and the Jewish world, as well as by making an indelibly Jewish and Israeli contribution to humanity.

We view Zionism as a dynamic ideology that seeks to realize the right of the Jewish People to self-determination in its own nation-state. We work to help Zionism and Israel continuously evolve, responding to internal and external developments and successfully addressing their toughest challenges. Central to our strategy has been grooming Flexigid leaders who themselves assume positions of authority, leadership and influence in Israel and the Jewish world.

We have been focused on issues that stem directly from the logic of Flexigidity: on the re-structuring of Israeli society as a network of prosperous and resilient communities led by vibrant local civic leadership; on ensuring the ideal of inclusive growth; on securing the fundamental legitimacy of the State of Israel; on imagining new ways to keep the State of Israel and Diaspora Jewry close, in spite of their growing rift; and on the responsibility and opportunity of the State of Israel and the Jewish People to make a significant contribution to humanity. Our work is founded upon thorough diagnosis, attempting to articulate compelling visions and strategies, testing and piloting our ideas on the ground, modeling new capacities and institutions, and partnering with other organizations in order to ensure the scalability of our initiatives.

In sinking our teeth into Israel's most daunting challenges, my colleagues and I at Reut believe that the Flexigid legacy of Judaism is vitally important and relevant to the challenges that face Israel as a society. It is also invaluable to Israel's future adaptability as the pace of change in the world only accelerates. In fact, we hold the legacy of a permanent and universal *talmudic* process of learning and interpretation, of inclusive growth and of a network of communities, to be key to Israel's future prosperity and resilience. They place Israel in a unique position of advantage in comparison to all other developed nations, endowed with the opportunity to rise to global leadership in the coming decades.

In fact, I view our Reut team as a member of the community of the Flexigid leaders of the Jewish world. We place our work within the broader context of Jewish history and society. We experiment with breakthrough concepts for the future of Israel and the Jewish world. We realize that the continued renaissance of the Jewish People will require merging old traditions with institutional and ideological innovations and for the State of Israel and world Jewry to work together across denominations.

The Jewish People – organized as a worldwide web of communities that are interconnected by shared values, texts, language, calendar and ceremonies – is outstandingly resilient. Jewish history shows that while we may have repeatedly experienced severe setbacks, we nevertheless reemerged powerful

Join the conversation www.flexigidity.com

and prosperous. In other words, while at any time some or many Jews may be suffering, we know with certainty that the Jewish People will not only survive but eventually thrive.

The collective leadership challenge is to place another link in that chain of Jewish legacy and Zionist success. For centuries, the Jewish People bewildered many with its resilience and leadership. For decades, Israel has outperformed many expectations. We can continue to do so if we correct our weaknesses and identify and focus on the secrets of our success: on leadership, communities, institutions and their interconnectedness; on education, lawmaking and society-building; on a healthy tension between Israel and the Diaspora. In one word: on our Flexigidity.

A Personal Prelude

About a year ago, when *Shmuel Rosner*, the editor of the Hebrew version of this book, read the manuscript, he asked me how long I had been working on the text. "Two and a half years," I answered. "No Gidi," he replied, "You have been writing this text in your head for a decade." He was right.

Indeed, the publication of this book is a major milestone in my personal life and career. The framework put forth summarizes and generalizes upon my personal experiences and research. I have had the privilege of visiting dozens of Jewish communities and meeting hundreds of rabbis, scholars, lay leaders and professionals from many countries. They make up an astounding diversity of philosophies, outlooks and activities. I struggled to understand Judaism, Zionism, Diaspora, Israel and their interaction with the world, trying to fit the pieces together. I believed that there must be logic and an order to the Jewish system, which I continued to seek. Slowly but surely, over the past few years, my insights came together into a conceptual framework, which is articulated in this book.

Naturally, my personal background, identity, outlook, motivation and objectives heavily influenced this project. I share this personal dimension not just for the sake of transparency and for the purpose of providing context for this project, but also because such accountability is integral to leadership in a Flexigid society, as I have argued.

I was born in 1970 to a secular middle-class and Zionist family in the Tel Aviv suburb of Holon, the eldest of three boys. My mother was born in Zion, then under the British Mandate, and has vague memories of the day when the State of Israel was established. She grew up and became an adult in the 1950s and 1960s when Israel went from austerity to prosperity and from vulnerability to becoming a regional power, while absorbing millions of immigrants and taking shape as a nation. My father was born during World War II in Bucharest, Romania, and came to Israel when he was twenty one years old to study at the Technion, in Haifa, where he met my mother. At the age of twenty five, in January 1967, he started active combat duty as an officer. He served on the front lines for the three years that included the astonishing victory of the Six-Day War of June 1967 and continued through the War of Attrition with Egypt and against Palestinian terrorism from Jordan and Lebanon.

The Shoah struck my family on both sides: on my father's side, my grandfather, Meir Grinstein, was held in seven labor camps in Romania, and my late grandmother, Sarah z"l, delivered and raised twin boys during the war. On my mother's side, my late grandmother, Diana Rapoport z"l, was brought up in a German Jewish family of Spanish origins *(Spharadim)*, who relocated to Poland before the War. She was sent in 1935 at the age of 14 to Zion, then under the British Mandatory Government, to join her Zionist uncle who came there in the 1920s. Her father and most of her family perished in the Nazi concentration and labor camps.

My immediate family chose Zionism and Israel again and again: Meir's journey to Zion began in 1934 and lasted twenty eight years, until the arrival of his family in 1962. My maternal great-grandparents, Moshe and Sarah Moscovitz HaCohen, traveled in 1910 from Romania to Jaffa, then under Ottoman rule, as part of the *Second Aliyah*. They built their home in Tel Aviv, where my grandfather, Avraham, was born in 1918, just as the British Mandate began. My parents re-chose the State of Israel in 1978, after having worked in Africa for six years.

Jewish religion and observance have always been present in our family. I grew up in a secular home, where non-observance was the practice. On the Romanian side of our family, my great-grandfather was a devoted scholar of Torah and my grandmother regularly sought intimate conversations with God. The German-Russian side of my mother represented a mix of assimilated, enlightened *(Maskilim)* and Zionist Jews, who had disregard and contempt toward the Jewish religion and God, which manifested in eating non-Kosher meals during the fast of the Day of Atonement *(Yom Kippur)*.

My world view was a product of so-called Classical Zionism. This was an atheist outlook, which saw the State of Israel as the epitome of the aspirations of the entire Jewish People and the realization of its inalienable right to self-determination. It negated Diaspora Jewish life, which it viewed as degrading and unsustainable due to antisemitism and assimilation, and called upon all Jews to move to Israel. Meanwhile, within the framework of the so-called 'blood-for-money deal,' it demanded unwavering financial and political support from world Jewry in exchange for us, Israelis, risking our lives in the service of the Jewish People by building its national home and safe haven. After the 1967 War, when Israel took over the Temple Mount *(Har HaBaiyt)* in Jerusalem and unified the city under its sovereignty, liberated ancestral lands in Judea and Samaria and conquered the Sinai Peninsula and the Golan Heights, Zionism took on a messianic aura and became domineering toward other Jewish outlooks, as well. Israel's self-perception at that time was captured by the late Prime Minister Levi Eshkol (1895-1969), who described the State of Israel in *Yiddish* as 'Shimshon the Nabech' ('Samson the

Weakling'), simultaneously assertive yet whining, proud yet needy.

My first visit to a Jewish institution outside of Israel shook this outlook. In July 1994, as a Navy Officer of the Israel Defense Forces, I participated in the Brandeis-Bardin Collegiate Institute in Simi Valley, California, known to many as BCI. The paradoxes of that place were striking. We sang Israeli songs, learned Israeli folk dancing, raised the Israeli flag and participated in a program called *Aliyah*, which would ordinarily connote relocating to Israel. Meanwhile, some of our staff were Israelis who had lived in the Los Angeles area for many years and whose children spoke to them in English. They had no intention of ever repatriating. Among the participants, some knew little or nothing about Israel and spoke no Hebrew. They were comfortably living in the USA and the thought of relocating to a distant Middle Eastern nation did not even occur to them. For many, their last significant Jewish experience was at the age of twelve or thirteen with their *Bat or Bar Mitzvah,* and they resented their time in Hebrew and Jewish Sunday schools. Some of them did not associate with any Jewish community, and were not even sure they were going to marry a fellow Jew or consecrate their union in a Jewish ceremony. In short, the people I met that summer did not fit in the worldview of my upbringing.

Shortly after that visit, I graduated from my military service and committed myself to public service. I worked in a non-governmental organization dedicated to advancing peace and co-existence between Israelis and Arabs by the name of the Economic Cooperation Foundation. I then joined the Office of the Prime Minister of Israel during a critical moment in Israel's modern history between 1999 and 2001, to serve as the secretary and coordinator of Israel's delegation to the negotiations with the PLO and to the Camp David Summit.

That experience of serving in the Bureau of the Prime Minister and the experience of being a Wexner Israel Fellow at the Harvard Kennedy School of Government during the following year were formative ones for me. In the Bureau of the PM I witnessed how societal matters of critical importance were systematically and repeatedly poorly handled by government. At the Harvard Kennedy School I realized that non-governmental work could fill voids which are created by failures of governments and markets. Those two experiences inspired me to establish the Reut Institute, which, as mentioned, is dedicated to addressing some of Israel's most critical and complex challenges.

Meanwhile, I have also visited numerous Jewish communities around the world, experiencing a dizzying array of commonality and dissimilarity, and have spent countless hours reading, discussing, visiting, observing and experiencing. I have been privileged to experience the Jewish world, both in Israel and outside of it, particularly in North America, in very significant doses.

This journey transformed my worldview regarding Israel, Zionism and the Jewish world. On the one hand, I was repeatedly perplexed by the sophistication and resilience of Jewish society in the Diaspora, which not only survived two millennia of exile but also managed to offer exceptional leadership to humanity. Amidst astonishing geographical, cultural, institutional and ethical diversity, I saw striking communal similarities. On the other hand, while the ideal of becoming a model society, which inspired the Heralds of Zionism, Herzl and Ben-Gurion, is yet to be fulfilled and remains amorphous and subject to deep disagreement, the structures and institutions of the State of Israel are worryingly underperforming.

Thus, I came to revisit key themes of the classical Zionism of my upbringing and indoctrination. There is no doubt in my mind that Zionism's negation of the Diaspora was legitimately rooted in the undeniable historical realities of nearly two centuries of oppression and poverty, particularly in Russia and Europe, which culminated in the Shoah. However, this approach also encouraged collective Israeli arrogance and ignorance regarding the legacy and reality of the Diaspora.

Over time, I realized that the State of Israel is reaching a tipping point where it will need to reverse its approach and begin to view a vibrant Jewish and Israeli Diaspora as a Zionist imperative. I began to see the heavy-handedness of Zionism toward Diaspora Jewry, and the legacy of this attitude. Zionism turned on Jewish history, traditions and heritage with an axe, where a surgeon's knife would have been more warranted and effective. It was quick to "throw out the baby with the bath water." It called for replacing a Jewish society that had consistently survived, repeatedly prospered and provided exceptional leadership for two millennia with a modern state that is yet to meet this tall order. Furthermore, Israel's future is overshadowed by a legacy of three past failures by the Jewish People to successfully eternalize sovereignty and develop a model society: during the Kingdom of Israel, the Kingdom of Judea and during the era of the Second Temple, which were destroyed and exiled in 722 BCE, 586 BCE, and 70 CE respectively.

My identity evolved, as well. At the beginning of my adult life and career, I was essentially an Israeli who happened to be Jewish. In 1994, when I left for BCI, I viewed the Jewish world in the context of Israel, expecting Diaspora Jews to support Israel and join us while letting go of their Diaspora mindset and way of being, which I viewed as provisional by the very nature of their exilic condition.

Over the past two decades, I have come to view Israel in the context of Jewish history, society, and legacy: I would like Israel to fulfill its aspiration and potential of leadership in the Jewish world and to remain a beacon for all Jews; I view the existence of a vibrant Diaspora as essential for Judaism and for Zionism, and not just a legacy of the past; I support activities and policies that engage world Jewry in Israel and vice versa, such as the Birthright Israel project; I view the integration of Israel's Arab minority as an ethical challenge for the entire Jewish People that is critical to its collective legacy, as much as it is a task of Israeli laws and policies; I believe that Israelis and world Jews must strive together to make an indelibly Jewish and Israeli contribution to humanity beginning, to the extent possible, with our immediate neighborhood in the Middle East.

My personal life, too, has become Jewishly multi-faceted. Whereas I do not meet Maimonides' standard of faith requiring wholehearted belief, I married into a religious family that observes *Shabbat* and *kashrut* and two of our sons are orthodoxly observant. I occasionally attend synagogue and observe the fast days during the Jewish year. I have chosen to live and build a family in the State of Israel, inspired by the opportunity to be a part of and to influence the most significant Jewish project of my time: the return of the Jewish People to Zion and the reestablishment of its sovereignty in its ancestral land. However, I have also been deeply involved with the Jewish Diaspora. While my professional career has been focused on serving Israel's prosperity and security, I am also committed to the vision of turning Israel into a model society that will make an indelible and distinct contribution to the Jewish People and the rest of humanity.

This Jewish journey led me to concrete action beginning with my role in shaping the Birthright Israel program between 1995 and 1999. While this idea has deep roots in Jewish history, its rationale has been that such a visit would have a lasting and positive impact on its participants in terms of their association with the Jewish People, its religion and traditions, as well as with the State of Israel. The radical twist of Birthright at that time, which earned us significant criticism, was that it called upon the Government of Israel to support a visit to Israel that was designed to strengthen Diaspora Jewish communities, rather than serve the ideal of *aliyah*. Birthright is now the largest project of the Jewish People, soon to bring 50,000 Jewish young adults to Israel each year, with over 300,000 participants to date.

My flagship project to serve this outlook has been the Reut Institute, which I established in 2004 and have been leading ever since. The ideological framework of Reut is captured in the phrase '21st Century Zionism,' which reflects our view of the Jewish national movement as dynamic and constantly evolving in the face of permanent adversity and exceptional volatility. As mentioned, the challenge of

Join the conversation www.flexigidity.com

21st Century Zionism is to draw upon the wisdom of the past in order to thrive in the future, and to optimize the pace of adaptation in Israeli society in order to ensure prosperity, security, leadership and social cohesion. Reut's purpose is to be an institution that is the most effective force of change in Israel and the Jewish world, and its mission is to lead in areas that are critically important for their security and prosperity, as well as to make an indelible Jewish and Israeli contribution to humanity within the spirit of *or la'goim* and *tikkun olam*.

The work of Reut requires a nuanced understanding of the broader context. Success hinges upon our ability to identify strategic threats and opportunities facing Israel and the Jewish world, to articulate new visions, as well as to design and effectuate innovative strategies. As Reut's founder, I regard my chief responsibility as infusing the organization with the worldview that led me to establish Reut in the first place. This outlook also inspired and informed Reut's vision, mission, structure, strategy and the values it seeks to bring to Israeli and Jewish societies. It also guided some of Reut's key efforts in the areas of national security, economic development, *Tikun Olam* and the future of Israel's relations with the Jewish world.

My objectives for the Flexigidity Project have been both personal and limited, as well as collective and broad. My original goal was narrowly defined as formulating the worldview that shaped the Reut Institute. To date, this outlook has been conveyed orally or scattered across numerous emails, lectures and other texts. Such an explication of our ideology is critical to Reut's institution-building and to developing new and successful leadership for the organization, thus escaping the so-called founder's syndrome. I envision Reut contributing to the development of the State of Israel and the Jewish People long after I am no longer at its helm. However, the broader relevance of the Flexigidity Project beyond the Reut Institute – to Jewish, Zionist and Israeli leaders and novices, as well as to non-Jews – was quick to surface, as described earlier.

Thousands of hours, a small financial fortune and countless little sacrifices went into the Flexigidity Project. During this journey, I often asked myself: what if only a handful of people buy this book, if its web-platform remains unpopulated and its impact insignificant? Now that this work is complete, my answer is clear. It has been well worth the effort. I now have a vision to guide my coming decade of work and service. the Ethics of our Fathers *(Pirkei Avot)* teaches, "while it is not upon us to finish the task, neither are we free to desist from it." This is the opening quote of this book. It is also its closing one.

Gidi Grinstein
Kislev 5774, December 2013

Acknowledgements

I began the Flexigidity Project on July 4, 2010, with the belief that it would require a few weeks, perhaps three months, to finalize the founding text. Three and a half years later, after thousands of hours and hundreds of thousands of words that were written, deleted, re-written and edited, it has now come to the critical milestone of the publication of the book and the launching of the web-platform. The there is still a long journey ahead until the full objectives of this project will be realized, but this is, nonetheless, a good moment to appreciate my good fortune and say thank you.

Expressing gratitude is a challenging task at this moment. The contents of this book build upon the intellectual legacy of giants, Jews and non-Jews whose work contributed to the richness of our understanding of Judaism and the Jewish People. I have only been able to scratch the surface of that wealth of wisdom, and my sources are scattered along the book and listed in its bibliography. It also builds upon countless little encounters, conversations, site visits and insights, which are too numerous to relay.

In between the few that are enshrined in this text and the many that have been forgotten, I would like to acknowledge the help, support, generosity and love of a few dozens of acquaintances, colleagues, friends and family. They are lay leaders, rabbis, professionals, philanthropists and academics, from Tel Aviv, Jerusalem, New York, Los Angeles, London and Melbourne, all part of the Jewish worldwide web.

The Flexigidity Project is ambitious and unique to a level that could discourage its author, and distance, frustrate and dishearten others. Under such circumstances, colleagues and friends that stand by you and a spouse that unwaveringly supports you are invaluably important. I have been privileged to have all of the above.

Indeed, there are a few individuals whose friendship, support, intellectual contribution and outstanding generosity were essential for the completion of this project, to a level where it may be difficult to imagine this moment without them. *Avraham Infeld*, who is a dear friend and mentor, spent numerous hours talking the ideas through with me, commenting on different versions of the text, encouraging me in moments of frustration while gently refraining from over-discouraging me with brutal criticism in the initial phases of the journey. His endorsement is invaluable to me, and I am honored and grateful that he agreed to write the foreword to this book. *Dr. Robert Wexler*, President of *American Jewish University* in Los Angeles, is a dear friend who believed in this project, and, one day in a phone call, offered me a fellowship to spend a sabbatical at AJU in Los Angeles dedicated to this project. This was the time when the Flexigidity Project took its final shape. Bob's generosity was matched by the *Younes & Suraya Nazarian Center for Israel Studies in UCLA*, led by *Dr. Aryeh Saposnik*. Finally, my dear friend and current Chairman of *American Friends of the Reut Institute, Adam Herz*, stood by me with close friendship and rock solid support.

The vision of a web platform, which builds on the legacy of the Talmud and supports mass-substantive engagement with the contents of this book, has been integral to this project since its inception. It would not be realized without the support of the *Charles & Lynn Schusterman Family Foundation* and *Mick Davis of the Davis Foundation*. In addition, I am grateful to *Amir Give'on and Naomi Leight of Rimona Consulting* in Los Angeles for their partnership in designing, building and operating the Flexigidity web-platform.

I also owe a debt of gratitude to the board and management team of the *Reut Institute*. In particular, Chairman of the Board, *Erez Meltzer* and my colleagues, *Roy Keidar* and *Netaly Ophir*, then Reut Chief Executive Officer and Vice President, respectively, whose steadfast support allowed me to take my sabbatical. This project also benefitted from the support of *American Friends of the Reut Institute*, particularly board members and close friends and confidants *Carol Aminoff, Michelle Kleinert Bader* and *Joel Mandel*, and Managing Director *Doris Schwartz*. I thank them for their countless acts of assistance and advice.

I am a novice in the areas covered by the Flexigidity Project. My ability to write this book depended upon intellectual engagement with and support from many people. In my attempt to make the book readable by all denominations of the Jewish People I have sought guidance, advice and teaching from *Rabbi Nachum Executive Director of Academic Exchange* in Los Angeles, *Rabbi Edward Feinstein* of *Valley Beth Shalom* in Los Angeles, *Rabbi Dr. Micha Goodman* of the *Ein Prat Academy for Leadership* in Israel, *Rabbi Steve Leder* of Wilshire Boulevard Temple in Los Angeles, *Rabbi Michael Paley*, the Pearl and Ira Meyer Scholar in Residence at the *Jewish Resource Center of UJA-Federation of New York*, and *Rabbi Chaim Seidler-Feller* of *Hillel UCLA*.

In addition, *Edgar Bronfman z"l*, President Emeritus of the *Samuel Bronfman Foundation* and Former President of the *World Jewish Congress*, was repeatedly and outstandingly generous with his time, sharpness and wisdom. I am also indebted to *David Avital, Esther Benton, Isaac Devash, Omri Dolev, Charles Gorodess, Rae and Richard Janvey, Tal Keinan, Michael Leffell, Nick Lyons,*

Dana Raucher, Jeff Solomon, David Suissa, Zvi Howard Rosenman, Rami Wernik and *Neri Zilber* for their substantive feedback. My colleagues at the Reut team in Israel helped me assess the usefulness of this effort and contributed to its development. They, too, deserve to be thanked, particularly *Martin Ben-Moreh, Talia Gorodess, Yotam HaCohen, Shirlee Harel, Dana Preisler* and *Yonatan Weinberg.*

In addition, a few friends have been exceptionally generous in supporting the Flexigidity Project. I am referring to *Brad Berger, Avi Friedman, Mitch Julis, Joel Mandel, Michael Leffell, Reagan Silber* and *Marilyn Ziering.* All of them are personal friends and long-term supporters of *American Friends of the Reut Institute* and of the *Reut Institute.* I also owe a particular debt of gratitude to *Zofia Yalovsky,* Vice President for Finance, Administration and Technology at AJU, for her help with all technical matters.

I hope we have been able to deliver a text that is polished, factually founded and thoroughly researched and sourced. This outcome would not have been possible without the assistance of three exceptional young men who supported me in different phases of this project. They are *Or Cohen, Gahl Rinat* and *Max Simchowitz.* In addition: *Ilana Kurshan* provided invaluable editorial inputs and translated the poem of Alterman; *Lior Holtzer* verified the factual accuracy of the text and enriched it with his insights; *Mike Lefkowitz,* volunteered to copyedit the manuscript and to provide critical feedback; and *Abigail Pickus* who gave it a final cover-to-cover polish. Finally, the beautiful cover of this book, capturing its essence in a single visual, was created by *Naomi Shoua* of *Firefly Media* in Los Angeles.

This list would not be complete without a few more people who were supportive and encouraging with their understanding, advice, introduction and guidance. They are *Debbie Dadon and Albert Dadon* for their hospitality and patience; *Mark Pearlman* for his vision for the visual side of this project that is yet to be realized; *Rick Rosen* and *Mel Berger* of *WME Entertainment* for their guidance; *Shep Rosenman* for his direction; *Michael Rudell* for his legal advice; *Eli Tene* for the warm introduction to *Eran Zmora,* who is now my publisher in Israel.

A particular gratitude goes to *Josh Gottesman,* of Houston, Texas, now Tel Aviv. I met Josh in the summer of 2012 following a random encounter and a Facebook post. Many hundreds of hours later, when I am often seated at the desk with Josh peeking over my left shoulder, he gradually became my assistant, advisor, co-editor and partner on this project. The fingerprints of his intellect, articulateness, diligence, discipline, integrity and hard work are spread all over this document, which could not have been as it is without him. As a close friend told me, "Gidi, you have a damn good editor." As Josh grows to pursue his passion as a Jewish educator, the logic and vision of Flexigidity will gain a powerful engine of progress.

I am also eternally grateful to *Raya Strauss Ben-Dror*. Fifteen years ago, Raya and I participated in co-authoring what would become the ISRAEL 15 vision, which called for Israel to be one of the fifteen leading nations in terms of quality of life. That vision inspired my work at the Harvard Kennedy School of Government and later became one of the key efforts of the Reut Institute. Together with her husband *Shmuel Ben-Dror*, Raya has been a dear friend to our family. She has been outstanding in her generosity, friendship and loyalty, a true partner in a long, challenging and deeply rewarding journey of leadership in Israel and the Jewish world.

Finally, Betty. Without my wife, mother of our children, partner, friend and greatest and staunchest supporter, this project may have never materialized. She believed in the vision of the Flexigidity Project as much as I did, often with a deeper sense of urgency. She was willing to relocate to Los Angeles with the kids far away from her work on the spur of the moment. She allowed me to be absent for long days and nights, particularly during the last few months, assuming the burden of caring for our children. Her wise advice and strong intuition have been invaluable.

As I was contemplating the dedication of this book, a few options came to mind. One was my ninety-eight-year-old grandfather, Meir, who is the most inspiring person I know and whose journey to Zion lasted twenty-eight years. A second option was my parents to whom I owe all that I have. Another option was the Reut Institute, with its vision and mission, to which I have dedicated the last eleven years of my career.

But ultimately, I decided to dedicate this book to Betty and our five children – Eliyahu, Yosef (Sefi), Michael, Noa Sarah and Yael – with the wish that they will grow to be powerful, creative, committed and unique links in the Jewish chain.

Gidi Grinstein
Tel-Aviv, Israel
Kislev 5774, December 2013

Bibliography

My Big Picture Books

* Heifetz Ronald A., *Leadership Without East Answers*, The Belknap Press of Harvard University Press, 1997

* Johnson Paul, *A History of the Jews*, Harper Perennial, 1988

* Dr. Zvi Lanir, *The Fox Pocket Notebook*, Mendele electronic Books, Tel-Aviv, 2013 (in Hebrew)

* Lau Rabbi Binyamin (Benny), *Sages – Volume 1: The Second Temple Period*, Miskal – Yedioth Ahronot Books and Chemed Books, 2006 (in Hebrew)

* Lau Rabbi Binyamin (Benny), *Sages – Volume 2: From Yavne to the Bar-Kokhba Revolt*, Miskal – Yedioth Ahronot Books and Chemed Books, 2007 (in Hebrew)

* Lau Rabbi Binyamin (Benny), *Sages – Volume 3: The Gallilean Period*, Miskal – Yedioth Ahronot Books and Chemed Books, 2008 (in Hebrew)

* Rabbi Jonathan Sacks, *Future Tense*, Hodder & Stoughton, 2009

Additional sources

* Avineri Shlomo, *Varieties of Zionist Thought*, Am Oved Publishers, Fifth Printing 1991

* Beinhocker Eric D., *The Origin of Wealth*, Harvard Business School Press, 2006

* Ben-Gurion David, *Uniqueness and Destny (Yichud v'Yiud)*, Israel Ministry of Defense, 2011 (in Hebrew)

* Botticini Maristella and Eckstein Zvi, *The Chosen Few: How Education Shaped Jewish History 70-1492*, Hebrew Translation, Princeton University Press, 2012

Join the conversation www.flexigidity.com

- Bronfman M. Edgar and Zasloff Beth, Hope, Not Fear: A Path to Jewish Renaissance, self-published, 2008, First Edition

- Cohn-Sherbok Dan, *Fifty Key Jewish Thinkers*, Resling Publishing, 2010

- Dror, Yehezkel, *Epistle to an Israeli Jewish-Zionist Leader*, Carmel Publishing House, 2005 (In Hebrew)

- Friedman Thomas L., *The World is Flat,* Penguin Books, 2006 Updated and Expanded

- Gafni Isaiah M., *The Jews of Babylonia in the Talmudic Era: A Social and Cultural History*, The Zalman Shazar Center for Jewish History, Jerusalem, 1990 (Hebrew translation)

- Goldsmith Emanuel S. and Scult Mel, *Dynamic Judaism: The Essential Writings of Mordecai M. Kaplan,* 2011 (Hebrew Translation)

- Heifetz Ronald, Grashaw Alexander and Linsky Marty, *The Practice of Adaptive Leadership: Tools and Tactics for Changing Your Organization and the World*, Harvard Business Press, Boston Massachusetts, 2009

- Kaplan Mordechai, *Judaism as a Civilization: Toward a Reconstruction of American Jewish Life*, Jewish Publication Society of America, 1994

- Keidar Nir, *Mamlakhtiyut: David Ben-Gurion Political-Civic Ideas*, Ben-Gurion University Press & Yad Ben-Zvi, 2009

- Kook Rabbi Avraham Isaac HaCohen, *Lights (Orot),* Hemed Publishin, 1992 (in Hebrew)

- Lau, Rabbi Israel Meir, *Foundations – One Hundred Concepts in Judaism*, Miskal – Yedioth Ahronoth Books and Chemed Books, 2008 (in Hebrew)

- Mearsheimer John J. and Walt Stephen M., *The Israel Lobby and U.S. Foreign Policy*, Farrar, Straus and Giroux, New York, First Edition, 2007

- Senor Dan Senor and Singer Saul, *Start-Up Nation: The Story of Israel's Economic Miracle*, a Council of Foreign Relations Book, Twelve Hachette Book Group, New York, First Edition, 2009

- Soloveitchik Joseph B., *Kol Dodi Dofek, Listen: My Beloved Knocks*, Yeshiva University Press, 2006

- Taleb Nassim Nicholas, *Antifragile: Things That Gain from Disorder*, Random House New York, 2012, First Edition

- Taleb Nassim Nicholas, *The Black Swan: The Impact of the Highly Improbable*, Random House Trade Paperbacks, 2010, Second Edition

- Taub Gadi, *What is Zionism*, Miskal – Yedioth Ahronoth Books and Chemed Books, 2010 (in Hebrew)

- Wald Shalom Salomon, *Rise and Decline of Civilizations: Lessons for the Jewish People*, Miskal – Yedioth Ahronoth Books and Chemed Books, 2013 (in Hebrew)

Articles

- Ahad Ha'Ahm, *The Jewish State and the Jewish Problem*, Jewish Virtual Library, see: http://www.jewishvirtuallibrary.org/jsource/Zionism/haam2.html

- Ahad Ha'Ahm, *On a Crossroads (Ahl Parashat Drachim),* (in Hebrew)

- Conversation between Rabbi Michael Paley and William Novak in "Kerem: Creative Explorations in Judaism", Jewish Study Center Press, Inc., Washington DC, 2012, volume no. 13 p. 31-59

לְעַרְבֵּב אֶת תְּחוּמֵי הַהֹוֶה וְהַזֵּכֶר,
אֶת גְּבוּלוֹת הַמֻּפְשָׁט וְנִכְסֵי הַמּוּחָשִׁי,
וְלִמְדֹד לְכֻלָּם בְּאוֹתָהּ מִדַּת שֵׂכֶל,
בְּאוֹתָהּ מְסִירוּת שֶׁל כֹּחוֹת נְחוּשִׁים.

וְלָתֵת בְּבוֹא יוֹם, בְּעַד אֵלֶּה אוֹ אֵלֶּה,
אֶת הַדָּם הוּא הַנֶּפֶשׁ, בְּלִי לַהֲג פְּתָאִים,
כִּבְעִנְיַן חֲלִיפִין שֶׁיָּאֶה לוֹ הָאֵלֶם,
לְאַחַר שֶׁנִּבְחַן וְנִמְצָא כְּדַאי.

(נתן אלתרמן, 'עיר היונה', שיר הרעות, בית ו')

To blend the worlds of the present and memory,
The borders abstract, and the assets concrete.
And to mete out to all with the same, equal measure,
Of unfaltering strength with devotion complete.

And to give, when the time comes, for these ones or those,
The blood ('tis the soul), and without foolish prattle.
As an exchange for which silence is golden,
After all is examined and deemed worth the battle.

(Natan Alterman, City of the Dove, Friendship Song, House 6)
Translated by Ilana Kurshan

Made in the USA
Middletown, DE
19 August 2015